T0384601

Uncertain Warriors

In an era where 'history' had supposedly ended, what was an army for? This question confronted the US Army at the end of the Cold War. Although public support for the military remained high, fewer were sending their children to enlist and questions were raised about the uncertainty of future operations: How would Army leaders prepare soldiers for difficult peacekeeping operations that called for a more human-oriented approach in light of the promises of high-tech warfare? What was the best way to navigate the broader debates about changing gender and sexual norms in American society? Pulled in different directions, the Army struggled to put forward a compelling vision of who and what the American soldier should be. In *Uncertain Warriors*, David Fitzgerald reveals how, in response to this uncertainty, they eventually fell back on an older vision of martial masculinity, embracing a 'warrior ethos' that was meant to define the contemporary American soldier.

David Fitzgerald is a lecturer in international politics at University College Cork. His first book, *Learning to Forget: US Army Counterinsurgency Doctrine and Practice from Vietnam to Iraq*, was a finalist for the Society of Military History's Edward M. Coffman prize.

MILITARY, WAR, AND SOCIETY IN MODERN
AMERICAN HISTORY

Series Editors
Beth Bailey, University of Kansas
Andrew Preston, University of Cambridge

Military, War, and Society in Modern American History is a new series that showcases original scholarship on the military, war, and society in modern US history. The series builds on recent innovations in the fields of military and diplomatic history and includes historical works on a broad range of topics, including civil–military relations and the militarisation of culture and society; the military's influence on policy, power, politics, and political economy; the military as a key institution in managing and shaping social change, both within the military and in broader American society; the effect the military has had on American political and economic development, whether in wartime or peacetime; and the military as a leading edge of American engagement with the wider world, including forms of soft power as well as the use of force.

Uncertain Warriors

The United States Army between the
Cold War and the War on Terror

David Fitzgerald

University College Cork

CAMBRIDGE
UNIVERSITY PRESS

Shaftesbury Road, Cambridge CB2 8EA, United Kingdom

One Liberty Plaza, 20th Floor, New York, NY 10006, USA

477 Williamstown Road, Port Melbourne, VIC 3207, Australia

314–321, 3rd Floor, Plot 3, Splendor Forum, Jasola District Centre, New Delhi – 110025, India

103 Penang Road, #05–06/07, Visioncrest Commercial, Singapore 238467

Cambridge University Press is part of Cambridge University Press & Assessment, a department of the University of Cambridge.

We share the University's mission to contribute to society through the pursuit of education, learning and research at the highest international levels of excellence.

www.cambridge.org
Information on this title: www.cambridge.org/9781009235808

DOI: 10.1017/9781009235822

First published 2024

Printed in the United Kingdom by TJ Books Limited, Padstow Cornwall

A catalogue record for this publication is available from the British Library

A Cataloging-in-Publication data record for this book is available from the Library of Congress

ISBN 978-1-009-23580-8 Hardback

For Daniel

Contents

Figures

Acknowledgements

Writing the acknowledgements is simultaneously one of the great joys and great agonies of finishing a book. It's a joy because you get the chance to publicly acknowledge all those who made the work possible; it's an agony not only because you need to find the right words to thank those to whom you owe gratitude (even where words are not enough), but also because it's accompanied by the nagging fear that you may well have forgotten to mention someone. In this case, the agony is particularly acute because the book has had such a long gestation period that I have accumulated debts to so many people.

I first started thinking about the ideas that ended up in this book in 2007 when, as a visiting graduate student in New York City, I found myself reckoning with the strange relationship that the United States seemed to have with its military, which was then off fighting wars in faraway places while leaving the rest of the country to get on with life as normal. If I was to identify a particular moment when the idea for this book began to form, it was probably in a conversation in a hostel living room with my friend Allison, as she explained to me the weirdness of signing up to serve in a peacetime military and then suddenly finding herself at war in the Middle East. The other reason I date the origins of the book to my time in New York is that that is where I first encountered Marilyn Young, whose unique combination of fierce intellect, political commitment, personal warmth, and inexhaustible generosity had a huge impact on me, as it did on many others. Marilyn pushed me to take culture seriously in my work and was characteristically supportive when I first began to think about this book in more detail.

The year I spent as a postdoctoral fellow at the Clinton Institute for American Studies in University College Dublin helped me to broaden my understanding of what history could look like. I am grateful to Liam Kennedy and Catherine Carey, who have together created a special institution, for making my time there a joyful and stimulating one. While the seed for this book was planted many years ago, I wrote all of it while at my present home in University College Cork. I am grateful to my current and former colleagues there for their camaraderie and support over the years, especially Chiara Bonfiglioli, John Borgonovo, Lindsey Earner-Byrne, Jonathan Evershed, Jason Harris, Dónal Hassett, Sabine Kriebel, Mervyn O'Driscoll, Maeve O'Riordan, Jill Rogers, and Jay Roszman. David Ryan remains as sage a mentor and as astute a reader as he was when I was a first-year PhD student. His comments on a draft of the Introduction were insightful and reassuring in equal measure, and I am eternally grateful for his support and friendship.

Ever since he came to Cork to give a talk and then spent what was surely more time than had he bargained for listening to me hold forth about my own work over pints of Beamish, Brian McAllister Linn has been with this book in one way or another. There is no better historian of the US Army than Brian, and his advice has made this work vastly better. He directed me to sources and urged me to never lose sight of the gap between the view from the E-Ring of the Pentagon and the realities of the Army in the field.

I have also been extremely fortunate to work with Andrew Preston and Beth Bailey, whose enthusiasm for the project led me to submit a proposal for consideration in the series they edit together for Cambridge University Press. I couldn't imagine a better home for this book and couldn't have asked for better or smarter interlocuters when it came to shaping the book proposal. At Cambridge, Cecelia Cancellaro has been unfailingly supportive throughout the whole experience, and Victoria Phillips has helped to keep the project on track. Andrew, Beth, and Cecelia's excitement over the book helped to sustain me throughout the writing process. Cecelia's predecessor at Cambridge, Debbie Gershenowitz, seems to appear in an inordinate number of book acknowledgements in the field of American foreign relations history and that is for good reason. When I was in the early stages of looking for a home for the book, Debbie gave me both encouragement and incisive advice over breakfast at a Society for Historians of American Foreign Relations (SHAFR) annual meeting.

I am grateful to audiences and fellow panel members at several conferences, especially at the annual meetings of SHAFR, the Society for Military History, the British International Studies Association US Foreign Policy Working Group, and the Historians of the Twentieth Century United States. Many different parts of this book received airings at these events, and audience feedback shaped the manuscript in ways both big and small. Two of my frequent co-conspirators at these conferences, David Kieran and Shaul Mitelpunkt, read parts of the manuscript and offered invaluable comments. Together with Simon Toner, Shaul also put together an excellent workshop on violence and the American century at Sheffield in September 2022 that was perfectly timed to coincide with my attempts to finalise a full draft of the book. Along with Simon and Shaul, Molly Avery, Oli Charbonneau, Molly Geidel, Miguel Hernandez, Andrew Johnstone, Althea Legal-Miller, Kaeten Mistry, Ilaria Scaglia, Bevan Sewell, and Nick Witham all provided insightful feedback as well as solidarity. Many in that group have also been participants in the SHAFR UK/Ireland seminar, a group assembled by Elisabeth Leake during the depths of the pandemic when the ability to share work with a likeminded group become a lifeline. I am grateful to Elisabeth for creating that space and for her comments on my work, as well as to Heather Dichter, Alessandro Iandolo, Jonathan Hunt, Matthew Jones, Marc Palen, Sean Fear and Sarah Miller-Davenport for their engagement in these sessions, one of which allowed me to polish a chapter before submitting it with my book proposal.

Some early versions of this book appeared, wholly or in part, in article form. I am grateful to the editors of those journals for their help and for their permission to use the material here: 'Support the Troops: Gulf War Homecomings and a New Politics of Military Celebration', *Modern American History* 2, no. 1 (2019): 1–22; and 'Warriors Who Don't Fight: The Post-Cold War United States Army and Debates over Peacekeeping Operations', *Journal of Military History* 85, no. 1 (2021): 1127–56.

I am also grateful to the US Army Military History Institute for a General and Mrs. Matthew B. Ridgway Military History Research Grant, and to both the School of History and the College of Arts, Celtic Studies, and Social Sciences at University College Cork for providing the financial support that made meaningful archival research possible despite the perpetually financially straitened circumstances of higher education in Ireland. Historians simply couldn't function without archivists, and I am thankful for the efforts of all the staff of the archives I visited throughout this project. Whether it was at the George H. W. Bush Presidential Library, Northwestern University Archives, the William J. Clinton Presidential Library, the Library of Congress, or the US Army Heritage and Education Center (AHEC), archivists were unfailingly generous with their time and advice, and very gracious in dealing with my sometimes jetlagged queries. I need to especially thank Rich Baker at AHEC and Rachel C. Altman at the Bush Library for going above and beyond in tracking down sources. At College Station, Jason Parker was kind enough not to laugh too much at my failure to rent a car and willingly ferried me between hotel and archive so that I didn't need to walk four miles every morning in the Texan August heat. At Carlisle, the Hume family generously hosted me and gave me the chance to realise that I really wasn't very good at wakeboarding over a memorable Fourth of July weekend.

Ruth Lawlor is (marginally) better at wakeboarding than I am, as she is at many things. She has been a companion through much of this journey, sharing archival expeditions and conference trips alike, as well as reading drafts of pretty much everything I produced. She read every line of this manuscript and suggested some of them. Ruth and I have talked at length about history, politics, and everything else for many years due in no small part to that fact our similarities and differences complement each other so well, and her interventions, both critical and supportive, have had a decisive influence on *Uncertain Warriors*. Every page of this book reflects her eye for detail, her curiosity, and her generosity of spirit. Words really do fail me when it comes to expressing the thanks that I owe Ruth, and I am beyond grateful for her brilliance and friendship.

My family have supported me longer than anyone else. I would be nowhere without my parents' love, faith, and support. Their bookshelves have been a source of fascination since childhood and even now I make sure to check in on a Sunday visit to see what new 700-page military history tome my dad has acquired. My sister Claire, taciturn as she is about her vast talents as a writer, has always been generous in putting up with my garrulousness about my own work, and she and my brother-in-law Felix have long been a source of encouragement and support. My nan passed away before this book was completed but, given that she enjoyed gently needling me about my seeming lack of progress on it (betraying a wildly unrealistic understanding of academic publishing timelines), I think she would have appreciated seeing the finished version.

Most of all, I am grateful to Sarah Thelen for her love, support, and encouragement. She listened, read, offered astute line edits that greatly improved my prose, and took care of so much while I was immersed in writing or away at the archives. I am endlessly thankful for the life we have made together. Our son Daniel has been a source of joy ever since he entered our lives. He is now just about old enough to understand that I've been writing a book this whole time and has been very clear in his disapproval of the fact that it has nothing to do with Lego or trucks. He is also old enough to be able to recognise his own name in print and so, in the hope that he will get a kick out of it and thus forgive me for writing something so uninteresting instead of drawing pictures with him, it is to him that I dedicate this book.

Introduction
Warriors at the End of History

What use was an army at the end of history? What would its soldiers be expected to do, and what kind of soldiers might they be? Many within the post–Cold War United States Army would have rejected the premise of the first question. Even though the Berlin Wall had fallen, and liberal capitalist democracy seemed triumphant, history, for them, had not ended and they talked instead of violent threats and of continuing geopolitical uncertainty and conflict. Some turned to the darker rhetoric of a clash of civilisations to map out the Army's future role, while others even took to the domestic culture wars to find purpose.[1] Still, the question nagged at them. The Soviet Union had been an ideological foil for the United States since 1917 and the Cold War was the organising principle around which its contemporary army had been built, so the sudden disappearance of both was bound to cause disorientation and anxiety.[2] Moreover, the Army was finding it hard to navigate a broader societal shift. As the intellectual historian Daniel Rodgers has argued, the last decades of the twentieth century were, in many ways, an 'age of fracture' where the ideas that had organised American life began to fragment into smaller and less coherent pieces and where the narratives that had bound the nation together began to lose their force.[3] Put together, the ongoing fragmentation of social reality in the United States and the geopolitical shock of the end of the Cold War posed a profound challenge to the Army's self-image as an institution that exemplified what was best about Americans.

[1] Samuel Huntington, *The Clash of Civilizations and the Remaking of World Order* (New York: Simon & Schuster, 1996).
[2] On the long-standing prominence of anti-communism in US foreign policy, see Walter LaFeber, *America, Russia, and the Cold War, 1945–2006* (Boston: McGraw-Hill, 2008); Walter LaFeber, 'An End to Which Cold War?' *Diplomatic History* 16, no. 1 (1 January 1992): 61–5; Douglas Little, 'Anti-Bolshevism and American Foreign Policy, 1919–1939: The Diplomacy of Self-Delusion', *American Quarterly* 35, no. 4 (1983): 376–90. On broader post–Cold War anxieties, see Penny M. Von Eschen, *Paradoxes of Nostalgia: Cold War Triumphalism and Global Disorder since 1989* (Durham, NC: Duke University Press, 2022).
[3] Daniel T. Rodgers, *Age of Fracture* (Cambridge, MA: Harvard University Press, 2011).

Ironically, these questions emerged at a time when it seemed as though the Army, like the American military as a whole, had recovered its standing in American society and indeed attained new heights of respectability. It had put behind the tumult of the Vietnam era, as the advent of the All-Volunteer Force and a series of successful reforms had produced a high-quality force that attracted excellent recruits and was capable of remarkable feats on the battlefield. Indeed, even as the Soviet Union staggered through its final months and Pentagon leaders began to talk with some uncertainty about the post–Cold War world, the United States Army demonstrated logistical, operational and tactical virtuosity in assembling a vast force in the Saudi Arabian desert and using it to thoroughly defeat the Iraqi Army in a lightning campaign of just 100 hours of ground combat.[4] Given that the victory in the Gulf War was the culmination of thirty years of transformation and reform, it seemed almost unfair that the Army would immediately have to turn to face a different world than the one it had been preparing for.

Yet the institution had no choice but to turn to these questions. Political scientist Francis Fukuyama's claim that the end of the Cold War signalled the end of history may have been controversial, but it captured the spirit of the age and pointed to the dilemmas faced by an organisation whose central activity – war – was the very stuff that history was made of.[5] Deprived of an obvious opponent, suffering from a budgetary drawdown and buffeted by culture wars, the Army suffered from deep disquiet about its future direction. What sort of wars it might fight, what sort of threats would it face and what political leaders might ask it to do were open questions, and ones that Army leaders failed to answer convincingly.

Fundamentally, these questions were, like so many others of the politics of the late twentieth century, about identity. In their attempts to answer existential questions about the Army's role, Army leaders, policymakers and ordinary soldiers all offered competing visions of who and what the American soldier should be. Much as budgets, doctrine, force structure and equipment mattered greatly to the Army, and were often at the forefront of conversations about the future, all of these were undergirded by questions about people. Put simply, the Army could not

---

[4] Rick Atkinson, *Crusade: The Untold Story of the Persian Gulf War* (Boston: Mariner Books, 1994); Tom Clancy and Fred Franks, *Into the Storm: A Study in Command* (New York: Putnam, 1998); James Kitfield, *Prodigal Soldiers: How the Generation of Officers Born of Vietnam Revolutionized the American Style of War* (Washington, DC: Potomac Books, 1997).

[5] Francis Fukuyama, 'The End of History', *The National Interest*, no. 16 (Summer 1989): 3–18.

function without recruiting and retaining the right type of soldier and, as had been the case for nearly two decades, it had to do so without the aid of a draft to help fill its ranks. As the torrid early years of the All-Volunteer Force had demonstrated, questions about personnel could never be very far from conversations about the Army's future.

Of all the military services, the Army has long been the one most concerned with its demographics and with the identity of its soldiers. Writing in 1989, the analyst Carl Builder argued that when the Army talked about itself, it tended to emphasise 'the depth of its roots in the citizenry, its long and intimate history of service to the nation, and its utter devotion to country'. As Builder put it, if the Navy worshipped at the altar of tradition, the Air Force at the altar of technology and the Marine Corps at the altar of combat, then 'the object of the Army's worship is the country; and the means of worship is service to the country'.[6] Thus, the particular character of debates over the Army's identity, focusing as they did on the Army as a unique institution that needed to stand apart from broader American society in some way, are significant, as they cut against the grain of a longstanding rhetorical tradition within the Army of celebrating citizen-soldiers, even when the actual Army was composed entirely of professionals.

Uncertain Warriors tells the story of how the Army confronted uncertainty over its role and identity in the decade between the end of the Cold War and the beginning of the War on Terror. It traces the Army's response to these challenges by focusing on the central figure in the institution's relationship with broader society and its self-image: the American soldier. It examines how – in doctrine, policy, speeches and popular culture – Army leaders, political leaders and soldiers themselves contested and sought to define that identity. In an effort to find coherence in what seemed to be a world without coordinates, the organisation eventually settled on a vague yet loaded term to describe the American soldier of the twenty-first century: warrior.

While the meaning of the term was ambiguous, it was a world away from the rhetoric of citizen-soldiers that had previously dominated, and even from the sort of quiet and steady proficiency implied in the equally popular phrase 'profession of arms'.[7] Even if the citizen-soldier rhetoric

---

[6] Carl Builder, *The Masks of War: American Military Styles in Strategy and Analysis: A RAND Corporation Research Study* (Baltimore: The Johns Hopkins University Press, 1989), 20.

[7] The literature on military professionalism is vast. For an introduction, see John Winthrop Hackett, *The Profession of Arms: The 1962 Lees Knowles Lectures Given at Trinity College, Cambridge* (London: The Times Publishing Company, 1962); Morris Janowitz, *The Professional Soldier: A Social and Political Portrait*, reissue edition (New York: Free Press,

had been detached from the reality of a professionalised force, the fact that Army leaders had felt the need to invoke it said something about their broader vision of military service and the Army's relationship to the nation. The 'profession of arms' obviously emphasised the distinctiveness of the military experience, but it understood soldiering to be a vocation like that of the doctor, the lawyer or the accountant. By contrast, the 'warrior ethos' that emerged from attempts to resolve the contradictions inherent in the Army's post–Cold War position by its very nature emphasised that soldiers were a distinct group which stood apart from the rest of society because of the risks they faced and the constraints they lived under. The book demonstrates that when faced with the question of whether the Army should seek to widen or shrink the gap between itself and broader society, Army leaders effectively chose the former course of action, a decision whose consequences would reverberate for years to come.

Efforts to preserve the military's enhanced post–Desert Storm reputation meant both defending the professional ethos and technocentric focus of the organisation and resisting pressure to adapt to evolving societal norms relating to gender and sexuality, as Army leaders felt that conforming to these standards might damage the organisation's ethos and cohesion. In response to complaints both from within the ranks and from conservative politicians about a military that was becoming 'politically correct', Army leaders rolled out a warrior ethos programme, a new effort to revamp basic training and instil warrior values into its soldiers. The warriors produced by this programme would be ready for anything, from peacekeeping to high-tech conventional war, and would be able to deploy as part of expeditionary force to anywhere in the world at a moment's notice. Crucially, warriors would be ready to fight on arrival, no matter what their specialisation. At its heart, the warrior ethos was about affirming that the central business of the Army was war, not the countless peacetime tasks that often made up the mundane reality of the soldier's existence. Even as the official 'warrior ethos' was silent on questions of gender and mission, it sought to break down barriers between elite and non-elite troops by focusing on close combat as the ultimate measure of the soldier. However, not only did it require all soldiers to orientate themselves towards combat, it also legitimated a growing subculture that saw soldiers as part of a special group that was distinct from – and superior to – their fellow Americans.

1964); Samuel P. Huntington, *The Soldier and the State: The Theory and Politics of Civil–Military Relations* (Cambridge, MA: Belknap Press of Harvard University Press, 1981); Allan Reed Millett, 'Military Professionalism and Officership in America', A Mershon Briefing Center Report (Columbus, OH: Mershon Center of the Ohio State University, 1977).

Arguments over who the force should look to recruit and who would be allowed to serve may have stemmed from differing visions of the Army's future missions, but they also touched upon these broader debates about changing norms in American society. Similarly, questions about how the organisation could prepare its soldiers for a life of frequent deployments, and what could it reasonably call upon them to do once they were deployed, were at once strategic, organisational and political. Leon Trotsky once claimed that 'the army is a copy of society and suffers from all its diseases, usually at a higher temperature', something that surely holds true for the United States Army, even for the professional force of the All-Volunteer era.[8] Thus, given demographic changes and changing cultural norms around issues such as gender, sexuality and military service itself – the 'age of fracture' that Rodgers wrote about – the Army found itself at a crossroads in terms of the type of soldier it wanted to recruit and train, and how, as an organisation, it wanted to relate to its country more broadly. While public support for the military remained at historically high levels, and the public almost universally looked upon soldiers with admiration, questions about the character of the American soldier were also political flashpoints. As the historian Andrew Hartman has noted, the culture wars were in essence a debate over the idea of America, so an institution that saw itself not only as defending the nation but as its embodiment on the battlefield was bound to find itself caught up in some of these disputes.[9]

The Army was not solely or even primarily navigating its post–Cold War dilemmas by reference to social or cultural debates. Among military theorists, there was a growing sense that the character of war had begun to fundamentally change, and geopolitical shifts meant that the Army found itself embroiled in a debate over how it might reinvent itself in the face of new challenges.[10] Even in the immediate aftermath of the Persian Gulf War, while soldiers were being fêted in the streets of American cities, Army leaders worried about what the future held. Senior leaders recognised that not every opponent would be as easy to fight as Saddam

---

[8] Leon Trotsky, *The Revolution Betrayed* (London: Faber and Faber, 1937), 211, http://archive.org/details/in.ernet.dli.2015.237974.

[9] Andrew Hartman, *A War for the Soul of America: A History of the Culture Wars* (Chicago: University of Chicago Press, 2016), 2.

[10] Martin Van Creveld, *The Transformation of War* (New York: The Free Press, 1991); Mary Kaldor, *New and Old Wars: Organized Violence in a Global Era* (Cambridge: Polity Press, 1999); Steven Metz, 'A Wake for Clausewitz: Toward a Philosophy of Twenty-First Century Warfare', *The US Army War College Quarterly: Parameters* 24, no. 1 (4 July 1994), https://doi.org/10.55540/0031-1723.1685; Hew Strachan, *The Direction of War: Contemporary Strategy in Historical Perspective* (Cambridge: Cambridge University Press, 2014).

Hussein had been. Not only that, but the end of the Cold War deprived
the Army of its mission of confronting the Warsaw Pact in Europe, meaning that the prospect of conventional warfare on that continent, which
had preoccupied the force for much of the twentieth century, was now
an exceedingly remote possibility. Accordingly, the Army had to reassess
its priorities, especially as budget cuts began to constrain the choices of
an organisation that had been lavishly funded during the final years of
the Cold War. On one end of the spectrum, the Army was troubled by
the fact that victory in the Gulf War seemed to be down to the precision
bombing of American airpower rather than the skills of ground combat
units; on the other, it faced a series of lengthy deployments to messy conflict zones with ambiguous missions. The Army simultaneously found
itself on peacekeeping duty in places such as Somalia, Haiti and Bosnia,
and being compelled to articulate a vision for how it would wage high-
tech war in the era of the 'Revolution in Military Affairs'.[11]

The historian Brian McAllister Linn has argued that the study of militaries in peacetime is plagued by a tendency to look for the causes of
future wars. This means that 'peacetime armed forces are more accurately
defined as the pre-war armed forces'.[12] However, foreknowledge of the
wars to come 'makes it relatively easy to pinpoint the weapons, the individuals, and the doctrines that proved important'. This can give a sense of
inevitability to these histories, where everything is prologue for the main
event that looms just off the stage. However, Linn notes that 'for those
who lack this historical hindsight, who are living through the aftermath
of the last war, and who lack a clear vision of the future – the challenges
of being a military professional in peacetime are much more complex'.[13]
This book attempts to recover that sense of uncertainty and complexity
that was inherent in the period that fell between the Cold War and War on
Terror. In the absence of the sort of clear structuring narratives provided
by these two conflicts, the Army had to articulate a strategy that was not
so much based on countering specific enemies but that was, in the words
of the 2001 'Quadrennial Defense Review', 'capabilities-based', ready to
be applied against any threat that emerged from an uncertain environment.[14] This post–Cold War era is particularly interesting both because

[11] The 'Revolution in Military Affairs' concept posits that new technologies combine with
doctrinal and tactical innovations to fundamentally alter the character of war.
[12] Brian McAllister Linn, 'Military Professionals and the Warrior Ethos in the Aftermath
of War', in *The Harmon Memorial Lectures in Military History, 1988–2017*, ed. Mark E.
Grotelueschen (Maxwell Air Force Base, AL: Air University Press, 2020), 591.
[13] Linn.
[14] 'Quadrennial Defense Review Report' (Washington, DC: US Department of Defense,
September 2001), iv.

it was a strange kind of peacetime – one that saw several armed American interventions around the world – and because the absolute degree of hegemony enjoyed by the United States in this 'unipolar moment' was surely historically unparalleled.[15] The headaches that this primacy gave the Army may have been ones that previous generations of leaders would have wished for, but they were very real nevertheless.

This book argues that the Army had three major responses to the unique dilemmas of the post–Cold War world. First, because planners struggled to envisage what future conflicts might look like and what US strategic priorities might be, they focused on building an adaptable, expeditionary force that could deploy quickly to anywhere in the world to further US aims, which could often be wide ranging. Unlike the Cold War–era Army, with its large overseas bases that housed military families and communities, the aim of reform efforts was to make sure that soldiers could be deployed on short notice, ready to carry out a huge range of tasks, including, for the first time, peacekeeping missions. Even as the Army downsized to a smaller, more expeditionary force, leaders refused to alter the overall mix of forces, keeping large numbers of armoured units on hand, and emphasising the need for sophisticated and well-trained soldiers who could handle any mission rather than focusing on specialised units equipped for particular contingencies. In the long arc of American military history, this was an unusual move, as the commitment to maintain a small Army at high levels of readiness and modernisation contrasted with past practices of maintaining a skeletal framework that could be quickly expanded into a much larger army in wartime.[16] Nonetheless, given the way the successes of the post-Vietnam reforms had been validated in Operation Desert Storm, maintaining a slightly smaller version of the Army of the 1980s seemed to make the most sense to Army leaders at the time.

---

[15] Hal Brands, *Making the Unipolar Moment: U.S. Foreign Policy and the Rise of the Post-Cold War Order* (Ithaca, NY: Cornell University Press, 2016); Charles Krauthammer, 'The Unipolar Moment', *Foreign Affairs* 70, no. 1 (1990): 23–33; Sidita Kushi and Monica Duffy Toft, 'Introducing the Military Intervention Project: A New Dataset on US Military Interventions, 1776–2019', *Journal of Conflict Resolution* (8 August 2022), https://doi.org/10.1177/00220027221117546.

[16] Richard H. Kohn, *Eagle and Sword: The Federalists and the Creation of the Military Establishment in America, 1783–1802* (New York: Free Press, 1975); William A. Taylor, *Military Service and American Democracy: From World War II to the Iraq and Afghanistan Wars* (Lawrence: University Press of Kansas, 2016); Christopher Capozzola, *Uncle Sam Wants You: World War I and the Making of the Modern American Citizen* (Oxford: Oxford University Press, 2010); David R. Segal, *Recruiting for Uncle Sam: Citizenship and Military Manpower Policy* (Lawrence: University Press of Kansas, 1989); J. P. Clark, *Preparing for War: The Emergence of the Modern U.S. Army, 1815–1917* (Cambridge, MA: Harvard University Press, 2017).

8   Uncertain Warriors

Second, in keeping with its preference for holding on to its existing force structure, the Army successfully resisted external pressures to rethink the nature of military service. The lesson of the Gulf War and the end of the Cold War had been that the All-Volunteer Force had worked.[17] Despite growing worries about a civil–military gap as a shrinking force made up of a less representative sample of the population concentrated more and more on large bases, half-hearted efforts to change the demographics of the military had little effect. The post-Vietnam notion that soldiers were inherently heroic was largely unshakeable and woven into American politics and popular culture.[18] Despite the changed strategic context and the new array of missions faced by the Army, calls to reintroduce the draft or move to a different model of military service fell on deaf ears, and even the Reserve Components of the Army became more professional and occupational in their outlook. Indeed, such was the emphasis on the 'profession of arms' that the concept of the citizen-soldier was effectively reduced to a rhetorical flourish deployed by military leaders and politicians in search of applause lines. Worries about recruiting and retention, which became more acute towards the end of the decade, did little to alter faith in the All-Volunteer Force.

Finally, if the Army successfully defended its model of military service, it had only partial success when it came to keeping the institution out of step with changes in broader society relating to gender and sexuality. Army leaders joined with other service chiefs to successfully oppose the Clinton administration's efforts to allow openly gay troops to serve but did so in a way that betrayed a lack of confidence that their resistance to this change could endure forever. The Army, like the rest of the military, also resisted attempts to open combat roles to women, but – in the wake of the 1996 Aberdeen Proving Ground sexual assault scandal – efforts to roll back progress and resegregate basic training failed. Not only that, but societal pressure and the more utilitarian question of what sort of skills would be needed for peacekeeping and non-combat missions, not to mention maintaining the Army's sophisticated technology, combined to create space for a critique of military masculinity in surprising places. Thus, while the Army's growing emphasis on a 'warrior ethos' that

---

[17] On the history of the All-Volunteer Force, see Beth Bailey, *America's Army: Making the All-Volunteer Force* (Cambridge, MA: Harvard University Press, 2009); Robert K. Griffith, *US Army's Transition to the All-Volunteer Force, 1968–1974* (Washington, DC: Center of Military History, 1996); Bernard Rostker, *I Want You! The Evolution of the All-Volunteer Force* (Santa Monica, CA: RAND, 2006).
[18] Andrew J. Bacevich, *The New American Militarism: How Americans Are Seduced by War* (New York: Oxford University Press, 2005); Walter L. Hixson, '"Red Storm Rising": Tom Clancy Novels and the Cult of National Security', *Diplomatic History* 17, no. 4 (1 October 1993): 599–614.

emerged towards the end of the decade was in part a backlash against the perceived threat of 'identity politics', ultimately this project sought to produce an ethos that, while not quite gender neutral in its focus, looked very different from the more traditional warrior ethos that many had hoped the Army would promote.

Debates over military service, roles and missions, and identity sometimes moved through different terrain and involved different protagonists but usually boiled down to two duelling impulses. One was to emphasise that professional American soldiers were something akin to Spartan warriors, where every soldier was psychologically committed to the demands of combat, regardless of specialty or distance from the battlefield. The other impulse was directly in opposition to this notion of a hypermasculine 'warrior culture'. Those who pushed back against discourse about warriors were a diverse group ranging from those who wanted to reinstate an all-male draft to those who wanted to fully end the gay ban and open all positions in the Army to women. In spite of their differences, they all emphasised not only the need for the Army to be broadly aligned with the values of American society but asserted that those very values had martial virtues of their own, given the ambiguities of modern conflict.

★★★★

There is something ironic in the fact that a period which supposedly marked the final triumph of liberal democracy saw the return of the warrior: a pre-modern and even primordial figure. This is doubly ironic because, as Linn notes, professional soldiers began to supplant warriors in early modern society precisely because warriors tended to contribute very little in peacetime and were unreliable, being more focused on their own personal honour than broader political goals, and often terrorised civilians.[19]

Even if the definition of warrior has been remarkably stable across cultures and time, the manner in which people have deployed the term and, crucially, understood its moral valence has differed. For instance, the classicist Bret Devereux argues that, contrary to popular understanding, warriors were not in fact common in ancient Roman or even Greek society.[20] In warrior societies such as Sparta, individuals might conflate their own sense of masculine honour with that of the *polis*, but as Greek

---

[19] Linn, 'Military Professionals and the Warrior Ethos in the Aftermath of War', 595.
[20] Bret Devereaux, 'The U.S. Military Needs Citizen-Soldiers, Not Warriors', *Foreign Policy*, 19 April 2021, https://foreignpolicy.com/2021/04/19/united-states-afghanistan-citizen-soldiers-warriors-forever-wars/.

city-states evolved into more complex polities, the division of labour became more specialised, and the warrior identity predominated less.[21] The Latin term for warrior, *bellator*, was rarely applied to Roman soldiers, who were known as *milites*, which, as Devereux points out, 'comes from the same mil-root as the word "mile," signifying a collection of things (a Roman mile being a collection of a thousand paces)'.[22] Roman *milites* were part of a collective. Soldiers were paid by, and thus subordinated to, a higher authority, 'a relationship that naturally placed them in groups raised by some other political entity – be it a king, parliament, or congress'.[23] For a soldier, fighting is an occupation carried out in service to a larger polity. In contrast, warriors are attached to war because it forms a central part of their own personal identity. This meant that even where societies required military service of all men, they did not expect them to be warriors. Soldiers become civilians again when they take off the uniform, but warriors can never truly retire. Even when the war ends, a warrior remains a warrior. Even when warriors fight in groups, they fight for individual reasons rooted in their own personal identity rather than for a greater cause. Thus, warriors are 'definitionally a class apart, individuals whose connection to war sets them outside civilian society'.[24] Inevitably, such a group, focused as it was on martial rather than other virtues, would look upon civilians with contempt. For Devereux, the re-emergence of rhetoric lauding warriors is a dangerous development: one that portends a threat to a free and democratic society.

Even if actual warrior societies were far less common than the popular imagination allows, the celebration of the values associated with warriors, such as courage, honour and glory in battle, was certainly ubiquitous across time and space. By the end of the twentieth century, though, it seemed like the balance between veneration of that warrior ethos and societal disgust at the absurdity and tragedy of war had tipped decisively towards the latter impulse. In 1999, the International Committee of the Red Cross commissioned a large-scale survey to commemorate the 50th anniversary of the signing of the Geneva Conventions. This survey, 'People on War', consisted of interviews with 12,860 people across twelve countries who had endured the effects of modern war in recent years.[25] These interviewees,

---

[21] Moshe Berent, 'Anthropology and the Classics: War, Violence, and the Stateless Polis', *The Classical Quarterly* 50, no. 1 (2000): 257–89.
[22] Devereaux, 'The U.S. Military Needs Citizen-Soldiers, Not Warriors'.
[23] Devereaux.
[24] Devereaux.
[25] International Committee of the Red Cross, 'The People on War Project: ICRC Worldwide Consultation on the Rules of War' (Geneva: ICRC, 1999), iii, www.icrc.org/en/doc/assets/files/other/globalreport.pdf.

both civilians and combatants, reflected on the psychological and social dimensions of war. In the words of one of the survey's authors, 'most of the respondents seemed to offer a sort of meta-narrative, telling of a kind of demoralization that appears common to all, fighters and civilians alike, regardless of the specific context and circumstances'.[26] They described war as a 'traumatic collective experience', not just because of the physical and psychological suffering they had endured, but 'connected with the aware-ness that war had lost its meaning as a social reality'. These interviewees spoke of being 'crushed by the absurdity and moral disgrace of the violent episodes they had been exposed to either as perpetrators, victims or spec-tators', and fighters emphasised their feelings of alienation and the impos-sibility of deriving any glory or nobility from armed conflict. Indeed, their experience of violence 'contradicted all principles, all representations, all values inherited from the past and traditionally associated with war'.[27] The depth of this disillusionment, which would have been intimately familiar to generations of scholars of war, seemed to suggest that, in the eyes of global public opinion at least, the warrior ethos had lost its utility.

There have, however, been attempts to rescue warriors from obsoles-cence. The international relations scholar Christopher Coker has argued that warriors have unfairly acquired a bad reputation in western culture in recent decades. Channelling Nietzsche, Coker argues that what sepa-rates warriors from soldiers is the question of will. Warriors are those who continue to fight, often with enthusiasm, even when the situation is impossible. For Coker, 'war is transformative' because it 'allows a war-rior to tap into the vein of his own heroism. It allows him to lead an authentic life'.[28] Coker is less concerned with warriors as a distinctive class than he is with the warrior as an individual, and he argues that we have always been able to find warriors in the ranks of soldiers, even if their presence has been unevenly distributed. He argues that warriors operate in both the instrumental and existential dimensions and that modern warriors do indeed serve the state as well as their own needs. However, Coker's analysis is not so much a celebration as it is a lament. He complains that 'soldiers these days are expected to be like oncolo-gists, whose professional speciality is studying cancer and whose profes-sional vocation is fighting it. A soldier's profession may be fighting, but his vocation, society believes, should be to combat war, not glory in it.'[29]

---

[26] Gilbert Holleufer, 'Heroic Memory and Contemporary War', *International Review of the Red Cross* 101, no. 910 (April 2019): 231.

[27] Holleufer, 231.

[28] Christopher Coker, *The Warrior Ethos: Military Culture and the War on Terror*, (Abingdon: Routledge, 2007), 4–5.

[29] Coker, 9.

He argues that war has lost its grandeur and that, far from being resurgent, contemporary warriors have become disenchanted with what war has become, claiming that 'war becomes soulless when it is more life-denying than life-affirming – a paradox which has haunted every warrior since Achilles'.[30] Where Devereux and the authors of the 'People on War' report see the warrior as a figure who should be confined to the past, Coker sees a society that is not honest with itself about what war is and what sort of values it requires. The contemporary re-emergence of the warrior ethos, in his view, is no more than a futile attempt to reinvigorate western appreciation for the ambiguous virtues of the warrior.

Coker derived some of his analysis from the work of the American strategist Edward Luttwak, who observed the developments of warfare in the 1990s and argued that the reluctance of western governments to accept casualties in war was not only a product of the low birth rate of post-industrial societies but of the fact that the goals of their military interventions were often quite limited and only weakly related to the sort of vital national interests that would bring about total commitment and a willingness to lose soldiers.[31] Moreover, standoff weapons, although expensive, offered governments a way to achieve their objectives without risking their own people, even if these tactics transferred risk to the civilian population on the receiving end of those very same weapons.[32] Luttwak coined the influential term 'post-heroic warfare' to describe this phenomenon. In this emerging way of war, there was no room for heroes or warriors.[33] Coker argued that 'soldiers are becoming their technology' and that this highly technocentric, risk-averse mode of fighting stripped war of 'that "religious" element which made the confrontation with the enemy and oneself in battle an epiphany for some, almost a religious experience'.[34]

However, these narratives of post-heroic warfare and of a west that has lost its appetite for war cannot account for the fact that western societies have been content to see their small professional militaries endlessly deployed on combat missions that can and do produce casualties. The sociologist Anthony King has a more convincing explanation for the decline of heroism in modern warfare. Focusing on contemporary

---

[30] Coker, 13.
[31] Edward N. Luttwak, 'Toward Post-Heroic Warfare', *Foreign Affairs* 74, no. 3 (1995): 109–22.
[32] Martin Shaw, *The New Western Way of War: Risk-Transfer War and Its Crisis in Iraq* (London: Polity Press, 2005).
[33] Luttwak's argument provoked a debate among scholars of the military about the nature of heroism in contemporary warfare. See Sibylle Scheipers, *Heroism and the Changing Character of War: Toward Post-Heroic Warfare?* (Basingstoke: Palgrave Macmillan, 2014).
[34] Coker, *The Warrior Ethos*, 12.

infantry tactics and cohesion, King offers an ethnographic account of the behaviour of the soldiers whose exposure to death and violence is similar to that faced by their predecessors throughout history.[35] He argues that, unlike the mass armies of poorly trained citizen-soldiers, modern professional militaries have little need for individual heroes. King argues that even if discourses of masculinity and patriotism still abound in these organisations, the actual source of cohesion and effectiveness is the shared ability to conduct tightly choreographed drills that require all members of the platoon to perfectly synchronise their actions in order to win the firefight. These drills, similar to those taught to professional athletes in team sports and inculcated through repeated and intensive training regimes, mean that technical competence in the minutiae of marksmanship and close-quarter battle drills is far more important than the willingness to jump out of a trench and single-handedly charge at the enemy in the hopes of inspiring comrades to follow. In this iteration of the professional military, there is still room for sacrifice and even heroism, but the basis for inclusion in the group has radically altered.[36] The point is not to rely on individual warriors having a near-religious experience in combat, but to have a well-drilled team capable of automatic reactions and acting cohesively as a single unit.

Even if we might still reasonably call these professionals warriors, given that the skill set they employ is incredibly specialised and that they still draw on many of the same martial virtues of courage, self-sacrifice, and loyalty as soldiers in earlier eras, it seems as though there is something qualitatively different about them in a way that separates them from the unhappy warriors that Coker describes. Indeed, the retired British general Sir John Kiszely has questioned the sloppy usage of the term, asking 'is a warrior just a military professional? Or is a warrior essentially a person with a strong habitual liking for fighting, an aggressive person whose job is to "destroy the enemy"?'[37] He argues that the term has 'a number of meanings and is potentially misleading', especially in the complex environment of 'postmodern war'.[38]

Thus, if there were tensions between those who feared the rise of a warrior class and those who thought that a warrior ethos would be vital

---

[35] Anthony King, *The Combat Soldier: Infantry Tactics and Cohesion in the Twentieth and Twenty-First Centuries* (Oxford: Oxford University Press, 2013).

[36] King also argues that the transformation of the armed forces has involved significant amounts of outsourcing and privatisation. See Anthony King, 'The Post-Fordist Military', *Journal of Political and Military Sociology* 34, no. 2 (Winter 2006): 359–74.

[37] John Kiszely, 'Postmodern Challenges for Modern Warriors', *Army History*, no. 71 (2009): 24.

[38] Kiszely, 31.

for success in twenty-first-century conflicts, there was also a split between those who thought of warriors as masculine throwbacks to older forms of society and those who were effectively using the term to describe highly competent professionals whose business happened to be war. While its utility as a concept that delineated the military as a separate and special group was clear, 'warrior' was still an ambiguous term that allowed groups to ascribe different meanings to it and to use it to advance agendas that conflicted with each other.

★★★★

The following chapters trace how tensions between these conflicting imperatives animated discussions both within and outside the Army over the organisation's future in the post–Cold War world. This book takes a broadly thematic approach, investigating the most important venues where the American soldier's identity was contested and produced. By drilling down into specific issues such public adulation of solders; gender and sexuality; peacekeeping; recruiting; technology and the soldier; and warrior culture, we can see more clearly how competing demands pulled Army leaders in different directions and produced articulations of 'warrior' identities that were riven with contradictions and tensions.

Chapter 1 examines the Army's post-Vietnam reconstruction of its image and explores how the triumphalism that followed the Gulf War encapsulated the notion that soldiers represented all that was best about the United States. The Army's reforms after defeat in South-east Asia and its attempts to build an All-Volunteer Force at the end of the draft were central to its self-image as a highly professional and competent force, dedicated to avoiding the mistakes that had led to defeat in Vietnam and malaise in the aftermath of that war. Even here, though, we can see how some within the Army worried about a force that was becoming too bureaucratic and too detached from the realities of war, as mid-ranking officers began to call for a 'warrior ethos' that would rededicate the Army to the essentials of its profession. This dissent, along with any doubts about the Army's post-Vietnam recovery, was quashed by the force's performance in Operation Desert Storm, where American soldiers displayed extraordinary skill and competence in winning a rapid victory. Crucially, Desert Storm also marked a moment when the broader American public joined in with celebrating the image of the volunteer soldier as an inherently heroic figure.

Chapter 2 demonstrates that, while that broader public regard for the military endured, the Gulf War's aftermath immediately saw a series of crises over who could serve in the Army. It begins with the Army's position in the 1993 debate over allowing gay personnel to serve openly in the US military. In particular, the chapter focuses on how the Army sold a vision of soldiers as a separate and unique group that had to be allowed to disregard wider social norms in order to be able to operate effectively. Debates about women in the military played out along very similar lines; halting moves by the Clinton administration to open up more roles for women in the armed forces were met with complaints about cohesion and the sanctity of the 'band of brothers', even when sexual assault scandals made clear what the consequences of this rhetoric were. Here, though, we can see how conservative complaints about a 'kinder, gentler military' were beginning to lose their purchase. Despite calls to do so, the Army did not resegregate its recruit training and roll back other forms of progress for women. In dealing with these complaints, Army leaders turned to a discourse about warriors and argued that being a warrior in the late twentieth century was more complicated than it used to be.

Chapter 3 examines how some of those complexities played out on deployments, by tracing debates over peacekeeping operations, missions that the Army had firmly committed to by the mid-1990s. Peacekeeping meant different things to policymakers, Army leaders, public intellectuals and those who served on such missions. Army leaders were generally not enthusiastic about participation in these operations, but most recognised that their complexities were indicative of future trends in conflict. Similarly, personnel deployed as peacekeepers accepted the role, even if they often struggled to understand how best to navigate the grey zone between peace and war. Peacekeeping missions may have been a central, if sometimes unwanted, concern of the US Army in the 1990s, but they also exposed deeper fissures within the Army and broader American society about the organisation's proper role and the sorts of attributes that American soldiers would need in the twenty-first century and heightened the tensions between notions of the soldier as violent warfighter or armed humanitarian, citizen-soldier or professional warrior. Some even used the opportunity to ask again who soldiers should be, advocating for a greater role in peacekeeping missions for reservist citizen-soldiers or even a new class of putative short-service soldiers, drawn from the ranks of college graduates, that would renew the bonds between the Army and the society it served.

Chapter 4 directly considers the questions of military service and recruiting that became particularly acute by the end of the decade, as the Army struggled to meet its recruiting quotas and to retain personnel. At the same time, the new pace of deployments and the diminished number of bases meant that soldiers and their families increasingly had less contact with the civilian world. When the Army missed its recruiting targets in 1998 and 1999, this prompted renewed concerns over the health of the All-Volunteer Force and its relationship with broader society. While Army leaders made heavy use of 'citizen-soldier' rhetoric and looked to movies such as *Saving Private Ryan* to promote these ideals, they fought back against attempts to change recruiting practices and terms of service to produce a more demographically balanced force. At the same time, tensions between the active duty Army and Reserve Components were at an all-time high, as both sides fought to maintain their position during budget cuts and Army leaders began to doubt whether these citizen-soldiers had the skills and training needed to succeed in the profession of arms.

Chapter 5 explores how technology and the drive for expertise helped foreclose some of these moves to rethink the nature of military service. While the Army as an institution was somewhat less enamoured of the putative 'Revolution in Military Affairs' than other services, there was nonetheless a move to digitise the force and acquire new precision weapons systems and communications platforms. This modernisation process envisioned soldiers being part of a sophisticated network of sensors, command nodes and weapons systems. Given the difficulties in recruiting and retaining such highly skilled soldiers, not to mention the proportion of the Army's budget that had been eaten up by research and development costs related to this transformation, Army leaders turned to private contractors both to operate and maintain some of the more sophisticated computer systems and to take over some of the more mundane parts of the Army's logistics and support services. These contractors would be expected to accompany an increasingly expeditionary Army overseas, as the result of this digitisation process was supposed to be a lethal force with a light footprint, capable of deploying anywhere in the world at short notice.

Chapter 6 examines the growth of the warrior ethos within the Army and ties it to this shift towards expeditionary operations. As the decade wore on, complaints both in the ranks and in the conservative media focused on how the Army's attempts to adapt to the post–Cold War world was producing a force bereft of the warriors it needed to succeed. Army Chief of Staff General Eric Shinseki used his tenure to try to reinvigorate Army culture to make it more hospitable to warriors. Shinseki's attempts to produce unity via the introduction of the black beret as the Army's working headdress were immensely controversial and even counterproductive, as critics charged him with devaluing the service of the Army Rangers who had previously worn the beret and of handing out honour too cheaply. He had more success with his 'warrior ethos' initiative, launched in the final weeks of his tenure and carried on by his successor, General Peter Schoomaker. Reflecting doctrinal developments that been brewing since the late 1990s, the 'warrior ethos' programme sought to directly embed that ethos within the Army, making it a central part of recruiting and training at all levels, while also affirming that close combat was both a fundamental task for all soldiers and the core undertaking that differentiated them from the rest of society. It may seem strange than an era that had begun with claims about the end of history ended with the Army invoking such a primordial term and telling its cooks and clerks that they, too, were warriors, but the sometimes existential anxieties unleashed by the Cold War's end could produce unexpected results and new ways to think about both the Army's identity and its purpose.

1   The Post-Vietnam Recovery, Operation Desert Storm and the Veneration of the Volunteer Soldier

In September 1989, *Parameters*, the journal of the US Army War College, published an article by Major Daniel P. Bolger so pungent in its criticism of the Army's culture that it provoked a note from the journal's editor to the War College's director of academic affairs to warn him about a possible backlash.[1] Bolger's article, 'Two Armies', opened with a famous quote from *The Centurions*, French author Jean Larteguy's novel about the experience of a French parachute battalion in Indochina and Algeria, in which the protagonist, a veteran of Dien Bien Phu, lamented, 'I'd like France to have two armies'. One would be 'for display, with lovely guns, tanks, little soldiers, fanfares, staffs, distinguished and doddering generals, and dear little regimental officers who would be deeply concerned over their general's bowel movements or their colonel's piles'. This was 'an army that would be shown for a modest fee on every fairground in the country', while the 'real' army would be 'composed entirely of young enthusiasts in camouflage battledress, who would not be put on display but from whom impossible efforts would be demanded, and to whom all sorts of tricks would be taught'.[2] Bolger's complaint was that the United States was now also fielding 'two armies, one for show and one for real fighting'. He critiqued the Army of the Cold War as being 'heavy with tanks, mechanized infantry, self-propelled guns, nimble helicopters, sophisticated electronics of all designs, and fleets of fuel and ammunition trucks'. This was 'America's demonstration army', ready for action 'if the Wehrmacht should resurrect'. Under the cloud of mutually assured destruction, though, they were 'strictly for show'.[3] The ethos of this 'display army' was dominated by bureaucratic routine and a 'preoccupation with quotidian detail'.[4]

---

[1] Lloyd Matthews, 'Memorandum for Colonel Lunday: Potentially Controversial Parameters Article', 19 July 1989, Lloyd Matthews Papers; Box 1A, Folder 10, notes for 'The Early Struggle, The Later Success' by Colonel Lloyd J. Matthews, 2nd binder [part 4 of 9], US Army Heritage and Education Center, Carlisle, PA (AHEC).

[2] Daniel Bolger, 'Two Armies', *Parameters: The US Army War College Quarterly* 19, no. 1 (4 July 1989): 24, https://press.armywarcollege.edu/parameters/vol19/iss1/5.

[3] Bolger, 26–7.

[4] Bolger, 32.

Less than two years later, this same army was indeed on display on the streets of American cities, but as the object of national adulation during the long months of victory parades that followed its evisceration of the Iraqi Army during Operation Desert Storm. The calls for such celebrations began even before the guns had finished firing in Iraq and Kuwait. On the very day that President Bush declared a ceasefire in the Middle East, popular author Tom Clancy took to the pages of the *Los Angeles Times* to ask: 'how about a few parades? How about the collective thank you that was cruelly denied to the last class of American warriors? .... The military has learned its lessons from Vietnam. What about the rest of us?'[5] This spirit of gratitude was widespread and, as Americans prepared to celebrate their military via mass spectacle, President Bush's speechwriters suggested that he invoke that spirit of gratitude for a national regeneration by asking Americans to 'honor those who have served us – those who have shown us all that America means to the world – by making certain that we here are worthy of them'.[6] Far from being a paper tiger, it seemed as though the 'demonstration army' that Bolger had criticised was for far more than show.

How, then, do we explain this discrepancy between the anxiety that Bolger and officers like him expressed in the late 1980s and the triumphalism that followed in 1991? Part of the reason is that Bolger was not claiming that the Army of the 1980s was a decrepit institution; he found much to admire in the 'real army' that he himself hailed from, but worried about the effects of focusing too much on the unlikely scenario of conventional war in Europe. Mostly, though, this disjuncture stems from the fact that, as historian Adrian Lewis argues, 'while the military may have recovered materially, technologically, and qualitatively from the Vietnam War ... it had not completely recovered emotionally and psychologically'.[7] Both the Army's own confidence in its abilities and public support for it were somewhat brittle until the full extent of the institution's recovery from its post-Vietnam nadir was made clear in the Persian Gulf. While most observers hailed vast improvements in the standard of the Army's recruits and training, many officers such as Bolger continued to worry that the force was not adapting quickly enough

---

[5] Tom Clancy, 'How About a Few Parades?' *Los Angeles Times*, 28 February 1991, B13, in folder 03195-008, Persian Gulf Working Group, Paul McNeill Files, White House Office of Communications, George Bush Presidential Library (GBPL).

[6] Dan McGroarty and Peggy Dooley, 'Draft Presidential Remarks: Joint Session of Congress, the Capitol, March 6, 1991', 5 March 1991, folder 29166-004 'Persian Gulf War [2]', Issues File, John Sununu Files, White House Office of the Chief Staff, GBPL.

[7] Adrian R. Lewis, *The American Culture of War: The History of U.S. Military Force from World War II to Operation Iraqi Freedom* (Abingdon: Routledge, 2006), 312.

for what would soon be a post–Cold War world. For these critics, the quality of the American soldier was not in doubt, but it was an open question whether the Army was producing the right sort of soldier for the missions they would likely face.

As we will see in later chapters, these debates would resurface in the 1990s and beyond, but the events of 1991 meant that they would take place on different terrain. After the success of Operation Desert Storm, the narrative of a redeemed Army was irrefutable. This chapter traces the Army's rehabilitation of its reputation in the wake of the Vietnam War and then focuses on how that rehabilitation created and then rei-fied the image of the soldier as inherently heroic and representative of all that was best about Americans. Through movies, advertising campaigns, institutional reforms and public discourse about veterans and soldiers, the soldier went from pariah to paragon.

Two features were central to this transformation. The first was the advent of the All-Volunteer Force and the post-Vietnam reforms to Army training, equipment and doctrine. After a shaky start, the All-Volunteer Force's success normalised the notion of soldiering as an occupation rather than an obligation, and the reforms seemed to create a much more professional and competent force than the one that had been wracked by unrest and uncertainty in the 1970s. Second, the Army's performance in Operation Desert Storm affirmed this narrative of professionalism and competence. Even as the Army stabilised, some, such as Bolger, ques-tioned whether it had gone far enough in its post-Vietnam reforms or whether it had lost something essential in its single-minded focus on one type of war. Any such doubts about the abilities of the American soldier were swept aside in both the public outpouring of support for the military during the build-up to war and the Army's performance during the campaign itself. This was even more apparent in the aftermath of the war. The celebrations that took place to welcome home Gulf War veterans stood out as the largest seen in the United States since the end of World War II, as hundreds of thousands of troops marched in trium-phant parades in almost every major American city and in hundreds of small towns. But the pageantry did not simply celebrate American mili-tary and technological prowess. Spectators at these parades also engaged in a novel form of patriotism that emphasised unquestioning support for the troops without necessarily affirming the legitimacy of the war itself.

The depth of this veneration meant that the 'stars' of Operation Desert Storm would be in hot demand in the war's aftermath. General Norman Schwarzkopf was fêted at both the Kentucky Derby and the Indianapolis 500, and his memoirs were a bestseller. Another general whose mem-oirs topped the *New York Times* bestseller lists, Chairman of the Joint

Chiefs of Staff Colin Powell, was the subject of feverish political specu-
lation, as pundits ventured that he would be a viable candidate for the
vice presidential ticket for either of the two parties in 1992.[8] Not since
Eisenhower had generals commanded such political respect across party
lines, a reflection of the fact that the military was regaining the reputation
it had enjoyed in the aftermath of World War II. While norms about civilian control of the military broadly held firm in this period, the 'celebrity
general' phenomenon made it clear that the Army's post-Vietnam trajectory now meant that soldiers had political currency and, as exemplars
of American values, would be objects of contestation during the culture
wars of the 1990s.[9] The victory in the Persian Gulf, and the subsequent
swell of emotion, thus represented a crucial moment in the American
public's deepening veneration for US soldiers and veterans. The Gulf
War celebrations made it clear that the Vietnam-era image of the soldier
as a broken or rebellious draftee was now finally and purposefully eclipsed
by the notion of the volunteer service member as hero, a powerful image
that would shape much of what was to come as the Army, along with the
other military services, began to reckon with the post–Cold War world.

1.1   The Fall and Rise of the Army after Vietnam

The notion of generals being star personalities was very far from reality in 1970. Long before the final collapse of the South Vietnamese
regime in Saigon, it was obvious that the war in South-east Asia had

---

[8] Colin L. Powell and Joseph E. Persico, *My American Journey: An Autobiography* (New
York: Random House, 1995); Norman Schwarzkopf, *It Doesn't Take a Hero: The
Autobiography of General H. Norman Schwarzkopf* (New York: Bantam, 1993); Victor
Gold, 'Will Colin Powell Be on the Ticket in '92?', *Tampa Bay Times*, 28 May 1991,
www.tampabay.com/archive/1991/04/28/will-colin-powell-be-on-the-ticket-in-92/
C1kX3QTaP0G28MhKT3Ue/Exmv0yhh22d; Cathleen Decker, 'The Ticket for
Clinton? Everyone Has an Idea: Campaign – Suggestions for the Vice Presidential Spot
Are Pouring in, but Few Fill That Combination of Glitz and Stability', *Los Angeles
Times*, 12 May 1992, www.latimes.com/archives/la-xpm-1992-05-12-mn-1721-story
.htmlC1kX3QTaP0G28MhKT3Ue/Exmv0yhh22d; Paul Galloway and Cheryl Lavin,
'A New No. 2 May Be Just the Ticket', *Chicago Tribune*, 28 July 1992.

[9] Even if these norms ultimately held, historians and political scientists nonetheless spent
much of the decade debating the extent to which they had frayed. Chapters 2 and 3 discuss
some of the areas where generals and politicians clashed. Richard H. Kohn, 'Out of Control:
The Crisis in Civil–Military Relations', *The National Interest* 35 (Spring 1994): 3; Russell
Weigley, 'The American Military and the Principle of Civilian Control from McClellan
to Powell', *Journal of Military History* 57 no. 5 (1993), 27–58; Peter D. Feaver, 'The
Civil–Military Problematique: Huntington, Janowitz, and the Question of Civilian Control',
Armed Forces & Society 23, no. 2 (1996): 149–78; Ole R. Holsti, 'A Widening Gap between
the U.S. Military and Civilian Society? Some Evidence, 1976–96', *International Security*
23, no. 3 (1998): 5–42; Deborah Avant, 'Conflicting Indicators of "Crisis" in American
Civil–Military Relations', *Armed Forces & Society* 24, no. 3 (1 April 1998): 375–87.

done serious damage to the Army as an institution.[10] Morale was low, the non-commissioned officer (NCO) cadre had been decimated by enlisted personnel opting not to re-enlist, the quality of draftees was poor, discipline problems abounded and Army combat units all over the world reported poor readiness.[11] By 1972, only four of thirteen divisions were rated as ready for combat.[12] Even those officers who were seen to have a bright future in the Army found that the 'heart and soul of the officer corps' was imperilled. A 1970 study by the Army War College on military professionalism in the officer corps found that the 450 participants surveyed, including the entire War College class of 1970, were scathing about the institution's ethos.[13] All reported a significant difference between the ideal values and the actual values of the officer corps, and reported a zero defects culture that was intolerant of any admission of problems, rampant careerism, a lack of integrity and a lack of care for subordinates. Officers talked about being forced to fake readiness reports, to lie to progress the careers of their commanding officers and even to carry spare rifles with them in Vietnam so that they could plant these weapons on the bodies of unarmed Vietnamese people killed by American patrols.[14] Crucially, the study's authors did not blame external 'fiscal, political, sociological or managerial influences' or the lack of public support for the war in Vietnam for this crisis.[15] The problems the Army was facing stemmed primarily from choices made by its own leaders.

While the officer corps' integrity had been badly damaged by the Vietnam War, the aftermath of that same war caused even greater problems in the enlisted ranks. In the words of the Army's official history of

---

[10] There was an extensive literature dedicated to exploring the Army's breakdown while it was ongoing. Cecil Currey, *Self-destruction: The Disintegration and Decay of the United States Army during the Vietnam Era* (New York: Norton, 1981); Stuart H. Loory, *Defeated: Inside America's Military Machine* (New York: Random House, 1973); Richard Boyle, *The Flower of the Dragon: The Breakdown of the U.S. Army in Vietnam* (San Francisco: Ramparts Press, 1972); Richard A. Gabriel and Paul Savage, *Crisis in Command: Mismanagement in the Army* (New York: Hill and Wang, 1978); William L. Hauser, *America's Army in Crisis: A Study in Civil–Military Relations* (Baltimore: The Johns Hopkins University Press, 1973); William R. Corson, *Consequences of Failure* (New York: W. W. Norton & Company, 1974).

[11] Robert H. Scales, *Certain Victory: The U.S. Army in the Gulf War* (Washington, DC: Potomac Books, Inc., 1998), 6–7, 15–16.

[12] Richard Lock-Pullan, *U.S. Intervention Policy and Army Innovation: From Vietnam to Iraq* (London: Routledge, 2005), 49.

[13] US Army War College, 'Study on Military Professionalism' (Carlisle Barracks, PA: US Army War College, 30 June 1970), Defense Technical Information Center, http://handle.dtic.mil/100.2/ADA063748.

[14] US Army War College, 28, B-1-3, B-1-14.

[15] US Army War College, v.

Figure 1.1 Military policemen being taught to recognise drug para-
phernalia, 1973

Operation Desert Storm, 'the American Army emerged from Vietnam
cloaked in anguish ... it was an institution fighting merely to maintain its
existence in the midst of growing, apathy, decay, and intolerance'.[16] By
1971, the *New York Times* was reporting on bases where commanders
needed to chain up vehicles lest they be stolen and where muggings took
place in unlit areas. Army leaders in both South Vietnam and Europe
reported increasing problems with drug use, and the desertion rate
climbed steadily higher, with 17.7 per cent of all soldiers in the Army
listed as having been absent without leave and fully 7.4 per cent classi-
fied as deserters (Figure 1.1).[17] Overseas, stagnating wages along with
the drop in the value of the dollar relative to the Deutschmark meant
that Germans began to comment on the poor quality of American military housing and the beat-up cars that soldiers were driving, while the
state of race relations in the US 7th Army drew the attention of the West
German government, as African American GIs protested against racist

[16] Robert H. Scales, *Certain Victory: The US Army in the Gulf War* (Washington, DC:
Potomac Books, 1998), 6.
[17] B. Drummond Ayres Jr., 'Army Is Shaken by Crisis in Morale and Discipline', *New York
Times*, 5 September 1971, www.nytimes.com/1971/09/05/archives/army-is-shaken-by-
crisis-in-morale-and-discipline-army-is-shaken-by.html.

treatment at the hands of both the Army and local authorities.[18] Some GIs looked to their counterparts in the Dutch military, who had successfully won the right to collective bargaining, and wondered whether such a move would help them improve their working and living conditions.[19] The need for some sort of radical intervention was made clear by the fact that a 1973 Harris Poll 'revealed that the American public ranked the military only above sanitation workers in relative order of respect'.[20] Given this state of affairs, attracting and retaining high-quality recruits would be increasingly difficult.

The recruiting problem was more acute than it had been in decades, as the Nixon administration moved to abolish the draft by 1973. Selective Service had been a vital source of manpower for over thirty years, not just in the raw number of draftees it provided but in motivating others to volunteer for the Army before being drafted, so as to have more control over their military specialisation.[21] Immediately, Army leaders worried about finding enough volunteers for combat units and began to invest both in initiatives to improve the quality of life for enlisted personnel and in a vastly expanded advertising budget. These measures, which included relaxing haircut regulations, allowing individual rooms in barracks, advertisements that highlighted job training opportunities and, most controversially of all, the slogan 'Today's Army wants to join you', created consternation in the officer and NCO ranks over a softening of the Army's image and seemingly did little to improve morale or the quality of recruits in what was now an All-Volunteer Force.[22]

As historian Beth Bailey notes in *America's Army*, her history of the All-Volunteer Force, these early years were difficult. While the Nixon administration raised salaries by 61 per cent in 1973 to aid with recruitment, wages stagnated after that, with a 10 per cent decline in military

18 Maria Höhn, 'The Racial Crisis of 1971 in the US Military: Finding Solutions in West Germany and South Korea', in *Over There: Living with the U.S. Military Empire from World War Two to the Present*, ed. Maria Höhn and Seungsook Moon (Durham, NC: Duke University Press, 2010), 267–9; Howard J. De Nike, 'The US Military and Dissenters in the Ranks', in *GIs in Germany: The Social, Economic, Cultural, and Political History of the American Military Presence*, ed. Thomas W. Maulucci and Detlef Junker (Washington, DC: German Historical Institute; Cambridge University Press, 2013), 277.
19 Jennifer Mittelstadt, '"The Army Is a Service, Not a Job": Unionization, Employment, and the Meaning of Military Service in the Late-Twentieth Century United States', *International Labor and Working-Class History* 80, no. 1 (2011): 29–52.
20 Scales, *Certain Victory*, 7.
21 Amy J. Rutenberg, *Rough Draft: Cold War Military Manpower Policy and the Origins of Vietnam-Era Draft Resistance* (Ithaca, NY: Cornell University Press, 2019).
22 Beth Bailey, *America's Army: Making the All-Volunteer Force* (Cambridge, MA: Harvard University Press, 2009); Bernard D. Rostker and K. C. Yeh, *I Want You! The Evolution of the All-Volunteer Force* (Santa Monica, CA: Rand Corporation, 2006).

pay relative to civilian pay between 1975 and 1979 compounded by the expiry of the Vietnam-era GI Bill.[23] Meanwhile, over 250 recruiters were disciplined in 1973 for falsifying high school diplomas and concealing the police records of potential recruits, and a further 5 officers and 187 NCOs were relieved of duty in 1979 for the same thing.[24] Retention among career soldiers also dropped precipitously, with re-enlistment rates falling from 83 per cent at the end of the draft to 69 per cent in 1979.[25] Concerns over 'quality' were deeply entangled with race, as complaints regarding the quality of recruits tracked the increase in the number of African Americans in the ranks.[26] The drop in intelligence test scores, though, was driven not by black recruits, who tended to come from the African American lower middle class, but by an influx of poor white soldiers. By 1978, an increasing number of soldiers were failing their qualification tests in their area of speciality and, writing in *The Atlantic Monthly* in 1981, the journalist James Fallows spoke about an Army in which 'such soldiers as do enlist stand befuddled before the space age machinery they must operate'.[27] By 1981, over 50 per cent of all Army recruits were classed as Category IV in intelligence tests, leading observers to complain that the All-Volunteer Force was 'too dumb, too black and too costly'.[28] It seemed to many observers as though the return of the draft was only a matter of time.

The combination of recruiting and morale problems, along with limited training and maintenance budgets, led Army Chief of Staff General Edward 'Shy' Meyer to tell President Carter that the United States had a 'hollow army' in November 1979, a warning he repeated before Congress in May 1980.[29] The immediate impetus for Meyer's declaration, which has since acquired immense weight as a trope within the military as a whole, was reporting that suggested that four of the Army's ten stateside divisions were incapable of deploying to Europe, with every

---

[23] Scales, *Certain Victory*, 15.

[24] Bailey, *America's Army*, 105–6; James Kitfield, *Prodigal Soldiers: How the Generation of Officers Born of Vietnam Revolutionized the American Style of War* (Washington, DC: Potomac Books, 1997), 208.

[25] Kitfield, *Prodigal Soldiers*, 208.

[26] By 1974, over 30 per cent of Army recruits were African American. In 1967, during a period where civil rights campaigners were protesting against disproportionate African American casualties in Vietnam, 16.3 per cent of draftees were Black. Bailey, *America's Army*, 115; Gerald F. Goodwin, 'Black and White in Vietnam', *New York Times*, 18 July 2017, www.nytimes.com/2017/07/18/opinion/racism-vietnam-war.html.

[27] Bailey, *America's Army*, 121.

[28] Bailey, 121, 125.

[29] Kitfield, *Prodigal Soldiers*, 197–208; Frank L. Jones, *A 'Hollow Army' Reappraised: President Carter, Defense Budgets, and the Politics of Military Readiness* (Carlisle Barracks, PA: Strategic Studies Institute, US Army War College, 2012).

unit bar the 82nd Airborne Division understrength, tank companies with only twelve tanks rather than the required seventeen, and battalions missing whole platoons and companies.[30] Meyer made his public 'hollow army' remarks before Congress in the immediate aftermath of the Desert One debacle: the failed attempt to rescue American hostages in Iran that resulted in a helicopter and aircraft being destroyed, five helicopters being abandoned in the Iranian desert and eight service members being killed. An interservice disaster, Desert One only underlined the fact that the military had yet to recover from its post-Vietnam nadir.[31]

Even as it struggled with morale and discipline, though, the Army was making several changes that would offset problems caused by the end of the draft and the post-Vietnam drawdown and chart a route to longer-term recovery. First, Army Chief of Staff General Creighton Abrams successfully resisted attempts at making big cuts to the Army's overall strength after Vietnam, which held at 785,000, and even managed to expand the Army's number of active combat divisions in 1973 from thirteen to sixteen.[32] He achieved this by advocating for a Total Force policy, where the Army would use Reserve Component units to help round out Active Component divisions. Reservists would increasingly take on combat service support functions, which both made it imperative to mobilise them during any future crisis and freed up more strength in the Active Force to concentrate on combat tasks.[33] While Abrams' policy was celebrated in later years as providing the bedrock for success during the Gulf War, it gave Army planners at the time a huge headache, as they had to struggle to make the numbers that had previously sustained thirteen Army divisions work for a sixteen-division force, with less funding available for training and maintenance.[34] In some ways, the ambition of Abrams' initiative led to the problems that caused Meyer to complain about readiness and the 'hollow army', but the strengthening

---

[30] Jones, A 'Hollow Army' Reappraised, 7.

[31] Charles Cogan, 'Desert One and Its Disorders', *The Journal of Military History* 67, no. 1 (2003): 201–16.

[32] Lewis Sorley, *Thunderbolt: General Creighton Abrams and the Army of His Times* (New York: Simon & Schuster, 1992), 363–5.

[33] Sorley claimed that Abrams' policy was intended to ensure that a future president would have to call up the reserves before going to war, but this claim has been disputed by scholars working with recently released archival sources. See Sorley, 365; Conrad C. Crane and Gian P. Gentile, 'Understanding the Abrams Doctrine: Myth versus Reality', *War on the Rocks*, 9 December 2015, https://warontherocks.com/2015/12/understanding-the-abrams-doctrine-myth-versus-reality/C1kX3QTaP0G28MhKT3Ue/Exmv0yhh22d; Brian D. Jones, 'The Abrams Doctrine: Total Force Foundation or Enduring Fallacy?', in *A Nation at War in an Era of Strategic Change*, ed. Williamson Muray (Carlisle Barracks, PA: Strategic Studies Institute, US Army War College, 2004), 201–26.

[34] Kitfield, *Prodigal Soldiers*, 150–1.

of the relationship between the Active and Reserve Components, which had become more distant when the latter effectively sat out the Vietnam War, paid long-term dividends.

The second significant move the Army made to alleviate recruiting difficulties was one that it had been under pressure to make for some time in any case. The cap on the number of women in the armed forces had been lifted in 1968 and, as the Equal Rights Amendment worked its way towards ratification, the Army along with the other military services moved to integrate women more fully into its ranks, abolishing the separate Women's Army Corps.[35] Given the recruiting pressure caused by the All-Volunteer Force, it only made sense to devote more attention to recruiting women to help make up for the shortfall in numbers.[36] While still heavily restricted in the roles they could take on, women moved from making up 1.3 per cent of the ranks by 1971 to 7.6 per cent in 1979, a figure that meant that the military could no longer function without them.[37] The scale of the contribution that women made to the All-Volunteer Force meant that they were able to survive the conservative backlash that leveraged the general crisis of standards in the Army to make the case that the increasing number of women in the ranks was a sign of the problems that the force was facing regarding quality and readiness. As retired Air Force Major General Jeanne Holm put it, many in the military thought that the expansion of women's roles and numbers in the All-Volunteer Force was 'a temporary condition that would pass with the demise of a misguided Carter administration', and the Army seized the opportunity provided by the election of Ronald Reagan to institute a 'womanpause' in 1981, halting the recruitment of women altogether.[38] They also proposed a return to the draft, which still excluded women from its reach. Secretary of Defense Caspar Weinberger immediately rejected any notion that the military would return to the draft and, as Beth Bailey put it, 'even Ronald Reagan's Pentagon believed [that women] were key to the survival of the All-Volunteer Force'.[39]

As the failed attempt at a 'womanpause' and aborted attempts to return to the draft made clear, neither the All-Volunteer Force nor the expansion of women's roles in the Army were universally welcomed at the time, even if they both ultimately proved crucial to the health of

---

[35] Bailey, *America's Army*, 157; Tanya L. Roth, *Her Cold War: Women in the U.S. Military, 1945–1980* (Chapel Hill: University of North Carolina Press, 2021).

[36] Bailey, *America's Army*, 154.

[37] Bailey, 133.

[38] Jeanne Holm, *Women in the Military: An Unfinished Revolution* (Novato, CA: Presidio Press, 1992), 387; Bailey, *America's Army*, 171.

[39] Bailey, *America's Army*, 216.

the Army. Other post-Vietnam changes were more immediately popular. Chief among them was the establishment of Training and Doctrine Command (TRADOC) under the leadership of General William E. DePuy. Designed to oversee all Army training and the development of operational doctrine, TRADOC became a vehicle for extensive reform. DePuy, a sometimes abrasive character who had been deeply affected by his experiences of combat with the 90th Division in Normandy during World War II, wanted to return the Army to what he saw as the basics.[40] Junior officer training would no longer focus on abstract topics such as the art of war, but on the construction of trenches and on tank gunnery, while in general terms training would take priority over education throughout the force, and a new approach to training, measured by passing standardised tests rather than hours put into training, took hold.[41]

An essential part of what an Army historian termed the Army's 'training revolution' was the establishment of much more realistic and less scripted combat exercises. Working with DePuy, Major General Paul Gorman overhauled the Army's training standards and established the Army's National Training Center (NTC) in Fort Irwin, California. Heavily influenced by the Air Force's 'Red Flag' exercises and the Navy's 'Top Gun' programme, the architects of the NTC made use of over 1,000 square miles of uninhabited desert to develop a huge area for whole brigades to conduct realistic tactical manoeuvres, while sophisticated sensors would record 'kills' on the simulated battlefield.[42] A well-trained and highly motivated 'opposition force' training cadre modelled themselves on Soviet doctrine, dressed in Soviet uniforms and modified their vehicles to look like Warsaw Pact vehicles. This combination of relatively free play exercises and rigorous post-exercise debriefings made Army units much more tactically proficient. At the staff officer level, the Army established the School of Advanced Military Studies at Fort Leavenworth in 1982 to offer a rigorous and intensive course designed to prepare officers to serve as divisional and corps-level planners and to offer as challenging an operational environment as the NTC was a tactical one.[43]

As the presence of Soviet uniforms in Fort Irwin indicated, all of this activity was singularly geared towards confronting the Red Army. The

[40] Henry G. Gole, *General William E. DePuy: Preparing the Army for Modern War* (Lexington: University Press of Kentucky, 2008).

[41] William E. DePuy, *Selected Papers of General William E. Depuy*, ed. Richard M. Swain (Fort Leavenworth, KS: Combat Studies Institute, 1994), 197, 221.

[42] Scales, *Certain Victory*, 39; Kitfield, *Prodigal Soldiers*, 191–3.

[43] Kevin C. M. Benson, *Educating the Army's Jedi: The School of Advanced Military Studies and the Introduction of Operational Art into U.S. Army Doctrine 1983–1994* (Lawrence: University of Kansas, 2010).

Astarita Study Group, convened by General Creighton Abrams in 1973, had recommended that the Army should focus its mission on providing conventional deterrence in Europe.[44] Warfare in Europe was something that the Army knew well, and many argued that the last time the Army had truly performed well in combat was during the campaigns of 1944 and 1945, where they pushed the *Wehrmacht* back to Germany. Writing about the report's findings a few years later, General Fred Weyand reflected on this return to the familiar by quoting T. S. Eliot's lines: 'At the end of all our exploring / Will be to arrive where we started / And know the place for the first time'.[45] Certainly, the Army dedicated some effort to knowing Europe again: the 1976 edition of FM 100-5 Operations contained detailed meteorological data for Germany and maps of urban density from the Ruhr to the Oder rivers, an unusually tight focus for a manual that was supposed to provide doctrinal guidance for the full range of Army operations.[46] In a letter to Weyand, DePuy clearly stated his intent, declaring that 'this manual takes the Army out of the rice paddies of Vietnam and places it on the Western European battlefield against the Warsaw Pact'.[47]

Like many of his initiatives, DePuy's edition of FM 100-5 proved controversial, but the debate it sparked led to the new doctrine of 'Air-Land battle', a term that appeared in the 1982 edition of FM 100-5.[48] This doctrine heavily emphasised a manoeuvre-based defence and tight integration between land forces confronting the first wave of Soviet attacks and air forces simultaneously attacking the enemy's rear echelons and follow-on echelons. Proponents of Air-Land battle explicitly drew on the experiences of the German *Wehrmacht* during World War II and emphasised the need for operational and tactical excellence, along with sophisticated new weapons systems.[49] These weapons systems, which had soaked up large portions of the Army's budget while they were in

---

[44] Harry G. Summers, Jr, *The Astarita Report: A Military Strategy for the Multipolar World* (Carlisle Barracks, PA: Strategic Studies Institute, US Army War College, 1981).

[45] Fred C. Weyand and Harry G. Summers, 'Serving the People: The Need for Military Power', *Military Review* 56 (1976): 10.

[46] US Army, *FM 100-5 Operations* (Washington, DC: Department of the Army, 1976); Richard Lock-Pullan, '"An Inward Looking Time": The United States Army, 1973–1976', *The Journal of Military History* 67, no. 2 (2003): 483–511; David Fitzgerald, *Learning to Forget: US Army Counterinsurgency Doctrine and Practice from Vietnam to Iraq* (Stanford: Stanford University Press, 2013), 39–59.

[47] DePuy, *Selected Papers of General William E. Depuy*, 194.

[48] Paul H. Herbert, *Deciding What Has to Be Done: General William E. DePuy and the 1976 Edition of FM 100-5, Operations* (Fort Leavenworth, KS: Combat Studies Institute, US Army Command and General Staff College, 1988); US Army, *FM 100-5 Operations*, 100–5.

[49] John L. Romjue, 'From Active Defense to AirLand Battle: The Development of Army Doctrine from 1973 to 1982', TRADOC Historical Monograph Series (Fort Monroe, VA: Historical Office, US Army Training and Doctrine Command, 1984).

development in the 1970s, began to be fielded by units in the early 1980s and represented a major improvement in capabilities.[50] Later termed the 'big five' after the role they played in the Gulf War, the emergence of the M1 Abrams tank, M2 Bradley Infantry Fighting Vehicle, AH-64 Apache attack helicopter, UH-60 Black Hawk utility helicopter and MIM-104 Patriot surface-to-air missile assuaged fears that the Army had fallen beyond their Soviet counterparts in technological terms and gave Army leaders confidence that they could win an armoured battle in Europe.

As Army doctrine, training and equipment improved, so did its recruiting and retention situation. General Maxwell Thurman took over Recruiting Command in 1979 and immediately reinvigorated it, using social science research to undergird recruiting efforts and working with advertising agencies to come up with the hugely successful 'Be All That You Can Be' advertising campaign and slogan.[51] Thurman was aided by the growing defence budgets of the Reagan era, as military pay increased significantly and the GI Bill was revitalised, even as the Reagan administration drastically cut college financial aid for civilians.[52] By the mid-1980s, the word 'college' seemed to be omnipresent in Army ads, in the hope that a focus on education rather than cash bonuses would attract more intelligent and ambitious recruits.[53] The military social welfare system grew more elaborate and generous, and focused more on family welfare, as the All-Volunteer military attracted older, longer-serving members who had a much higher marriage rate than their predecessors in the Selective Service Era.[54] The combined effects of more effective advertising and more generous compensation were remarkable: whereas only 54 per cent of recruits in 1980 were high school graduates and over half were Category IV, by 1987, 91 per cent of recruits were high school graduates and only 4 per cent were Category IV.[55] The contrast with the early 1970s image of the rebellious draftee or reluctant and ill-disciplined recruit was striking. The soldier of the 1980s was educated, highly disciplined and seemingly highly proficient.

Some observers such as the sociologist Charles Moskos began to argue that the military could provide an example for broader society. By 1986, Moskos was reporting that the racial tensions that had roiled the Army

---

[50] Scales, *Certain Victory*, 19–20.

[51] Bailey, *America's Army*, 180–92.

[52] Jennifer Mittelstadt, *The Rise of the Military Welfare State* (Cambridge, MA: Harvard University Press, 2015), 98, 104.

[53] Bailey, *America's Army*, 195.

[54] John Worsencroft, 'A Family Affair: Military Service in the Postwar Era' (PhD dissertation, Philadelphia, Temple University, 2017), 125.

[55] Bailey, *America's Army*, 197.

of the 1970s had now vanished and that the service provided a model for what racial integration could look like, with no signs of de facto segregation on Army bases, and African American soldiers rising through the ranks to take on high command with little fuss.[56] Certainly, the Army's broader image had improved. While West German politicians of the 1970s had worried about race riots, German observers in the 1980s noted that American armoured forces were much more competent than they previously had been, no longer littering German roadways during exercises and damaging crops and buildings with their tanks, while American units began to outperform their West German counterparts in tank gunnery exercises.[57] This operational improvement took place alongside a cultural rehabilitation of the armed forces, with Hollywood churning out movies that celebrated a highly competent and heroic military.[58] Opinion polling reflected this shift too. While the Harris Poll of the early 1970s had indicated that soldiers were about as well regarded as sanitation workers, Gallup polling in August 1990 indicated that 68 per cent of Americans had a 'great deal' or 'quite a lot' of confidence in the military, up from a 1979 low point of 50 per cent.[59]

1.2   Dissent: Bureaucracy and the Missing 'Warrior Spirit'

This story of the Army's recovery from its Vietnam trauma is well known. Scholars often understandably draw a straight line between the reforms of the 1970s and 1980s and the overwhelming success of Operation Desert Storm.[60] Not for nothing is the Army's official history of that conflict called *Certain Victory*. General Barry McCaffrey captured the essence of this sentiment when he testified before the Senate Armed Services Committee in the aftermath of the Gulf War that 'this war didn't take 100 hours to win, it took 15 years'.[61] However, this post-1991 triumphalism misses

---

[56] Charles C. Moskos, 'Success Story: Blacks in the Military', *The Atlantic*, May 1986, www.theatlantic.com/ideastour/military/moskos-full.html.

[57] Scales, *Certain Victory*, 32.

[58] Susan Jeffords, *Hard Bodies: Hollywood Masculinity in the Reagan Era* (New Brunswick, NJ: Rutgers University Press, 1994); Lawrence Howard Suid, *Guts and Glory: The Making of the American Military Image in Film*, 2nd edition (Lexington: The University Press of Kentucky, 2002); Walter L. Hixson, '"Red Storm Rising": Tom Clancy Novels and the Cult of National Security', *Diplomatic History* 17, no. 4 (1993): 599–614.

[59] Gallup Inc., 'Confidence in Institutions', www.gallup.com/poll/1597/Confidence-Institutions.aspx.

[60] James F. Dunnigan and Raymond M. Macedonia, *Getting It Right: American Military Reforms after Vietnam to the Gulf War and beyond* (New York: William Morrow & Co., 1993); Kitfield, *Prodigal Soldiers*.

[61] Barry R. McCaffrey, 'Desert Shield and Desert Storm Operations Overview', testimony before the Committee on Armed Services, United States Senate, 102nd Congress, 1st session, 9 May 1991.

something about the uncertainty and the ongoing lack of confidence felt by many in the Army, even throughout the military build-up of the Reagan administration. We can see something of this nervousness in the fact that the Army awarded over 9,000 medals for bravery and valour for Operation Urgent Fury, the 1983 invasion of tiny Grenada, even though no more than 7,000 soldiers were ever on the island in the first place.[62] The invasion of Grenada also highlighted a slew of problems with intelligence and interservice communication and coordination.[63] More broadly, even as the US Army in Europe began to rehabilitate its reputation, officers took to the pages of professional journals to complain that many of the issues that had plagued the Army in the Vietnam era still remained unresolved.

Perhaps the most scathing critic of the Army of the late 1980s was Christopher Bassford, an artillery officer who had left the Army after a five-year stint and who would later go on to become a widely respected scholar of Clausewitz. In 1988, he published *The Spit-Shine Syndrome: Organizational Irrationality in the American Field Army*, a book that recounted his frustrations as a junior artillery officer while offering a wider critique of the Army as a whole.[64] Bassford claimed that 'the organizational pathologies that led to disaster in Vietnam are still alive in the army of the 1980s' and his study echoed many of the same complaints of the 1970 Army War College study on professionalism.[65] For Bassford, the Army's reporting systems were still broken, as they 'mandate a fatal level of dishonesty, distort the chain of command, create a tremendous waste of time and resources, forbid tactical or organizational flexibility or creativity, compartmentalize units into jealously competing fragments, and drive wedges between commanders and their troops'.[66] He claimed that units in Germany were falsifying readiness reports by failing to report equipment breakdowns, which then caused supply NCOs to lose faith in the supply system and hoard spare parts by double-ordering, scrounging and theft so that they could repair their vehicles without formally requisitioning the parts that would tip off higher headquarters that something wasn't right.[67] As a result, trust between different elements of the Army's component parts was breaking down, and the logistics system was becoming more inefficient.

[62] Kitfield, *Prodigal Soldiers*, 268.
[63] Philip Kukielski, *The U.S. Invasion of Grenada: Legacy of a Flawed Victory* (Jefferson, NC: McFarland, 2019).
[64] Christopher Bassford, *The Spit-Shine Syndrome: Organizational Irrationality in the American Field Army* (New York: Praeger, 1988).
[65] Bassford, 1.
[66] Bassford, 14.
[67] Bassford, 60.

The Officer Efficiency Report system was similarly irrational. Bassford's description of the system came strikingly close to repeating almost verbatim the complaints of the Vietnam-era professionalism study; he argued that it 'could not be better designed to produce a class of timid, dishonest paper shuffler, far more concerned about their individual promotion chances than about producing effective military units'.[68] He noted that a 1984 army survey showed that 49 per cent of Army officers took the position that a 'bold, creative officer could not survive in the army', and argued that the Army's vast command superstructure 'exerts a crushing weight on subordinate units through gross over-supervision'.[69] All of this produced what Bassford called a 'spit shine syndrome': an obsession with appearances at the expense of reality, where 'the mirror polish of a spit shine combat boot is taken as an analogue for dedication to the unit and military professionalism, because those doing the evaluating either cannot judge, do not have time to worry about, or have no interest in the actual capability of the soldier'.[70] Bassford thought that the 'hollow army' described by General Edward C. Meyer still existed, albeit it was 'hidden under a layer of shoe polish'.

Bassford pinned much of the blame for this state of affairs on a personnel system that created far too much churn, which then encouraged both extensive bureaucratic oversight and an emphasis on the individual rather than the collective. In his foreword to the book, retired Lieutenant General Robert M. Elton celebrated contemporary American soldiers, claiming that 'as individuals, they are the most outstanding today that I have ever seen' and that 'the potential is there to mold a truly great army'. However, like Bassford, Elton worried that 'in a sophisticated army with great lethality, we will drive away those very individuals who would make us great'.[71] Elton believed that future wars would not rely on general mobilisation but would be 'come as you are', which meant that the Army needed to focus on building and testing cohesive units where soldiers were not equated to spare parts in an inventory, and where 'replacements come as cohesive packages rather than parceled out in poker chips one at a time to meet monthly readiness paper requirements'.[72] An Army that kept units together for an extended period and whose primary form of evaluation was a collective one based on realistic field exercises would be one that could truly meet its potential.

---

[68] Bassford, 79.
[69] Bassford, 8, 14.
[70] Bassford, 32.
[71] Robert M. Elton, 'Foreword', in *The Spit-Shine Syndrome: Organizational Irrationality in the American Field Army*, ed. Christopher Bassford (New York: Praeger, 1988), xi.
[72] Elton, xi.

Many in the upper ranks of the Army agreed. Indeed, Meyer had thought reforms along these lines were on a par with the establishment of TRADOC, the fielding of new weapons systems and doctrine, and the creation of the NTC in terms of their importance for the Army's future. Under his leadership, in 1981, the Army created a pilot programme known as Cohesion, Operational Readiness and Training (COHORT), which was intended to reorient the Army's personnel policy towards a unit-based system rather than one based on the individual. Meyer wanted to slow down personnel turbulence by creating units that would stay together for a minimum of three years.[73] Recruits would start basic training together and then join up with a cadre of officers and NCOs who would lead those same soldiers for the duration of their first enlistment, with the makeup of every squad and platoon remaining unchanged from start to finish. The objective was to create cohesive small units where personnel were accustomed to training and working closely together.[74] Speaking of the then-proposed changes in 1979, the military sociologist Morris Janowitz claimed that the move was an obvious one to make and that the 'the question is not how to create cohesion. Armies have known how for centuries. The question is why the American Army doesn't want cohesive units.'[75]

The subsequent failure of COHORT seemed to pose that same question yet again. From an initial pilot of twenty companies, the Army expanded the programme to 110 COHORT companies by 1983 and 281 companies by 1988.[76] Along with a parallel development of a new regimental system, which would group all soldiers in the Army into regionally based and culturally distinctive regiments where they could expect to serve the bulk of their careers both at home and overseas, COHORT was supposed to be rolled out to the entire Army.[77] However, critics such as Bassford claimed that the pace of change was far too timid and slow, and while studies demonstrated that COHORT units had much greater horizontal cohesion than their non-COHORT counterparts, officers and NCOs did not buy into the system in the same way, and turbulence at

---

[73] Kitfield, *Prodigal Soldiers*, 206.

[74] Brad Knickerbocker, 'Army's COHORT Plan Keeps Units Together, Builds Morale', *Christian Science Monitor*, 22 December 1982, www.csmonitor.com/1982/1222/122243.html.

[75] Michael R. Kearnes, 'Lessons in Unit Cohesion from the United States Armys COHORT (Cohesion, Operational Readiness, and Training) Experiment of 1981 to 1995' (Fort Leavenworth KS: US Army Command and General Staff College, 12 June 2020), 72, https://apps.dtic.mil/sti/citations/AD1124784.

[76] Kearnes, 87, 96.

[77] Richard Halloran, 'Army Is Reviving Use of Regiments', *New York Times*, 22 December 1982, www.nytimes.com/1982/12/22/us/army-is-reviving-use-of-regiments.html.

the level of unit leadership never really improved.[78] The rhythm of regular deployments to Europe and Korea meant that commanders preferred to think in terms of individual personnel slots that they needed to fill rather than rotating an entire unchanging unit.[79]

Looking back on his career, Maxwell Thurman, the general credited with saving the All-Volunteer Force with his overhaul of Recruiting Command, commented that 'if I look and say what did I fail to get accomplished, the answer is that I failed to get accomplished the institutionalization of COHORT. I had too many people against me on that. The commanders in Europe didn't like it. Armor didn't like it ... I wouldn't say they sabotaged it, but they fought it tooth and nail every step of the way and it succumbed on those grounds.'[80] More broadly, the Army's reporting and evaluation systems never adapted to account for the new policy, and, as one study of COHORT put it, 'an underlying assumption of the Army's culture is the individual system is so entrenched is because leaders succeed in an environment, and subconsciously become skeptical of change'.[81] Given the significance that so many studies of military effectiveness assign to small-unit cohesion, the failure of the COHORT project, which had the strong support of three different chiefs of staff, in the face of bureaucratic inertia indicates that all was not well in the Army in the late 1980s, despite all the reforms that took place in the aftermath of defeat in Vietnam.

The fundamental immovability of Army bureaucracy was one of the issues that most vexed critical mid-ranking officers, especially those that were associated with the Military Reform movement.[82] This group, which was largely made up of civilian analysts and disgruntled Air Force officers, critiqued careerism in the officer corps, the military's tendency to develop complex and expensive weapons systems, and a focus on attrition as a strategy, an approach they characterised as mindlessly focusing on grinding the enemy down over time.[83] Many within this group took

---

[78] Kearnes, 'Lessons in Unit Cohesion from the United States Armys COHORT (Cohesion, Operational Readiness, and Training) Experiment of 1981 to 1995', 109–23.
[79] Kearnes, 96, 130.
[80] Kearnes, 133–4.
[81] Kearnes, 139.
[82] For an account of the movement and its origins in the US Air Force, see Michael W. Hankins, *Flying Camelot: The F-15, the F-16, and the Weaponization of Fighter Pilot Nostalgia* (Ithaca, NY: Cornell University Press, 2021).
[83] James G. Burton, *The Pentagon Wars: Reformers Challenge the Old Guard* (Annapolis, MD: Naval Institute Press, 1993); James Fallows, 'Muscle-Bound Superpower: The State of America's Defense', *Atlantic Monthly*, October 1979. The British historian Paul Kennedy made a similar argument about the tendency of the United States to overspend on unnecessarily complex weapons systems in his highly influential book, *The Rise and Fall of the Great Powers* (New York: Random House, 1987).

inspiration from Air Force Colonel John Boyd's 'patterns of conflict' briefing, which drew on an impressionistic understanding of German tactics in World War II to make the case for a 'manoeuvrist' approach to warfare that would seek to throw the enemy off balance by avoiding their strong points and attacking their weaknesses and critical vulnerability, destroying their cohesion and ability to cope by a series of rapid and unexpected actions.[84]

While Boyd and his acolytes shared an admiration for the *Wehrmacht* with the generals who devised Air-Land battle, they were critical of Air-Land battle's focus on synchronisation, which necessitated tight control to integrate Air Force and Army actions more effectively.[85] Instead, they focused on command as an art form, where individual commanders would be empowered to act in accordance with their own assessment of the situation. This doctrine of 'mission command' was derived from an American understanding of the German concept of *Auftragstaktik*.[86] With its emphasis on individual creativity and skill, mission command was, as the historian Adam Tooze put it, both the hallmark of western individualism and freedom put consciously into opposition to the unthinking automatons of the Red Army, and 'the gothic scissors that cut through the threads that suspended the American fighting-man like a puppet from the dead hand of McNamara's Pentagon'.[87] The US military had seen the results of bureaucracy in Vietnam and they needed to do everything in their power to move away from it.

Mission command made it into American doctrine and was an artefact of the almost universal celebration of the *Wehrmacht* in the Army of the

---

[84] John Boyd, *A Discourse on Winning and Losing* (Maxwell Air Force Base, AL: Air University Press, 2018), www.airuniversity.af.edu/Portals/10/AUPress/Books/B_0151_Boyd_Discourse_Winning_Losing.pdf; Frans P. B. Osinga, *Science, Strategy and War: The Strategic Theory of John Boyd* (Cheltenham: Routledge, 2007); Robert Coram, *Boyd: The Fighter Pilot Who Changed the Art of War* (New York: Back Bay Books, 2004). Stephen Robinson's revisionist account demonstrates that Boyd and manoeuvre warfare theorists misunderstood the nature of the German approach to war and misrepresented that history in order to promote their own theories about the potency of manoeuvre. Stephen Robinson, *The Blind Strategist: John Boyd and the American Art of War* (Dunedin, New Zealand: Exisle, 2021).
[85] Saul Bronfeld, 'Did TRADOC Outmanoeuvre the Manoeuvrists? A Comment', *War & Society* 27, no. 2 (1 October 2008): 111–25.
[86] Ricardo Herrera has argued that the American infatuation with *Aufstragstakik* began with the publication of Trevor Dupuy's *A Genius for War* in 1977, but that this infatuation represents a fundamental misunderstanding of both German and American military history. Trevor N. Dupuy, *A Genius for War: The German Army and General Staff, 1807–1945* (London: Macdonald and Jane's, 1984); Ricardo A. Herrera, 'History, Mission Command, and the Auftragstaktik Infatuation', *Military Review*, August 2022, 53–66.
[87] Adam Tooze, 'Chartbook #128: Mission Command – NATO's Strangelove Vision of Freedom Enacted on the Ukraine Battlefield', Substack newsletter, *Chartbook* (blog), 12 June 2022, https://adamtooze.substack.com/p/chartbook-128-mission-command-natos.

1980s, but for the military reformers, Army leadership was only paying lip service to the concept.[88] They argued that the Army's focus on high-tech weaponry, its careerist promotion system and its failure to improve unit cohesion via the COHORT system meant that the organisation was far more rigid and hidebound than those who celebrated post-Vietnam reforms cared to admit.

Many blamed this inertia on the post-Vietnam Army's overwhelming focus on its mission in Europe and its sense that the outbreak of war there was not in fact likely. Colonel Walther E. Mather complained that too many senior commanders saw deterrence and the preservation of peace as being their primary mission, which contributed 'to a peacetime-oriented professional, more concerned with peacetime management manifest in DoD's [Department of Defense] planning-programming-budgeting system and "How the Army Runs" courses than with the serious study of war'.[89] Similarly, Air Force Lieutenant Colonel G. Murphy Donovan argued in *Parameters* that the military's recent rhetorical emphasis on 'warfighting' was hollow and that military education focused too 'much on producing managers', while the promotion system produced careerists who tended 'to confuse rank with achievement, promotion with competence' and who believed that 'their personal success is a validation of their way of doing things, even if their way includes ignoring the obvious'.[90] Moreover, while the post-Vietnam military had spent heavily on new equipment, 'the difficult problems of military competence concern strategy and operational art, not just procurement and logistics where necessities are often confused with sufficiencies'.[91] Donovan believed that none of this would change without 'radical changes in the ways that officers think about warrior preparation'.[92]

Daniel Bolger's 'Two Armies' article, which opened this chapter, appeared in the same issue of *Parameters* as Donovan's piece. Bolger took the critique even further and claimed that the heavy forces which predominated in Europe were nothing but 'show troopers', reliant on 'extensive synchronization' and 'inch-thick operations orders', who might be dedicated and competent but who tended to be preoccupied

[88] For an account of the US Army's incorporation of mission command into their doctrine, see Eitan Shamir, 'The Long and Winding Road: The US Army Managerial Approach to Command and the Adoption of Mission Command (Auftragstaktik)', *Journal of Strategic Studies* 33, no. 5 (1 October 2010): 645–72.

[89] Walter Mather, 'Peace Is Not My Profession; Deterrence Is Not My Mission', *Armed Forces Journal International* 125, no. 11 (June 1988).

[90] G. Murphy Donovan, 'Sustaining the Military Arts', *Parameters: The US Army War College Quarterly* 19, no. 1 (4 July 1989): 21.

[91] Donovan, 15.

[92] Donovan, 21.

with 'quotidian detail' rather than 'readiness for a war that the commanders have begun to suspect will never happen'.[93] He believed that
the 'real fighting' since 1945 had been done by the Army's light units
along with the Marine Corps, who together made up 'the expeditionary
army'.[94] These were a different breed: 'paratroopers might be quaffing
beer at a pizza parlour near Fort Bragg one night and be in a desperate
firefight in a distant hostile land the next afternoon. These regulars go
into action as they are, with no mobilization'. The speed of their deployments meant that they would expect to 'fight outnumbered far from
friendly bases and must rely on the collective skills imparted by sound
leadership, demanding training, and shared pre-battle hardship' rather
than the traditional American advantages in technology and numbers.[95]
These expeditionary soldiers could not afford to 'conform to prevailing
social norms of self-serving comfort; they conform instead to the pitiless
calculus of armed struggle'. Unlike the display Army in Europe, they
'must eschew bureaucratic miasma and exude the ethos of the pure warrior. That which does not contribute directly to success in battle must be
ruthlessly excised. Warriorship is a way of life.'[96]

Bolger's concern was that the 'show army' and the 'expeditionary
army' had not been fully divorced and that the Army's priorities tended
towards satisfying the needs of the wrong part of the force. In this, he
was not alone. Participants in ExcelOpers, an early internet-based Army
discussion forum, similarly mused that the contemporary Army wasn't
doing enough to promote the 'warrior spirit', with some claiming that if
'the warrior exists in the Army today, it exists only in a few units at best'
and that 'we simply struggle with the making of warrior. Our raw materi-
als come from a soft society.' Others noted that this 'warrior spirit' was
hard to sustain in peacetime and that 'the only way to catch the warrior
fever is through spirited, aggressive live firing ... which unfortunately
often runs counter to a safety-conscious Army'.[97]

These complaints were echoed by no less a figure than the novelist
Tom Clancy. In a surprising move for someone who played his own role
in the rehabilitation of the military's post-Vietnam public image through
depictions of extreme military competence in his best-selling techno-
thriller novels, Clancy published an opinion piece in the *Washington Post*

---

[93] Bolger, 'Two Armies', 31, 32.
[94] Bolger, 27.
[95] Bolger, 30.
[96] Bolger, 33.
[97] 'Transcript: Regarding the Nebulous and Esoteric Warrior "Spirit"', 21 May 1985, Gordon R. Sullivan Papers, Box 64, Folder 7, Discussions with Colleagues on Training of Officer Corps, May 1985, AHEC.

in December 1988 that excoriated both the Navy and the Army for not adequately training its commanders and for producing a climate where command had 'become a mere adjunct to career advancement – and therefore a place of passage, a place to play safe and make no mistakes'.[98] Clancy argued that the 'current system militates towards homogenized mediocrity' and that military leaders had forgotten that 'the military was meant to be neither a jobs programme nor another federal bureaucracy'.[99] Ironically for someone whose work focused with exquisite detail on the working of military machinery, Clancy argued that public debates over military budgets were missing the point because they focused too much on weapons rather than people, and that the military needed to 'return to fundamentals' and to 'restore the warrior ethic'. For Clancy, 'not all officers are or can be warriors, but only those who are deserve to command at any level'.[100] Therefore, the military had to change its training programmes to identify and nurture these people before giving them the support and experience they would need to succeed in combat. The crucial issue undergirding all this anxiety about incomplete reforms and about persistent bureaucratic pathologies was the sense that, however much the Army had overhauled itself after Vietnam, it remained essentially untested in the crucible of war.

1.3   A Revolution Validated: Operation Desert Storm

That test was not long in coming. While the interventions in tiny Grenada and Panama had been facile, Iraq's invasion of Kuwait in August 1990 set the United States on course for confrontation with what analysts were quick to note was the fourth largest army in the world, battle hardened by a decade of war with Iran. The Bush administration quickly launched Operation Desert Shield to ensure that Iraqi advances would not continue further south into Saudi oilfields, and deployed the XVIII Airborne Corps, beginning with the 82nd Airborne Division, to Saudi Arabia. As the administration began to build an international coalition to eject Iraq from Kuwait, and more and more soldiers poured into the Persian Gulf through the autumn and winter of 1990, it was becoming clear that war, and with it a serious test of the Army's capabilities, was likely.

Both the military and broader American society took the situation seriously. The Veterans Administration made arrangements to clear

[98] Tom Clancy, 'Look Who's Sinking Our Navy', *Washington Post*, 25 December 1988, www.washingtonpost.com/archive/opinions/1988/12/25/look-whos-sinking-our-navy/be6f11f3-a21d-4bbf-b738-72868af8f412/.C1kX3QTaP0G28MhKT3Ue/Exmv0yhh22d
[99] Clancy.
[100] Clancy.

hospital beds for the anticipated flow of wounded soldiers.[101] Some analysts estimated that the war would result in between 10,000 and 20,000 American casualties.[102] While not on the scale of Vietnam-era protests, a substantial anti-war movement emerged, largely driven by grassroots peace organisations but also featuring large-scale protests in cities such as San Francisco and Washington, DC. The political debate over intervention was fraught, and the Senate only narrowly voted to authorise the use of military force, with the resolution passing fifty-two votes to forty-seven.[103] In some quarters, there were even fears of a more a general war: sales of gas masks boomed in January 1991, and some wrote to local newspapers to suggest that the crisis called for the planting of World War II–type 'victory gardens'.[104] While the Department of Defense strongly denied that the military build-up in the Gulf was prompting them to think about reinstating the draft, some members of local Selective Service boards openly speculated about its return.[105] With question marks still hanging over the success of the military's post-Vietnam reforms, some allowed their imaginations to run wild.

While few in the Army shared these sentiments, Army leaders were certainly attuned to what was at stake. Speaking to students in Fort Leavenworth in November 1990, Army Chief of Staff General Carl Vuono claimed that 'this is not a minor league operation. If we don't fire a shot, it's been a demanding scenario.'[106] As a service chief, Vuono was not part of the chain of command for operations in the Persian Gulf, and he kept his focus on the potential impact of the crisis on the broader institution. For Vuono, the challenge would be to maintain global readiness,

---

[101] 'Is the VA Ready?' *DAV Magazine*, October 1990, folder 03194-004 'Persian Gulf Working Group', Paul McNeill Files, White House Office of Communications, GBPL.

[102] 'Potential War Casualties Put at 100,000', *Los Angeles Times*, 5 September 1990, 2.

[103] W. Lance Bennett and David L. Paletz, eds, *Taken by Storm: The Media, Public Opinion and U.S. Foreign Policy in the Gulf War* (Chicago: Chicago University Press, 1994); Frederick Fico, Linlin Ku and Stan Soffin, 'Fairness, Balance of Newspaper Coverage of U.S. in Gulf War', *Newspaper Research Journal* 15, no. 1 (January 1994): 30–43; Robert A. Hackett and Yuezhi Zhao, 'Challenging a Master Narrative: Peace Protest and Opinion/Editorial Discourse in the US Press During the Gulf War', *Discourse & Society* 5, no. 4 (October 1994): 509–41; John E. Mueller, *Policy and Opinion in the Gulf War* (Chicago: Chicago University Press, 1994).

[104] David Treadwell, 'Americans Willing to Pay for Bit of Security', *Los Angeles Times*, 23 January 1991, A11; Ivetta Burch, 'Readers Write – It's Time Again for Victory Garden', *Owensboro Messenger-Inquirer*, 6 February 1991, 7A.

[105] Rosemary Weathers, 'Gulf Crisis – Next in Line? – Young Men Wait on Return of U.S. Draft – Threat of War Rekindles Draft Fears', *Kentucky Post*, 12 January 1991; Rosemary Weathers, 'Gulf Crisis – Draft-Board Members Search Their Souls', *Kentucky Post*, 12 January 1991.

[106] Carl E. Vuono, 'Address to CASSS 91-1/2', 1 November 1990, Carl E. Vuono Papers: Box 33A, Folder 9, Speeches and Remarks, 1991, AHEC.

observing that 'while we are keeping our eye on Desert Shield, we have to keep our eye on the rest of the Army and strike the right balance in terms of how we mix the forces'. He recalled that when he was a more junior officer, 'we didn't do that … and it took us 10–12 years to recover from it'. What was at stake was the success of the All-Volunteer Force. Vuono emphasised to the student officers that 'we have an Army today of volunteers; everybody in the ranks today volunteered. We didn't have to go out looking and forcing people into the Army, they volunteered. They raised their hands.'[107] If the Army allowed Operation Desert Shield to run down readiness within the force, then fewer hands might be raised in the future. Moreover, he reminded his audience that 'the American people have entrusted to you the most precious commodity that this country has – its son and daughters'.[108] Vuono had lived through a time when that trust had been broken and had no intention of repeating the experience.

The initial public reaction to Operation Desert Shield suggested that this time the military could count on public support. In August 1990, a convoy of soldiers from the 101st Airborne Division at Fort Campbell on their way to Atlanta to be airlifted to the Persian Gulf was met by cheering crowds along Interstate 75, with every overpass for 110 miles, from Chattanooga, Tennessee to Atlanta, Georgia, packed with flag-waving well-wishers.[109] Media commentators covering these deployments highlighted the more racially diverse, mature and well-trained volunteer force as a symbol of the strength and diversity of the United States – a move that the historian Melani McAlister has termed 'military multiculturalism'.[110] While debates over the wisdom of going to war with Iraq may have been fraught, all sides emphasised support for the troops. Senate Majority Whip, Senator Wendell Ford (D-KY), who had voted against the war, declared that 'we have a profound responsibility to ensure that the tragedy of the Vietnam veterans is not repeated' and called for every American to 'reach out personally to let our service men and women and veterans know that their essential contribution to democracy is appreciated'.[111]

---

[107] Vuono.
[108] Vuono.
[109] Larry Lewis, 'Pro or Con, Flag Means Patriotism to All', *Philadelphia Inquirer*, 22 January 1991.
[110] Melani McAlister, *Epic Encounters: Culture, Media, and U.S. Interests in the Middle East since 1945* (Berkeley: University of California Press, 2005), 235–59.
[111] Wendell F. Ford, 'Press Release: Ford Urges Kentucky Towns and Cities to "Adopt" Servicemen and Women in the Persian Gulf', 17 December 1990, White House Office of Media Affairs, Subject Files: Congress, GBPL.

Indeed, Americans sent thousands of care packages to soldiers stationed in Saudi Arabia and elsewhere, and many displayed yellow ribbons in front yards and on jacket lapels.[112] Celebrities embraced those serving in the Gulf, releasing charity singles to raise the morale of those deployed and embarking on USO trips to the Middle East to entertain the troops.[113] The pinnacle of the entertainment industry's embrace of the troops was Whitney Houston's bravura Super Bowl rendition of 'The Star-Spangled Banner', aired ten days into the conflict.[114] Such messages sent fundamentally emotional, apolitical messages of support to the troops and their families. Indeed, even those who opposed the war made a point of publicly displaying their support for the troops. Todd Gitlin, for example, a prominent anti-war figure during the Vietnam War and an opponent of US military intervention in the Gulf, donated blood with *NBC News* cameras rolling.[115] That Gitlin made such a gesture demonstrates how the notion of American soldiers as apolitical and worthy professionals had become an article of faith in American politics.[116] This shift in public attitudes had little to do with Air-Land battle or close scrutiny of the performance of manoeuvre units at the NTC; rather it emerged from a widespread sense that the soldiers of the All-Volunteer Force were of a higher calibre than their Vietnam-era counterparts, as well as a feeling that the nation had treated these Vietnam veterans poorly. From Reagan's declaration that the war in Vietnam had been a 'noble cause' to the building of the Vietnam Veterans' memorial to the staging of a large parade for Vietnam veterans in

---

[112] For the history of the yellow ribbon and its use during the Gulf War, see Jack Santino, 'Yellow Ribbons and Seasonal Flags: The Folk Assemblage of War', *The Journal of American Folklore* 105, no. 415 (Winter 1992): 19–33; George Mariscal, 'In the Wake of the Gulf War: Untying the Yellow Ribbon', *Cultural Critique*, no. 19 (Autumn 1991): 97–117; Gerald E. Parsons, 'How the Yellow Ribbon Became a National Folk Symbol', *Library of Congress American Folklife Center: Folklife Center News* 13, no. 3 (Summer 1991): 9–11.

[113] Chuck Philips, 'Stars Voice Their Support of Gulf Forces', *Los Angeles Times*, 6 February 1991, http://articles.latimes.com/1991-02-06/entertainment/ca-794_1_gulf-forces.

[114] Danyel Smith, 'When Whitney Hit the High Note', ESPN.com, 1 February 2016, www.espn.com/espn/feature/story/_/id/14673003/the-story-whitney-houston-epic-national-anthem-performance-1991-super-bowl; Chuck Philips, 'Stars Voice Their Support of Gulf Forces', *Los Angeles Times*, 6 February 1991, F1.

[115] Gitlin argued that the selective use of images from his blood donation effectively cancelled out his stance against the war. Todd Gitlin, 'On Being Sound-Bitten: Reflections on Truth, Impression, and Belief in a Time of Media Saturation', *Boston Review* 16, no. 6 (December 1991): 15–17.

[116] On the debate over the extent to which the Vietnam-era media was 'anti-troop' and the extent to which memories of that war hamstrung the Gulf War protestors, see Thomas D. Beamish, Harvey Molotch and Richard Flacks, 'Who Supports the Troops? Vietnam, the Gulf War, and the Making of Collective Memory', *Social Problems* 42, no. 3 (August 1995): 344–60.

Houston in 1988, the image of the veteran was rehabilitated alongside the reputation of the US military.[117]

This success of this rehabilitation was now at stake in the Persian Gulf. While most senior officers deployed to Saudi Arabia were confident that the coalition assembled to fight the war would easily defeat Saddam Hussein's army and that some of the figures circulating in the press about potential American casualties were overblown, all of this would be hypothetical until the first shots were fired. For Major General Barry McCaffrey, commander of the 24th Mechanized Infantry Division, the moment he realised that this time would be different was when he attended CENTCOM (United States Central Command) commander General Norman Schwarzkopf's briefing on what would be called Operation Desert Storm: the plan of attack to liberate Kuwait. As Schwarzkopf described a campaign that would feature massive aerial bombardment before the launch of a huge multi-corps wheel into the desert to outflank Iraqi forces, McCaffrey was overcome with emotion. As the journalist James Kitfield described it, 'the briefing had left McCaffrey slightly stunned ... he had one overriding thought. We're not going to fight a war of attrition, or a limited war. It was a revelation. He saw now that the Army was going to play to its strengths and the enemy's weakness. By God, we learned. We learned.' When he turned to his counterpart General Binford Peay, commander of the 101st Airborne Division, 'there were tears in McCaffrey's eyes. Peay just nodded his head in confirmation: "That's it, Barry. That's what we'll do."'[118]

And indeed, Army units deployed to the Persian Gulf did just what the plan called for them to do. The flanking movement was a stunning success, and Army divisions carved their way through Iraqi defensive positions without difficulty. After only 100 hours of ground combat, President Bush declared a ceasefire and declared that Kuwait had been liberated. As the Army's official history of the conflict puts it, 'only 100 ground combat hours were necessary for the Army to re-establish itself convincingly

---

[117] Ronald Reagan, 'Peace: Restoring the Margain of Safety' (Veterans of Foreign Wars Convention, Chicago, 18 August 1980), www.reagan.utexas.edu/archives/reference/8.18.80.htmlC1kX3QTaP0G28MhKT3Ue/Exmv0yhh22d; Patrick Hagopian, *The Vietnam War in American Memory: Veterans, Memorials, and the Politics of Healing* (Amherst: University of Massachusetts Press, 2009); David Ryan, 'Vietnam in the American Mind: Narratives of the Nation and the Sources of Collective Memory', in *Cultural Memory and Multiple Identities* (Berlin: Lit Verlag, 2008); David Kieran, *Forever Vietnam: How a Divisive War Changed American Public Memory* (Amherst: University of Massachusetts Press, 2014); Jerry Lembcke, *The Spitting Image: Myth, Memory, and the Legacy of Vietnam* (New York: NYU Press, 2000); Viet Thanh Nguyen, *Nothing Ever Dies: Vietnam and the Memory of War* (Cambridge, MA: Harvard University Press, 2016).

[118] Kitfield, *Prodigal Soldiers*, 24.

as a successful land combat force'. The Army's mechanised forces had advanced at a speed of more than ninety-five kilometres per day, double what the *Wehrmacht* had achieved during the heyday of blitzkrieg warfare in 1941.[119] If there had been any doubts as to the extent of the Army's renaissance, then Operation Desert Storm seemingly put them to rest.

Like most of the people attending Schwarzkopf's pre-war briefing, McCaffrey had served multiple tours in Vietnam, and his sentiments about what Desert Storm meant were far from unique. An entire generation of Army leaders had lived through the Vietnam experience and its aftermath and so saw the Gulf War as the conclusion of a narrative arc of redemption. In their memoirs, generals such as Colin Powell, Norman Schwarzkopf, Jr and Tommy Franks told stories of their frustrations in Vietnam followed by years of hard work to rebuild the military before finding vindication in the deserts of the Arabian Peninsula.[120] As the scholar Andrew Bacevich observes, 'virtually every one of these narratives conforms to a prescribed formula … From his experience in a lost war, the protagonist derives certain essential truths that he vows to apply if ever called upon in some future crisis to serve in a position of authority.' In these memoirs, the protagonist returns home from war to find his fellow citizens shunning those who serve, but commits himself to the military, 'rising through the ranks during a lengthy apprenticeship. When his moment finally arrives, he orchestrates a great victory, by implication showing how Vietnam ought to have been fought. In vanquishing the enemy, he also helps heal old wounds at home, promoting both reconciliation and national renewal.'[121] The most vivid example of this genre is *Into the Storm*, an account of the ground war in the Persian Gulf co-authored by Tom Clancy and General Fred Franks, who commanded VII Corps throughout the conflict. After losing a leg in Vietnam in 1971, Franks underwent his personal 'Valley Forge' of recovery. As his own body healed, the Army itself was healed and rebuilt by veterans of Vietnam. Franks then took command of a well-trained and well-equipped Armored Corps and defeated Saddam Hussein's vast army in just 100 hours of combat.[122]

The Army's official history of the conflict, *Certain Victory*, followed the same narrative arc by focusing on the figure of Steven Slocum, who had

---

[119] Scales, *Certain Victory*, 5.

[120] Tommy R. Franks, *American Soldier* (New York: HarperCollins, 2005); Colin L. Powell and Joseph E. Persico, *My American Journey: An Autobiography* (New York: Ballantine Books, 1995); Norman Schwarzkopf, *It Doesn't Take a Hero: The Autobiography of General H. Norman Schwarzkopf* (New York: Bantam Books, 1993); Hugh Shelton, Ronald Levinson and Malcolm McConnell, *Without Hesitation: The Odyssey of an American Warrior* (New York: St Martins Press, 2010).

[121] Andrew Bacevich, 'A Modern Major General', *New Left Review* 29 (October 2004).

[122] Tom Clancy and Fred Franks, *Into the Storm: A Study in Command* (New York, 1998).

served in Vietnam as a specialist fourth class and in the Gulf as a command sergeant major. As a young soldier, his unit had been decimated
by fighting during the 1968 Tet Offensive, but this time, 'Slocum took
2,000 young paratroopers to the Gulf and brought them all back'. While
his brigade took part in an assault on an Iraqi airfield, 'he watched the
young infantrymen he had trained go about their business with a professionalism and self-confidence far different from what he had seen [in
Vietnam]'.[123] American tactical proficiency was not the only thing that
separated the two experiences. Whereas Specialist Slocum had returned
from Vietnam in 1968 on his own and to no fanfare, Command Sergeant
Major Slocum returned from the Gulf decades later with his unit and to
'thank you's' from everyone from the flight attendant on his chartered
Pan Am 747 to the thousands waiting 'with fluttering flags and banners'
at Pope Air Force Base, North Carolina.[124] For the authors of *Certain
Victory*, it was the presence of that crowd of thousands at the homecoming as much as the performance of the troops in the desert that affirmed
that the post-Vietnam redemption was now complete.

1.4   Operation Welcome Home

On the very day that President Bush declared a ceasefire in the Gulf,
The Los Angeles Times published a piece by Tom Clancy calling for victory parades for the veterans of Operation Desert Storm. Whereas in
1988 Clancy had worried that an overly bureaucratic military had lost
the 'warrior spirit', he now returned to familiar themes and rhetorically
asked 'does America still have it?' before answering his own question with
the retort: 'ask the Iraqis'. He acknowledged 'how effective our weapons
were' but also argued that 'there is no truer measure of any society than
its armed forces. In uniform you will find the best and worst, the tools,
the people, the ideas, all distilled in one place.'[125] He told his readers
that 'when they come home, it's your job to remember who they are, and
whom they worked for .... And they're coming home winners. We owe
them.' Clancy's appeal fell on fertile ground: in a *USA Today* poll taken
in early March, 86 per cent of respondents said that they would go to a
parade for hometown soldiers.[126] Moreover, even as Clancy published

---

[123] Scales, *Certain Victory*, 356.

[124] Scales, *Certain Victory*, 355–7.

[125] Tom Clancy, 'How About a Few Parades?', *Los Angeles Times*, 28 February 1991, B13,
in folder 03195-008, Persian Gulf Working Group, Paul McNeill Files, White House
Office of Communications, George fBPL.

[126] 'Communities Make Homecoming Plans', n.d., folder 03195-014 'Persian Gulf Working
Group: Surrogates [2]', Paul McNeill files, White House Office of Communications
Files, GBPL.

his piece, White House Chief of Staff John H. Sununu kept on his desk a draft schedule of homecoming events. He had solicited ideas for managing the celebrations from a Washington public relations consultant on 22 February, two days before the ground campaign in Kuwait started.[127]

The festivities that ensued are a useful barometer of the public's regard for the military. Much as Army leaders became increasingly confident about the success of their reform efforts as the years wore on, and much as opinion polling had indicated a strong recovery in the military's public image since the low point of the 1970s, the aftermath of Operation Desert Storm was the clearest indication yet that the military's post-Vietnam overhaul had been noticed by the broader American public. Moreover, the fact that many of these celebrations specifically emphasised the volunteer status of the military and that they gave a prominent place to high-tech weaponry gives some sense as to which reforms had most resonated with Americans.

Indeed, politicians made a point of celebrating volunteerism as one of the cardinal virtues of the force that had won the war. Writing to President Bush, House Minority Whip Newt Gingrich offered ideas for the president's upcoming address to a Joint Session of Congress, using the volunteer ethos of the military to advance conservative policies. Gingrich urged Bush to tell Congress that 'one thing we must not forget is that the brave men and women who participated in Operation Desert storm did so as volunteers – they chose to risk their lives for principle, for honor, for country and for a better, safer world. They volunteered to do the hard work of freedom.' He wanted Bush to call on Americans to 'join with that volunteer army of freedom' to make the twenty-first century the next 'American Century'.[128] While White House staffers did not use Gingrich's suggested language in the actual address to Congress, Bush agreed with Gingrich's claim that 'our military today is fundamentally better than it was ten years ago'. He celebrated the 'first-class talent' that 'went halfway around the world to do what is moral and just and right', and claimed that the victory belonged to 'the privates and the pilots, to the sergeants and the supply officers, to the men and women in the machines and the men and women who made them work'.[129] For both

[127] Roy Pfautch, 'Memorandum to John Sununu: The National Welcome Home', 22 February 1991, folder 04733-005 'Desert Storm: Events', Sig Rogich Files, White House Office of Public Events and Initiatives, GBPL.
[128] Newt Gingrich, 'Memorandum to John Sununu: Suggested Rhetoric for 3/6 Joint Speech', 4 March 1991, folder 29166-004 'Persian Gulf War [2]', Issues File, John Sununu Files, White House Office of the Chief Staff, GBPL.
[129] George H. W. Bush, 'Address Before a Joint Session of the Congress on the Cessation of the Persian Gulf Conflict' (Online by Gerhard Peters and John T. Woolley, The American Presidency Project, 6 March 1991), www.presidency.ucsb.edu/ws/?pid=19364.

Bush and Gingrich, the volunteer military stood at the heart of what had gone right in Desert Storm.

Others emphasised volunteerism as a quintessentially American trait. A concept paper sent to the White House Office of National Service made the connection between the skills displayed by the military in the Gulf and the needs of modern American capitalism. According to the paper's author, 'American enterprises increasingly require employees with the experience and qualities shown by the troops. To compete in the global marketplace, most US manufacturers and service industries find they must delegate responsibility for precision operations to employees well down the line'. Desert Storm veterans fit the bill perfectly because, 'as volunteer recruits they performed on time, in time and in teams …. They exercised savvy, courage and leadership in performing their missions.'[130]

This analysis drew heavily on a *Washington Post* column by Steven Rosenfeld that celebrated the victory over Iraq as springing from the democratic ideology of the US military. Rosenfeld cited Marine Corps Colonel W. C. Gregson, who claimed that US military doctrine 'counts heavily on and encourages the initiative, skills and courage of the individual and the small-unit leaders'. According to Gregson, this worked only because 'our armed forces personnel are not "simple soldiers" who slavishly serve the hierarchy, as in totalitarian forces. In the democratic tradition, they are the purpose around which all our efforts revolve.' Rosenfeld concluded by arguing that 'to walk in American footsteps, other governments must change their basic political ways – loosen up central control, devolve authority to lower levels, reward individual initiative …. Let us ship our field manuals – and the Bill of Rights. This is the wonderfully subversive lesson of the war.'[131] For Rosenfeld and other observers, the volunteer soldiers of Desert Storm not only displayed tactical and operational mastery, but also the best American capitalist values of personal responsibility and individual enterprise.

Such was the admiration for the victors of Desert Storm that several public relations firms believed the administration should use them to advance its domestic policy goals of shrinking the size of the federal government and promoting private volunteerism. Hill + Knowlton Strategies, a firm with close ties to both the administration and the Kuwaiti government, suggested that Bush appoint a hero of Desert Storm, such as General Schwarzkopf or Powell, to run 'Operation Domestic

---

[130] Frances Brigham Johnson to Clark Irvin, 'Welcoming the Troops Home to New Opportunities: Hometown Volunteers Can Make a Difference', 2 April 1991, folder 03630, General Files: Veteran and Operation Desert Storm Information, Clark Kent Irvin Files, White House Office of National Service, GBPL.

[131] Stephen S. Rosenfeld, 'Democracy's War', *Washington Post*, 29 March 1991, A21.

Prosperity', a 100-day initiative to make the United States a 'home fit for heroes' by pressuring Congress to pass the Bush administration's domestic agenda.[132] Recalling the 'freedom trains' of the early Cold War, they also suggested a 'victory train' stocked with veterans to tour the nation and celebrate 'the men, women and technology of Desert Storm'.[133] This would be accompanied by a 'freedom flotilla' of US Navy and merchant marine vessels sailing around the United States, and a giant yellow ribbon stretching completely across it.[134] Burson-Marsteller, a rival to Hill + Knowlton, proposed that the Department of Defense should carefully hand-pick and give media training to returning service members and then send them out to 'maintain and expand in a meaningful way the national sense of pride, accomplishment and good feeling generated by Operation Desert Storm'.[135] Most ambitious of all was a suggestion from Kenneth Smith, CEO of a private consulting firm with ties to the Republican Party.[136] He suggested that the administration train the more than 500,000 Gulf War veterans as 'Desert Storm Community Service Volunteers' for an unspecified purpose. According to Smith:

The people who participated in Desert Storm are truly an enormous national asset …. America's young people desperately need heroes – real heroes. Real people in real walks of life who do the real things that make America what it is. People who serve their country. People who earn their money, people who have a commitment to excellence and competence, people who believe in the value of service.[137]

---

[132] On behalf of Kuwait, Hill and Knowlton coordinated false testimony given to the House Human Rights Caucus in October 1990, where a fifteen-year-old Kuwaiti girl claimed to have witnessed Iraqi soldiers taking babies out of incubators in a Kuwaiti hospital and leaving them to die. John R. MacArthur, 'Remember Nayirah, Witness for Kuwait?', *New York Times*, 6 January 1992, A17.

[133] The 1947–9 'freedom train' was a travelling exhibit designed to 'sell America to Americans' by displaying artifacts such as original copies of the Constitution, the Bill of Rights, and the Declaration of Independence. Fried, *The Russians Are Coming!*, 29–50.

[134] Craig L. Fuller, 'Memorandum for John Sununu', 27 March 1991, folder 04733-005 'Desert Storm: Events', Sig Rogich Files, White House Office of Public Events and Initiatives, GBPL.

[135] Thomas D. Bell, 'Memorandum for Ed Rogers: Expanding the Spirit of Desert Storm', 2 April 1991, folder 04733-005 'Desert Storm: Events', Sig Rogich Files, White House Office of Public Events and Initiatives, GBPL.

[136] Smith was the founder and CEO of the International Development and Management Group, a consulting firm based in Alexandria, VA. Formerly a Nixon White House staffer, he had been appointed to various national advisory councils by President Reagan. His firm specialised in building 'strategic partnerships' between industry and government.

[137] Kenneth Smith, 'Memorandum for David Demarest: Desert Storm Heroes as Community Service Leaders', 15 March 1991, folder 07637-09, White House Office of National Service, GBPL.

Unlike previous homecomings, in which the public and government officials worried about how to reintegrate veterans back into society and what sort of supports they would need, the Gulf War veterans would instead be the ones to provide support and inspiration to broader American society.

The initial celebrations, such as an event in Texas Stadium, home of the Dallas Cowboys, that attracted 30,000 revellers, were often pro-troop rallies that had been scheduled before the end of hostilities and then turned into improvised victory parties, and thus emphasised flag-waving and patriotism rather than military hardware. For later homecomings, martial pageantry formed a prominent part of the festivities, even in locations as small as Hueytown, Alabama (population: 15,000). The mayor of Hueytown sent the White House an invitation to the 18 May celebration, describing a military display including 'helicopters, tanks, artillery' and a day of festivities that would open with an 'Army Special Forces flyover, followed by two squads of troops rappelling from hovering helicopters onto field in full battle dress to engage in mock battle, complete with blank ammo'.[138] While not everyone opted for a full-scale mock combat demonstration, almost every city across the United States put on some sort of homecoming celebration. The major cities and communities adjacent to large military bases attracted the most direct military involvement, and virtually all of them hosted some sort of large-scale parade featuring several thousand troops.

Writing in 1987, the sociologist Michael Mann pointedly described the modern military, which relies on advanced technology and a smaller, professional armed force, as lending itself to 'spectator sport militarism', in which the general population mobilised for war 'not as players but as spectators'.[139] The events organised by large American cities after the Gulf War affirmed this profound shift. In New York City, Mayor David Dinkins planned a 'Mother of All Parades' – a traditional tickertape parade up Broadway on 10 June. Such events – where Wall Street workers threw tickertape (or, in later years, computer paper sheets) out of office windows onto returning heroes – had been in recent years reserved for sports teams, such as the New York Mets when they won the World Series in 1969 and 1986. This one would attract between 1 million and 4.7 million spectators.[140] Five thousand

[138] Richard Shelby, 'A Patriot's Day Celebration in Hueytown, Alabama', 7 May 1991, document 208848, ME002 Messages (Sent to Groups/Organizations), Subject File – General, WHORM files, GBPL.

[139] Michael Mann, 'The Roots and Contradictions of Modern Militarism', *New Left Review* 162 (March–April 1987): 35–50, 48.

[140] Robert D. McFadden, 'New York Salutes in a Ticker-Tape Blizzard, New York Honors the Troops', *New York Times*, 11 June 1991, A1.

Figure 1.2 A soldier waves an American flag during a ticker tape parade in New York City to welcome troops home from the Persian Gulf, June 1991

soldiers, led by Secretary of Defense Dick Cheney and Generals Colin Powell and Norman Schwarzkopf, kicked off the start of a 24,000-strong procession featuring various veterans' organisations, diverse community groups and bands (Figure 1.2).[141]

While New York City may have attracted the most spectators, Washington, DC's National Victory Celebration displayed by far the most military hardware. The parade organisers, the 'Desert Storm Homecoming Foundation', consisted of the three major veterans' organisations: the Veterans of Foreign Wars, the American Legion and Disabled American Veterans. They initially scheduled the parade for 4 July but moved it to 8 June, ostensibly because Congress would still be in session then, but, in reality, to upstage New York's parade.[142] General Schwarzkopf led 8,800 troops on their march through DC, and then joined President Bush on the reviewing stand. A twelve-minute-long flyby of over eighty

---

[141] Michael Specter and Laurie Goodstein, 'Millions Honor Gulf Vets at Parade in New York', *Washington Post*, 11 June 1991, A1.
[142] Leigh Ann Metzger, 'Memorandum for the President: Meeting with Desert Storm Homecoming Foundation', 18 April 1991, folder 12918 Iraq [1991] [4], Alphabetical Subject Files, Marlin Fitzwater Files, White House Press Office, GBPL.

aircraft, led by a lone F-117 stealth fighter, an icon of the war, capped off the event, which also included thirty-one heavy military vehicles, among them the M1A1 Abrams main battle tank and the Patriot missile system.[143] Major General William Streeter, Commanding General of the Military District of Washington, provided commentary on both the troop formations and various weapons and vehicles for C-SPAN, while *CBS News* correspondent Eric Engsberg reported that there was 'so much military hardware moving, at times it seemed as if Washington was under attack'.[144] Seven blocks of the National Mall were also dedicated to what bemused reporters called a 'military petting zoo' of weaponry and equipment. One exhibit tent contained every type of bomb and missile used in the war, while others allowed visitors to try on a gas mask or practice laying a howitzer on the Washington Monument.

Indeed, such was the scale and bulk of the hardware on display that National Park Service personnel worried about tanks tearing up the Mall and damaging the sprinkler system underneath. Some asked questions about whether the bridges over the Potomac, designed for civilian traffic, could bear the weight of the seventy-tonne Abrams tanks. The military put in place traffic regulations allowing only one tank to cross the bridge at a time, keeping to under thirty miles per hour and at least two feet away from the curb on either side. Electric and phone companies worried about damage to their cables and several streetlights had to be removed so that the Patriot Missile Launcher vehicle could get through. Designing a parade route that did not cross any of Washington, DC's metro tunnels and stations, as engineers feared they might collapse under the weight of the vehicles, proved most difficult of all.[145]

The eventual parade route stretched just over two and a half miles long, but the event attracted only around 200,000 spectators, far below the one million that organisers had hoped for. The crowd featured a heavy contingent of federal employees and defence contractors, a group that one reporter observed was 'tightly connected to the military and the bureaucracy, closer than most of the country to weapons and the workaday of war'.[146] Along with the 'military petting zoo' on the Mall and the

---

[143] 'Bush Unfurls Desert Storm Day of Pride Gulf War Veterans Get Extravaganza', *Baltimore Sun*, 9 June 1991, 1A.

[144] 'National Victory Celebration Parade', C-SPAN, 8 June 1991, www.c-span.org/video/?18328-1/national-victory-celebration-parade (accessed 25 November 2018); Caroline Linton, 'How CBS News Reported the Last National Military Parade in 1991', *CBS News*, 7 February 2018, www.cbsnews.com/news/how-cbs-news-reported-the-last-national-military-parade-in-1991/ (accessed 25 November 2018).

[145] Mary Jordan, 'D.C. Parade Plans Roar into Focus', *Washington Post*, 16 May 1991, A1.

[146] Associated Press, '200,000 View War Victory Parade', *Pittsburgh Press*, 9 June 1991, A1.

hardware-heavy parade and flyby, the Pentagon chose to use the week following the parade to promote its budget priorities. It promoted an 'Air Force Stealth Week' at nearby Andrews Air Force Base where reporters could visit the base and see a selection of stealth aircraft, including a prototype of the F-22 Raptor, the F-117 Nighthawk and the B-2 Spirit. Not coincidentally, Congress had recently threatened to cancel the B-2's building programme.[147] For the Pentagon, then, the National Victory Celebration was a chance not just to welcome home the 'half million heroes' their Public Affairs Office invoked in discussions with the White House, but also to aggressively promote budget priorities in the post–Cold War spending drawdown.

While the White House wanted to emphasise the importance of volunteers and the military used the parades as an occasion to make the case for maintaining spending on equipment, the celebrations also served as an opportunity to emphasise their story of post-Vietnam redemption and to implore the American people to extend gratitude not just to the contemporary armed forces but to veterans of all American wars. The commemorative pamphlet produced for Washington, DC's National Victory Celebration made this clear when it included an account from a Gulf War veteran of the welcome he received from a wheelchair-bound Vietnam veteran. The Desert Storm veteran hoped and prayed that 'our welcome home will in some small way make up for the one he and his brother never got'.[148]

Vietnam veterans played prominent roles in the planning and execution of many of the parades. During the Philadelphia celebrations, for example, two Vietnam veterans symbolically passed a US flag and a POW-MIA flag to two Gulf veterans.[149] Other parades also featured marching Vietnam veterans: in Chicago, Chairman of the Joint Chiefs of Staff General Colin Powell and Secretary of Veterans Affairs Edwin Derwinksi, both veterans, served as grand marshals, and a group of 350 Vietnam veterans received loud cheers as they marched.[150] In Hollywood,

---

[147] Fred Kaplan, 'Air Force Opens up to Save Its Stealth Capitol Hill Pitch Plays on Gulf War Parades', *Boston Globe*, 11 June 1991, 3.

[148] 'Desert Storm: A Commemorative Salute' (Grabhorn Studio Inc, 8 June 1991), folder 08809-02 Miscellaneous Files: Desert Storm [2], White House Office of National Service, GBPL.

[149] The POW-MIA flag is the symbol of the National League of Families of American Prisoners and Missing in Southeast Asia. Weightman Public Relations, 'Press Release: Vietnam Veterans Salute Persian Gulf Veterans in an Emotional Independence Day in Philadelphia', 19 June 1991, folder 04733-005 'Desert Storm: Events', Sig Rogich Files, White House Office of Public Events and Initiatives, GBPL.

[150] 'Chicagoans Line Up 15 Rows Deep for Parade Honoring Gulf Veterans', *Los Angeles Times*, 11 May 1991, 18; Edward Walsh and Lauren Ina, 'Chicago Cheers Gulf Vets; Parade Also Salutes Vietnam Soldiers', *Washington Post*, 11 May 1991, A3.

none other than General William Westmoreland, the former commander of US forces in Vietnam, led a large contingent of Vietnam veterans. Westmoreland told reporters that 'any time I can be with the troops it's an exhilarating experience ... there's lots of camaraderie'. He also noted that 'I don't think we've ever seen a time in history when the country is so elated and so happy about the great success of a war'.[151] Westmoreland received loud cheers from Vietnam veterans when he appeared on parade, even as some veteran groups refused to participate because of his presence.[152]

Some veterans of earlier wars found the adulation for Gulf War veterans harder to stomach. In Orange County, California, Vietnam veteran Dan Baldwin spoke about the Desert Storm veterans to reporters as he attended a homecoming parade: 'These guys did a hell of a fine job over there ... I'm proud of them, but there's a bit of jealousy.' Baldwin saw a stark difference between the two wars: 'here they are getting a parade, well-deserved as it is, for eight months of work and 100 hours of war. I was in Vietnam for 13 months, wounded twice. There was nothing for us. But it's a different society today.'[153] Writing to the *Louisville Courier-Journal* on Veterans Day and looking back at the summer of celebratory homecomings, World War II veteran Frank O'Rourke complained about both the adulation for the Gulf War veterans and the grievances of Vietnam veterans. O'Rourke pointed out that the vast majority of veterans did not actually see combat and that the 'war for them will be remembered as an experience from their youth that they can reminisce about the way college students do about a big football game'.[154] Further, there was something off-putting about these parades, where 'soldiers looked the way civilians thought victorious soldiers should look – clean shaven, pressed uniforms, shiny boots, bands playing, and flags flying', more like a championship-winning football or baseball team.

In contrast, O'Rourke recalled his own experience, when he, like most experienced combat veterans, opted to leave the 82nd Airborne Division early rather than delay his discharge to take part in the homecoming parade. When he attended the division's 1946 parade down Fifth Avenue in New York City as a civilian onlooker, he saw a division full of fresh recruits that the Army had rushed in to replace the departed veterans.

[151] Associated Press, 'Tinseltown Gives Gulf Vets Huge Parade', *Northwest Florida Daily News*, 20 May 1991.

[152] Harris and Meyer, 'Gulf Troops Welcomed with Hollywood Flair Parade'; Rosenberg, 'A Parade of TV Praise for Gulf Warriors, War'.

[153] Gary A. Warner, 'Hero's Welcome Far Cry from Vietnam', *Orange County Register*, 19 May 1991, A14.

[154] Frank J. O'Rourke, 'Parade of Veterans', *The Courier-Journal*, 11 November 1991, 6.

O'Rourke wished instead for a less sanitised parade, one that featured his unit when they came out of the Battle of the Bulge: 'just columns of guys straggling down Fifth Avenue, shuffling along on frostbitten feet, with hand grenades tucked in the webbing of their harnesses, M-1s slung over their shoulders, bearded faces, gaunt eyes, hollow eyes, fatigued, exhausted physically and emotionally'.[155] Instead, he saw the Gulf War homecomings as a continuation of a deception about the nature of war.

Generally, though, the wave of celebrations across the country drowned out perspectives such as O'Rourke's. Given the ubiquity and intensity of these celebrations, it is clear that they represented widespread popular sentiment. Perhaps the most striking demonstration of the ways in which Americans embraced veterans in 1991 took place at Bangor International Airport, Maine. Bangor became a major transit point for troops returning from the Middle East. Throughout the spring and summer of 1991, approximately 220 flights landed there, containing some 60,000 veterans of Operation Desert Storm. Local civic groups organised a roster of greeters so that every flight, whether it landed in the middle of the night or during the working day, would be met with an enthusiastic crowd of locals offering coffee, small gifts, free phone calls, embraces and handshakes.[156] The mood at the airport was generally euphoric: greeters pinned yellow ribbons on the veterans, and soldiers autographed children's commemorative Desert Storm T-shirts. On one of the initial flights, on 8 March, Sergeant Kevin Tillman grabbed a saxophone and played a rendition of the 'Star-Spangled Banner' from the steps of the plane to a cheering crowd.[157]

The organisers made the point that their greeting party had 'nary a politician or bureaucrat in its ranks'.[158] One greeter claimed that 'we as a nation can't afford to repeat the mistakes we made with the troops in Vietnam. It's time to welcome home a new generation of veterans'.[159] Similarly, local journalist Brian Swartz argued that the Bangor homecomings 'had flipped the page historically by welcoming home our veterans, not by castigating them for obeying their civilian superiors' orders and policies' and that the greeters honoured 'them for what they

---

[155] O'Rourke.
[156] Brian Swartz, *An American Homecoming* (Bangor, ME: Bangor Pub Co, 1996); Lynne Junkins Cole, *Goodbye Desert Storm, Hello Bangor, Maine: Experience Welcoming the Troops through the Eyes of the Greeters* (Hampden, ME: Lynne Cole Pub, 1991).
[157] '20 Years Later, Sax-Playing Soldier Helps John Bapst Band Send off Troops', *Bangor Daily News*, 19 October 2011, https://bangordailynews.com/2011/10/19/news/bangor/20-years-later-sax-playing-soldier-helps-john-bapst-band-send-off-troops/ (accessed 19 December 2018)
[158] Swartz, *An American Homecoming*, 2.
[159] Swartz, 15.

were: the best of the best, American men and women who had gone into harm's way for the rest of us'.[160] Some members of the American Legion and Veterans of Foreign Wars even made a point of chasing any service members embarrassed by the welcome out from the ramp and into the waiting arms of the crowd 'where they belonged'.[161] Whether they wanted it or not, Gulf War veterans would receive a loud and public welcome home in Bangor. So extensive were the homecoming celebrations, which continued until September 1991, that the city held a special ceremony to thank the greeters in August 1991. At that ceremony, Lieutenant General John Yeosock, who had commanded the US 3rd Army in the Gulf, told the crowd that, much as he had been heartened by the groundswell of public support marked by the volume of care packages and mail sent to the troops, the scale of the phenomenon had not occurred to him until he landed in Bangor. But now he had no doubt that the greeters 'manifested the totality of what it was that this great nation of ours came to believe, feel, understand and do'.[162]

1.5   The Lessons of Desert Storm

In June 1991, officers within the Army Staff's think tank, the Chief's Analysis and Initiatives Group (CAIG), began circulating memos that offered broad reflections on what had transpired over the past few months. These remarkably candid musings offer valuable insights as to how some of the Army's most promising mid-ranking officers were processing the events of the war and its aftermath. One staff officer talked about his shock at being handed an anti-war pamphlet in the foyer of his church before Sunday Mass and hearing his deacon preach against the military build-up in the Gulf. He pointed out that in the run-up to war, there 'was reason to be concerned that the American public would remain seriously divided about going to war' and that 'the administration and the military both found themselves not only watching the polls to find out what the prevailing sentiment was, but carefully considering how and when to make various statements and policy moves to elicit the most favourable public impression'.[163] The outpouring of support for the troops seen during both Operation Desert Shield and Operation Desert Storm was therefore not a foregone conclusion. As the build-up to

---

[160] Swartz, v.
[161] Swartz, 26.
[162] Swartz, 227.
[163] Jim Narel, 'Protests, Parades and Polarization', June 1991, Carl E. Vuono Papers: Box 41, Folder 2, Issues Book [part 2 of 2], June 1991, AHEC.

war continued and media coverage paid attention to the stories of troops deployed to Saudi Arabia, the anti-war pamphlets disappeared from the church and the homilies became more balanced, but the incident reminded the officer that public support could not be taken for granted.

Another staffer, Colonel Robert Killebrew, also focused on the question of public support, noting just how much of that support focused on the figure of the soldier. Marvelling at the 'public reaction to Desert Shield', he claimed that 'Americans didn't react as if the soldiers over there were mercenaries; the troops were "our boys and girls," exactly as if they had been draftees'. He asked: 'with the draft dead as a dodo for nearly twenty years, why did the public react that way?'[164] The answer was that the All-Volunteer Force was a unique institution in American history; it was qualitatively different from the old 'Regular Army' of the 1930s that had been largely cut off from the American public, or the draftee armies of the world wars and Cold War and was instead 'a different kind of volunteer Army'. Killebrew argued that:

The citizen-soldier is alive and well in the ranks, but the basis for entering service has changed. What has passed is that coercion is no longer used to bring the citizen to the ranks. ... today's high-quality soldier is closer (not the same, but closer) to the tradition of the Greeks (or the volunteers on both sides of the American civil war) who saw voluntary service as a condition of citizenship than did his uncle who was drafted, or his grandfather who was an old-time Regular.[165]

This provided 'a new basis for military service in this democracy ... one that affects how the nation perceives *and uses* its Army over the long haul'. He noted that 'although soldiering is still basically a blue-collar profession, the world has changed, and the Army has thankfully changed along with it'. A professional army required discipline and toughness, but armies in democracies, 'islands of authoritarianism in a liberal sea', could only do this via a focus on service to the nation and on the tough, realistic training that had marked the organisation's ascent out of the nadir of the 'Hollow Army' days. Killebrew believed that volunteer recruits offered 'themselves freely to their country' because they wanted that tough training, and that the Army had to avoid losing that focus and giving into the temptation of creating 'a very nice Army ... that spends more time looking after itself and avoiding bureaucratic snarls than doing the messy and hard stuff out in the rain that makes tough,

---

[164] Robert Killebrew, 'Thought Piece: Continuity and Change', June 1991, Carl E. Vuono Papers: Box 41, Folder 2, Issues Book [part 2 of 2], June 1991, AHEC.
[165] Killebrew.

cocky soldiers'. To maintain the unusual alchemy that sustained an All-Volunteer Army that was seen by the American public as representative of its ideals, Army leaders would need to build a force 'dedicated to winning, dedicated to the point that we are all first soldiers and only then transporters or radio repairmen, or colonels, for that matter'.[166] Paradoxically, only by embracing this warrior ethos could the true spirit of the citizen-soldier be preserved.

Some policymakers made the same point. While CAIG officers were penning their reflections on Operation Desert Storm, Representative Les Aspin (D-WI), then chairman of the House Committee on Armed Services, gave a speech to the Center for Strategic and International Studies in Washington, DC. In it, he offered what he styled as not only his own views but those of his House committee as a whole. Much of Aspin's analysis followed along conventional lines. This included the claim that 'the men and women of the U.S. military today may be the best ever', his praise of the salutary effects of the Goldwater–Nichols Act, the 1986 legislation that reorganised the military chain of command and strengthened the role the chairman of Joint Chiefs of Staff, and his assertion that military 'high technology was vindicated in Desert Storm'.[167]

In the last part of his analysis, though, he broke with the arguments that had appeared in the military's official accounts of the war and reflected on the role of the Military Reform movement. While much coverage of this movement had focused on debates over weapons systems, Aspin noted that 'their programme was people first, ideas second and weapons only third' and that their agenda focused on promoting warriors over managers, 'agile, unpredictable manoeuvre warfare', and unit cohesion, 'the fighting spirit that comes when men train and fight together, for each other'. For Aspin, Desert Storm had validated these ideas, but only by accident. Certainly, the military 'clearly had warriors in General Powell and General Schwarzkopf', and unit cohesion appeared to be strong, but this cohesion was never really tested, given the brevity of the war. He pointed to the failure of the COHORT system and noted that many military reformers still argued that Army units clearly lacked natural cohesion and 'stumbled into it more by chance than by conscious adaptation'. If cohesion existed, it was because units spent six months together in the desert waiting for the war to start, so 'unit cohesion was developed on the scene rather than developed through Army policy'. In Aspin's mind,

---

[166] Killebrew.

[167] Les Aspin, 'Desert One to Desert Storm: Making Ready for Victory: Speech to Center for Strategic and International Studies, Washington, D.C.', 20 June 1991, Gordon R. Sullivan Papers: Box 88, Folder 9, Memorandum [part 1 of 2], July 1991, AHEC.

'the jury was still out' on whether the Pentagon would accept this key part of the Military Reform movement's agenda.[168] In emphasising questions of cohesion and the warrior spirit, Aspin was hinting that, despite all of euphoria brought about by the swift victory in the Gulf, some of the cultural problems highlighted by dissident officers in the late 1980s had not gone away.

1.6   Conclusion

Aspin's brief reflections on cohesion aside, the aftermath of Operation Desert Storm was about celebration. 'Lessons learned' studies would later go into more detail about what had worked well and what hadn't, but the overwhelming public message was that the military had reached new heights of competence and even brilliance. For Army leaders, Desert Storm and its celebratory aftermath confirmed that the All-Volunteer Force had been a success and that its bonds with the American people had been thoroughly rebuilt. Part of the message of the homecoming parades was that never again would these bonds be allowed to break. In reflecting on the meaning of these events, Army leaders felt that their duty was to ensure that any post–Cold War drawdown preserved the essentials of the post-Vietnam reforms and embraced the things that had made the Gulf War go so well for the United States. This meant that any fundamental rethinking of the Army's roles, missions or culture would be out of the question, even in a world without the Cold War.

For the broader public, the military's post-Vietnam reforms and its triumph in the Persian Gulf elevated the figure of the soldier as representative of all that was best about the United States. The jubilation of the summer of 1991 would not last, but this heroic image would, in large part, endure, even as the actual experience of military service was the preserve of fewer and fewer Americans. Since the soldier being idealised was a volunteer professional, not a draftee, political rhetoric emphasised that soldiers embodied American values to conform to the 'citizen-soldier' ideal. Even if the military's makeup did not map precisely onto the demographic contours of the country, soldiers could act as symbols for the nation. If soldiers were supposed to be paragons of American ideals, then it was all the more important for different political groups to claim soldiers as their own, and to ensure that the values of the military were indeed in keeping with those of broader society. This situation also made it imperative for the broad swathes of American society

[168] Aspin.

that had been excluded from the possibility of full military service to demand the right to don the uniform so that they could access all the symbolic and material benefits that came with it. The tensions between a military leadership that was determined to preserve what it saw as a hard-won restoration and the social forces both within the ranks of the Army and in broader society who sought to make the institution a more equitable one would soon spill over into a dispute that would take some of the gloss off the successes of Desert Storm.

2   Gender, Sexuality and the Profession of Arms

Don't Ask Don't Tell, Women in
Combat and the 'Band of Brothers'

In early February 1993, the Chairman of the Joint Chiefs of Staff General Colin Powell sat down for an interview with CNN's Bernard Shaw. While much of the interview consisted of Powell parrying suggestions that he might be interested in a presidential run, it started with something of a softball exchange. Shaw noted that the military as an institution enjoyed incredible popularity and widespread respect. Powell agreed, stating that 'the armed forces of the United States are in exquisite condition now and I think the American people have every reason to be very, very proud of them'.[1] As the interview went on, though, Shaw began to home in on rumours of tensions between the military and the Clinton White House. On every issue bar one, Powell denied that there were difficulties. However, when it came to Clinton's proposal to allow openly gay personnel to serve in the military, Powell was quick to admit disagreement. He claimed that 'it is a very controversial subject throughout the nation' and that 'in my culture, not to have told the President in candid, direct terms what the feelings were of his military leaders and what the feelings were of the troops out there – that would have been insubordination'.[2] Indeed, Powell had already made his position on the issue clear, telling an audience of midshipmen in a January 1993 address at the Naval Academy that 'the presence of homosexuals in the force would be detrimental to good order and discipline, for a variety of reasons', and advising his audience that they should consider resigning if they could not stomach serving in the military alongside openly gay colleagues.[3]

---

[1] 'Interview with General Colin Powell, Chairman, Joint Chiefs of Staff', *CNN Today*, 10 February 1993.

[2] 'Interview with General Colin Powell, Chairman, Joint Chiefs of Staff'.

[3] Eric Schmitt, 'Military Cites Wide Range of Reasons for Its Gay Ban: Joint Chiefs Stress Morale, Privacy and Discipline Armed Services Cite a Wide Range of Reasons for Ban on Homosexuality Some Officers Say Easing the Gay Policy Would Change Little', *New York Times*, 26 January 1993, www.proquest.com/docview/109230833/abstract/D4198017B6A34C37PQ/1.

In Powell's mind, the 'exquisite condition' of the military in the early 1990s and the ban on gay military service were closely related. For Powell and his colleagues, the military was essentially where it needed to be, and – while they were reconciled to post–Cold War budget cuts and drawdowns – any attempt to alter its social makeup had to be fiercely resisted. In this understanding, the achievements of the post-Vietnam era were fragile and could easily be lost if civilians interfered with military prerogatives. The post-Vietnam reforms had combined a new culture of professionalism with older martial virtues such as courage, self-sacrifice and loyalty. Powell and other military leaders questioned whether bonds of loyalty and self-sacrifice could be maintained if politicians mandated that previously all-male and all-heterosexual spaces be opened to others. They argued that such changes would inevitably have a negative impact on unit cohesion and morale.[4]

The debate over gay military service was one of only several crises that began to eat away at the warm afterglow of the Gulf War. In some ways, these crises were a product of the success of Operation Desert Storm. The presence of thousands of servicewomen in the Persian Gulf led to questions about whether the services should open combat roles to them. Similarly, the presence of gay men and women in their desert combat uniforms in Pride parades around the country, many of whom who had received discharges on their return from the Gulf, raised the temperature on the political debate over gay military service. This meant that the Army, along with the other services, was faced with two nearly simultaneous challenges to its personnel policies. Here, the Army's fate was bound up with those of the other branches of the military. More than any other issue, debates over who should serve and under what conditions took place on the terrain of politics. This means that while other chapters in this book exclusively focus on the Army, parts of this chapter necessarily treat discussions of gender and sexuality as an interservice issue. As one group of scholars put it, 'the military had complete control over very little when it came to sex. Decisions about who could serve and under what conditions were made by Congress, in its role of civilian oversight. They were adjudicated by the courts. They were subject

---

[4] Scholars across disciplines have noted both how frequently arguments about cohesion have been invoked to defend a particular type of military masculinity, but also how vulnerable those arguments are to being undermined when units that do not conform to these norms outperform expectations. Beth Bailey, 'The Politics of Dancing: "Don't Ask, Don't Tell", and the Role of Moral Claims', *Journal of Policy History* 25, no. 1 (2013): 89–113; Megan MacKenzie, *Beyond the Band of Brothers: The US Military and the Myth that Women Can't Fight* (New York: Cambridge University Press, 2015); Anthony King, *The Combat Soldier: Infantry Tactics and Cohesion in the Twentieth and Twenty-First Centuries* (Oxford: Oxford University Press, 2013).

to executive order.'[5] While the military had to implement decisions on gender, sex and sexuality by developing policy and creating regulations, it did so under political and juridical constraints. These constraints only seemed to tighten in the aftermath of the Gulf War, as the service chiefs confronted a slew of court cases, political initiatives and complaints from marginalised service members about both the unfairness and ineffectiveness of current restrictions on service.

The generals' arguments for maintaining the status quo centred on the notion that the military was an exceptional institution within US society, with claims about the need for combat cohesion and the maintenance of a 'band of brothers' paramount in their approach to the issue. At the same time, even as senior leaders positioned the military as a site that needed some immunity from broader American society and general social and cultural trends, when it came to the question of gay military service, there was a paradox in their approach as they often fell back on opinion surveys of enlisted personnel and claims about possible recruiting difficulties to make the case for the continuing exclusion of openly gay people from the Army. There was a clear tension between claiming the Army was somehow set apart from the rest of American society and on relying on claims about deviating from 'widely accepted social norms' to continue the exclusionary policy. Both this contradiction and the tension between claims that the military was an organisation full of disciplined professionals and fears that introducing gay personnel into the ranks could produce violence can be understood by reference to a warrior ethos that took on a particular gendered form.

2.1   Don't Ask, Don't Tell

When Bill Clinton, then governor of Arkansas and running for president, declared in a speech at Harvard in 1991 that he would end the military's controversial ban on gay service members, he did not foresee the controversy that lay ahead. While his transition team in November 1992 may have believed that the policy change would be an uncomplicated move to adapt the military to the demands of modern society, they naively assumed that basic legislation and the stroke of a pen could somehow eradicate the structural inequality that decades of arcane and harmful regulations and attitudes had wrought. A quick consultation with military leaders, though, led to a realisation that this would not be so simple. One staffer, sent to gather the views of senior generals, reported that 'there has been

---

[5] Beth Bailey et al., eds, 'Introduction', in *Managing Sex in the U.S. Military: Gender, Identity, and Behavior* (Lincoln: University of Nebraska Press, 2022), 4.

no abatement in opposition. No one I spoke with favored allowing homo-sexuals into the military …. Virtually all were more interested in telling me why the action should not be taken than in how to do it', but added opti-mistically, 'no-one was hostile personally'.[6] Following these initial probes and several meetings with joint chiefs of staff both before and after his inauguration, Clinton agreed to a six-month process of consultation that would end up with the watered down compromise of 'Don't Ask, Don't Tell', wherein military authorities would no longer ask service members about their sexual orientation but any service members openly declaring their status as gay would receive a dishonourable discharge (Figure 2.1).[7]

Opponents of gay military service within the military, and within the Army in particular, used two distinctive and sometimes contradictory arguments about military identity to make their case. First, they and their outside allies argued that a 'people's army' would have to reflect the broader mores of the society from which it was drawn and that it should not be the site of 'social experiments' where marginal groups would be integrated. Second, they portrayed the military as an exceptional insti-tution that stood apart from civil society; one built around a vital but fragile sense of cohesion. Given the downsizing of the armed forces and the increased tempo of deployments, nothing should be done to risk cohesion and military readiness, and all other claims would have to be subordinated to the needs of the nation's defence.

Gay rights activists understood the move to end the ban in terms of equality, fairness and citizenship. The movement was in the process of shifting towards the political mainstream, with activists such as the conservative editor of the *New Republic*, Andrew Sullivan, disavowing earlier ideas of a radically separate gay identity and beginning to argue for the embrace of more conventional institutions such as marriage.[8]

---

[6] John Holum, 'Report to President-Elect Clinton: Homosexuals in the Military', 14 January 1993, OA/ID CF384, Counsel's Office – Neuwirth, Folder: Gays in Military, FOIA 2006-0227-F, William J. Clinton Presidential Library (Clinton Library).

[7] The story of how that weak compromise came about, from the continuing opposition of the generals to a huge mobilisation of the religious right to the highly effective Congressional opposition led by Democratic Senator Sam Nunn has been recounted in Nathaniel Frank, *Unfriendly Fire: How the Gay Ban Undermines the Military and Weakens America* (New York: Thomas Dunne Books, 2009); Randy Shilts, *Conduct Unbecoming: Lesbians and Gays in the U.S. Military: Vietnam to the Persian Gulf* (New York: St. Martin's Press, 1993); Bailey, 'The Politics of Dancing'; Aaron Belkin and Geoffrey Bateman, *Don't Ask, Don't Tell: Debating the Gay Ban in the Military* (Boulder, CO: Lynne Rienner Publishers, 2003). Jacqueline Whitt notes, however, that we still lack a comprehensive, holistic history of the Don't Ask Don't Tell era. Jacqueline E. Whitt, 'Queering American Military History', *International Journal of Military History and Historiography* 1 (17 May 2021): 14.

[8] Andrew Sullivan, 'Here Comes the Groom', *The New Republic*, 28 August 1989, https://newrepublic.com/article/79054/here-comes-the-groom.

Figure 2.1 Extract from the Army's 2001 publication *Dignity and Respect: A Training Guide on Homosexual Conduct Policy*

The military became a place to advance the idea of gay Americans being full and equal participants in American society and during the Gulf War more and more service members came out as they deployed to the Arabian Peninsula. The military considered these declarations to be attempts to avoid service in a combat zone but, in the words of Randy Shilts, many of them simply didn't 'want a coffin to be their final closet'.[9] These service members were lauded in the gay press and several led Gay Pride parades in uniform in the aftermath of the war (although virtually all had been discharged from the military upon return to the USA). These gay veterans and other prominent gay former service members such as Vernon Berg, Joseph Steffan, Leonard Matlovich and Perry Watkins made the case that gay Americans had always served in their country's military and that now was the time – in keeping with the growing acceptance of the idea that gay rights were simply human rights – for them to be able to openly acknowledge their sexual orientation as they served.[10] Writing in the *New Republic*, Sullivan argued that such a move would have a powerful impact because 'the acceptance of gay people at the heart of the state, at the core of the notion of patriotism, is anathema to those who wish to consign homosexuals to the margins of society'.[11]

Many proponents of the ban on gay service in the military understood the argument in the same terms. Commenting to RAND Corporation researchers completing a study on how to implement a lifting of the ban for the Office of the Secretary of Defence, some soldiers argued that the move to lift the ban was about politics, not what was best for the military: 'this is a gay rights movement, they want to put it in your face. They want to come in so they can say they can come in', and 'we're pawns, they want the military to accept it so they can get the rest of the country to accept it.' These troops believed that the military was being forced to undertake something that civilians were unwilling to do: 'we're the experimental testing ground', and 'this is about symbolism. The population will listen to us; they will say this is not right.'[12] For these soldiers, the important thing was that the military should not be made to move first on these issues in a way that would separate them from mainstream

[9] Shilts, *Conduct Unbecoming*, 736.
[10] Shilts, *Conduct Unbecoming*; Simon Hall, 'Leonard Matlovich: From Military Hero to Gay Rights Poster Boy', in *Warring over Valor: How Race and Gender Shaped American Military Heroism in the Twentieth and Twenty-First Centuries*, ed. Simon Wendt (New Brunswick, NJ: Rutgers University Press, 2018).
[11] Andrew Sullivan, 'The Politics of Homosexuality: A Case for a New Beginning', *The New Republic*, 10 May 1993.
[12] National Defense Research Institute, 'Sexual Orientation and US Military Personnel Policy: Options and Assessment: Prepared for the Office of the Secretary of Defense' (Santa Monica, CA: RAND, 1993).

society. One argued that 'it's not fair to be exposed to something like that when society shuns that type of behavior. People need to consider these things when making decisions on people's career and lifestyle.'[13]

Senior officers agreed with this critique, with Clinton transition team staffers discovering a deep-seated unease among the senior leadership about anything that hinted at the military being used for what they termed 'social engineering'.[14] Several invoked the memory of 'Project 100,000', an ill-fated Johnson-era programme where the military took in 100,000 below-standard draftees.[15] All argued that the military was not a social laboratory and that the primary criteria for deciding on the merits of any change was its impact on the combat effectiveness of the military.[16] Indeed, some argued that moving away from the agreed norms of American society would badly damage the military's effectiveness. The Military Working Group, a taskforce convened by Secretary of Defense Les Aspin to study the effects of lifting the ban, argued that 'as citizen soldiers, military members bring their values with them when they enter the Service. Whether based on moral, religious, cultural, or ethical considerations, those values and beliefs are often strongly held and not amenable to change.' It was not the military's role to make people change those values and beliefs because 'while we indoctrinate and train recruits, leadership and discipline cannot ... and generally should not ... attempt to counter the basic values which parents and society have taught. Indeed, efforts to do so will likely prove counterproductive.'[17]

Others sought to make the case that there really weren't that many gay people to accommodate in the first place. Briefing notes for Army Chief of Staff General Gordon R. Sullivan's December 1992 meeting with Clinton transition staffer John Holum contained passages drawn directly from material supplied by the fundamentalist Christian outfit the Family Research Council, and claimed that there was 'no basis in fact for the claim that 10% of the population is homosexual', and that

[13] Laura Miller and Charles C. Moskos, 'Sociological Survey of US Army Soldiers Serving in Bosnia in 1996 and 1998: Questionnaire Results', n.d., Charles C. Moskos Papers, Northwestern University Archives (Moskos Papers).

[14] For a useful critique of the 'social experiment' trope, see Jacqueline E. Whitt and Elizabeth A. Perazzo, 'The Military as Social Experiment: Challenging a Trope', *Parameters* 48, no. 2 (22 June 2018): 5.

[15] Christian G. Appy, *Working-Class War: American Combat Soldiers and Vietnam* (Chapel Hill: University of North Carolina Press, 1993), 32–3.

[16] Dick Klass, 'Memorandum to John Holum, Subject: Summary of Responses to Gay Issue by Flag Officers Who Endorsed Governor Clinton', 23 December 1992, OA/ID CF384, Counsel's Office – Neuwirth, Folder: Gays in Military, FOIA 2006-0227-F, Clinton Library.

[17] Office of the Secretary of Defense, 'Summary Report of the Military Working Group', 1 July 1993, 4658 – Counsel's Office – Cliff Sloan [3], FOIA 2006-0227-F, Clinton Library.

'the homosexual community pushes the 10% figure as another way to force acceptance of homosexuality and advance their political agenda'.[18] A few months later, Senator John Warner (R-VA) claimed at a congressional hearing that '[the homosexual] lifestyle is very very different. Society hasn't changed. I think we're here because gay activists capitalised on this as a campaign issue.' Speaking of the 'Don't Ask, Don't Tell' compromise, Warner argued that 'we all have to give up something to serve. We're asking homosexuals to give up a little something, that is to actively profess their sexuality. Give that up, we'll let them serve. But many don't have that inner strength or control to deal with this struggle and carry out their military duties.'[19]

His colleague Senator John McCain (R-AZ) took a slightly different tack on the issue at the same hearing, noting that he was 'concerned about the All-Volunteer Force and the impact of on it if the policy is changed'.[20] Based on his conversations with parents of potential recruits, McCain thought that recruiting and retention could be badly affected if the ban was rescinded. Therefore, attempts to move away from the mores of American society would cause grave damage to the military's ability to function. General Powell pointed out to Clinton at their first meeting after the inauguration that a 'people's army' must reflect society and that a volunteer army must compete economically for those people.[21] The Military Working Group argued that 'open homosexuality in the military would likely reduce the propensity of many young men and women to enlist due to parental concerns, peer pressure, and a military image that would be tarnished in the eyes of much of the population from which we recruit'.[22] The fear was not only that 'mothers in Iowa' would discourage their children from joining but that experienced NCOs and officers would leave the military if gays were allowed in. Some studies claimed that over 11 per cent of the service members could leave the force if the ban was lifted, with Commandant of the Marine Corps

---

[18] Daniel J. Sullivan, 'Memorandum Thru Colonel Harper for General Sullivan: Meeting with Mr. Holum on Homosexuality', 15 December 1992, Gordon R. Sullivan Papers; Box 125B, Folder 10, CSA General Office Files [part 1 of 2], December 1992, AHEC.

[19] Raymond W. O'Keeffe, 'Memorandum Thru Colonel Harper for General Sullivan: Homosexual Questions from SASC (By Senator by Date)', 18 May 1993, 7, Gordon R. Sullivan Papers; Box 159, Folder 7, Preparation Book for the Chief of Staff, Army for his Testimony on Homosexuals in the Military [Part 1 of 2], AHEC.

[20] O'Keeffe, 12.

[21] 'Handwritten Notes of President Clinton's Meeting with the Joint Chiefs of Staff', 25 January 1993, National Security Council, Richard Beardsworth (Defense Policy), OA/ Box Number: 3154, Folder: Gays in the Military, 1993–1999 [1], FOIA 2006-0227-F, Clinton Library.

[22] Office of the Secretary of Defense, 'Summary Report of the Military Working Group'.

General Charles Mundy reporting to Clinton that young leaders had written to him saying that 'we should disband the United States Marine Corps' before accepting this decision.[23]

In a January 1993 meeting with Clinton, Mundy had claimed that 'proclaiming I'm gay' was the 'same as I'm KKK, Nazi, rapist' because it's a declaration that 'I commit acts that America doesn't accept'.[24] Others within the military saw things in similarly catastrophic terms, with one Army major general worrying that ending the ban would be 'a foot in the door' and that 'soon they will force open the doors of West Point, the other academies and the ROTC [Reserve Officers' Training Corps]'. In this scenario, there would not be 'a great influx of homosexuals, but there will be an influx of those who are radical ... the drug/discipline/ race problems we had some years ago will be nothing compared to the problems they will bring'.[25] Another major general (this one retired) predicted that the military justice system would favour homosexuals and that 'the military services will become the happy hunting ground the homosexuals have always sought'. He predicted that 'there will be a push for affirmative action' and that the military's guaranteed lifetime health service and 'service-connected disability pensions for sexually transmitted diseases' would 'empty the bath houses of San Francisco'. Given all of this, he predicted that the US Army would be 30 per cent homosexual by the year 2000 unless Army leaders took preventative measures.[26]

Powell himself thought that this catastrophising was unhelpful and believed that while there would be an initial spike of resistance, most in the military would come to accept the change over time, albeit at the expense of diminished prestige in the eyes of the American public and, crucially, a gradual chipping away of combat effectiveness and cohesion over time.[27] It was this point about combat effectiveness and cohesion that was in fact the one made the most frequently by opponents of lifting the ban. While, as we have seen, many resisted the idea that the military be used as a social laboratory or forced to accept norms that mainstream US society did not yet accept, most made a different argument, one that did not so much

---

[23] 'Handwritten Notes of President Clinton's Meeting with the Joint Chiefs of Staff'.
[24] 'Handwritten Notes of President Clinton's Meeting with the Joint Chiefs of Staff'.
[25] Pat Brady, 'Letter to Gordon R. Sullivan', 29 January 1993, Gordon R. Sullivan Papers; Box 126A, Folder 3, CSA Correspondence Files [20–31 January] (Part 3 of 3), January 1993, AHEC.
[26] George Kuttas, 'Letter to Gordon R. Sullivan', 18 January 1993, Gordon R. Sullivan Papers; Box 127, Folder 1, CSA Correspondence Files (Part 1 of 3), February 1993, AHEC.
[27] John Holum, 'Memorandum to File, Clinton-Gore Transition, Ccs Admiral Crowe, George Stephanopoulos, Sandy Berger, Jeff Smith, Subject: Meeting with Joint Chiefs of Staff', 9 December 1992, OA/ID CF384, Counsel's Office – Neuwirth, Folder: Gays in Military, FOIA 2006-0227-F, Clinton Library.

focus on the idea of citizen-soldiers or a people's army – for in the late twentieth century, any people's army would surely have to include soldiers of different sexual orientations – but on the military as a site of exception, as a body somehow apart from civilian society and subject to different rules because of the unique challenges they faced as an organisation. For instance, while many proponents of lifting the ban used the analogy of the integration of African American soldiers in the aftermath of World War II to argue that the military *could* in fact function effectively as a social laboratory and be at the forefront of societal change, the response of opponents was telling. In the eyes of those who opposed open gay service, the integration of African Americans took place only because it aided combat effectiveness, and for no other reason. One flag officer told a Clinton staffer tasked with gathering views on the issue before the inauguration that 'we needed women to fill out the ranks, we don't need gays'. Another put it: 'You may not be able to prove that gays hurt combat effectiveness, but you certainly cannot prove that they help it.'[28]

This idea that only a few Americans could have the privilege of serving was an important one for those opposed to open gay service. The Military Working Group pointed out that 'the "terms of employment" for an individual service-member include the real possibility that he or she will be called upon to make the ultimate sacrifice in service to our country' and that there was no 'right to serve' in the armed forces. Military service was not so much an obligation but a privilege afforded only to those who were qualified. Homosexuality was a disqualifying feature, just like 'height, weight, prior conduct record, membership in groups with certain objectives, or mental category'.[29] As the first African American Chairman of the Joint Chiefs of Staff, Colin Powell played a vitally important role in parrying civil rights arguments about gay military service. He told students at American University that he got 'testy' when people drew comparisons between race and sexuality, arguing that skin colour was a 'benign characteristic' whereas homosexuality went 'to one of the most fundamental aspects of human behaviour'.[30] Northwestern

[28] Klass, 'Memorandum to John Holum, Subject: Summary of Responses to Gay Issue by Flag Officers Who Endorsed Governor Clinton'.

[29] Office of the Secretary of Defense, 'Summary Report of the Military Working Group'.

[30] 'Powell: Military "Struggling" Over Gays', *Washington Post*, 1 December 1992, www .washingtonpost.com/archive/politics/1992/12/01/powell-military-struggling-over-gays/1e92238a-c117-4203-acd7-fad60bf96ea8/; A. M. Rosenthal, 'On My Mind; General Powell and the Gays', *New York Times*, 26 January 1993, www.nytimes .com/1993/01/26/opinion/on-my-mind-general-powell-and-the-gays.html. What Powell didn't mention was that while the military had been one of the first institutions to racially integrate, it was very much behind the rest of society when it came to equal opportunity in terms of both gender and sexuality.

University sociologist Charles Moskos wrote to Senator Sam Nunn that he believed allowing gays to either marry or serve in the military 'means according gays a certain measure of honor. That we need not honor gays does not mean we disrespect them.'[31] Honouring gay service members or affording them the privilege of military service could not be allowed to interfere with unit cohesion, especially for military leaders who had a moral imperative to accomplish the mission with the least loss of life possible.[32]

Army leaders frequently made the social experiment argument in tandem with claims about how ending the ban would damage cohesion. Sullivan's May 1993 briefing book on 'homosexual issues' claimed that 'it is ludicrous to ... involve the Army in an attempt to change the cultural mores of a majority of Americans. Focusing on this issue would divert attention from our primary mission of providing a trained, ready, and cohesive fighting force.'[33] The Association of the United States Army, the influential Army-linked advocacy group, declared that 'this issue is emerging as one of the most critical social debates of our time' and that 'the role of our military is to protect and defend the nation, not to serve as a laboratory for social change'. Their position paper also brought up the issue of cohesion, arguing that 'units are a special segment of the military environment. They live, train, and fight together. Bonding is important.' This bonding was only possible because of shared values, which would be diminished by the presence of 'publicly avowed homosexuals', who would find it difficult to 'bond with and be fully accepted by the group'.[34] Tellingly, even the Family Research Council, an organisation whose objections to repealing the ban were decidedly based on moral arguments, chose to foreground these claims about cohesion and professionalism as well, arguing that 'the homosexual exclusion is based largely upon the considered professional judgment of military commanders responsible for raising, maintaining, training, and employing a military force'.[35]

---

[31] Charles C. Moskos, 'Letter to Sam Nunn', 25 January 1993, Moskos Papers.

[32] Honouring gay Americans also meant allowing gay advocacy organisations to lay a wreath at the tomb of the Unknown Soldier, an act which the Secretary of Defense refused to allow for years as he argued it constituted a political act.

[33] 'Questions and Answers', 19 May 1993, 3-1, Gordon R. Sullivan Papers; Box 159, Folder 7, Preparation Book for the Chief of Staff, Army for his Testimony on Homosexuals in the Military [Part 1 of 2], AHEC.

[34] Jack N. Merritt, 'AUSA Issues: The Department of Defense Homosexual Exclusion Policy', 1 February 1993, Gordon R. Sullivan Papers; Box 127, Folder 8, CSA General Office Files (Part 1 of 2), February 1993, AHEC.

[35] William A. Woodruff, 'The Battle over Homosexuality: Why the Military's Ban Should Not Be Lifted', February 1993, Gordon R. Sullivan Papers; Box 127, Folder 9, CSA General Office Files (Part 1 of 2), February 1993, AHEC.

As historian Beth Bailey has pointed out, the idea that nothing could be allowed to jeopardise combat effectiveness was a convenient one for the senior military leadership as it allowed them to say nothing in public about their own personal views about homosexuality but to still argue that most service members would not accept openly gay service members and thus that the presence of such personnel would in itself badly damage cohesion.[36] Sullivan told Congress that his judgement was based on '33 years of active service, 17 of those overseas and 24 months of combat duty' and that he knew 'what it has taken to build today's Army .... Small cohesive units are the cornerstone ... there will be degradation if the ban is lifted is certain.' Ultimately, this degradation would cost lives by reducing combat effectiveness. He argued that lifting the ban would champion 'the desires of the homosexual community over the needs of the Nation' and that these activists misunderstood the nature of military service. He argued that any public support for ending the ban was predicated on a belief that the military was a nine to five job like any other, but that extended deployment and the privations they brought with them meant that soldiers would be living together 24/7 and that camaraderie and cohesion were vital to getting through tough times.[37] In testimony before the Senate Armed Services Committee, Powell made similar claims and argued that:

To win wars, we create cohesive teams of warriors who will bond so tightly that they are prepared to go into battle and give their lives if necessary for the accomplishment of the mission and for the cohesion of the group and for their individual buddies. We cannot allow anything to happen which would disrupt that feeling of cohesion within the force. We are the best force in the world, and to be the best requires subjugating individual rights to the benefit of the group and the benefit of the team.[38]

But what Powell left unsaid was exactly what it was about homosexuality that made it so destructive to unit cohesion.

For the Military Working Group, it was that homosexuals lacked 'the shared moral values of the institution – the collective sense of right and wrong' that ensured the military's unique licence to kill and destroy would not be abused. This foundation was the essential difference between a

[36] Bailey, 'The Politics of Dancing'.
[37] Gordon R. Sullivan, 'Preparation Book for the Chief of Staff, Army, for His Testimony before the Senate Armed Services Committee on Implementing the Homosexual Conduct Policy', February 1994, Gordon R. Sullivan Papers, Box 68, Folder 4: Preparation Book, February 1994, AHEC.
[38] 'Hearing to Receive Testimony on Department of Defense Policy on the Service of Gay Men and Lesbians in the Armed Forces. Statement of General Colin Powell, Chairman of the Joint Chiefs of Staff', 20 July 1993.

professional armed force and a mercenary force. It provided to 'individual service-members the moral basis for personal service, commitment, and sacrifice in a profession which is demanding in the extreme'.[39] Homosexuality was, in their view, disruptive behaviour. Even undeclared homosexuals were dangerous because they formed subgroups and cliques that could not be detected by commanders. Others argued that the homosexual lifestyle was unhealthy and that allowing gays to openly serve would facilitate the spread of AIDS throughout the force.[40] Sullivan argued that in a small and shrinking army, 'it is becoming increasingly important that every soldier be deployable worldwide. Introducing a segment of the population that has a propensity to develop the AIDS virus would be self-defeating.' Army position papers also claimed that homosexuals were more promiscuous, had more propensity to develop sexually transmitted infections and would prey on younger soldiers.[41]

Some soldiers feared sexual violence at the hands of their gay comrades-in-arms, telling the Military Working Group that 'I'd be afraid to be in a foxhole with a gay person. I don't trust them. I'd be afraid that if I looked the other way, he'd do something' and 'I'm worried that when I'm holding up a piece of armament, someone might come over and grab me'. Some felt it would be a problem only in extreme situations: 'what happens if we are deployed for an exceptionally long time? Sexual urges will cause problems at the worst possible time. A soldier shouldn't have to be watching his back for more than a bullet.'[42] Still others reported that they felt that allowing gay soldiers to openly serve would undermine both the macho and moral basis of military service, telling RAND researchers that 'I have a hard time thinking about the image of a military where two gay guys can be out sunbathing. What am I going to tell my son if he sees this and asks if it is OK?' and 'no one will want to join the [military]. Morale will go down. We join because of the image, because we do the job right, are macho.'[43]

Charles Moskos had a unique explanation for why this focus on macho culture mattered. Arguing in favour of the ban in testimony before the Senate Armed Services Committee, Moskos referred to an influential 1948 article by Edward Shils and Morris Janowitz on cohesion and disintegration in the German *Wehrmacht* during World War II. Shils and

---

[39] Office of the Secretary of Defense, 'Summary Report of the Military Working Group'.
[40] M. J. McCauley, 'Letter to President Clinton', 27 May 1993, OA/ID 12138, scan ID: 020289, FOIA 2006-0227-F, Clinton Library.
[41] Sullivan, 'Memorandum Thru Colonel Harper for General Sullivan: Meeting with Mr. Holum on Homosexuality'.
[42] National Defense Research Institute, 'Sexual Orientation and US Military Personnel Policy: Options and Assessment: Prepared for the Office of the Secretary of Defense'.
[43] National Defense Research Institute.

Janowitz found that the soldiers in the *Wehrmacht*, commonly acknowledged by military historians to be an incredibly cohesive fighting force, had a strong propensity towards homoerotic behaviour, although homosexuals were obviously not publicly tolerated in Nazi Germany.[44] For Moskos, this was evidence in support of the ban. He said that 'precisely because there are homoerotic tendencies in all-male groups, this is exactly why the ban. Once these homoerotic tendencies are out, the cat is out of the bag: then you have all kinds of negative effects on unit cohesion.'[45] In a later interview, Moskos argued that 'the point is that in the Nazi army, you could not be a gay ... it might even be that the more homoerotic tendencies there are in a group ... the more homophobic it will be'.[46]

Moskos found some support in this position from a fellow scholar, the anthropologist Anna Simons. In a letter to Moskos that he immediately forwarded on to Army leaders, Simons claimed that military leaders had not done enough to make the case that there was such a thing as a 'military lifestyle' and to explain how cohesion actually occurred. In her view, 'what is integral to male bonding and small unit cohesion is discussion about and acknowledged (and sometimes even witnessed) participation in heterosexual sex'. This was the only shared universal value beyond the experience of passing through the same training and so was vital in providing a foundation for cohesion. Simons claimed that 'as an anthropologist, I would argue that until someone can effectively demonstrate what the components of "warrior-ness" are ... then the burden of proof remains with gay advocates as to how the gay "lifestyle" *is* a warrior lifestyle'. For Simons, the military lifestyle was itself a distinct way of life that was simply not compatible with any other.[47]

This argument could help explain the widespread fears of anti-gay violence in the military following the lifting of the ban. In a letter to President Clinton, one correspondent argued that 'if [gays] had any idea of what military integration would bring on them, they would be *protesting*, not *demanding* military integration: we can sit and dispassionately discuss such matters here at home, but in battle, among men trained to kill, patience and understanding are not common virtues'.[48] Similarly, participants in the RAND focus groups claimed that 'it will be healthier

[44] Edward A. Shils and Morris Janowitz, 'Cohesion and Disintegration in the Wehrmacht in World War II', *The Public Opinion Quarterly* 12, no. 2 (1948): 280–315.

[45] Cited in Frank, *Unfriendly Fire*, 134.

[46] Nathaniel Frank, 'What's Love Got to Do with It? The Real Story of Military Sociology and "Don't Ask, Don't Tell"', *Lingua Franca*, October 2000, Moskos Papers.

[47] Anna Simons, 'Letter to Charles Moskos', 9 February 1993, Gordon R. Sullivan Papers; Box 127, Folder 9, CSA General Office Files (Part 1 of 2), February 1993, AHEC.

[48] Raymond S. Moore, 'Letter to President Clinton', 20 January 1993, OA/ID 12138, scan ID: 008440, FOIA 2006-0227-F, Clinton Library.

for gays if they don't say anything. It will just be pain and heartache for gays', and 'it's hurting them more than helping them by removing the ban, because they're going to get hurt. Personally, if they leave me alone it's OK. But it's already happening that when they come out, they get beaten up.' One participant argued that 'no sane gay person would come out – he would get slipped overboard'. The most extreme form of this focus on violence was the threat that soldiers would give gay colleagues 'a blanket party' (a form of hazing where the victim is restrained by having a blanket flung over them while other members of the group beat them with bars of soap) 'over and over until they leave. The drill instructor will not tell you to do it – but you will clean up your own. It's not what should happen, but it will happen.'[49]

What is remarkable about all of this is that none of those who argued in favour of the ban, from enlisted focus group participants to four-star generals thought the experience of any other force – such as the Dutch and Israeli militaries which had successfully integrated gay service members without any mass violence – had any bearing on such fears. The Military Working Group argued that 'no other country has the global responsibilities, operational tempo, or worldwide deployment commitments of the Armed Forces of the United States'[50] and a survey of flag officers who had supported Clinton during the election campaign reported that 'no one thinks the "best military in the world" should follow someone else's lead on this subject'.[51] Unlike foreign militaries, 'the best educated, best trained, most cohesive military force in the history of the United States' was simply not ready to countenance the possibility of openly homosexual service members.

One of the few veterans' groups to support lifting the ban, the American Veterans Committee, noted that this did not reflect well on senior military leadership, reflecting in testimony to the Senate Armed Services Committee that 'sadly, from the statements of many highly placed officers, what the public has heard is a potential scenario of troops gone amok and leaders unable to control them'. The frequency with which this scenario was invoked 'must cast doubts on their effectiveness as leaders to direct and lead their troops. Surely this is not the impression they wish to leave with the American public, that they cannot be held accountable for the behavior of those under their command.'[52] Military

[49] National Defense Research Institute, 'Sexual Orientation and US Military Personnel Policy: Options and Assessment – Prepared for the Office of the Secretary of Defense'.

[50] Office of the Secretary of Defense, 'Summary Report of the Military Working Group'.

[51] Holum, 'Report to President-Elect Clinton: Homosexuals in the Military'.

[52] 'Statement of the American Veterans Committee (AVC) to the Senate Armed Services Committee on the Question of Lifting or Sustaining the Ban on Gays and Lesbians

leaders may not have meant to give this impression, but the manner in which their arguments about maintaining the ban shifted from old lines about the military not being a 'social laboratory' expected to implement changes that the rest of society was not ready for towards a series of claims that sacralised 'unit cohesion' and military readiness served the purpose of setting the military as a place apart, an institution that was deliberately and consciously out of step with civilian society.

2.2   Women in Combat

When Army leaders met with the staffers from the Clinton transition team to discuss ending the gay ban, they did so armed with briefing documents that drew directly on talking points provided by the religious conservative advocacy group, the Family Research Council (FRC). However, one particular argument from the FRC's document did not make it into their meeting binders. The FRC paper included advice on how to handle analogies between the experiences of women in the military and the prospects for openly gay service members. Tellingly, it did not completely dismiss the analogy, but argued that while 'the official view is that women have been fully accepted at all levels of the military services … the real situation is not publicly acknowledged'. Instead, the FRC claimed, 'servicemen often grumble about double standards, sex-normed testing, affirmative action in promotions, and even delays to upgrading technology' but that 'so strong is feminist intimidation that in many cases, they cannot say so without risking their careers'. Nonetheless, ultimately, they argued that 'the comparison between women and homosexuals is flawed' because women and men lived in separate quarters since 'sexual tension would devastate morale'.[53] These complaints point to the fact that the place of women within the military was far from settled. Indeed, it is striking to see how many of the same arguments about cohesion, morale and combat effectiveness were deployed when it came to both homosexuals and women.

Progress for women had always been fraught.[54] When the service academies began to admit women in the late 1970s, critics such as Marine

Serving in the Armed Forces', 30 June 1993, OA/ID 12138, scan ID: 034481, FOIA 2006-0227-F, Clinton Library.

[53] Family Research Council, 'Homosexuals in the Military: Talking Points', January 1993, Gordon R. Sullivan Papers; Box 126A, Folder 3, CSA Correspondence Files [20–31 January] (Part 3 of 3), January 1993, AHEC.

[54] On this longer history, see Holm, *Women in the Military*; Leisa D. Meyer, *Creating GI Jane: Sexuality and Power in the Women's Army Corps During World War II* (New York: Columbia University Press, 1996); Roth, *Her Cold War*; Linda Kerber, *No Constitutional Right to Be Ladies* (New York: Hill and Wang, 1999), 221–2; Beth Bailey et al., eds,

veteran (and soon-to-be Secretary of the Navy in the Reagan administration) James Webb argued that they should shut down rather than accept such an indignity.[55] The Army even briefly instituted a 'womanpause' in 1981, halting the recruitment of women altogether, an experiment that was doomed to failure if only because the All-Volunteer Force could not survive without women making up the ranks.[56] In 1982, it also ended the five-year-old practice of gender-integrated initial entry training. In 1988, the Department of Defense formalised what they called the 'risk rule', a policy that permitted the exclusion of women from any role, combat or non-combat, if the risks of exposure to direct combat, hostile fire or capture were equal to, or greater than, the risk in the units they supported.[57]

The end of the Cold War and the experience of combat in Panama and, more significantly, the Persian Gulf meant that the viability of the 'risk rule' was in question almost as soon as it was formalised. Given the nature of the contemporary battlefield, it seemed like it would be impossible to sort out exactly which units would be exposed to the risk of hostile fire, and indeed Captain Linda Bray, a Military Police officer, became the first American woman to command troops in combat during the invasion of Panama in 1989. Shortly thereafter, 41,000 women deployed overseas during the Persian Gulf War of 1990–1, where virtually all of them were within range of potential Iraqi Scud missile attacks (Figure 2.2).[58] The media ran stories about 'mom's war', focusing on mothers having to leave behind their children to deploy to the Gulf, but also celebrated competent military women capable of taking on any number of tasks, in stark contrast to their oppressed Saudi counterparts.[59] Polling suggested that the

Managing Sex in the U.S. Military: Gender, Identity, and Behavior (Lincoln: University of Nebraska Press, 2022); Douglas Bristol and Heather Marie Stur, eds, *Integrating the US Military: Race, Gender and Sexual Orientation since World War II* (Baltimore: Johns Hopkins University Press, 2017); Kara Dixon Vuic, ed., *The Routledge History of Gender, War, and the U.S. Military* (New York: Routledge, 2017); Kara Dixon Vuic, *Officer, Nurse, Woman: The Army Nurse Corps in the Vietnam War* (Baltimore: Johns Hopkins University Press, 2010); Heather Marie Stur, *Beyond Combat: Women and Gender in the Vietnam War Era* (New York: Cambridge University Press, 2011).

[55] Jim Webb, 'Women Can't Fight', *Washingtonian*, 1 November 1979, www.washingtonian .com/1979/11/01/jim-webb-women-cant-fight/.

[56] Bailey, *America's Army*, 171; Holm, *Women in the Military*, 387–95.

[57] MacKenzie, *Beyond the Band of Brothers*, 24–5.

[58] Michael R. Gordon, 'Noriega's Surrender: Army; For First Time, a Woman Leads G.I.'s in Combat', *New York Times*, 4 January 1990, www.nytimes.com/1990/01/04/ world/noriega-s-surrender-army-for-first-time-a-woman-leads-gi-s-in-combat.html; 'Report to the Secretary of Defense: Women in the Military: Deployment in the Persian Gulf' (Washington, DC: General Accounting Office, 1993), 2, http://archive.gao.gov/ t2pbat5/149552.pdf.

[59] Elizabeth Mesok, 'Combat Exclusion Policies and the Management of Gender Difference in the U.S. Military', in *Managing Sex in the U.S. Military: Gender, Identity,*

Figure 2.2 Female soldiers of the 82nd Airborne Division put on gas masks as they prepare for a nuclear-biological-chemical warfare exercise during Operation Desert Shield

American public was broadly supportive of women being allowed to serve in combat units even before the Gulf War. A January 1990 *CBS News/New York Times* poll showed that 72 per cent were in favour of women serving in combat units, while a February 1990 poll commissioned by Representative Patricia Schroeder, a key advocate for military women, reported that 79 per cent of American women approved of combat duty for women, while 60 per cent said that they would not oppose it for their daughters.[60]

In the wake of the Gulf War, several members of Congress, including Schroeder, introduced legislation to allow women to take up combat roles in the military. In response to that pressure, congressional leadership established the Presidential Commission on the Assignment of Women in the Armed Forces to examine the implications of changing existing laws and policies that restricted the assignment of female service members. The commission's report, issued in 1992, recommended that

and Behavior, ed. Beth Bailey et al. (Lincoln: University of Nebraska Press, 2022), 260; Melani McAlister, *Epic Encounters: Culture, Media, and U.S. Interests in the Middle East Since 1945* (Berkeley: University of California Press, 2001), 255–7.

[60] Rosemarie Skaine, *Women at War: Gender Issues of Americans in Combat* (Jefferson, NC: McFarland & Company, 1999), 121.

women be allowed to serve on combatant ships in the Navy, but upheld the ban on women flying in combat mission aircraft or serving in ground combat units.[61] In order to reach those conclusions, the commission spent a year visiting military installations, consulting with members of the public and active duty personnel, reviewing documents and conducting surveys. Most notably, the commission surveyed all retired general and flag officers, receiving 3,200 responses, which ran heavily in favour of maintaining the status quo, with 92 per cent of those respondents opposing women being assigned to the infantry.[62]

Among the 8 per cent who thought that women should be permitted in the infantry was Lieutenant General (retired) Charles W. Dyke. Dyke was apparently the only Army general officer, serving or retired, to hold this position and he laid out his reasoning in a letter to the commission.[63] He argued that not only was the risk rule absurd given the absence of defined front lines in modern combat, but that women in fact were perfectly capable of serving in combat units, including in the infantry. Dyke recalled his three years in combat with the 101st Airborne Division in Vietnam and argued that the experience proved to him that 'the qualities we desire in good people in garrison, in school, in the motor pool and on the training fields are the same qualities we look for and prize on the battlefield. We need soldiers with competence, courage, candour and conviction.'[64] He claimed that 'those who meet the combat unit's standards and who thus belong are part of the bond, whether they are black, white, brown, male, female, indigenous scout or a "tech rep" from industry'.[65] For Dyke, 'the concept of a "warrior" being a macho, two fisted, hard drinking, tough talking hombre is simply not true'.[66]

Polling of the broader military population indicates that there was slightly more support for this position than in the upper echelons of the force. In a poll of active duty military personnel conducted on behalf of the commission, 74 per cent of respondents opposed women being assigned to infantry units, 66 per cent opposed women in Special Operations Forces, 59

---

[61] Robert T. Herres, *The Presidential Commission on the Assignment of Women in the Armed Forces: Report to the President, 15 November 1992* (Washington, DC: Government Printing Office, 1992), https://catalog.hathitrust.org/Record/002635968.

[62] Herres, 66.

[63] Charles W. Dyke, 'Letter to Denis J. Reimer', 20 February 1997, Denis J. Reimer Papers: 1mm Reading Files, Box 1, Folder 2, February 1997, AHEC.

[64] Charles W. Dyke, 'Letter to Robert T. Herres', 22 September 1992, 6, Denis J. Reimer Papers: 1mm Reading Files, Box 1, Folder 2, February 1997, AHEC.

[65] Dyke, 3. Dyke's arguments foreshadowed scholarly work based on the twenty-first-century battlefields of Iraq and Afghanistan that argued that cohesion in combat units comes not from shared identities but through professional competence. See King, *The Combat Soldier*.

[66] Dyke, 'Letter to Robert T. Herres', 5.

per cent opposed women in tank crews and 54 per cent opposed women in the artillery.[67] A survey of the general public showed a 50/50 split on the question of ending the combat exclusion, while the commission also heard extensive testimony from commanders of mixed-gender units who believed that having women serve in combat units would have no negative effect on unit cohesion.[68]

Notwithstanding this testimony, the bulk of the commission was unsympathetic to these arguments. By an eight to seven vote, the commission agreed to continue to bar women from ground combat and from flying combat missions, even while allowing women to serve on combat ships. A large conservative faction was strongly opposed to even discussing how integration had worked in practice, and often refused to attend sessions where military personnel testified in favour of it. Some of these commissioners even argued that Operation Desert Storm couldn't count as real war and therefore said nothing about the suitability of women for combat. Such was the tension between commissioners that five of the fifteen filed a minority report to dissent from the majority's findings, as they felt that the report did not go far enough in defending the combat exclusion, and several individual commissioners added personal statements to the report, where they attacked each other for obstructiveness.[69] One commissioner, Army Captain Mary M. Finch, claimed that 'as a Commission member and active duty Army officer, I believe that the work of this Commission has been an insult to all servicewomen'.[70] Another commissioner, Ronald D. Ray, a former Marine who had served as Deputy Assistant Secretary of Defense in the Reagan administration, took the opportunity to say that he had 'sought direction from the Bible' throughout the process and that he was keenly aware that 'feminism and Christianity are in opposition'.[71] Even though the conservative faction's

---

[67] Maxwell R. Thurman, 'Section III: Commissioner Statements', in *The Presidential Commission on the Assignment of Women in the Armed Forces: Report to the President, 15 November 1992* (Washington, DC: Government Printing Office, 1992), 117, https://catalog.hathitrust.org/Record/002635968.

[68] Herres, *The Presidential Commission on the Assignment of Women in the Armed Forces*, D-1.

[69] Samuel G. Cockerham et al., 'Section II – Alternative Views: The Case Against Women in Combat', in *The Presidential Commission on the Assignment of Women in the Armed Forces: Report to the President, 15 November 1992* (Washington, DC: Government Printing Office, 1992), https://catalog.hathitrust.org/Record/002635968.

[70] Mary M. Finch, 'Section III: Commissioner Statements', in *The Presidential Commission on the Assignment of Women in the Armed Forces: Report to the President, 15 November 1992* (Washington, DC: Government Printing Office, 1992), 106, https://catalog.hathitrust.org/Record/002635968.

[71] Ronald D. Ray, 'Section III: Commissioner Statements', in *The Presidential Commission on the Assignment of Women in the Armed Forces: Report to the President, 15 November 1992* (Washington, DC: Government Printing Office, 1992), 116, https://catalog.hathitrust.org/Record/002635968.

opposition to integration was clearly based on moral beliefs, they made their arguments in terms of unit cohesion. Their key argument was that it didn't matter if some women might be excellent candidates for combat roles because the unit of analysis was not the individual but the group. According to their dissent, 'in combat training and in war, an individual's desires, interests or career aspirations are totally subordinated to the accomplishment of the military mission' and that in order for 'the military as a whole to function as a capable fighting force, each unit, from the smallest up must operate cohesively and in harmony with other units'.[72] This meant that any changes that would disrupt that harmony in any way would harm readiness.

If moral arguments about women's role in society had little sway with the majority of the commission, the cohesion argument certainly resonated. Marine Corps Brigadier General Thomas V. Draude wrote that he had reported to the commission with an open mind, had taken his duty very seriously and even took a swipe at the more conservative commissioners for displaying their bias. Draude noted that his own daughter was currently a trainee pilot with the US Navy. Nonetheless, while he supported opening up combat aviation and combatant vessel slots to women, he recoiled from assigning them to ground units, claiming that 'the fabric of unqualified love necessary to hold men together in infantry combat would be torn by the sexual tension caused by the presence of women'. Draude argued that 'it's not anyone's fault, it's just the way men are', before admitting that the fact 'that women are forced to pay the price for this reality is unfortunate to say the least'.[73]

Commission member Charles Moskos, who had also voted to maintain restrictions, later complained that 'we heard interminable testimony on physiological differences and after $4 million learned that: most men are stronger than most women, [and] some women are stronger than some men'.[74] Moskos claimed that his own surveys demonstrated that enlisted women did not want to serve in the combat arms because they felt that this would lead to increased sexual harassment. On the other hand, female officers wanted a change in policy because 'without women in combat arms, there will never be a proportionate number of female

---

[72] Cockerham et al., 'Section II – Alternative Views: The Case Against Women in Combat', 44.

[73] Thomas V. Draude, 'Section III: Commissioner Statements', in *The Presidential Commission on the Assignment of Women in the Armed Forces: Report to the President, 15 November 1992* (Washington, DC: Government Printing Office, 1992), 104, https://catalog.hathitrust.org/Record/002635968.

[74] Charles C. Moskos, 'Achieving Racial and Gender Equity in the Military: Are They the Same? [Undated Lecture]', n.d., 2, Moskos Papers.

generals at the highest levels'. For Moskos, the dilemma was 'do we want more female generals or less sexual harassment?' His view was that the Army should be attentive to physiological differences and should 'worry more about breaking bones than breaking glass ceilings'. He did not see a way to avoid the sexual harassment issue, claiming not to understand what critics meant when they talked about 'macho culture'. Like others, Moskos thought that unit cohesion in combat units would be harmed if women were included in their ranks.[75]

Given that the commission's deliberations preceded the 'Don't Ask, Don't Tell' debate by a matter of months, it is perhaps no surprise that the same arguments about cohesion, health and the safety of new members in the ranks played out in both cases. Indeed, many of the key protagonists, such as Charles Moskos and the conservative activist Elaine Donnelly, featured in both debates. Ultimately, though, the defenders of the status quo had less success here than they did with the gay ban. The commission's report hardly ended discussion on the issue. A *New York Times* editorial condemned it as a 'hash', full of 'inconclusive and contradictory' recommendations, and argued that 'once in office, President Clinton could do women, and men, a favour by asking for a steadier, more coherent report'.[76] Indeed, the Clinton administration paid little heed to the specifics of the report. In April 1993, the new Secretary of Defense Les Aspin, ignoring some of the commission's recommendations, directed the services to open up combat aircraft slots to women and rescinded the 'risk rule'.[77] From now on, female soldiers would only be excluded from direct ground combat assignments.[78] Meanwhile, the Army, along with the Navy and Air Force, began to integrate basic training, starting with a pilot project in Fort Jackson in 1993. Following the success of the pilot, the Army moved to Army-wide, gender-integrated basic training in 1994, and senior leaders felt relieved that a new equilibrium had finally been reached after years of uncertainty about women's place in the Army.

---

[75] Moskos, 9.

[76] 'Women in Combat: Maybe? Yes?', *New York Times*, 28 November 1992, www.nytimes.com/1992/11/28/opinion/women-in-combat-maybe-yes.html.

[77] 'Women in Combat: News Conference with Secretary of Defense Les Aspin', *C-Span*, 28 April 1993, www.c-span.org/video/?40217-1/women-combat.

[78] The decade also saw a deluge of publications on the debate over women in combat. For a representative sample, see Melissa S. Herbert, *Camouflage Isn't Only for Combat: Gender, Sexuality, and Women in the Military* (New York: NYU Press, 1998); Brian Mitchell, *Women in the Military: Flirting with Disaster* (Washington, DC: Regnery Publishing, 1997); Stephanie Gutman, *The Kinder, Gentler Military: Can America's Gender-Neutral Fighting Force Still Win Wars?* (New York: Scribner, 2000); Lorry Fenner and Marie deYoung, *Women in Combat: Civic Duty or Military Liability?* (Washington, DC: Georgetown University Press, 2001).

2.3   Sexual Assault and Gender-Integrated Training

This equilibrium was shattered in November 1996 with the news from Aberdeen. The Army announced that three male instructors responsible for Advanced Individual Training at Aberdeen Proving Grounds, Maryland had been charged with rape, abuse and harassment of female soldiers under their supervision. Eventually, twelve drill instructors were charged with a variety of crimes, exposing a pattern of sexual exploitation and the abuse of authority by male NCOs and officers.[79] At the same time, the Army announced they were opening an investigation into similar abuses at Fort Leonard Wood, where three instructors were accused of abusing twenty-two female trainees. Army leaders, mindful of the reputational damage suffered by the Navy in the aftermath of the 1991 Tailhook scandal, where Navy and Marine Corps aviators were alleged to have sexually assaulted more than eighty women at a convention at the Las Vegas Hilton, moved quickly to commission several inquiries about sexual abuse within the Army.[80] The Army set up a hotline for soldiers to report sexual harassment in the Army, which was soon overwhelmed with over 6,000 calls. Surveys of women in the Army revealed that at least 55 per cent of female soldiers had been sexually harassed, and political pressure for action grew.[81]

Public reaction to the Aberdeen scandal was not straightforward, however. All twelve of the instructors who went before courts-martial were black, and their victims were all white. Questions about racial targeting in a downsizing Army prompted the National Association for the Advancement of Colored People (NAACP) to take up the instructors' cause. In March 1997, the NAACP organised a press conference where

---

[79] 'The Army Investigates Rape', *New York Times*, 10 November 1996, www.nytimes .com/1996/11/10/opinion/the-army-investigates-rape.html.

[80] At the 1991 Tailhook Association symposium – a gathering of naval aviators in the Las Vegas Hilton – US Navy and Marine aviation officers sexually assaulted eighty-three women and seven men, which was then inadequately investigated by the Navy, leading to public outcry. Norman Kempster, 'What Really Happened at Tailhook Convention Scandal: The Pentagon Report Graphically Describes How Fraternity-Style Hi-Jinks Turned into Hall of Horrors', *Los Angeles Times*, 24 April 1993, www.latimes.com/ archives/la-xpm-1993-04-24-mn-26672-story.html; Jean Zimmerman, *Tailspin: Women at War in the Wake of Tailhook* (New York: Doubleday, 1995), http://archive.org/details/ isbn_9780385477895; William H. McMichael, *The Mother of All Hooks: Story of the U.S. Navy's Tailhook Scandal* (New Brunswick, NJ: Transaction Publishers, 1997); Michael Winerip, 'Revisiting the Military's Tailhook Scandal', *New York Times*, 13 May 2013, www.nytimes.com/2013/05/13/booming/revisiting-the-militarys-tailhook-scandal-video.html.

[81] Peter T. Kilborn, 'Sex Abuse Cases Sting Pentagon, but the Problem Has Deep Roots', *New York Times*, 10 February 1997, www.nytimes.com/1997/02/10/us/sex-abuse-cases-sting-pentagon-but-the-problem-has-deep-roots.html.

five women alleged that they were pressured and coerced by Criminal Investigation Command into making false statements. These women admitted to having sex with drill instructors but claimed that the sex was consensual and that they were never raped.[82] Writing in the *New Republic*, the commentator Hanna Rosin found the scandal perplexing, claiming that the 'most tradition-minded, socially conservative and over-whelmingly male institution in America has in fact embraced a theory of sexual intercourse that belongs not only to feminism, but to feminism's more radical wing'. Because there was no direct physical coercion, then there was no rape to report. For Rosin, 'on the central question of the trials – whether or not the sex was consensual – the United States Army has proved itself less a disciple of Rambo than of Andrea Dworkin and Susan Brownmiller'.[83]

While it was true that Secretary of the Army Togo West hired the Duke University legal academic Madeline Morris to advise him on sexual assault issues based on her work on rape and military culture, Army investigators and leaders drew their understanding of power and consent not from feminist texts but from the experience of command and training.[84] During the trial of one of the accused, Sergeant Delmar Simpson, prosecutors used Simpson's badge and cap as props to explain the almost unquestioned authority that drill instructors had over their trainees. This meant that Simpson did not have to use any force to get his victims to submit; he just had to order them to do so.[85] Similarly, senior leaders were concerned about the effects such abuses would have on unit cohesion. The Army's Senior Review Panel reported that their interviewees frequently cited an erosion of trust in their unit because of sexual abuse and that 'in one unit with significant levels of sexual harassment, none of the female soldiers wanted to come to work'.[86]

The Senior Review panel also blamed elements of Army culture for the pervasiveness of the problem. They argued that once sexual assault or harassment claims made it to brigade or battalion commanders, the

[82] Paul W. Valentine and Jackie Spinner, 'Race Raised Again as Aberdeen Issue: Something Is Wrong, Congressional Black Caucus Leader Says', *Washington Post*, 17 March 1997.

[83] Hanna Rosin, 'Sleeping with the Enemy: How the Army Learned to Love Andrea Dworkin', *The New Republic*, 23 June 1997.

[84] Eric Schmitt, 'Army Is Criticized on Harassment Survey', *New York Times*, 27 June 1997, www.nytimes.com/1997/06/27/us/army-is-criticized-on-harassment-survey.html; Madeline Morris, 'By Force of Arms: Rape, War, and Military Culture', *Duke Law Journal* 45, no. 4 (1996): 651–781.

[85] Elaine Sciolino, 'Army Trial Raises Questions of Sex, Power and Discipline', *New York Times*, 12 April 1997, www.nytimes.com/1997/04/12/us/army-trial-raises-questions-of-sex-power-and-discipline.html.

[86] *The Secretary of the Army's Senior Review Panel Report on Sexual Harassment*, vol. 1 (Washington, DC: Department of the Army, 1997), 65.

problem was usually dealt with, but that leaders at this level were too focused on other priorities, which meant that they were not adequately supervising subordinates. Meanwhile, a 'zero defects' mentality meant that local leaders saw such complaints 'as an adverse reflection on their leadership and a "defect" from which they can never recover if it becomes known higher up the chain of command'.[87] The National Organization for Women (NOW) saw similar problems with Army culture. Like the NAACP, they doubted whether Army commanders at Aberdeen were capable of dealing with allegations of harassment and abuse. Because the chain of command would inevitably be implicated in contributing to a culture of abuse that grew under their command, these leaders could not be expected to be impartial in dealing with any complaints. Shortly after news about the abuses at Aberdeen became public, NOW asked the Department of Defense, without success, to create a permanent team of sexual harassment investigators that would operate outside of the Army's chain of command to investigate and resolve claims of abuse.[88]

In the middle of all this controversy was Army Chief of Staff General Denis Reimer. Reimer's own views on both sexual assault in the military and gender-integrated training were complicated. In response to a letter from a friend who claimed that the sexual assault scandal was 'another example of the media and certain people on "The Hill" [trying] to portray our Army – and all the services – in a very ugly light', he replied: 'times are tough, but we won't let the bastards grind us down'.[89] Writing to another friend in May 1997, the Army chief of staff complained: 'here I am a 57-year-old man and all anybody wants to talk to me about is sex'. Reimer was responding to a warning that the Army Criminal Investigative Division had ignored allegations that a group of soldiers had gang raped a woman at Fort Carson.[90] The allegations had been

[87] *The Secretary of the Army's Senior Review Panel Report on Sexual Harassment*, 1:48.
[88] Jackie Spinner, 'NOW, NAACP Remain at Odds with Aberdeen', *Washington Post*, 9 March 1997, www.washingtonpost.com/archive/local/1997/03/09/now-naacp-remain-at-odds-with-aberdeen/29a9f2ec-deed-40a3-848b-f82329bf10c4/. As of 2022, the chain of command issue remained unresolved. Jennifer Steinhauer, 'With Biden's Backing, Austin Prepares to Tackle Military's Sexual Assault Problem', *New York Times*, 26 January 2021, www.nytimes.com/2021/01/26/us/politics/military-sexual-assault-lloyd-austin.html; Jackie Speier, 'Removing Sexual Harassment from Military Chain-of-Command', *The Hill*, 23 April 2022, https://thehill.com/opinion/congress-blog/3461117-removing-sexual-harassment-from-military-chain-of-command/.
[89] Phillip J. Zeiler, 'Letter to Dennis J. Reimer', 6 February 1997, Denis J. Reimer Papers: 1mm Reading Files, Box 1, Folder 2, February 1997, AHEC; Dennis J. Reimer, 'Letter to Phillip J. Zeiler', 17 February 1997, Denis J. Reimer Papers: 1mm Reading Files, Box 1, Folder 2, February 1997, AHEC.
[90] A memo from the commanding general at Fort Carson to Reimer's office indicated that the Army Criminal Investigative Division were now investigating the issue but that 'as is so often the case, many of the perceptions … were not accurate'. No further

brought to Reimer's attention by an old friend who was also the attorney for the woman's parents. In his response, Reimer also joked that 'I feel like the male version of Dr. Ruth, only I'm not making those kinds of bucks' before becoming more serious and promising that the Army would 'come down hard on the sexual misconduct issues such as rape'.[91] Reimer thought that there was a difference between sexual misconduct and sexual harassment, and that each needed to be dealt with differently. The former was a result of 'the real cancer' of the abuse of authority by the chain of command and necessitated a tough disciplinary response, whereas the latter could be addressed via training and education.

Writing to a subordinate who had raised the sexual harassment issue with him, Reimer admitted that 'it's very complex and I have learned a lot about it in the last six months. It's Jody calls, it's posters on the wall, it's the way we dress when we go to the gymnasium – all of these things contribute to this environment.'[92] While visiting Aberdeen Proving Ground (where, to his chagrin, he was advised not to speak about sexual assault by his legal advisor, lest he be seen to be prejudicing an investigation), Reimer responded to a question about whether adult magazines should be sold at PXs[93] by reiterating his comments about marching cadences and gym uniforms and by announcing that the Army needed to 'desexualize the environment we live in' and that 'if we're really going to have an environment where people can be all they can be, we've got to try and reduce the pressure in terms of the things that lead to sexual harassment'.[94] Elsewhere he noted that 'as we look at sexual harassment, we find less of it occurring in the individual unit than outside'. Reimer noted that unit cohesion meant that mixed-gender sleeping arrangements in the field didn't seem to be a problem and that 'most of the female soldiers I've talked to prefer to stay with their particular squad or platoon as long as we provide them some type of privacy'.[95]

records of the case exist in Reimer's papers. John M. Pickler, 'Memo to CW5 Tony Ecleava', 9 May 1997, 5, Dennis J. Reimer Papers: Series III: 5 General Management Correspondence Files, Box 9: May 1997, AHEC.

[91] Dennis J. Reimer, 'Letter to Rose Mary Allmendinger', 20 May 1997, Dennis J. Reimer Papers: Series III: 5 General Management Correspondence Files, Box 9: May 1997, AHEC.

[92] Dennis J. Reimer, 'Letter to Antoinette Smart', 17 March 1997, Dennis J. Reimer Papers: Series III: 5 General Management Correspondence Files, Box 8: March 1997, AHEC. 'Jody calls' refers to marching cadences sung by soldiers that traditionally focus on their girlfriends or wives cheating on them while they are deployed.

[93] PX refers to the Army's Post Exchange.

[94] Dennis J. Reimer, 'Speech at Aberdeen Proving Ground', 12 February 1997, Dennis J. Reimer Papers: 870-5f Organization Historical Files, VCSA, CGFORSCOM, CSA – Box 69 CSA, 12 February 1997, Drill Sergeants, Aberdeen Proving Ground, AHEC.

[95] Reimer, 'Letter to Antoinette Smart', 17 March 1997.

Reimer also recognised that the issue was a potentially corrosive one. Writing to Senator Barbara Mikulski (D-MD) after a meeting about sexual assault, he noted that what was at stake was 'retaining the trust and confidence of the American people' and that 'most of us spent too much time rebuilding an Army after Vietnam to let it slip away now'. He told Mikulski that while he was 'not looking for any politically correct solution and will not recommend such for a lot of reasons', it was clear that they both agreed on the fundamentals of the issue, which were about leadership and values. Mikulski had emphasised to Reimer that the United States set an example for other nations and armies. Reimer agreed and noted that this point 'ties in nicely to the new military strategy which talks about shaping the environment ... we want the new emerging democratic nations to pattern after our Army'.[96]

Part of the response to the sexual abuse scandals was therefore a new rhetorical emphasis on values. Army headquarters produced a fifteen-minute-long video on Army values as part of what it called the 'Character XXI' programme. The video opened with a short address from Reimer, who proclaimed that 'as good as the last several years have been for the Army, we have not been perfect' and that 'the time has come to refocus and rededicate ourselves to Army values. We want to reaffirm and retain the Army's ethical base.'[97] The video, which was shown to all soldiers in the Army, then went on to talk through the Army's core values of duty, integrity, loyalty, selfless service, courage and honour. This video package was preceded by an Army-wide training packet on sexual harassment that had to be delivered by brigade or battalion commanders to their troops. This packet also included a video from Reimer (along with the sergeant major of the Army) that emphasised a zero-tolerance policy on sexual harassment.[98]

This emphasis on rhetoric and education, though, was not enough to satisfy the Army's critics. Given the complaints from both NOW and the NAACP, the Senate Armed Services Committee demanded a meeting with Army leaders to ask if an independent commission to investigate Aberdeen would be more appropriate. Congressional interest in

---

[96] Dennis J. Reimer, 'Letter to Senator Barbara Mikulski', 20 May 1997, Denis J. Reimer Papers: General Management Correspondence Files: Box 11: May 1998 [2 of 2], AHEC.

[97] W. K. Sutey, 'Recommended CSA Remarks Character Development XXI Video', 20 March 1997, Dennis J. Reimer Papers: Series VI: 870-5f Organization Historical Files, VCSA, CGFORSCOM, CSA, Box 70 CSA 24 March 1997, Video Script: Character Development XXI, AHEC.

[98] Dennis J. Reimer, 'Email to Henry A. Leonard. Re: Statement for the Record – SASC Hearing', 31 January 1997, Dennis J. Reimer Papers: 870-5f Organization Historical Files, VCSA, CGFORSCOM, CSA, Box 69 CSA 4 February 1997, Testimony, SASC: Sexual Harassment and Misconduct, AHEC.

this issue was of a different nature to that which had prompted the Presidential Commission on the Assignment of Women in the Armed Forces. Calls for the opening of combat assignments to women in the aftermath of the Gulf War had come from a Congress in which both chambers were controlled by Democrats, and the Army and other services made their moves to begin gender-integrated training in the early months of the new Clinton administration. The 1994 midterm elections, though, not only delivered both the House and Senate to the Republican Party but brought with it a new generation of extremely conservative lawmakers, led by new Speaker of the House Newt Gingrich. Gingrich made his feelings about women in ground combat clear when he argued that combat meant being in a ditch and that 'females have biological problems staying in a ditch for 30 days because they get infections, and they don't have upper body strength', whereas men 'are basically little piglets; you drop them in the ditch, they roll around in it'.[99] His views were not an outlier in the Republican congressional caucuses. When the Senate Armed Services Committee held hearings on sexual assault in the military in February 1997, freshman Senator Rick Santorum (R-PA) argued that the Army needed to segregate its training in order to separate 'the match and the gunpowder'. While Reimer was broadly supportive of gender-integrated training in his testimony, he also signalled a willingness to 'take a hard look' at the practice if any of the reports commissioned into sexual assault concluded that it was a contributory factor.[100]

Some women in the military immediately recognised the danger posed by this concession. A group of female military White House Fellows wrote to Reimer and warned that this focus on gender-integrated training was an exercise in victim blaming. They were concerned that 'a move to "study" the issue of mixed-gender training may not only be misplaced but might also be a setback' because it would focus attention on the wrong issue and reopen old and well-worn debates.[101] Retired Brigadier

---

[99] Gingrich thought that these dynamics might reverse with more technologically-driven warfare, claiming that if combat 'means being on an Aegis class cruiser managing the computer controls for 12 ships and their rockets, a female again may be dramatically better than a male who gets very, very frustrated sitting in a chair all the time because males are biologically driven to go out and hunt giraffes'. Katharine Q. Seelye, 'Gingrich's "Piggies" Poked', *New York Times*, 19 January 1995, www.nytimes .com/1995/01/19/us/gingrich-s-piggies-poked.html.

[100] Dana Priest, 'Army May Restudy Mixed-Sex Training; Chief of Staff Suggests It's Time to Weigh Benefits, Drawbacks', *Washington Post*, 5 February 1997.

[101] Brenda Berkman, Susan Fink, and Loree Sutton, 'Letter to Dennis J. Reimer', 11 February 1997, Dennis J. Reimer Papers: Series III: 5 General Management Correspondence Files, Box 8: February 1997, AHEC.

General Evelyn 'Pat' Foote, now serving on the Army's Senior Review Panel on Sexual Harassment, expressed similar frustration. In testimony before a congressional committee, she complained:

In my nearly forty years of affiliation with the United States Army, women soldiers have been the subject of an unending array of studies, tests, and more recently, congressionally or presidentially directed commissions. The inference so often in these studies is that somehow, women negatively impact readiness. I know of no study to date which supports such a contention.

Foote also noted that 'a very serious consequence of this parade of studies is that the flames of dissent and contention between genders is never permitted to die down. The emphasis is forever focused on gender differences, not on what is common to all soldiers.'[102] The Congressional Women's Caucus also picked up on this issue and held a meeting with Secretary of the Army Togo West both to voice their concerns about Aberdeen and to emphasise, in the words of Rep. Jane Harman (D-CA), that 'gender integrated training is not the subject of these investigations and should not be another victim in this sad story'.[103] Reimer followed up with Harman in a letter where he assured her that 'although I know from personal experience that basic training is a very stressful time, I still feel the United States Army can properly conduct gender-integrated training in the training base', although he said that if a Department of Defense taskforce concluded otherwise, then 'we should obviously review the policy'.[104]

Much of the correspondence to Reimer, though, indicated that there were plenty of committed opponents of gender-integrated training who were eager to reopen the debate. A common refrain among letters from retired officers to Reimer was that the only service to get the balance right was the Marine Corps, which alone had declined to institute gender-integrated training in 1993. One retired colonel wrote to Reimer to praise the Marine approach as pragmatic and complained that the Army was attempting 'to make the concept of gender-integrated basic training work', a concept that he believed was dreamed up by 'social engineers'. He continued: 'yes, there were some bad apples at Aberdeen and perhaps some leadership failures. But it would be far simpler to

---

[102] Evelyn Foote, 'Statement of BG Evelyn "Pat" Foote, US Army (Retired) before Congressional Commission on Military Training and Gender-Related Issues', 21 December 1998, Dennis J. Reimer Papers: Series III: 5 General Management Correspondence Files, Box 13: December 1998, AHEC.

[103] 'Congressional Women's Caucus Press Conference', 19 March 1997, Denis J. Reimer Papers: General Management Correspondence Files: Box 8: March 1997, AHEC.

[104] Denis J. Reimer, 'Letter to Rep. Jane Harman', 13 February 1997, Denis J. Reimer Papers: 1mm Reading Files, Box 1, Folder 2, February 1997, AHEC.

bring men and women through their initial Army training separately.'[105] An active duty female captain wrote to Reimer to advocate for more self-defence classes to take care of the problem of sexual harassment, claiming that 'if anyone, man or woman, does not handle situations with aggression and boldness regarding sexual encounters, then, personally, I do not believe they should be in the Army'. She then went on to critique grooming standards, claiming the women in the Army needed to 'start looking like soldiers again, not cosmetologists'.[106]

Reimer's predecessor as chief of staff, Gordon R. Sullivan, who had made the decision to integrate men and women during basic training, wrote to Congress to say that he had no regrets. Sullivan argued that 'young men and women, entering the Army from an environment where the genders are certainly mixed, training to serve in an environment where the genders will be routinely mixed, do not benefit from a brief period of artificial separation'.[107] Others supported this position and went further to claim that the Army had, in fact, tried too hard to mirror Marine practices in basic training and that this had fostered a culture of abuse. Lieutenant General (ret.) DeWitt Smith, former deputy chief of staff of the Army, argued to Reimer that any attempt to copy the Marine Corps model would be a mistake. In his view, training that 'strip[ped] soldiers of their dignity, decency, personality, and individuality' was wrong, and he argued that the Army didn't need 'hyper-macho loudmouths or insensitive, shout-kick-shove "leaders"' in charge of basic training.[108]

The bulk of retired officer opinion on basic training, though, went in the opposite direction. Lieutenant General (ret.) Hal Moore consulted with Reimer on his experiences of commanding basic training at Fort Ord in the early days of the All-Volunteer Force in the 1970s. For Moore, the same lessons applied in the 1990s as they did in his day. The Army needed to place emphasis on NCO authority and responsibility and emphasise discipline and military appearance. While not advocating it as a solution for sexual harassment, Moore argued that hand-to-hand combat should get more time on the curriculum, as should more rigorous

---

[105] Charles K. Nichols, 'Letter to Dennis J. Reimer', 26 June 1997, Dennis J. Reimer Papers: General Organization and Functions Correspondence Files – Box 14: 1997 [folder 3 of 3], AHEC.

[106] Jalesia M. Griffin, 'To Army Leadership', 26 November 1998, Dennis J. Reimer Papers: General Organization and Functions Correspondence Files – Box 15: April-May 1999, AHEC.

[107] Gordon R. Sullivan, 'Letter to Marty Meehan', 15 May 1998, Denis J. Reimer Papers: General Management Correspondence Files: Box 11: May 1998 [2 of 2], AHEC.

[108] DeWitt C. Smith, 'Letter to Evelyn P. Foote', 10 March 1997, Dennis J. Reimer Papers: Series III: 5 General Management Correspondence Files, Box 8: March 1997, AHEC.

physical training.[109] Indeed, Moore's opinions reflected the views of the Senior Review Panel on Sexual Harassment, which argued that the problems at Aberdeen had partly been caused by Advanced Individual Training focusing too much on technical skills and too little on 'soldierisation', that is, soldier skills and attitudes. The panel concluded that Advanced Individual Training had adopted a 'campus' orientation and that this must change.[110]

These findings were echoed by yet another report, this one commissioned by Secretary of Defense William Cohen, who wanted an independent advisory committee to investigate the gender-integrated training issue. The committee was chaired by former Senator Nancy Kassebaum Baker (R-KS) and included senior figures from both sides of the aisle, including Stanford University Provost Condoleezza Rice and former Assistant Attorney General for Civil Rights Deval Patrick. Many of the committee's findings mirrored conversations that had been taking place within the Army. It recommended toughening basic training and physical training requirements and doing more to enforce standards. It also called for less of an emphasis on monetary incentives in military recruiting campaigns, hoping that such a move would attract more patriotic and (presumably) more disciplined recruits. While these and other recommendations caused few difficulties for the military services, two of their thirty findings caused considerable consternation for the service chiefs and affirmed the fears of the women who felt that even agreeing to study the issue in the first place would be a retrograde step. First, the committee recommended that male and female recruits be housed in separate barracks during basic training, and second 'that the Army, Navy, and Air Force organise all their operational training units by gender in platoons, divisions, and flights', arguing that this move would 'recapture the cohesion, discipline, and team-building of living and training together as an operational unit'.[111] The committee felt that gender integration at the operational training unit level was 'causing confusion and a less cohesive environment', mirroring many of the claims made by the Presidential Commission on women in the armed forces five years previously.

Secretary Cohen received the report in late December 1997 and passed it on to the services for comment without accepting or rejecting it.

---

[109] Dennis J. Reimer, 'Letter to Harold G. Moore', 24 March 1998, Dennis J. Reimer Papers: 1mm Reading Files – Box 6: March 1998, AHEC.

[110] *The Secretary of the Army's Senior Review Panel Report on Sexual Harassment*, 1:29.

[111] 'Report of the Federal Advisory Committee on Gender-Integrated Training and Related Issues to the Secretary of Defense' (Washington, DC: Federal Advisory Committee on gender-integrated training and related issues, 16 December 1997), 10–11, https://apps .dtic.mil/sti/pdfs/ADA344122.pdf

The Army, Navy and Air Force all concurred with the first twenty-eight recommendations but rejected the final two. In March 1998, Cohen announced that he had rejected the committee's recommendation on resegregating basic training and housing.[112] This did not entirely end the controversy. Congressional Republicans continued to hold hearings on gender-integrated training and even set up another commission to examine the issue, the Blair Commission, in the hopes of producing a stronger condemnation of all forms of gender-integrated training.[113] The fact that the Army, Navy and Air Force were unanimous in their resolve to continue with gender-integrated training, though, ensured that the prospects for any significant rollback were dim.

Cohen did, though, direct the services to review and toughen their physical fitness standards to 'produce fit disciplined, motivated soldiers, sailors, airmen, and Marines' and ordered them to 'ensure that their training exercises are realistic, challenging, and instructive while also pushing individuals to achieve their maximum potential'.[114] In response to this, the Army made changes to its basic training, extending it from eight to nine weeks and increasing time spent on physical training, while a seventy-two-hour Warrior Field Training Exercise was to be introduced as a 'rite of passage' with rigorous physical and skills requirements. In addition, the syllabus now put greater emphasis on core military values, with each week of training beginning with a class on one of the Army values, while all trainees were issued with a 'soldier values card' to be worn at all times alongside their dog tags.[115] Faced with public scrutiny over sexual assault, the Army fell back on old habits and patterns in the hope that recommitting to soldier values would produce a better culture for its trainees.

To put it mildly, this did not solve the problem. According to Major General (ret.) Robert Shadley, commander of the Ordnance School at

---

[112] Steven Lee Myers, 'Call to Halt Mixed-Sex Training Is Opposed by 3 Armed Services', *New York Times*, 11 March 1998, www.nytimes.com/1998/03/11/us/call-to-halt-mixed-sex-training-is-opposed-by-3-armed-services.html.

[113] Anne Chapman's monograph offers the best account of the myriad studies and commissions that examined gender-integrated training. Anne W. Chapman, *Mixed-Gender Basic Training: The U.S. Army Experience, 1973–2004* (Fort Monroe, VA: U.S. Army Training and Doctrine Command, 2008), 132–9; Vince Crawley, 'Conservatives Push Return to Same-Sex Training', *Army Times*, 6 August 2001.

[114] William Cohen, 'Secretary Cohen Issues Guidance to Services on Kassebaum Baker Panel Recommendations' (Office of the Assistant Secretary of Defense (Public Affairs), 16 March 1998).

[115] Undersecretary of Defense, 'Report on the Responses of the Armed Services to the Federal Advisory Committee on Gender-Integrated Training and Related Issues and Additional Direction by the Secretary of Defense' (Washington, DC: Department of Defense, 1 May 1998).

Aberdeen in 1996, in the twenty-year period after the Aberdeen scandal, over 400,000 service members were the victims of sexual assault.[116] Yet, if the Army failed to adequately act on sexual abuse, we should also pay attention to other roads not taken. Despite the impulse to revert to tradition, as seen in recommendations to toughen training, there was no real impetus within the Army to return to gender-segregated training, as there had been in 1982. With the Kassebaum Baker Report, a path opened up for the Army to return to the way things had been before, yet they, along with the other services, chose not to go down that path. Certainly, senior leaders had some sympathy for those who wanted to resegregate training. Writing to one of the members of the Kassebaum Baker Committee, Reimer confessed that 'I believe that sexual harassment concerns may be a little overstated', but that he thought the committee's recommendations were 'right on target and confirm some of my own observations based upon recent visits with the training base'. In considering the problem, Reimer admitted that he was 'wrestling with how we correct without overcompensating'.[117]

So why did the Army's response not involve resegregating training? Politics surely had something to do with it. Even a Clinton White House that had folded on the question of ending the ban on openly gay service members was unlikely to stand by if services chose to erode gender integration so drastically in the military. However, in a town hall session with soldiers at Aberdeen, Reimer denied that these calculations weighed heavily on him, claiming that there had 'not been the political pressure on us to make judgements that are different than what we think is right for that particular service at that particular point in time' and that certainly the Army wasn't 'trying to lose the warfighting ethos'. Instead, what mattered was that 'the world has changed dramatically' and that the Army had to 'recognize the world out there as we see it, not as we wish it to be'.[118]

Ultimately, for Reimer, this meant that the 'warrior spirit is slightly more complex than it used to be. Fighting the nation's battles requires soldiers who are smart, disciplined, and well trained.'[119] Therefore, soldiers deserved 'to be treated with dignity and respect'. This more complex world meant that the Army could not go back to the certainties of

---

[116] Karl Hawkins, 'Retired General Speaks out on Stopping Sexual Abuse in the Workplace', Defense Visual Distribution Service, 11 February 2019, www.dvidshub .net/news/310306/retired-general-speaks-out-stopping-sexual-abuse-workplace.

[117] Dennis J. Reimer, 'Letter to Lieutenant General Robert H. Forman', 30 December 1997, Dennis J. Reimer Papers: 1mm Reading Files – Box 5: December 1997, AHEC.

[118] Reimer, 'Speech at Aberdeen Proving Ground'.

[119] Dennis J. Reimer, 'Letter to James A. Donovan', 23 October 1997, Dennis J. Reimer Papers: 1mm Reading Files – Box 4: October 1997, AHEC.

an imagined past, much as they might have wanted to. The service simply would not be able to face the challenges of conflict in the late twentieth century without women in its ranks, and therefore soldiers would have to train as they fought. The Army's attempt to reconcile that reality with conservative critiques of a supposedly soft military by increasingly emphasising 'Army values' in basic training may have helped to preserve women's place within the Army, but it also left these tensions unresolved. The very fact that a controversy that had begun with the arrest of several male drill sergeants for sexual assault had ended up with a response that largely focused on whether women and men should train together at all indicated just how much work was left to do.

2.4   'A Fight for the Army's Soul and Future'

While public attention focused on the fallout from Aberdeen, the journalist Tom Ricks of the *Wall Street Journal* broke another story that would highlight tensions surrounding the Army's values and its focus in training and education. On 13 March 1997, the newspaper published a lengthy article entitled 'Army at Odds' about the fate of Colonel Jim Hallums, whose tenure as chair of the Leadership and Behavioural Science Department at West Point came to an abrupt end when he was sacked for abusive leadership and sexual harassment.[120] The story described West Point as an institution riven with tensions between those with an academic focus and those who prioritised 'muddy boots' and instilling 'the warrior spirit' in cadets. Hallums had indeed been brought to the Military Academy because of his combat experience, which included fighting in the battle of Hue and a tour as a military advisor in El Salvador. Within months of arrival, though, Hallums split opinion in the Leadership Department by attempting to bring an infantry ethos to bear in what was an academic department. Hallums openly disdained the non-combat arms, judged faculty members by their fitness for combat, 'amused himself by showing others he could undulate chest muscles beneath his shirt', walked through the department in a sleeveless shirt and spandex shorts and occasionally invited female officers to touch his biceps.[121] He was also verbally abusive to his subordinates, brooking no dissent, and made a point of asking the department's civilian female teachers 'if they had any romantic entanglements he should know about', while also telling faculty that divorced people lacked commitment. Critics of Hallums, which

---

[120] Thomas E. Ricks, 'Army Colonel Loses His Career in Fight Over Academy's Vision', *Wall Street Journal*, 13 March 1997, www.wsj.com/articles/SB858206074489518000.
[121] Ricks.

evidently included the leadership of West Point, considered him to be a 'macho, oafish officer out of step with the reality of a peacetime Army whose purpose is now more complicated than storming a machine-gun nest' and as someone who was a fundamentally abusive leader.[122]

For all of this, Hallums was found guilty of sexual harassment for creating 'an intimidating, hostile or offensive environment' and removed from his post. He clearly had many defenders within both West Point and the broader Army though, as the large number of on-the-record quotes in the Ricks article made clear. Hallums' retirement ceremony was sponsored by General David Bramlett, head of United States Army Forces Command (FORSCOM), who told the crowd at the Fort Campbell ceremony that 'Jim Hallums went where the Army sent him and he did his duty' before telling Hallums 'your example stands for all of us'.[123] Defenders of Hallums told Ricks that he was facing a 'viscerally anti-military atmosphere' at West Point. Ricks summed up this viewpoint thus: 'he didn't pass muster with the "weenie" element of the modern Army. Too gruff, blunt and demanding for the academics around him; too proud of his warrior past. He was, they charge, drummed out of the service for being politically incorrect.'[124] His supporters repeatedly referred to him as a 'genuine warrior' who had been 'plenty good enough to lead men into deadly combat and win medals of valor' but not good enough to handle a group of entitled academics.[125] In Ricks' telling, all of this was evidence that the 'the same divisive culture wars that have been raging in the corridors of U.S. education, religion and the workplace have now broken out in the military' and that all protagonists agreed that this was 'a fight for the Army's soul and future'.[126]

The story made a splash, and the *Journal* ran a follow-up piece consisting of letters from the public a few weeks later, where opinion ran heavily in Hallums' favour. The former US ambassador to Bolivia wrote to say that he had worked with Hallums in Latin America and found him to be a '"warrior officer" in the very best sense of that the word', although he admitted that Hallums had 'a personality so forceful [that it] can be misperceived as intolerant'.[127] Other correspondents bemoaned that careers were 'being sacrificed on the altar of military feminization by soft-headed bureaucrats' and that West Point had become 'a finishing school for the effete', a place that had become 'an Ivy League-like

---

[122] Ricks.
[123] Ricks.
[124] Ricks.
[125] Ricks.
[126] Ricks.
[127] 'Letters to the Editor: For Wars, We Need Warriors', *Wall Street Journal*, 4 April 1997.

campus that shuns its once proud tradition of building tough war-riors'.[128] These writers variously worried that 'the nation would pay a high price' because the 'brutal nature of war hadn't changed' and that 'failing to instil the warrior spirit in our military leaders weakens the military's ability to perform its primary function – to fight and win wars'. They drew a stark contrast between 'officers who look pretty, salute well, have good social graces and offend no one' and 'killers [who] win battles and keep troops alive' and who 'are not adept at caressing tender egos or singing Kumbaya'.[129] They blamed the 'sterile academics of West Point' and the 'sullen egalitarian mavens of gender and racial politics and their intellectual statist standard-bearers who proclaim a floating morality that adheres to no absolutes' for ending the career of a 'warrior officer', and who would, if not stopped, 'doom our armed forces to second-rate status or worse'.[130]

Evidently, correspondents expressed similar sentiments directly to the leadership at the Military Academy and West Point Superintendent, Lieutenant General Daniel Christman put out a statement on the West Point website, noting that he had seen a 'large volume of letters and e-mails from graduates and the general public on the recent *Wall Street Journal* article'. Christman noted that Ricks had not included the views of West Point leadership on the issue and claimed that the article lacked context and the complete picture. He reassured his readers that 'despite what some of you have concluded, we haven't lost sight of our mission to produce officers for our Army, nor have we become a "touchy-feely" haven for leadership theoreticians'.[131] Christman went on to disagree point by point with some of the article's characterisations. He argued that 'the warrior spirit is not dead at West Point. But I will be frank and tell you that warriors who are abusive to their subordinates and fail to accord them proper respect cannot successfully lead. They have no place at West Point or in our Army.'[132] For Christman, the Hallums incident had nothing to do with 'political correctness' and everything to do with leadership. He put complaints about political correctness into context by arguing that they were similar to complaints by graduates about previous 'final blows' to the Military Academy, such 'as the elimination of horses, Christmas leave for Plebes, or admission of women'. Christman argued

---

[128] 'Letters to the Editor: For Wars, We Need Warriors'.
[129] 'Letters to the Editor: For Wars, We Need Warriors'.
[130] 'Letters to the Editor: For Wars, We Need Warriors'.
[131] Daniel W. Christman, 'Open Letter To Friends of the Military Academy', 1 April 1997, Dennis J. Reimer Papers: General Management Correspondence Files – Box 9: April 1997, AHEC.
[132] Christman.

that change was inevitable, but that West Point would always train warriors, albeit 'warriors drawn from the deepest traditions of America – and American warriors don't abuse subordinates!'[133] In Christman's mind, what was at stake was not the warrior spirit but the basic principles of professionalism.

This controversy did not go unnoticed in Army headquarters. Reimer sent a note to Christman to say that he had read his message on Hallums and agreed with it.[134] He himself had been receiving correspondence about the affair, including a note from retired General Bruce Palmer, former deputy commander of US forces in Vietnam. Palmer informed Reimer that the controversy had a 'major topic of discussion among West Pointers' and that he and other graduates both felt that Hallums had been badly treated and that, more broadly, 'that the Academy we knew no longer exists' and that West Point had become 'the wimp academy'.[135] Reimer forwarded Christman's message to Palmer, along with a note to assure him that the decision to relieve Hallums had not been made lightly but that the leadership at West Point had had no other choice, given his behaviour. In a handwritten addendum to the note, he added that he had looked into the case and spoken to trusted friends who knew Hallums and who had been surprised that he had been appointed to the West Point job in the first place.[136]

As both Reimer and Christman's inboxes attested, the Hallums affair stirred up a level of interest that went way far beyond what one might normally expect of the internal disciplinary processes of the Military Academy, but this level of interest was indicative of a broader sense of foreboding felt by conservatives as both the Hallums affair and the much larger controversy over sexual assault rumbled on. Much of the rhetoric attacking the Army's halting attempts to deal with sexual assault and its refusal to resegregate basic training focused on the notion of soldiers as 'warriors'. One retired Marine Corps colonel wrote to Reimer to say that it pained him 'to see the Army so distracted from its main missions and business by the various problems caused by females in the Army'. He argued that the Army should be made up of 'disciplined, tough warriors' who by definition must be male. 'Sexual and social problems' would not be a concern if 'the roles of females are properly limited and

---

[133] Christman.

[134] Dennis J. Reimer, 'Note to Daniel W. Christman', 20 March 1997, Dennis J. Reimer Papers: General Management Correspondence Files, Box 8: March 1997, AHEC.

[135] Bruce Palmer, 'Letter to Dennis J. Reimer', 19 March 1997, Dennis J. Reimer Papers: General Management Correspondence Files – Box 9: April 1997, AHEC.

[136] Dennis J. Reimer, 'Letter to Bruce Palmer Jr.', 1 April 1997, Dennis J. Reimer Papers: General Management Correspondence Files – Box 9: April 1997, AHEC.

understood'. This meant that women in the military needed 'to help the male warriors – not to become female warriors'.[137]

Along with his letter to Reimer, this correspondent attached newspaper clippings, including an August 1997 opinion piece in the *Conservative Chronicle* entitled 'American's Ruling Elite Is Effeminate'. The author of the piece, Charley Reese, approvingly quoted a British colonial official who had said that 'the rise of feminism is one of the certain signs of a declining empire' before going on to offer a paean to the virtues of a 'manly society', which included the 'love of a good tale and good song, an eye for beauty, a taste for war and worship and wine and women'. For Reese, 'it is the warrior who is sensitive to beauty and the sweetness of life … because the warrior knows how fleeting and short life is'. Reese wanted a society where 'the civilians become more like the military' not one 'where the military becomes more like the civilians, as the politicians in Washington are trying mightily to bring about'.[138]

Other conservative publications directly attacked Reimer. An article entitled 'America's Domestic Cold War' in *Strategic Review*, the outlet of the United States Strategic Institute, began with an image of Reimer at the Senate Armed Services Committee hearings on sexual assault: 'there he stood, contrite and confused, with head bowed and shoulders stooped, military bearing brought low indeed'.[139] The author, William J. Corliss, advised that 'defenders of America's national interests will not regain their composure until they identify as their true enemies the cultural priorities of postmodernism'. Corliss warned that members of the armed forces could no longer 'hunker down to be left alone … this is one cold war, a domestic cold war that they are about to lose'. Corliss likened the military to 'the last Spartan at Thermopylae', the only thing preventing 'the collapse of patriotic America, its tradition and its ethos'.[140] He warned that 'the hour is late' and that members of Congress and the military had to once and for all ban women from combat forces. Notably, he felt that they needed to do so on moral grounds, since arguments about efficiency and utility were not holding sway. What was at issue, again, was the sacred bond between male soldiers, a bond that was built on 'supreme sacrifice of one's private good, one's life, on behalf of a good that is intensively better because it is a good common to many, with exigencies altogether

---

[137] James A. Donovan, 'Letter to Dennis J. Reimer', 15 September 1997, Dennis J. Reimer Papers: 1mm Reading Files – Box 4: October 1997, AHEC.

[138] Charley Reese, 'America's Ruling Elite Is Effeminate', *Conservative Chronicle*, 6 August 1997, Dennis J. Reimer Papers: 1mm Reading Files – Box 4: October 1997, AHEC.

[139] William J. Corliss, 'Editorial: America's Domestic Cold War', Fall 1997, 3, Dennis J. Reimer Papers: 1mm Reading Files – Box 5: November 1997, AHEC.

[140] Corliss, 3.

different from a person's proper good alone'. Any women, 'however qualified otherwise', should not enter this space if her presence would disturb it, even 'if she shared the ethos of the common good'.[141]

This piece was incendiary enough that it drew a personal apology from the chairman of the United States Strategic Studies Institute, retired Marine General Victor Krulak, who wrote to Reimer to say that he found the piece offensive.[142] Reimer was relatively used to this sort of commentary, though. A few months earlier, retired Army Colonel Harry Summers had published a piece in the *Washington Times* about both Hallums and sexual assault, entitled 'A Disease of the Soul'. Reimer paid enough attention to it to send it to Christman with the note: 'Dan, Harry Summers is usually pretty good – you might consider giving him your side of the case.'[143] Summers argued that the sexual harassment scandals were indeed 'disturbing and disfiguring', but they were 'primarily diseases of the skin that – with proper treatment – can and will be cured'. Far more serious was 'the reported "wimpification" of leadership at West Point', something that constituted 'a fight for the Army's very soul and future'.[144] Even as he brushed off Aberdeen and other scandals, Summers decried the treatment of Hallums as the product of a climate of political correctness and fondly recalled General Colin Powell's line from 1993 that 'we're warriors … and we have this mission to fight and win this nation's wars'. Summers wondered whether it was Hallums or the West Point faculty who had truly internalised what Powell's words had meant. The Hallums affair clearly revealed deep tensions within the Army as to what exactly being a warrior meant at the close of the twentieth century. For Summers and other conservatives, the thousands of cases of sexual assault within the military were merely a skin-deep problem that said nothing about that warrior identity, whereas the alleged persecution of a West Point faculty member was indicative of something deeply wrong with the institution.

2.5   Conclusion

The difference in tone between Powell's sunny optimism about the 'exquisite condition' of the armed forces in early 1993 and Harry Summers' laments about an institution being afflicted by a 'disease of the

---

[141] Corliss, 4.

[142] Victor H. Krulak, 'Letter to Dennis J. Reimer', 27 October 1997, Dennis J. Reimer Papers: 1mm Reading Files – Box 5: November 1997, AHEC.

[143] Reimer, 'Note to Daniel W. Christman'.

[144] Harry G. Summers, 'Disease of the Soul', *Washington Times*, 20 March 1997, Dennis J. Reimer Papers: General Management Correspondence Files, Box 8: March 1997, AHEC.

soul' just four years later is striking. Equally striking is the difference between the way the debates over gay military service and the combat exclusion for women played out compared to the subsequent controversy over sexual assault and gender-integrated training. Throughout, Army leaders used the same language about cohesion and the sacred bonds between soldiers, but on the issue of gender-integrated training, they broke decisively with the conservative faction that wanted to use the documented problems with sexual assault as an excuse to further restrict women's role in the military. Similarly, the Hallums affair demonstrated that there was not only a significant number within the Army who yearned for a certain type of 'warrior' masculinity, but also that the West Point and Army leadership were not willing to countenance its most extreme form.

In their partially successful defence of the gay ban and in their move to keep women out of ground combat units, Army leaders and advocates for the status quo had repeatedly emphasised the importance of small group cohesion and the deep bonds of affection that were necessary to accomplish the mission. Contained within that definition of 'cohesion' were all sorts of gendered norms and expectations about what it took to maintain this fragile and yet vital bond between soldiers. Ironically, even as worries about the overall stability and effectiveness of the post–Cold War army grew, the actions of Army leaders demonstrated that they were beginning to become slightly less concerned about the effect of women on this delicate balance. Proponents of full integration had argued that professionalism should ultimately mean that men and women were able to work together, and while Army leadership did not fully follow the logic of that argument to its conclusion by ending the combat exclusion or rethinking their opposition to openly gay people serving in the military, they did employ similar language themselves against those who wanted further restrictions.

The most significant indicator that things were changing was the Army's reaction to the Kassebaum Baker Report. When presented with a recommendation from a DoD-commissioned high-level group to resegregate basic training, the Army, along with the Navy and Air Force, had simply refused. The Army did move to toughen its basic training requirements, in some sort of nod to arguments about needing to promote a warrior ethos, but this move came with the recognition that all-male spaces in the Army were shrinking. The Army's reaction to sexual assault scandals within the force were undeniably inadequate, as their continued refusal to remove the chain of command from investigations into sexual violence made clear, but by focusing on professionalism in both their response to that particular crisis and in their reaction to the

Kassebaum Baker Report, they were beginning to articulate a different vision of the profession from the one espoused by conservative commentators. Army leaders certainly spoke about cultivating 'warriors', but they were far less clear about what the term meant than the most vocal opponents of change in the Army had been.

3   Warriors Who Don't Fight
The Dilemmas of Peacekeeping Operations

From September 1994 to March 1995, over 20,000 US soldiers deployed to Haiti as part of Operation Uphold Democracy, an intervention to support the newly reinstated civilian government of Jean-Bertrand Aristide. This mission, with its focus on peacekeeping and reconstruction, was a relatively new departure for many of the American troops deployed to the Caribbean nation. Newspaper coverage reflected the novelty of the deployment, with much of the reporting dwelling on the strangeness of the experience for Americans. Writing about his experience of being embedded with a platoon of soldiers from the 101st Airborne Division, Rick Bragg of the *New York Times* reported that 'here, in the muck and murk of the poorest nation in the Western Hemisphere, a few young soldiers of the post–Cold War have found something not too far from glory'. He spoke of the soldiers' pride at the adoration they received from the civilians of Port-au-Prince and how they knew 'that the people feel safe under their guns'. One African American soldier asked 'how often in a black man's life … does he walk through a crowd of people of his own color and see them throw flowers at his feet?' For Bragg, Haiti was a place where 'the American soldiers will play peacekeeper and god'.[1]

Yet he also recorded the soldiers' ambivalence about what they were doing. The platoon sergeant told him that 'my job is to make sure they are prepared', to which Bragg added, 'but for what, no one is quite sure'. These soldiers were acutely aware of the experience of their counterparts in Somalia just over a year earlier. There, crowds had also greeted American troops with smiles before something went wrong and the mission ended with the mutilated bodies of American soldiers being dragged through the streets. This was an image 'burned into the mind of every soldier in the Third Platoon'.[2] Haiti, in their view, was a dangerous and mysterious place too, where soldiers couldn't afford to relax. For Bragg,

---

[1] Rick Bragg, '"I Never Seen Nothing Like That"', *New York Times*, 6 November 1994, www.nytimes.com/1994/11/06/magazine/i-never-seen-nothing-like-that.html.
[2] Bragg.

Figure 3.1 A soldier from the 555th Military Police Company attempting to hold back a crowd in Port-au-Prince, Haiti, 1994

it was also a place that highlighted the inherent goodness of the soldiers of the 101st Airborne. He acknowledged that 'they sound too good to be true, angels with M-16's', before admitting that 'they are not. They curse in Technicolor. Some speak fondly about being knee-walking drunk, of regrettable trifles with mean women and general all-around sorriness.' He claimed, though, that 'when seen against the backdrop of cruel and exotic Haiti, they are innocent. Haiti at once makes them feel like they are doing something pure and scares them half to death' (Figure 3.1).[3]

While this combination of an exoticised Haiti and innocent Americans abroad is familiar to scholars of the history of American overseas intervention, what was unusual about 1990s interventions such as Operation Restore Democracy in Haiti was the extent to which media coverage emphasised the uncertainty with which American soldiers faced this new conflict environment.[4] Some, such as Major Ernst Lubin, searched for domestic analogies to make sense of the deployment. Speaking to the

[3] Bragg.
[4] The historiography of American military occupation is vast, but for a representative sample see Mary A. Renda, *Taking Haiti: Military Occupation and the Culture of U.S. Imperialism, 1915–1940* (Chapel Hill: University of North Carolina Press, 2001); Brian McAllister Linn, *The Philippine War, 1899–1902* (Lawrence: University Press of Kansas, 2000); Melani McAlister, *Epic Encounters: Culture, Media, and U.S. Interests in the*

Washington Post, Lubin, the second in command of a Marine battalion training Haitian police, argued that 'the Haitian people need to see strength' and wondered why the Haitian military had been vilified for employing the same tactics used by the Los Angeles Police Department to suppress the 1992 riots in South-Central Los Angeles.[5] Others simply expressed bewilderment and frustration to reporters, with one soldier telling the *Los Angeles Times* that 'when we first got here, we didn't know what to expect. First, we were told we were going on an invasion. And then it was a peacekeeping mission.' Another admitted that these operations took a psychological toll, stating that 'it's rougher here. Even though I was under threat in Saudi, this is rougher and more frustrating mentally.' Indeed, the Army deployed extra psychologists and mental health workers to Haiti after the suicides of three soldiers in as many weeks in October 1994.[6]

The doubts expressed by soldiers and Marines to reporters in Haiti were echoed throughout the US military in different ways throughout the decade. Without the Cold War, and in the absence of any peer competitor, the armed forces struggled to articulate a coherent vision of their place in this new world order, amid claims about the 'end of history' and debates about whether or not war's fundamental character was changing.[7] For some, these deployments were harbingers of the conflicts of the twenty-first century, and for others, they were unnecessary distractions from the real business of soldiering. More than any of the other services, the Army was riven by tensions about what its future might look like. The Marines were well used to expeditionary operations, while the Air Force and Navy were largely content to highlight their capabilities in high-tech conventional warfare. The Army, however, was less sure about how to relate to these missions. The costs of this uncertainty fell most heavily on soldiers deployed to places such as Haiti, who, in the absence of clear guidance, had to reconcile the often vague political ends of these

---

Middle East since 1945 (Berkeley: University of California Press, 2005); John W. Dower, *Embracing Defeat: Japan in the Wake of World War II* (New York: W. W. Norton & Company, 2000); Susan L. Carruthers, *The Good Occupation: American Soldiers and the Hazards of Peace* (Cambridge, MA: Harvard University Press, 2016).

[5] William Booth, 'U.S., Haitian Troops: Scarcely a Team', *Washington Post*, 24 September 1994, www.washingtonpost.com/archive/politics/1994/09/24/us-haitian-troops-scarcely-a-team/865f6171-27ae-424c-aeff-470b3db14a3a/.

[6] Tracy Wilkinson, 'GI Suicides in Haiti Alert Army to the Enemy Within', *Los Angeles Times*, 21 October 1994, http://articles.latimes.com/1994-10-21/news/mn-53023_1_military-police.

[7] For more on this debate, see Thomas X. Hammes, 'The Evolution of War: The Fourth Generation', *Marine Corps Gazette* 78, no. 9 (n.d.): 35–44; Mary Kaldor, *New and Old Wars: Organized Violence in a Global Era* (Cambridge: Polity Press, 1999); Martin Van Creveld, *The Transformation of War* (New York: The Free Press, 1991).

missions with means that had not been designed to achieve them. Soldiers wrestled with questions about the utility of force, the need for proficiency in non-combat tasks and whether such missions were appropriate for American soldiers at all.

Certainly, the Army had a long history of undertaking constabulary operations, but now, for the first time since World War II, the question of whether such missions would be one of the organisation's core functions was an open one. Army leaders might not have had much of an appetite for them, but large-scale conventional war, which had seemed improbable even in the mid-1980s, was now vanishingly unlikely, leaving the Army in search of new missions. For a time, it seemed like peacekeeping might be a central role for the Army of the twenty-first century. The 1990s marked the first (and to date only) time that the Army participated in peacekeeping missions – operations that posed particular challenges when it came to the use of force – on a large scale. In the decade between the end of the Cold War and the attacks of 11 September 2001, soldiers deployed on peacekeeping missions to places as diverse as northern Iraq, Somalia, Macedonia, Bosnia and Kosovo, and encountered widely varying levels of instability, complexity and fluidity in these operations. This pattern of deployment, coupled with broader uncertainties about the future of conflict, led to significant anxieties both within and outside the Army about what participation in peacekeeping operations meant for readiness and the ability to fight conventional wars.

Peacekeeping meant different things to policymakers, Army leaders, public intellectuals and those who served on such missions. Army leaders were generally not enthusiastic about participation in these operations but most recognised that the complex nature of peacekeeping was a harbinger of future trends in conflict. Similarly, personnel deployed as peacekeepers accepted the role, even if they often struggled to understand how best to navigate the grey zone between peace and war. Political commentators tended to be much less ambivalent about peacekeeping, with some neoconservative observers enthusiastic about using such operations to practice skills that would be useful in later wars, while most conservatives displayed a deep antipathy for such interventions, arguing that they corroded valuable warfighting skills and were symptomatic of an Army that had lost its way. For the few liberal commentators engaged in debates over Army policy, peacekeeping operations represented an opportunity to showcase American values and even to promote a deeper connection between the US military and broader American society.

Given the range of issues at stake, these debates focused not only on questions of doctrine, training and education but on the individual soldier as well. Peacekeeping missions may have been a central, if sometimes unwanted, concern of the US Army in the 1990s, but they also exposed deeper fissures within the Army and broader American society about the organisation's proper role and the sort of attributes that American soldiers would need in the twenty-first century. Participation in peacekeeping operations heightened the tensions between notions of the soldier as violent warfighter or armed humanitarian, citizen-soldier or professional warrior, and these contrasts became the subject of widespread debate. Senior Army leaders, ordinary soldiers, academics and political commentators alike wrestled with the ambiguities and anxieties raised by these missions. Ultimately, all were concerned with the same question: in an era with little prospect of conventional war, what were soldiers for?

3.1   A New World Order?

The historian Hew Strachan has written that the end of the Cold War was a much more important turning point in strategic affairs than the attacks of 11 September 2001. For Strachan, the collapse of the Soviet Union created an 'intellectual vacuum' and robbed western militaries of the scenarios around which they had organised their training, doctrine and procurement.[8] Certainly, to read the professional journals of the US Army in the early 1990s is to get a sense of the unease caused by this vacuum. While there was certainly plenty of triumphalism after the swift victory in the Persian Gulf that validated so many of the Army's post-Vietnam reforms, strategists, planners and theorists still struggled to understand how to best reposition the American military for a post–Cold War world. Despite the recent overwhelming victory in Kuwait and Iraq, journals published article after article warning that Operation Desert Storm was a once-off and would not be a precursor of the decade to come. Writing in *Parameters*, Daniel Bolger drew historical parallels with the pre-World War I British Army:

Just as Omdurman rang with the last stirrings of the Scots Greys' headlong dash at Waterloo, so the American Army's brilliantly successful Gulf War is a final echo of the Third Army's great wheel across France. The British soon found Boers out there as well as Dervishes, and Americans will shortly find Boers of their own to confront in El Salvador, the Philippines, or a dozen other hot, grimy flashpoints.[9]

Bolger warned that the U.S. Army 'must turn from the warm and well-deserved glow of its Persian Gulf victory and embrace, once more, the

---

[8] Hew Strachan, *The Direction of War: Contemporary Strategy in Historical Perspective* (Cambridge: Cambridge University Press, 2014), 156.
[9] Daniel P. Bolger, 'The Ghosts of Omdurman', *Parameters* 21, no. 3 (1991): 31.

real business of regulars, the stinking gray shadow world of "savage wars of peace" as Rudyard Kipling called them'.[10] There was a sense that what had clearly worked so well in Kuwait and southern Iraq was already irrelevant.[11]

Indeed, the immediate aftermath of Operation Desert Storm saw 9,000 troops deployed to protect newly established Kurdish enclaves in northern Iraq. Soldiers in Operation Provide Comfort were expected to deal with very fluid situations, ambiguous rules of engagement and an environment where the identities of friend and foe were often blurred.[12] This operation was only the first of many. Between January 1989 and December 1993 the Army deployed on no fewer than forty-eight 'named' operations, ranging from hurricane relief (Hurricane Andrew) to peace-keeping and peace enforcement operations (Operation Provide Comfort in Iraq and Operation Restore Hope in Somalia).[13] This operational tempo reflected hopes for a 'new world order' of superpower cooperation and optimism in Washington that, following the end of the Cold War and the victory in the Gulf War, the United Nations could be used as a vehicle to promote peace and security. Peacekeeping operations would be an integral part of this new world order.[14]

Indeed, many shared the hope that the end of the Cold War would open up new possibilities, particularly for the United Nations. No longer would Cold War tensions cause gridlock at the Security Council; world powers could now act together to promote peace and security. Between 1987 and 1993, the number of UN peacekeeping missions jumped from five to twenty-three and, for the first time, these missions included large contingents of troops from the major powers.[15] Building on these developments, UN Secretary-General Boutros Boutros Ghali

---

[10] Bolger, 32.

[11] The political scientist Rebecca Lissner argues that Operation Desert Storm marked an endpoint rather than a beginning because US performance during the war ushered in an entirely new grand strategy that was more ambitious and aggressively interventionist. Rebecca Lissner, *Wars of Revelation: The Transformative Effects of Military Intervention on Grand Strategy* (Oxford: Oxford University Press, 2021), 108–51.

[12] Mary Elizabeth Walters, '"Tree Hugging Work": The Shifting Attitudes and Practices of the U.S. Marine Corps Toward Peace Operations in the 1990s', *Marine Corps History* 5, no. 2 (Winter 2019): 56–61.

[13] Francis M. Doyle, Karen J. Lewis, and Leslie A. Williams, 'Named Military Operations from January 1989 to December 1993' (TRADOC, April 1994).

[14] George H. W. Bush, 'Towards a New World Order: Address before a Joint Session of the Congress on the Persian Gulf Crisis and the Federal Budget Deficit', 11 September 1990.

[15] Alex J. Bellamy and Paul D. Williams, 'Trends in Peace Operations, 1947–2013' in *The Oxford Handbook of United Nations Peacekeeping Operations*, ed. Joachim A. Koops, Norrie MacQueen, Thierry Tardy and Paul D. Williams (New York: Oxford University Press, 2015), 20.

proposed a standing UN force that would deploy on peacekeeping and peace enforcement missions, made up of units provided by member states.[16] The lukewarm responses of Security Council members might have betrayed an unwillingness to firmly commit to robust UN control over national militaries, but the fact that the proposal was even advanced spoke to the changing geopolitical context.[17] Indeed, most major western militaries recognised that they needed to reorient their forces towards peacekeeping and stability operations. As the sociologist Christopher Dandeker has documented, the British government established 'promoting the United Kingdom's wider security interests through maintenance of international peace and stability by acting under mandates issued by the UN' as one of their three core defence roles.[18] Similarly, the 1994 French Defence White Paper emphasised the need to contribute to multinational peacekeeping operations, while the German *Bundeswehr* also began to think about the role it could play beyond its traditional one of territorial defence.[19] Throughout NATO, member states were revising their strategy documents to include new missions and priorities. Crucially, unlike the United States, virtually all of these other militaries put multilateralism, if not UN control, at the centre of their analysis.[20]

American political leaders partly embraced this trend, and this seeming post–Cold War consensus was reflected in the 1992 presidential campaign with both major party candidates proclaiming optimism about prospects for US involvement in peacekeeping missions. President George H. W. Bush spelled out his ambition for future US participation in UN peacekeeping operations in a September 1992 address to the General Assembly of the United Nations. Bush told the General Assembly that 'because of peacekeeping's growing importance as a mission

---

[16] Boutros Boutros Ghali, 'An Agenda for Peace: Preventive Diplomacy, Peacemaking and Peace-Keeping: Report of the Secretary-General Pursuant to the Statement Adopted by the Summit Meeting of the Security Council on 31 January 1992' (New York: The United Nations, 17 June 1992), www.un.org/ruleoflaw/files/A_47_277.pdf, 33.

[17] John M. Goshko and Barton Gellman, 'Idea of a Potent UN Army Receives a Mixed Responses', *Washington Post*, 29 October 1992, www.washingtonpost.com/archive/politics/1992/10/29/idea-of-a-potent-un-army-receives-a-mixed-response/2e43e766-2c20-4591-b3f6-b756296dabfc/.

[18] Christopher Dandeker, 'The United Kingdom: The Over-Stretched Military', in *The Postmodern Military: Armed Forces after the Cold War*, ed. Charles C. Moskos, John Allen Williams and David R. Segal (New York: Oxford University Press, 2000), 33.

[19] Bernard Boëne and Michel Lous Martin, 'France: In the Throes of Epoch-Making Change' in Moskos, Williams and Segal, *The Postmodern Military*, 51–79; Bernhard Fleckenstein, 'Germany: Forerunner of a Postnational Military?', in ibid., 80–100.

[20] For a comparative analysis of post-Cold War military transformations, see Theo Farrell, Sten Rynning and Terry Terriff, *Transforming Military Power since the Cold War: Britain, France, and the United States, 1991–2012* (Cambridge: Cambridge University Press, 2013).

for the United States military, we will emphasize training of combat, engineering, and logistical units for the full range of peacekeeping and humanitarian activities'. More importantly, he declared that he had 'further directed the establishment of a permanent peacekeeping curriculum in US military schools'.[21] During the campaign, Governor Bill Clinton declared his support for US involvement in a 'voluntary UN Rapid Deployment Force' and, on taking office as president, approved Presidential Review Directive (PRD) 13, which called for a greatly expanded military role for the United Nations, and permitted American troops to be placed under the operational control of a UN force commander.[22]

Despite enthusiasm in both the Bush and Clinton White Houses for peacekeeping missions, many within the military were sceptical of the merits of such operations. The tension between Chairman of the Joint Chiefs of Staff General Colin Powell and civilians within the Clinton administration is well known, and Powell used his public appearances to emphasise that any military interventions should employ overwhelming force and come with clearly defined objectives, congressional and public support, and an exit strategy. In his most striking remarks, Powell told reporters at a press briefing on the Clinton administration's 'bottom-up review' of the Pentagon that he was 'going to give them a little bit of a tutorial about what an armed force is all about'. Powell argued that 'notwithstanding all of the changes that have taken place in the world, notwithstanding the new emphasis on peacekeeping, peace enforcement, peace engagement, preventative diplomacy, we have a value system and a culture system within the armed forces of the United States. We have this mission: to fight and win the Nation's wars.'[23] For Powell, missions such as Haiti, Somalia and Bosnia were traps to be avoided. Reflecting on the US intervention in Haiti, Powell's successor as chairman of the joint chiefs, General John Shalikashvili, cautioned that 'we need to remember that the primary mission of the armed forces of the United

---

[21] George H. W. Bush, 'Address before the General Assembly of the United Nations', 22 September 1992.

[22] William J. Clinton, 'Strategic Security in a Changing World' (Los Angeles World Affairs Council, Los Angeles, California: C-Span, 13 August 1992), www.c-span.org/video/?31119-1/clinton-campaign-speech; Goshko and Gellman, 'Idea of a Potent UN Army Receives a Mixed Responses'; Barton Gellman, 'Wider UN Police Role Supported', *Washington Post*, 5 August 1993.

[23] Colin Powell, cited in William J. Durch, *UN Peacekeeping, American Politics, and the Uncivil Wars of the 1990s* (London: Palgrave Macmillan, 1996), 41. For more on the Powell Doctrine, see Colin Powell, 'U.S. Forces: The Challenges Ahead', *Foreign Affairs*, Winter 1992–3; Colin L. Powell and Joseph E. Persico, *My American Journey: An Autobiography* (New York: Random House, 1995); Gail E. S. Yoshitani, *Reagan on War: A Reappraisal of the Weinberger Doctrine, 1980–1984* (College Station: Texas A&M University Press, 2011).

States is to fight and win on the battlefield, and we ought not to get in the habit of this sort of thing'.[24] That Shalikashvili felt the need to remind his audience of the US military's prime mission even in the aftermath of a successful (from an American perspective) peacekeeping operation demonstrates not only the antipathy of many senior leaders towards these missions but the anxiety they felt about them as well.

This particular strain of resistance to peacekeeping among senior officers may have been uniquely American, but the travails of the 1990s certainly meant that other forces suffered doubts about how they would cope with the demands of these operations. Reflecting on his experience of peace-keeping in Kosovo, British General Sir Mike Jackson argued that politi-cians were relying too heavily on soldiers to solve what were fundamentally political problems: 'I fear that the soldiers are now more and more police-men .... Other means are needed; it is not a security job .... You cannot expect soldiers to change people's minds. That has to be done in other ways.'[25] Even forces with a relatively long track record of peacekeeping found these new missions to be challenging. Infamously, the Dutch Army, which had extensive experience of peacekeeping in Lebanon, was unable to prevent the massacre of Bosnian Muslims at Srebenica, while the Canadian General Roméo Dallaire found himself struggling with a limited mandate and unclear orders as the Rwandan genocide unfolded around both him and his lightly armed and undersized peacekeeping force.[26] Indeed, Cana-dian peacekeepers also struggled badly in Somalia, where two paratroopers were found guilty of beating a teenager to death, sparking a controversy that led to the disbandment of the Canadian Airborne Regiment and the partial withdrawal of Canada from peacekeeping operations.[27]

For Americans, the Somalia experience was just as harrowing, and US forces withdrew from their peacekeeping mission there after the death of eighteen soldiers in a day-long running firefight in downtown Mogadishu

[24] John Shalikashvili, cited in Harry G. Summers, Military Strategy: Conversations with Harry G. Summers, interview by Harry Kreisler and Thomas G. Barnes, 6 March 1996, Conversations with History; Institute of International Studies, UC Berkeley, http://globetrotter.berkeley.edu/conversations/Summers/summers4.html.

[25] Carlotta Gall, 'NATO Commander in Kosovo Says Peacekeeping Force Has Reached Its Limit', New York Times, 13 September 1999, www.nytimes.com/1999/09/13/world/nato-commander-in-kosovo-says-peacekeeping-force-has-reached-its-limit.html.

[26] Daniel Boffey, 'Srebrenica Massacre: Dutch Soldiers Let 300 Muslims Die, Court Rules', The Guardian, 27 June 2017, www.theguardian.com/world/2017/jun/28/dutch-soldiers-let-300-muslims-die-in-bosnian-war-court-rules; Cedric Ryngaert, 'Peacekeepers Facilitating Human Rights Violations: The Liability of the Dutch State in the Mothers of Srebrenica Cases', Netherlands International Law Review; Dordrecht, December 2017, 1–83, http://dx.doi.org/10.1007/s40802-017-0101-6, Roméo Dallaire, Shake Hands with the Devil: The Failure of Humanity in Rwanda (London: Arrow, 2005).

[27] Grant Dawson, 'Here Is Hell': Canada's Engagement in Somalia (Vancouver: UBC Press, 2011).

in October 1993. The mission, which began in 1992 as an effort to secure food supplies for the Somali populace, had morphed to a broader nation-building role and then to a hunt for Somali warlord Mohammed Farrah Adid.[28] Speaking of the disaster, Senator Richard Lugar of the Senate Foreign Relations Committee argued that 'the Mogadishu incident dramatically indicated that Americans were not tolerant of losing American lives, and grossly intolerant if it appeared that American leadership had no idea of what we were doing, and why they were lost and what sort of control we had'.[29] The Army's after-action report focused on a dysfunctional chain of command, critiquing 'a poorly organized United Nations nation-building operation' and ruefully complaining about the fact that 'in a country where the United States, perhaps naively, expected some measure of gratitude for its help, its forces received increasing hostility as they became more deeply embroiled into trying to establish a stable government'.[30] Such was the report's frustration with the UN, it suggested that 'for the immediate future, ... operations sanctioned and funded by the UN should be led by a single nation or an established military alliance', and recommended that Operation Desert Storm 'be a model for such interventions'.[31] A similar study of lessons learned, commissioned by the National Defense University, argued that the United States needed to avoid 'indefinite commitments at the expense of its other responsibilities worldwide' and to be mindful of 'bright lines' that should not be crossed in peace operations, including 'indefinite commitments at the expense of its other responsibilities worldwide'.[32]

Somalia did cause the Clinton administration to partially back away from its commitment to peacekeeping operations and the 1994 National Security Strategy declared that 'in ... situations posing a less immediate threat, our military engagement must be targeted selectively on those areas that most affect our national interests'.[33] Furthermore, Clinton's

[28] Mark Bowden, *Black Hawk Down: A Story of Modern War* (New York: Atlantic Monthly Press, 1999); John L. Hirsch and Robert B. Oakley, *Somalia and Operation Restore Hope: Reflections on Peacemaking and Peacekeeping* (Washington, DC: United States Institute of Peace, 1995).

[29] Richard Lugar, 'Frontline: Ambush in Mogadishu – Interviews – Senator Richard Lugar', *Frontline* (PBS), n.d., www.pbs.org/wgbh/pages/frontline/shows/ambush/interviews/lugar .html.

[30] *United States Forces, Somalia: After Action Report and Historical Overview: The United States Army in Somalia, 1992–1994* (Washington, DC: US Army Center of Military History, 2003), 14.

[31] *United States Forces, Somalia*, 45.

[32] Kenneth Allard, 'Somalia Operations: Lessons Learned' (Washington, DC: National Defense University, January 1995), 79, 80.

[33] William J. Clinton, *National Security Strategy of the United States, 1994–1995: Engagement and Enlargement* (Washington, DC: The White House, 1995), 12.

May 1994 Presidential Decision Directive 'PDD 25: Reforming Multi-lateral Peace Operations' affirmed that US forces would only be commit-ted to peace operations when participation would advance US interests, the risk to US forces was considered acceptable, US participation was considered necessary for the mission's success, a clear endpoint for that participation could be identified and other nations were willing to com-mit sufficient forces to achieve clearly defined objectives.[34] Not only that, but the directive put strict limits on the circumstances under which US troops would be placed under UN command. This marked a rapid retreat from the ambition of PRD-13, which had allowed for US partici-pation in such missions if they advanced US interests or would catalyse involvement of other countries and had opened the door to US troops being under the operational control of UN commanders.

Nonetheless, US involvement in peacekeeping missions did not cease after Somalia. Certainly, US forces deployed on such operations with a renewed sense of caution, but Shalikashvili's plea to 'not make a habit of this sort of thing' largely fell on deaf ears. Indeed, comparing the National Military Strategy (NMS) of 1995, published under Shalikash-vili's tenure, to the 1992 edition, there is a clear shift towards embracing, albeit reluctantly, a broader role. While the 1992 NMS largely focused on conventional threats, the 1995 NMS instead emphasised peacetime engagement and conflict prevention, while still embracing the need to maintain forces capable of simultaneously fighting two regional con-flicts.[35] Even though it was couched in the cautious language of PDD 25, the NMS also declared that the USA stood ready to support both tra-ditional peacekeeping and peace enforcement operations, and that this support 'may include participation of US combat units'.[36] The authors claimed to have learned the 'lessons of Somalia' and pointed to the US deployment in Haiti as an example of their determination to commit suf-ficient forces to these operations and to carefully tailor the disposition of those forces to achieve US objectives.[37]

This sort of policy, which both accepted the inevitability of participa-tion in peace operations and attempted to attach a string of caveats to it, was typical of the way that most senior Army leaders talked about peace-keeping. Writing in *Military Review*, one group of officers acknowledged

---

[34] 'Presidential Decision Directive/NSC 25: Reforming Multilateral Peace Operations' (Washington, DC: The White House, 1994), https://fas.org/irp/offdocs/pdd/pdd-25.pdf.

[35] Colin Powell, 'National Military Strategy of the United States' (Washington, DC: Department of Defense, January 1992); John M. Shalikashvili, 'National Military Strategy of the United States' (Washington, DC: Department of Defense, 1995).

[36] Shalikashvili, 'National Military Strategy of the United States', 9.

[37] Shalikashvili, 12.

that 'reading the tea leaves ... the Army will participate in peacekeeping and peace enforcement (like it or not)', and, in general, speeches from Army leaders emphasised that preparing for such missions was not something that could be avoided.[38] In the wake of intervention in Somalia, Army Chief of Staff Gordon R. Sullivan wrote that, when writing doctrine, the Army must resist the urge to focus solely on conventional operations and that 'we will no longer be able to understand war simply as the armies of one nation-state or group of nation-states fighting one another. Somalia again demonstrates that this understanding is too narrow – it always has been.' Sullivan recognised that 'we must learn to deal with reality as it is, not as we want it to be ... in not facing reality as it is, we could prepare the Army for the wrong war'.[39] General George Joulwan, commander of US European Command, went further and argued that 'one might say that the US military is returning to normal at the conclusion of the anomalous Cold War era because, historically, "normal" operations for US Forces are operations other than war'.[40] Joulwan believed that US forces must be ready to fight conventional war if required, but that securing the peace would be more important in a post–Cold War world.

Considering this uncertainty, senior leaders repeatedly stressed the need for adaptability and flexibility. In the absence of any peer competitor or a clear sense of where they might be called upon to deploy, Sullivan wanted the Army to be a 'power projection force', ready to deploy and sustain itself with little notice. Flexibility, however, did not mean fundamentally rethinking Army force structure. Writing in *Parameters*, Lieutenant Colonel David Fastabend complained that 'we digitize tanks. We slash force structure. We revise our doctrine. But we do not reorganize.'[41] In contrast, Army leaders generally argued that existing units could handle the entire spectrum of conflict without the need to create specialised units or to make major changes to the organisation of the force: well-trained combat units could handle whatever missions were thrown at them.

Army leaders would spend the next decade and beyond attempting to create a lighter and more flexible all-purpose 'power projection' force that could be deployed quickly, but in the meantime sought a compromise

---

[38] William W. Allen, Antione D. Johnson and John T. Nelsen, 'Peacekeeping and Peace Enforcement Operations', *Military Review* 73, no. 10 (1993): 59.

[39] Gordon Sullivan and James Dubik, *Envisioning Future Warfare* (Fort Leavenworth, KS: U.S. Army Command and General Staff College Press, 1995), 52.

[40] George A. Joulwan, 'Operations Other than War: A CINC's Perspective', *Military Review* 74, no. 2 (February 1994): 5.

[41] David A. Fastabend, 'Checking the Doctrinal Map: Can We Get There from Here with FM 100-5?', *Parameters* 25 (Summer 1995): 39.

between those who doubted that the Army should have a role in peace-keeping or Operations Other Than War (OOTW) and those who thought that such deployments were inevitable. The eventual solution was that training, doctrine and education could make some concessions in order to train soldiers for these missions, but Army force structure would remain unchanged. This refusal to make choices about what mix of units would be most appropriate to meet contemporary challenges led to a prevalence of terms such as 'full spectrum dominance' in doctrine and policy documents: in an era without serious peer competitors, the Army would attempt to excel at a vast range of missions, from conventional war to peacekeeping to peacetime engagement, and general-purpose forces would be expected to excel at them all.

This meant that the burden of adapting to this range of missions increasingly fell on junior soldiers. The soldiers themselves were expected to be nimble, intelligent and capable of handling a huge range of complex scenarios. Versatility became enshrined as a key doctrinal tenet and Army units would be required to be 'skilled and ready for war at all times [but also] prepared to commit to a variety of operations that may or may not include warfighting'.[42] The commander of US Army forces in Operation Restore Hope, General Steve Arnold, argued that 'well-trained, combat-ready, disciplined soldiers can easily adapt to peacekeeping or peace enforcement missions. Train them for war; they adapt quickly and easily to Somalia–type situations.'[43] The Center for Army Lessons Learned report on operations in Somalia made a similar point and argued that 'with operational tempos continuing to increase in the face of diminishing resources, units cannot afford OOTW requirements creeping into unit METLs [mission essential task lists]'.[44] Focusing Army training too much on peacekeeping-type missions would degrade combat readiness and imperil American soldiers.

This message meant that Army training for peacekeeping operations was ad hoc and piecemeal. Combat Training Centers did integrate some peace operations training into their exercises, but the quality varied. The NTC at Fort Irwin, California included training events such as media interviews and crowd control in their scenarios, but commanders treated this aspect of their NTC training as a minor sideshow and it

---

[42] Frederick M. Franks Jr, 'Full-Dimensional Operations: A Doctrine for an Era of Change', *Military Review* 73, no. 12 (1993): 5–10; James R. McDonough, 'Versatility: The Fifth Tenet', *Military Review* 73, no. 12 (December 1993): 13.

[43] Steven G. Arnold, 'Somalia: An Operation Other than War', *Military Review* 73, no. 12 (1993): 39.

[44] US Army Center for Lessons Learned, Fort Leavenworth, Kansas, 'US Army Operations in Support of UNISOM II: Operations Other than War', October 1994, Historical Resources Collection 2, US Army Center for Military History, Washington, DC.

was the first thing to be dropped from the schedule if the pre-exercise unloading of equipment went slowly.[45] Similarly, the Joint Readiness Training Center (JRTC) in Fort Polk, Louisiana allowed commanders to choose between a combat-oriented or a peace operations–oriented exercise when their units rotated through, but most commanders preferred to maintain an exclusive combat focus until their units were formally assigned to a peacekeeping operation.[46] This was in keeping with US Army peacekeeping doctrine, which called for a 'just-in-time' approach to training that would be specifically tailored to each mission.[47] Often, the lead-up time prior to a deployment was too tight for even that mission-specific training to take place, with units deploying to Haiti and Macedonia sometimes receiving as little as fifteen days' notice before arriving in-country.[48] Given such limited preparation time, commanders often preferred to focus their pre-deployment training on the worst-case, combat-oriented scenarios, practising things like close-quarter battle drills and convoy procedures rather than their negotiation and liaison functions.[49] Some units did not even do that, with one Germany-based battalion deploying to Macedonia continuing with their garrison taskings, including participating in a 4th of July parade, despite only having fifteen days to prepare for their new mission.[50]

Even where there was more extensive pre-deployment training, Army leaders at all ranks found it wanting. The Army's third Combat Training Center, the Combat Maneuver Training Center at Hohenfels, Germany, took the lead in training units due to deploy to Bosnia. With its Mountain Eagle exercise series, it offered intensive five-week-long mission readiness exercises that put units through a wide range of scenarios involving civilian role players and simulated villages and base camps that

---

[45] Michael F. Pappal, 'Preparation of Leaders to Make Decisions in Peacekeeping Operations' (Fort Leavenworth, KS: Army Command and General Staff College School of Advanced Military Studies, 15 May 2002), 48, https://apps.dtic.mil/sti/citations/ADA403349.

[46] J. T. Ford, S. H. Sternlieb and M. E. Guran, 'Peace Operations: Effect of Training, Equipment, and Other Factors on Unit Capability' (Washington, DC: General Accounting Office, 1995), 20, www.dtic.mil/docs/citations/ADA344826.

[47] US Army, FM 100–23 Peace Operations (Washington, DC: Department of the Army, 1994), 86.

[48] Ford, Sternlieb and Guran, 'Peace Operations', 23.

[49] Bruce E. Stanley, 'Where's Cap Haitien? Validating the Principles of Peace Operations' (Fort Leavenworth, KS: Army Command and General Staff College School of Advanced Military Studies, 17 December 1999), 17, https://apps.dtic.mil/sti/citations/ADA374956.

[50] Michael J. Flynn, 'Battle Focused Training for Peacekeeping Operations: A METL Adjustment for Infantry Battalions' (Fort Leavenworth, KS: Army Command and General Staff College School of Advanced Military Studies, 20 December 1996), 24, https://apps.dtic.mil/sti/citations/ADA324388.

represented specific locations in Bosnia.[51] Despite this effort, though, multiple general officers who deployed to Bosnia, including Generals Eric Shinseki and Montgomery Meigs and Major Generals Larry Ellis and William Nash, reported that they were not prepared for the experiences they had in Bosnia. Ellis claimed that his mission readiness exercise prepared him 'for an environment that did not exist in Bosnia'.[52] Nash described the challenge of training for peacekeeping as an 'inner ear problem', where officers who had trained for their entire careers to read a battlefield were now being asked to read a 'peace field'.[53] Meigs complained that, despite being second in command of the SFOR (Stabilisation Force in Bosnia and Herzegovina) mission in Bosnia, he had 'had no preparation other than what I did personally and the last job I had here. I had a lot of experience as a soldier, but other than a right-seat ride and a lot of guidance from my boss, I had no specific training for this mission. I got nothing ... for this mission. I visited a lot of folks, but the army didn't sit me down and say, "Listen, here is what you need to know."'[54]

Similar complaints came from mid-ranking officers and NCOs alike, with many focusing on the fact that they did not feel prepared to undertake negotiations or mediation or to make important decisions on the spot. One soldier commanding a checkpoint in Bosnia attempted to apply the rigid drills he had learned in Hohenfels to a busy road outside Tuzla, causing traffic to build up 4 km in either direction, angering local commuters in the process.[55] More darkly, an infantry company that deployed to Kosovo with no pre-deployment training in peacekeeping whatsoever saw eleven of its members convicted for intimidating, beating and abusing the local Albanian population.[56]

Despite these experiences, Army doctrine held that the ingenuity of the American soldier would have to be enough to see the Army through such trials. A TRADOC report claimed that 'the common sense, flexibility, and adaptability of the American soldier are sufficient to ensure a proper

[51] Charles Edward Kirkpatrick, 'Ruck It up!': The Post-Cold War Transformation of V Corps, 1990–2001 (Washington, DC: Government Printing Office, 2006), 59–67.
[52] G. S. McConnell, 'Formal Mediation and Negotiation Training, Providing Greater Skills for Commanders in Bosnia' (Fort Leavenworth, KS: Army Command and General Staff College School of Advanced Military Studies, 1 December 1999), 24, 31–2, 49, https://apps.dtic.mil/sti/citations/ADA375031.
[53] Howard Olsen and John Davis, 'Training U.S. Army Officers for Peace Operations: Lessons from Bosnia' (Washington, DC: United States Institute of Peace, 1 October 1999), 4, 1/19 www.usip.org /publications/1999/10/training-us-army-officers-peace-operations-lessons-bosnia.
[54] Olsen and Davis, 4.
[55] Pappal, 'Preparation of Leaders to Make Decisions in Peacekeeping Operations', 36.
[56] Pappal, 37.

response fitting the conditions in OOTW' while General Arnold argued
that leaders could adjust to the complexities of OOTW with ease, claiming that 'versatile units with flexible leaders ... are able to adjust to the
complexities faced in operations other than war' and that 'we are blessed
with some great colonels, lieutenant colonels and majors in our army. I
cannot say enough about them and the job they have done in Somalia.'[57]
The experience in Somalia influenced the emergence of concepts such
as the 'three block war', a phrase that came from General Charles Krulak, commandant of the Marine Corps. Krulak wrote of the role of the
'strategic corporal' and described a situation where soldiers conducted a
full-scale firefight, peacekeeping and humanitarian aid within the space
of three contiguous blocks.[58] These scenarios meant that junior leaders
would have to be given both the training and the freedom to take major
decisions, as their actions were likely to have strategic repercussions in
such an environment. Subtle changes in Army doctrine reflected such
sentiments. The 1994 edition of FM 100-1 *The Army* defined the traits
of the American soldier in a slightly different way to the 1991 edition –
noting that 'American soldiers have a long tradition of readiness and
adaptability that began with the Minutemen', where the older version
of that sentence mentioned only readiness – and stressed the need to be
able to endure 'the brutal realities of combat and tolerate the ambiguities
of military operations where war has not been declared'.[59] In short, these
types of conflicts would require soldiers who were equally comfortable
with warfighting and peacekeeping.

The career of General Wesley Clark provides some sense of how difficult it could be to adapt to the demands of peacekeeping. Clark was
involved in negotiating the Dayton Accords that ended the Bosnian
War and then, as head of US European Command, oversaw the SFOR
peacekeeping mission in Bosnia and the NATO bombing campaign in
Kosovo. In his memoirs, Clark reflected that his experiences taught him
that the 'the old separations in time between the military and political and between the echelons of military command were no longer the
same ... what we discovered was that the political and strategic levels impinged on the operational and tactical levels ... sometimes even

---

[57] Hugo E. Mayer, 'Operations Other than War', Technical Report (Fort Leavenworth,
KS: TRADOC Analysis Center, Operations Analysis Center, February 1995), 5–1,
https://apps.dtic.mil/sti/pdfs/ADA292507.pdf; Arnold, 'Somalia', 35.
[58] Charles Krulak, 'The Strategic Corporal: Leadership in the Three-Block War', *Marines
Magazine*, January 1999.
[59] *FM 100-1 The Army* (Washington, DC: Headquarters, Department of the Army,
1991); *FM 100-1 The Army* (Washington, DC: Headquarters, Department of the
Army, 1994), 6, 25.

insignificant tactical events packed a huge wallop'.[60] In Clark's case, this new reality was illustrated by an event in Bosnia that nearly ended his career. Despite warnings from American diplomats, he visited Bosnian Serb military headquarters in August 1994, where he met General Ratko Mladić, an already notorious figure who was later convicted for crimes of genocide, and drank wine with him and exchanged hats. Such was the furore when photographs of the exchange were published that the State Department allegedly instituted the 'Clark Rule', where generals would never be left to talk alone with any of the combatants in the Bosnian War.[61]

Clark applied these lessons during his tenure as commander in chief of European Command, focusing on the most minor of details where he felt they might have political consequences. In one incident, both he and General Eric Shinseki, commander of the US Army Europe and of SFOR, spent days deliberating about the presence of a checkpoint on a bridge in the town of Brčko, an operation that tied up a single infantry company.[62] The spectacle of two four-star generals, one of them holding the office of Supreme Allied Commander Europe that had originated with Eisenhower, making decisions that would ordinarily be left up to a battalion commander showed that, for all of the doctrinal discussion of 'three block war', adaptability and the 'strategic corporal', the reality of these operations was they were just as likely to produce hyper-cautious leaders who would end up intervening in decision-making at the lowest level.[63]

3.2   Soldiers in Peacekeeping

In light of this heavy emphasis on the flexibility and adaptability of American soldiers and the essentially unresolved tensions within the Army about the suitability of American forces for peacekeeping, it is no surprise that soldiers' views of these operations became the subject of extensive research among military sociologists, including those working under Department of Defense contract for bodies such as the US Army Research Institute for the Behavioral and Social Sciences and those pursuing their own scholarly research agendas. The Army commissioned

[60] Wesley K. Clark, *Waging Modern War: Bosnia, Kosovo, and the Future of Conflict* (New York: PublicAffairs, 2002), 10.
[61] Robert D. Novak, 'The Trouble with Wesley Clark', *Washington Post*, 22 September 2003, www.washingtonpost.com/archive/opinions/2003/09/22/the-trouble-with-wesley-clark/aa1c2c0d-cc09-4437-80a4-48f507a62af5/.
[62] Clark, *Waging Modern War*, 87–8.
[63] For an account of Clark's command of NATO forces during the Kosovo campaign, see Lawrence Freedman, *Command: The Politics of Military Operations from Korea to Ukraine* (Oxford and New York: Oxford University Press, 2022), 335–60.

several surveys to examine how peacekeeping missions affected readiness and how Army personnel felt about such missions, and to ask what types of soldiers were needed for these deployments.[64] This research demonstrated that those serving on such missions had a more nuanced view of peacekeeping than critics had allowed. Peacekeeping looked different to those deployed than it did to senior Army leadership. Soldiers certainly found these missions challenging in different ways, but they felt that peacekeeping missions didn't degrade readiness for conventional war. Their biggest difficulty, though, was in making sense of Army policies on both the use of force and force protection, issues that provoked complaints on virtually every deployment.

Northwestern University sociologist Charles Moskos carried out several of these studies for the Army, and he sought to determine whether peacekeeping deployments affected readiness for combat missions. Based on surveys and interviews with soldiers in Haiti, Somalia, Bosnia, Kosovo and Macedonia, he concluded that while there was some loss of skills on things such as crew-served weapons, soldiers thought that 'these skills can be quickly relearned upon returning to home station'.[65] Further, soldiers welcomed the opportunity to put some of their skills into practice. Moskos argued that 'nowhere else in the Army do mid-level NCOs organize patrols, record border incursions, and take care of the health, welfare and discipline of soldiers in isolated areas'.[66]

Moskos' surveys gave a quantitative basis for his conclusions. In Haiti, 44 per cent of soldiers thought the mission would better prepare them for a combat role, 40 per cent said it would have little effect and 7 per cent thought it make them less prepared.[67] In Kosovo, 35 per cent of soldiers agreed or strongly agreed with the statement that 'peacekeeping weakens the warrior spirit' but only 14 per cent thought the mission made them less ready for fighting conventional war.[68] Similarly, the sociologist David Segal's research on American peacekeepers in the Sinai demonstrated that they thought about peacekeeping in more

---

[64] See for instance: David R. Segal and Dana P. Eyre, *The U.S. Army in Peace Operations at the Dawning of the Twenty-First Century* (Alexandria, VA: U.S. Army Research Institute for the Behavioral and Social Sciences, 1996); Beatrice J. Farr and Ruth H. Phelps, *Reserve Component Soldiers as Peacekeepers* (Alexandria, VA: U.S. Army Research Institute for the Behavioral and Social Sciences, 1996).

[65] Charles C. Moskos, 'Memo to Gordon R. Sullivan: Soldiers and OOTW', 12 February 1995, Moskos Papers.

[66] Moskos.

[67] Charles Moskos and Laura Miller, 'Survey of U.S. Support Group, Port-au-Prince, Haiti', 27 August 1997, Moskos Papers.

[68] Charles Moskos, 'Memorandum for General Joseph W. Ralston, SACEUR: Report on Task Force Eagle', 21 October 2000, Moskos Papers.

martial terms than a lay audience might, but they were able to make sense of these missions by emphasising military values such as the need for discipline.[69] Like Moskos, Segal found that most of those deployed thought that soldiers could be effective at peacekeeping, even if they could not use force except in self-defence, and that the percentage of those who thought that this task was appropriate generally increased as the deployment went on.[70] The troops in the Sinai were deployed on a much less complex peacekeeping mission than those in Kosovo, Haiti or Somalia, with very restrictive rules of engagement and a much more passive posture and mission. Thus, even in a very traditional peacekeeping mission such as Sinai, soldiers were able to make sense of their mission in military terms.

The ambiguity inherent in these missions led to an interesting divide among soldiers. Sociologists working for the Army reported that those deployed on peacekeeping operations tended to go through three different phases in their feelings about the mission. First there was an idealism that Americans could help fix problems, typified by the pride that American soldiers in Haiti felt when local civilians fêted their arrival. The second stage involved a growing cynicism, as the mundane realities of the mission took hold. Soldiers several weeks or months into a deployment – and this was true of peacekeepers from all nations – tended to be very pessimistic about any suggestions that what they were doing was worthwhile.[71]

Certainly, peacekeeping operations brought with them a particular set of frustrations for the soldiers deployed on them. Many resented the lengthy separation from their families and questioned the utility of such missions. Indeed, a 1995 report by the *New York Times* reported dissatisfaction among the partners and children of the first wave of US troops set to deploy to Bosnia, with one seventh grader at Smith Barracks in Baumholder, Germany complaining that 'Clinton didn't go to the war he was supposed to go to … he had connections, so he wouldn't have to be away for a year' and others claiming that the US shouldn't be the 'parent of the world'.[72] The complaints of these schoolchildren surely

[69] David R. Segal, *Army Missions for the Twenty-First Century: Peacekeeping and Beyond* (Washington, DC: US Army Research Institute, 1998), 5.
[70] David R. Segal and Ronald B. Tiggle, 'Attitudes of Citizen-Soldiers toward Military Missions in the Post-Cold War World', *Armed Forces & Society* 23, no. 3 (1997): 387.
[71] Laura L. Miller and Charles Moskos, 'Humanitarians or Warriors? Race, Gender, and Combat Status in Operation Restore Hope', *Armed Forces & Society* 21, no. 4 (1 July 1995): 617.
[72] Alan Cowell, 'Army Children Express Their Doubts', *New York Times*, 2 December 1995, with www.nytimes.com/1995/12/02/world/army-children-express-their-doubts.html.

echoed some of the sentiments of their parents. Indeed, some of Segal's research argued that peacekeeping operations caused particular stress for military families because the national interest was not always as clear as it was in war, thus 'raising questions about the justification for the sacrifices that soldiers' families are asked to make when the soldiers deploy for peacekeeping duty'.[73] Army psychologists found that leaders on peacekeeping missions had a difficult task because their soldiers would inevitably 'look to them to validate the deployment, their discomfort, and their separation from their families', and providing this validation was difficult in environments where the everyday actions of units often seemed unmoored from the overall purpose of the mission.[74]

The third stage involved a reconsideration, where soldiers attempted to reconcile themselves to the mission as they reflected on what they'd learned towards the end of their deployment. It is at this third stage where a fascinating split occurred. According to sociologists Charles Moskos and Laura Miller, a stark divide emerged between two different groups of soldiers in Somalia: the 'warriors' and the 'humanitarians'. Based on a survey of just under 800 soldiers in Somalia and a series of interviews, Moskos and Miller found that a large subset of soldiers held very negative views of the Somalis, seeing the locals as lazy, uncivilised and as 'ungrateful bastards'.[75] This group also felt that they needed to meet violence with violence, lest they become a laughingstock among UN forces. Beating locals was a way of gaining respect. One interviewee reported of his colleagues: 'I've noticed that some of the women over here have been very gentle with the society around them and are putting too much trust in the (Somalis) they associate with. Men are far better suited to adjust to harsh situations ... I have become a real "asshole" to the people in this country.'[76]

By contrast, the 'humanitarians' were much more sympathetic to the plight of Somalis, whom they saw as simply unfortunate and were reluctant to use force unless they felt it strictly necessary for self-preservation. One interview participant reported that 'sometimes it's hard to feel sorry for the people over here ... when they are throwing rocks at you, but when you see the little children on the road so happy that we are here ... It changes the way you feel.'[77] Notably, there were clear demographic correlations for both the warriors and

---

[73] Segal, *Army Missions for the Twenty-First Century*, 8.
[74] Faris R. Kirkland, Ronald R. Halverson and Paul D. Bliese, 'Stress and Psychological Readiness in Post-Cold War Operations', *Parameters* 26, no. 2 (1996): 79.
[75] Miller and Moskos, 'Humanitarians or Warriors?', 626.
[76] Miller and Moskos, 627.
[77] Miller and Moskos, 630.

humanitarians, with black and female soldiers, along with support troops, all far more likely to be 'humanitarian' than whites, males and combat troops. The US contingent in Somalia was quite unusual as it was relatively gender-integrated and very multiracial: 12 per cent of those deployed were female and over one-third were black.[78] Most other contingents were all-male and tended to be racially homogenous (i.e., all-white European contingents, all-South Asian Pakistani contingents, etc.). For Moskos and Miller then, the very demographic diversity of US forces in Somalia was a tactical asset.

Soldiers were divided when it came to the question of what type of units might be appropriate for these missions. The 82nd Airborne troops surveyed by Segal thought that Military Police might be more appropriate than infantry for the Sinai mission due to the sort of duties they were assigned.[79] Writing in *Military Review*, Lawrence Yates surveyed the literature on peacekeeping and noted that 'virtually every non-traditional operation case study involving combat units is replete with a litany of complaints that the troops were not prepared or trained to perform many of the non-combat tasks assigned to them'. These tasks included 'distributing food, manning checkpoints, collecting money for weapons, quelling civil disturbances, reassuring local inhabitants, negotiating with civic leaders, arbitrating between contending factions, and rebuilding infrastructure', and Yates noted that 'the "warrior" mindset so essential to combat can be the source of anger, confusion, frustration and failure when applied to OOTW operations'.[80]

Indeed, many infantry units in places such as Haiti, Bosnia and Macedonia expressed frustration that 'they didn't come in shooting' and in places such as Somalia, where there was shooting, soldiers complained about the American public's lack of appreciation for the dangers they faced and the lack of clarity from Army leadership about the nature of the mission. Many of those deployed to Somalia had come straight from the humanitarian relief effort for Hurricane Andrew and were surprised to find that Somalia involved more combat than humanitarian action.[81] Indeed, many thought that their experience was similar to Operation Desert Storm, with one veteran of that operation declaring that 'Saudi

[78] Miller and Moskos, 616.

[79] David R. Segal, 'The Social Construction of Peacekeeping by US Soldiers', *Tocqueville Review* 17 (1996): 14.

[80] Lawrence A. Yates, 'Military Stability and Support Operations: Analogies, Patterns and Recurring Themes', *Military Review* 77, no. 4 (August 1997): 58.

[81] Moskos, 'Memo to Gordon R. Sullivan: Soldiers and OOTW', 12 February 1995; Miller and Moskos, 'Sociological Survey of US Army Soldiers Serving in Bosnia in 1996 and 1998: Questionnaire Results'.

was Disneyland compared to this. There we were never shot at.'[82] This ambiguity occurred elsewhere, with a report to Army Chief of Staff General Gordon R. Sullivan noting that, in Haiti, 'in October 1994, the 10th Mountain Division came in expecting to shoot, but did not. The 25th Infantry Division began to replace the 10th in December 1994, with the expectation of not shooting, though it might.'[83] Veterans of these operations wanted a combat patch to recognise their service, a crucially important marker of status in the military world. Those who served in Somalia eventually did receive a combat patch although the mission itself didn't get its own campaign medal until 2014, despite the deployment resulting in a large number of individual combat awards, including 103 Bronze Stars for Valor, 188 Purple Hearts, 41 Silver Stars and posthumous Medals of Honor for Master Sergeant Gary Gordon and Sergeant 1st Class Randall Shugart.[84] Segal interviewed fifty-five veterans of Somalia and found that they believed that 'they had not been in an "operation other than combat". They had been in combat.'[85]

After Somalia, US policy shifted to de-emphasise both combat and humanitarian action. US troops stood ready to use violence, if necessary, but they would accept far less risk in their day-to-day operations, and soldiers often had to limit their contacts with civilians due to security concerns. Morale among peacekeepers varied considerably, with those with the least amount of contact with the locals often having the lowest morale. Support troops restricted to their bases tended to be jealous of troops from combat units who could circulate in the countryside and enjoy a slightly more relaxed form of discipline. For both groups, boredom was a serious issue and soldiers complained about micromanagement and the byzantine command structures associated with multinational peacekeeping missions.[86] The American experience in Bosnia neatly encapsulated those dilemmas, with troops rarely allowed to leave their compounds, in contrast to their British colleagues, who were allowed to socialise in Sarajevo in civilian attire. Not only that, but American soldiers were also required to wear body armour at all times,

[82] Laura L. Miller and Charles Moskos, 'Humanitarians or Warriors? Race, Gender, and Combat Status in Operation Restore Hope', *Armed Forces & Society* 21, no. 4 (1 July 1995): 615–37.
[83] Charles C. Moskos, 'Letter to Gordon R. Sullivan: OOTW: Haiti Particulars and General Observations', 27 January 1995, Moskos Papers.
[84] Staff Report, 'It's Official: Units Credited for Somalia Campaign', *Army Times*, 17 December 2014, www.armytimes.com/pb/news/your-army/2014/12/17/it-s-official-units-credited-for-somalia-campaign/.
[85] Segal, 'The Social Construction of Peacekeeping by US Soldiers', 16.
[86] Kirkland, Halverson and Bliese, 'Stress and Psychological Readiness in Post-Cold War Operations'; Segal, 'The Social Construction of Peacekeeping by US Soldiers', 14.

which further aggravated complaints about being micromanaged. In a particularly absurd example of the problems associated with the chain of command and force protection, US soldiers serving under the British-led Allied Rapid Response Corps in Sarajevo were not required to wear body armour, while their V Corps colleagues serving in the same location but under a different chain of command were, resulting in a force protection policy that looked 'schizophrenic' to the US Army soldiers who endured it.[87]

This conservatism often led to difficult working relationships with other militaries, especially when it came to the use of force and force protection. Working with soldiers from other militaries did not seem to improve American soldiers' attitudes towards foreigners and Segal's studies showed that over two-thirds of American soldiers thought that it was more difficult to work with foreigners than Americans by the end of their deployment; a considerable increase on the start of the mission.[88] A Center for Army Lessons Learned after-action review on Operation Able Sentry in Macedonia noted stark differences between American and Nordic troops in terms of how they approached rules of engagement. The report cited a Finnish officer 'who boasted he had never fired his weapon, despite having been fired on "many times in various [peacekeeping operations]."' In another instance, 'a Nordic instructor training US troops in border patrol techniques told his class, "You've got to be shot [as opposed to shot at] first before you can return fire." To which one American soldier laconically replied, "Ain't gonna be that way."'[89]

The American approach to peacekeeping bemused other contingents. British Army Lieutenant Colonel Graeme Hazlewood wrote to his friend Charles Moskos that he failed to understand the American insistence on being always armed and in body armour. Hazlewood argued that 'the controlled relaxation of the need for these protective measures is a sign of confidence on the part of our forces, not weakness, and demonstrates a normalization of conditions' and that 'it is our view that peacekeeping is about confidence building, not just militarily dominating an area with bodies and guns'. Hazlewood thought that the American approach was ineffective, arguing that 'if your soldiers withdraw to their bases after their patrols, and only emerge in uniform and carrying weapons, we

[87] Walter E. Kretchik, 'Force Protection Disparities', *Military Review* 77, no. 4 (August 1997): 75.

[88] Segal and Tiggle, 'Attitudes of Citizen-Soldiers toward Military Missions in the Post-Cold War World'.

[89] Cited in Douglas Scalard, 'People of Whom We Know Nothing: When Doctrine Isn't Enough', *Military Review* 77, no. 4 (1997): 4–11.

believe they are isolating themselves from a key aspect of the job: meeting the community'.[90]

Moskos forwarded this correspondence to Major General Larry Ellis, who had commanded a division in Bosnia, and Ellis' response gives us some flavour of the attitudes of senior officers towards these deployments. Ellis wrote that 'I disagree with his observations that we are taking too hard a line with the dress and approach we take to peacekeeping, which comes from two distinctly different backgrounds between [the] British and U.S. armies'. Ellis argued that the British 'relaxed approach' reflected their 'it's just another mission' approach to peacekeeping, whereas, as the lone superpower, the United States had a very different set of responsibilities. For Ellis, peacekeeping was 'a violent process that requires credible, overwhelming force to be successful in keeping former warmakers compliant and deterring a return to paramilitary operations', and that US forces in Bosnia needed to 'maintain high standards of force protection, security, and presence which leaves no illusions to the local populace and Entity Armed Forces leaders that we mean business'. Ellis even argued that the more relaxed British approach to dress was causing problems unrelated to security. He noted that from 20 November 1996 through August 1998, there were 631 traffic accidents in the British sector in Bosnia but only 341 in the American sector, and argued that 'one must come to the conclusion that such statistical differences can be tied to the discipline of the force'.[91]

Other American commanders echoed Ellis' arguments. For them, American force protection measures were not a sign of excess caution but of discipline and toughness. General George Joulwan, commander in chief of European Command and Supreme Allied Commander, argued that when it came to peacekeeping operations, 'I'd look for the best warfighter in the world. I'd look for the best guy that can fight. You ought not to think that you can develop somebody that's got this political-military experience that can't go quickly to the next step. I want a warrior. I'll train him to the mission. We have no hostile deaths in Bosnia because we have warriors who are able to understand the next step.'[92] Army Chief of Staff General Denis Reimer noted of the initial American deployment into Bosnia that 'they watched how we came across. They knew we lead with the tanks. They knew we lead with the soldiers who had their flak vests on and their Kevlars buckled and it was a new way of doing business.' Reimer related that senior leaders in the Hungarian military had told him that '"there's a lot of forces in Bosnia, but there's only one Army, the U.S. Army" … and

[90] Graeme Hazlewood, 'RE: This and That', n.d., Moskos Papers.
[91] Larry Ellis, 'Comments', n.d., Moskos Papers.
[92] Olsen and Davis, 'Training U.S. Army Officers for Peace Operations: Lessons from Bosnia', 7.

Figure 3.2 An M1A1 Abrams tank from the 1st Armored Division crosses into Bosnia, 1995

that is terribly important and the way you deter war is you remain strong' (Figure 3.2).[93] In almost identical language, Brigadier General Stanley Cherrie reported that a Bosnian Corps commander told him that 'all my men out there are fighters, not yet soldiers. You Americans are soldiers. You all dress alike, you all have discipline, you have clean weapons at the ready, you always travel in four vehicle convoys, even your helicopters fly in formation. Soldiers do that and we notice it.'[94] For the US military leadership, being an effective soldier in this environment meant adhering strictly to traditional martial virtues such as discipline, virtues that were very much in tune with the self-image they had had before the Army became involved in these operations.

3.3   Peacekeeping and the Future of War

For some of the more radical internal critics of the late twentieth-century military, though, this approach was a deeply worrying one. Ralph Peters, a recently retired lieutenant colonel and now a media commentator, had,

[93] Denis J. Reimer, 'Address to the Adjutant General Association. U.S.', 8 September 1998, Denis J. Reimer Papers: 870-51 CSA, AHEC.
[94] Stanley F. Cherrie, 'Task Force Eagle', *Military Review* 77, no. 4 (August 1997): 72.

like some other neoconservatives, supported intervention in the Balkans and largely welcomed the US deployment to Bosnia, not because he was necessarily interested in remaking the Balkans, but because he felt these sorts of conflicts were the wave of the future and the US military needed to adapt to these missions sooner rather than later. Peters argued that 'an Army's peacetime mission is to acquire the skills and knowledge that enable it to win in war' and that Bosnia was an ideal learning environment. He argued, like Hazlewood, that US leaders in Bosnia were simply interested in bringing their troops home without taking any casualties and that all other priorities were a distant second to this; the shadow of Vietnam still hung over Army generals.

For Peters, this was a sign not only of a caution born of bitter experience in Indochina and Somalia, but a sign of a larger moral decay. He wrote that 'most Americans today – including soldiers – have lived incredibly sheltered lives by global or historical standards. We must expose them to foreign reality ... the notion of sheltering our soldiers from the big, bad world is a politically correct absurdism.'[95] Writing to Charles Moskos, he argued that soldiers needed to take risks in Bosnia to learn from the experience: 'now I'm not advocating sending them out to look for trouble ... but I do argue that they should get a good look at the destruction, the efforts to reconstruct communities, the "structures of everyday life" ... and a sense of who they might have to fight, of who "those people" are'. Peters was quite sanguine about the risks that might entail, claiming that 'frankly, if an officer or two were assassinated or kidnapped, that's the price of doing business. If that sounds coldblooded, I suggest the perception tells us how far we have come from the realities of military service.'[96] He saw no such courage in Bosnia and decried an Army that suffered from 'that worst of all military diseases, the fear of making a mistake'. He complained to Moskos that 'we have the vision of spoiled children' and that 'since we have entered a new age of an American expeditionary military, I suggest that, if we leave the Balkans without any broad, deep understanding of the place, we will have failed as a military'.[97]

Peters' vision of future war was a dark one. Laying it out in a series of articles in *Parameters*, he argued that while the USA would have no peer competitors for a decade, wars would come from 'collective emotions, sub-state interests, and systemic collapse' and 'there will be no peace. At any given moment for the rest of our lifetimes, there will be multiple

---

[95] Ralph Peters to Charles Moskos, 'Your Task Force Eagle Report', December 1998, Moskos Papers.
[96] Ralph Peters to Charles Moskos.
[97] Ralph Peters to Charles Moskos.

conflicts in mutating forms around the globe.' In this environment, the role of the US armed forces would be 'to keep the world safe for our economy and open to our cultural assault. To those ends, we will do a fair amount of killing.'[98] While his interventionism was far removed from the caution of senior Army leaders, he did share their (unrealised) ideas about empowering junior ranks to make decisions in these complex environments. For Peters, transformation into a force capable of operating in this new world would come from below. He claimed that 'even as traditionalists resist the reformation of the force, the "anarchy" of lieutenants is shaping the Army of tomorrow. Battalion commanders do not understand what their lieutenants are up to, and generals would not be able to sleep at night if they knew what the battalion commanders know.'[99]

Peters believed that the worldwide presence of the US military was an effective deterrent and was exuberant about the possibilities of combining Hollywood and the US military to great effect:

Everybody is afraid of us. They really believe we can do all the stuff in the movies. If the Trojans 'saw' Athena guiding the Greeks in battle, then the Iraqis saw Luke Skywalker precede McCaffrey's tanks. Our unconscious alliance of culture with killing power is a combat multiplier no government, including our own, could design or afford. We are magic. And we're going to keep it that way.[100]

This hegemony could be maintained not only by learning about contemporary substate conflict in the Balkans but by practising it at home. In one of his *Parameters* articles, he argued that cities were the most likely battlefields of the future and that the most effective way to train for urban combat would be for the US military to use the impoverished areas of major American cities as training grounds. In Peters' telling, 'city and state governments would likely compete to gain a U.S. Army (and Marine) presence, since it would bring money, jobs, and development – as well as a measure of social discipline'.[101] For Peters, Tuzla and the South Side of Chicago alike were excellent opportunities for American soldiers to prepare themselves for future wars, although he worried that in the case of Tuzla, this opportunity was being missed by an overly cautious and overly conservative US military that had not yet managed to grasp the extent of the transformation wrought by the end of the Cold War. Other neoconservatives had similar ideas, even if they

---

[98] Ralph Peters, 'Constant Conflict', *Parameters: Journal of the US Army War College*, Summer 1997, 4–14.

[99] Peters.

[100] Peters.

[101] Ralph Peters, 'Our Soldiers, Their Cities', *Parameters: Journal of the US Army War College*, Spring 1996, 43–50.

put their arguments in less strident terms. Alvin Bernstein, writing in the *Weekly Standard*, argued that 'carrying out these kinds of operations is part of what it means to be a superpower in today's world, and we cannot click our heels three times and simply wish away these messier aspects of global leadership'.[102] For Bernstein, there was an urgent need to reorient the US military towards these new missions while still retaining the ability to fight conventional wars.

Generally though, while most conservatives may have shared Peters' concerns about American society, they were much less supportive of peacekeeping missions.[103] Charles Krauthammer – hardly a dove given that he was the author of the *Foreign Affairs* article that had proclaimed the 'unipolar moment' – noted that the ultimate objective of US peacekeepers in Haiti was simply not getting shot.[104] For Krauthammer, this was 'as insane a purpose as sending American Marines in 1982 to sit in Beirut airport. If we are not sending the military to pacify, control and remake countries, as we did after the Second World War, why in God's name are we there? If "force protection is job one", it is a job best done at Fort Dix, New Jersey.'[105] Like Peters, he thought the peacekeeping status quo of the late 1990s was an absurdity, but unlike Peters, he thought that withdrawal from such operations, not deeper engagement, was the best solution. The key concern for Krauthammer and other critics, and indeed senior Army leaders, was the extent to which such missions atrophied warfighting skills. During the 2000 presidential election campaign, Republican candidate George W. Bush ran on a platform of global retrenchment and disengagement from peacekeeping while his foreign policy advisor Condoleezza Rice argued that 'carrying out civil administration and police functions is simply going to degrade the American capability to do the things America has to do. We don't need to have the 82nd Airborne escorting kids to kindergarten.'[106]

In a similar vein, Krauthammer decried 'Clintonian do-goodism' in his *Washington Post* column and claimed that 'the world's sole superpower

[102] Alvin H. Bernstein, 'The Truth about Peacekeeping', *Weekly Standard*, 22 September 1997, www.weeklystandard.com/the-truth-about-peacekeeping/article/10209.

[103] For a detailed discussion of neoconservative debates on US involvement in peacekeeping missions, especially in the Balkans, see Maria Ryan, *Neoconservatism and the New American Century* (Basingstoke and New York: Palgrave Macmillan, 2010).

[104] Charles Krauthammer, 'The Unipolar Moment', *Foreign Affairs* 70, no. 1 (1990): 23–33.

[105] Charles Krauthammer, 'The Short, Unhappy Life of Humanitarian War', *The National Interest; Washington*, Fall 1999, 8.

[106] Michael R. Gordon, 'The 2000 Campaign: The Military; Bush Would Stop U.S. Peacekeeping In Balkan Fights', *New York Times*, 21 October 2000, http://query .nytimes.com/gst/fullpage.html?res=9C07E4DE1E3EF932A15753C1A9669C8B63& sec=&spon=&pagewanted=1.

has no business squandering its resources and diluting its military doing police work and hand-holding in places like Haiti, Bosnia and Kosovo'. For Krauthammer, 'Americans make lousy peacekeepers – not because they are not great soldiers but precisely because they are .... Many nations can do police work; only we can drop thousand-pound bombs with the precision of a medieval archer.'[107] Echoing fellow neoconservative Robert Kagan's argument that there had been a sharp divergence between the United States and Europe in recent years and that Europeans were from 'Venus' and Americans from 'Mars', Krauthammer closed his column by declaring 'we fight the wars. Our friends should patrol the peace.'[108] In this vision of contemporary operations, soldiering and peacekeeping were inherently antithetical activities.

Such sentiments appeared regularly in the syndicated columns of David Hackworth. Hackworth, a former US Army colonel and Korea and Vietnam veteran, was generally sceptical of the value of such missions, but he also thought that the Pentagon needed to be able to fight both high-tech and low-tech war. While accepting that more Somalias and more Bosnias lay in the future, he worried that peacekeeping missions overstretched the US military and degraded soldiers' fighting abilities, arguing that 'here we are taking a well-trained prizefighter and putting him on a line to hand out chow at the Salvation Army .... We have got our warrior built up to fight wars, but he is doing missions where he has to pull his punch – and this pulls all his muscles.'[109] Hackworth argued that 'if our leaders don't soon get their priorities straight and stop mirroring the Roman Empire, our valiant warriors will again pay the grim price for not being ready when the war whistle blows'.[110] A frequent theme of Hackworth's columns on the US military in the 1990s was corruption and imperial overstretch; he referred to the Pentagon bureaucracy as the 'perfumed princes' whose self-interested behaviour undermined the 'romping, stomping warriors' and 'real studs' that he so admired.[111] The solution was to empower the tough, smart warriors

---

[107] Charles Krauthammer, 'We Don't Peacekeep', *Washington Post*, 18 December 2001, www.washingtonpost.com/archive/opinions/2001/12/18/we-dont-peacekeep/45dd2154-c2ac-474a-a9ca-03499d0a0c0e/.

[108] Robert Kagan, *Of Paradise and Power: America and Europe in the New World Order* (New York: Vintage, 2004).

[109] David H. Hackworth, *Hazardous Duty* (New York: William Morrow Paperbacks, 1997), 283.

[110] David H. Hackworth, 'What Got the Roman Empire Is About to Get Us', accessed 21 July 2017, www.hackworth.com/22jun99.html.

[111] Hackworth's description of a drinking session with a team of US Navy SEALs is typical of his writing: 'There is no better company than these rare and unique fighting men. Being in the vicinity of their testosterone levels would even recharge the batteries of a eunuch.' Hackworth, *Hazardous Duty*, 255.

that he saw at the junior levels of the armed forces: the highly educated soldiers who could participate in Charles Krulak's 'three block war' but who were also tough enough to fight North Korea if needs be.

While Hackworth respected the difficulties with which peacekeeping missions presented soldiers and he certainly didn't view them as beneath American capabilities the same way that Krauthammer did, he did see these deployments as a symptom of a broader malaise in US foreign policy: 'charity begins at home. We need to take care of America first, deal with our own domestic problems, before we continue rushing off to try to solve every global disaster because bleeding hearts, unmindful of the consequences, watch the tube and decide "America should do something."' For Hackworth, all of this was a distraction from the true purpose of the American military, which was simply to 'defend America'.[112]

Hackworth's critique went further than the standard conservative unease with peacekeeping in that he looked for structural explanations for this malaise and found them in the All-Volunteer Force. He pointed to Imperial Rome and argued that 'the past shows states like Rome that depended on mercenaries eventually bellied up'. By contrast, for Hackworth, the citizen-soldiers of the Early Republic were willing to push back against foolish decisions and helped to both prevent corruption and to steer strategy in a useful way. He claimed that 'if an order was bullshit, the troops sounded off: "Look, Captain, this doesn't make a damned bit of sense." We had a democratic army, not a Prussian military machine that clicks heels to all orders right or wrong.' This more democratic force was a more effective one, because 'back then the tooth was long and sharp and could bite like hell and inflict great pain on our enemies. There was little tail.' Since then, the US military had been in decline, as it attracted more and more 'perfumed princes' and failed to reward its warriors. Hackworth put this in explicitly emasculating terms when he argued that 'from 1776 to now we've grown an incredible bureaucratic tail and the teeth have been getting smaller and smaller. If we keep going this way, we will end up trying to gum our future enemies to death.'[113]

Air Force Colonel Charles Dunlap shared Hackworth's disquiet and saw a negative feedback loop where a more isolated military was taking on more and more non-traditional missions that took it further and further away from its proper role. Dunlap saw the increase in non-traditional missions as a threat to democracy. Counter-drug operations, hurricane relief, civil affairs operations, peacekeeping missions and any

---

[112] Hackworth, 284.
[113] Hackworth, 305.

relationship with civilian law enforcement were all things that the military should not be doing. In Dunlap's eyes, the only reason the US military was being given these tasks was because of the high esteem in which the military was now held as an American institution.[114] The military's perceived ability to solve any problem thrown at it meant that the Army was not only losing combat skills but was becoming more and more of a politicised organisation. Indeed, Dunlap's most famous piece of writing was another work of fiction, an article entitled 'The Origins of the Military Coup of 2012', a catastrophe for which he blamed the post–Cold War trend towards peacekeeping and OOTW.[115] The stakes for critics such as Hackworth and Dunlap were incredibly high: if the Army did not rethink its involvement in peacekeeping operations, then the foundations of civil–military relations and ultimately the health of American democracy were under threat.

It is no surprise that Dunlap and Hackworth's critique of peacekeeping missions resonated with the American far right. White power militia groups promoted conspiracy theories about a 'New World Order' where an emerging totalitarian world government was engineering a takeover of the United States by the United Nations, resuscitating narratives promoted by conservative organisations such as the John Birch Society during the Cold War.[116] Contemporary anxieties about this 'new world order' often took the form of paranoia about UN 'black helicopters' spying on US citizens and a US military that was being unwittingly co-opted into the command structures of this shadowy and sinister organisation.[117] This rhetoric sometimes had an effect on the ranks, as could be seen in October 1995: American soldiers from 1/15 Infantry, 3rd Infantry Division formed up in their barracks in Schweinfurt, Germany, in preparation for a peacekeeping deployment to the Former Yugoslav Republic of Macedonia. On the morning of 10 October the 550 troops scheduled to deploy as part of Task Force Able Sentry were arrayed on the parade square, awaiting a uniform inspection. One soldier, 22-year-old Specialist Michael New, stood out in the ranks as he was the only one

---

[114] For more on the issue of esteem, see David Fitzgerald, 'Support the Troops: Gulf War Homecomings and a New Politics of Military Celebration', *Modern American History* 2, no. 1 (March 2019): 1–22.

[115] Charles Dunlap, *The Origins of the American Military Coup of 2012* (Washington, DC: National Defense University National War College, 1992).

[116] Edward H. Miller, *A Conspiratorial Life: Robert Welch, the John Birch Society, and the Revolution of American Conservatism* (Chicago: University of Chicago Press, 2022); D. J. Mulloy, *The World of the John Birch Society: Conspiracy, Conservatism, and the Cold War* (Nashville: Vanderbilt University Press, 2014).

[117] Kathleen Belew, *Bring the War Home: The White Power Movement and Paramilitary America* (Cambridge, MA: Harvard University Press, 2018), 193–4.

not wearing the blue beret and the UN insignia. New was immediately dismissed from the parade and subsequently charged with disobeying a lawful order. His chain of command had been anticipating this disobedience, as he had penned a letter to his commander explaining his stance once he heard in August 1995 that the unit was deploying to Macedonia, and, more significantly, given an interview to the far-right publication the *New American* that had been published on 2 October.[118] His father had also posted about the situation on an internet bulletin board back in the United States, prompting a flood of mail from conservative activists supporting New's actions.[119]

New ultimately received a dishonourable discharge from the military, which made his case a conservative *cause célèbre*.[120] The incident provided fuel for talk radio hosts who believed that the UN was undermining US sovereignty, while candidates running in the 1996 Republican presidential primary repeatedly referenced the young soldier's plight in their campaign speeches.[121] One hundred members of Congress co-sponsored legislation that would prohibit a president from ordering US soldiers to wear UN insignia. Republican House Majority Whip Rep. Tom DeLay argued that 'forcing soldiers to wear the uniform of the United Nations effectively asks the soldier to serve another power. No American soldier should be put in Michael New's position – forced to choose allegiances between the United States and the United Nations.'[122]

This wave of support allowed New to pursue a series of legal appeals against his dismissal, which ran for well over a decade and only ended in 2007 when the US Supreme Court refused to hear the case, the final defeat in a streak of unsuccessful suits against the Army. New's defence rested on a series of assertions about the Army's uniform regulations, but also on the more consequential issue of whether the president had

---

[118] 'I Am Not a UN Soldier', *The New American*, 2 October 1995. The case had also been the subject of an article in a local North Carolina newspaper in mid-September. Dennis Cuddy, 'The Case for Army Specialist New', *Fayetteville Observer-Times*, 14 September 1995.

[119] Alan Cowell, 'G.I. Gets Support for Shunning U.N. Insignia', *New York Times*, 24 November 1995, www.nytimes.com/1995/11/24/world/gi-gets-support-for-shunning-un-insignia.html.

[120] 'U.S. Convicts G.I. Who Refused to Serve Under U.N. in Balkans', *New York Times*, 25 January 1996, www.nytimes.com/1996/01/25/world/us-convicts-gi-who-refused-to-serve-under-un-in-balkans.html.

[121] Marc Fisher, 'War and Peacekeeping', *Washington Post*, 4 March 1996, www.washingtonpost.com/archive/lifestyle/1996/03/04/war-and-peacekeeping/adfd68e7-9be7-4e16-94fb-ea566ec3fd03/.

[122] Imre Karacs, 'U.S. Medic Who Would Not Wear the Blue Beret Goes on Trial', *The Independent*, 18 November 1995, www.independent.co.uk/news/world/us-medic-who-would-not-wear-the-blue-beret-goes-on-trial-1582468.html.

the authority to put soldiers under the operational control of foreign officers (or, in the defence team's telling, in a non-American chain of command).[123] At the heart of the issue lay questions of sovereignty but also questions surrounding the ambiguity of these missions. If captured by armed actors, would New be a prisoner of war and thus entitled to Geneva Convention protections, or something else? New argued that President Clinton was effectively ordering him into a situation that might end in combat without following the correct legal procedures that should pertain to such risky missions.[124] His legal team's arguments found no purchase with the various judges that they appeared before, but they did capture a segment of the public imagination, revealing a deep-seated apprehension about the nature of such deployments. The New case was very straightforward as a matter of law, since there was clearly nothing unlawful about the order to don UN insignia, but the outsized attention it received from politicians, media figures, activists and members of the public demonstrates that peacekeeping missions were the site of fierce political contestation in the 1990s United States.

3.4   Citizen-Soldiers and Peacekeeping

Other observers recognised that the need for proficiency in both peacekeeping and conventional warfare posed challenges for Army capabilities and called into question the Army's role in a post–Cold War world, even if they understood the problem in less drastic terms. However, unlike Dunlap and Hackworth, they saw peacekeeping operations not as a threat to civil–military relations but as an opportunity to remake the All-Volunteer Force. Crucial to this effort was the question of who should serve on such operations. Not only did most US soldiers surveyed by military sociologists agree that the job was better suited to Military Police than infantry, but many felt that reserve forces, with their mix of civilian skill sets and a mentality that was often less aggressive than their Active Component counterparts, would be ideal for peacekeeping operations. Senior officers tended to prefer reserve forces for such missions too, although not necessarily due to any perceived suitability for peacekeeping. Rather, the Army had been greatly reduced in size since the

---

[123] Robert S. Winner, 'Spc. Michael New v. William Perry, Secretary of Defense: The Constitutionality of U.S. Forces Serving under U.N. Command', *DePaul Digest of International Law* 30, no. 3 (Spring 1997), www.kentlaw.edu/academics/courses/admin-perritt/winner.htm.

[124] New maintains a website that includes court documents that give an extensive accounting of the case. 'United States v. Michael G. New: Legal Documents', MikeNew.com, accessed 8 December 2020, www.mikenew.com/courtdocs.html.

end of the Cold War and a stretched force leaned heavily on its Reserve Component as the tempo of deployments increased. The 1995 NMS made this policy clear when it stated that 'reserve component elements will take on increased responsibility for participating in and supporting peacekeeping missions'.[125]

By 1998, one-third of the American soldiers in Bosnia were reservists or National Guardsmen, most of them on a compulsory deployment. Deputy Commander of Forces Command Brigadier General Pat O'Neal told the *New York Times* that, unlike the Cold War years, 'everyone is in the pool ... they are all eligible to go. That's the change.'[126] Due to the reforms of the 1970s, reservists and National Guardsmen tended to hold appointments in areas that were lightly staffed but critical for peacekeeping, such as civil affairs, public affairs, psychological operations, water purification and medical units.[127] Some within the Department of Defense also argued that, contrary to worries about peacekeeping operations' negative effects on readiness, these deployments could actually *increase* Reserve Component readiness, since these part-time units would be placed on a full-time footing for the duration of the deployment.[128] Reserve units allowed the Army to meet the needs of peacekeeping missions without having to confront broader questions about restructuring the Active Component to face these new challenges.

Indeed, even as the large-scale deployment of US forces on peacekeeping missions was in its early days, the Army experimented with deploying reserve forces on a large scale by sending a battalion of military observers, composed largely of reservist volunteers, to the peacekeeping mission in the Sinai. Writing to Army Chief of Staff General Gordon R. Sullivan, Charles Moskos argued that there was a strong political as well as military rationale for such a force. For Moskos, this 'rainbow battalion' would connect the mission to a broader cross-section of the American people, it would increase political support for such missions because it enhanced the role of the National Guard (an organisation beloved

---

[125] Shalikashvili, 'National Military Strategy of the United States', 9.
[126] Mike O'Connor, 'A Downsized Army Leans on Reserves for Duty in Bosnia', *New York Times*, 25 May 1998, www.nytimes.com/1998/05/25/world/a-downsized-army-leans-on-reserves-for-duty-in-bosnia.html.
[127] Jennifer M. Taw, David Persselin and Maren Leed, 'Meeting Peace Operations' Requirements While Maintaining MTW Readiness' (Santa Monica, CA: RAND Corporation, 1998), 20, www.dtic.mil/docs/citations/ADA342429.
[128] J. T. Ford, S. H. Sternlieb and M. E. Guran, 'Peace Operations: Effect of Training, Equipment, and Other Factors on Unit Capability' (Washington, DC: General Accounting Office, 1995), 48–9, www.dtic.mil/docs/citations/ADA344826.

of many in Congress) and, perhaps most importantly, 'in the event of casualties, the political fallout will be less for a dedicated battalion of "double volunteers" than for a standard ... unit'.[129] For proponents of such missions, the more diverse the unit deployed on peacekeeping operations, the more operationally effective and politically viable these missions would be.

The diversity of such 'rainbow battalions' had a usefulness beyond increasing political support for such operations. Many proponents took a more idealistic view of peacekeeping operations and the role of individual soldiers in such missions. For instance, Secretary of the Army Louis Caldera frequently emphasised the value of soldiers as ambassadors in his speeches and he argued that soldiers deployed on peacekeeping missions 'demonstrate our Nation's commitment to the principles of diversity and pluralism and the strength we derive from drawing on the talents of all our people'. For Caldera, this was 'a tremendously important message to send to places like Bosnia and Kosovo where people are having a hard time making a pluralistic society work'.[130]

The idea that American soldiers might serve as an example for others circulated within the Pentagon as early as 1992: Army Chief of Staff General Gordon R. Sullivan was surprised to learn that the Commonwealth of Independent States' (soon to be the Russian Federation) Minister for Defence Marshal Yevgeny Shaposhnikov had been speaking to retired American generals, requesting help in building 'a professional army ... like the American army'.[131] In response to Sullivan, Major General David C. Meade argued that 'in my view, an army very strongly reflects its society. The Soviet communist society was brutal, repressive, catered to political elites, ignored the rule of law, limited initiative, and discriminated against minorities', characteristics shared by its army. Meade noted that 'this communist society has disintegrated, and its army is shredding away with substantial desertions and poor morale. It must change and if we are fortunate, we can help to change it in a manner that will benefit us.'[132] Throughout the decade, Army leaders pointed to joint deployments with the Russians on peacekeeping

[129] Charles C. Moskos, 'Memorandum for Gordon R. Sullivan: Dedicated "Rainbow" Battalion for Peacekeeping Missions', 2 November 1993, Moskos Papers.
[130] Louis Caldera, 'Remarks by Honorable Louis Caldera, Comstock Club, Sacramento, California', 24 February 2000, Louis Caldera Collection, Box 10, Folder 2, AHEC.
[131] Gordon R. Sullivan, 'Memorandum', 2 February 1992, Gordon R. Sullivan Papers: CSA Memorandums, February 1992, AHEC.
[132] David C. Meade, 'Note for General Sullivan: Helping the CIS/Russian Army', 7 February 1992, Gordon R. Sullivan Papers: CSA Memorandums, February 1992, AHEC.

missions as an example of the potential for military-to-military contacts to shape international relations more broadly.[133]

Reservists played a central role in this idea of the American soldier as role model. In speeches on soldier-to-soldier engagement, Caldera frequently invoked both the importance of civilian control of the military and the ideal of the citizen-soldier, which for him was embodied in the National Guard. The Guard had, in fact, established partnership pro-grammes with former Warsaw Pact nations, which Army officers saw as creating 'ties between citizen soldiers who can show foreign armies not only how a professional military works in a democratic society, but how the civil fabric of America works and they can take those lessons back to their own countries'.[134] Reservists and Guardsmen therefore were useful in a number of ways in peacekeeping missions: they took the pressure off Active Component units struggling with a high tempo of deployments; they often provided skill sets that were in short supply; and more broadly, they offered both a connection with the American public and a model for democratic military service to foreign audiences. US soldiers, therefore, served as role models to the populations of the countries to which they deployed as well as the other militaries they deployed alongside.

Charles Moskos believed that not only were these missions particularly suited to reservists, but that they could be used as a means through which to reintroduce the ideals of the citizen-soldiers to both the Army and American society at large. Since the advent of the All-Volunteer Force, Moskos had worried about the changing demographics of the Army, with fewer urban, middle-class college students interested in joining and the burden of service therefore falling on the rural and urban working class and military families. Moskos argued that peacekeeping missions were ideal ways to attract college graduates in search of adventure, as such mis-sions did not necessarily require the sorts of skills that would necessitate lengthy technical training. Moskos proposed a new form of short-term enlistment, eighteen months to two years in length, with basic and then mission-specific training followed by a six-month deployment overseas before a return to the United States and civilian life. In the absence of any realistic hope of reinstituting the draft, Moskos made the case for a short-service enlistment repeatedly throughout the decade (and indeed right up

---

[133] Russian peacekeeping deployments were linked more to national security than to a desire to further cooperation with western powers. See S. Neil MacFarlane and Albrecht Schnabel, 'Russia's Approach to Peacekeeping', *International Journal* 50, no. 2 (1995): 294–324.

[134] William Morgan, 'Info Received from COL William Morgan, DUSA-IA', 16 February 2000, Louis Caldera Collection, Box 10, Folder 2, AHEC.

until his death in 2008) in correspondence with politicians and generals and in op-eds for national newspapers, where he published articles with such titles such as 'From College to Kosovo'.[135]

Ultimately, Moskos was far more sanguine about US involvement in peacekeeping missions than many observers; his surveys of personnel deployed on such missions had demonstrated that most were able to reconcile their identity as soldiers with the tasks of peacekeeping. Nonetheless, that his response to concerns about such deployments was one that sought to significantly change the makeup of the All-Volunteer Force indicates that Moskos had his own anxieties about the status of the Army in a time of peace. For Moskos, peacekeeping operations represented an opportunity to restore and enrich the connection between civilians and soldiers. By using reservists and short-term enlistees for these deployments, the Army could both reinforce the ideal of the citizen-soldier and become more operationally effective. Much as these missions encouraged neoconservatives such as Ralph Peters to push the Army to adapt itself to fight 'small wars', Moskos' call to broaden the recruiting pool was as much about broader visions about the role and status of the organisation as it was about efficacy in peacekeeping operations. As we will see in Chapter 4, questions about recruiting only become more acute by the end of the decade.

3.5   Conclusion

The fact that Moskos thought to use peacekeeping deployments as an opportunity to revisit something as fundamental as the All-Volunteer Force speaks to the potential that these missions had for unsettling basic assumptions about the Army's purpose. Peacekeeping missions may have been a central, if sometimes unwanted, concern of the Army in the 1990s, but they also exposed deeper fissures within the Army and broader society about the organisation's proper role and the sort of attributes that American soldiers would need in the twenty-first century. Army leaders and personnel deployed on peacekeeping operations struggled to articulate which martial values best applied to peacekeeping. Did being tough mean wearing body armour and having an alert posture on patrols, or an inclination to take risks and engage with locals? Did it mean restraint when it came to the use of force or a willingness to use violence when the situation called for it? How one answered those questions determined views regarding the sort of soldiers that would be needed for these missions.

For their part, Army leaders found themselves essentially unable to answer these questions. Their public rhetoric, their reluctance to adapt

---

[135] Charles Moskos, 'From College to Kosovo', *Wall Street Journal*, 25 August 2000.

force structures for these missions, the relative paucity of doctrine and the ad hoc and 'just-in-time' nature of pre-deployment training indicated an unease with these missions, but they did accept that peacekeeping deployments were likely to be more common in the future and commissioned research to evaluate how best to conduct them. Studies of soldiers serving on peacekeeping operations indicated that they felt more ambivalence than hostility towards this work, reflecting a similar note of equivocation in the Army's professional journals. In the absence of a clear prioritisation of the immediate demands of peacekeeping over the long-term need to train for conventional warfare, Army leaders preferred instead to rely on the ingenuity and adaptability of their soldiers and hoped that they would be able to successfully make their way through this ambiguity.

Critics outside of the military also focused on the impact of peacekeeping operations on the American soldier, although their views radically diverged depending on their standpoint on such interventions and their own politics. For Peters and other interventionists, the dilemmas of peacekeeping demonstrated a need to instil a warrior ethos into professionals, who would learn invaluable 'soft skills' from these missions that could be applied in more war-like scenarios in the future. The danger for Peters was political correctness and a lack of courage on the part of military leaders. Other conservatives, such as Dunlap, thought that not only did a focus on these 'soft skills' degrade important military capabilities, but that this 'mission creep' risked a dangerous politicisation of the US military as they increasingly took on roles that were rightly civilian in nature. Most ambitious of all was the project of liberal nationalists such as Charles Moskos to use peacekeeping missions as an opportunity to remake the Army's identity into a more democratic one. The proposals to use more Reserve and National Guard forces and to encourage short-term enlistments to attract more middle-class college graduates clearly demonstrated a shared concern with Dunlap about a growing gap between the military and civilians, but also proposed a more creative solution, albeit one that was never adopted.

Clearly, even in this relatively peaceful era, there were deep undercurrents of anxiety both within and outside the Army about the role of the force in a changing world and about the qualities that would be needed by American soldiers. The ongoing debates about peacekeeping spoke to a wider identity crisis within the Army. This crisis played itself out across multiple deployments, and indeed continued beyond the decade and up until the attacks of 11 September 2001, changed the conversation. Ultimately though, no one was able to define a clear vision for US involvement in peacekeeping missions, and a series of Army leaders were unable to use these debates over peacekeeping to rearticulate what American soldiers would be expected to do in a post–Cold War world.

4   Downsizing, Recruiting and Debates over Military Service

On 5 May 1998, Congressman Ike Skelton rose to address the House of Representatives. Recalling his experiences visiting US peacekeepers in Skopje, Macedonia, Skelton spoke of the conversations he had with soldiers at 'one of the far outposts of Americans keeping watch' and his worries about what he saw on his trip. For Skelton, these peacekeepers were 'the finest that we have ever had and yet the ironic and sad situation in which we find ourselves is that we are not able to support them as they should be'.[1] While not questioning the deployment to the Balkans, he worried that there were too few soldiers to meet the demands of these missions and that the Department of Defense and the nation were not doing enough to take care of them and their families. Skelton partly blamed the Army for this state of affairs, and he had previously written to Army Chief of Staff General Dennis Reimer to complain about what he saw as the serious danger of individual and organisational burnout caused by the high tempo of operations around the world.[2] Soldiers were simply being asked to deploy too frequently and on too many missions. More fundamentally though, Skelton thought that the root of this problem was the gap between resources and mission requirements caused by a more serious rift: between American society and its military. He argued that 'when the draft was in force, nearly every family had some experience with someone wearing a uniform', whereas now, 'fewer and fewer young people coming from fewer and fewer families across our country' served in the military and this meant that fewer Americans were writing to their Member of Congress to ask them to act on matters such as military pay, welfare and appropriations for training, equipment and deployments. Speaking of the broader American public, Skelton declared,

---

[1] Ike Skelton, 'Speaking on Issues Related to National Security' (105th Congress, 2nd Session: Congressional Record – Vol.144, No.54 – Daily Edition, 5 May 1998), H2784, www.congress.gov/congressional-record/volume-144/house-section/page/H2784.

[2] Ike Skelton, 'Letter to Dennis Reimer', 21 January 1998, Dennis J. Reimer Papers: General Organization and Functions Correspondence Files, Box 14, January–March 1998, AHEC.

'I know their heart is with the young people in uniform, but out of sight, out of mind'.[3]

Skelton's address went down well with Army leadership. Despite Skelton's disagreements with Reimer over operational tempo, Reimer sent him a note thanking him for the speech and telling him that 'as usual, you are right on target'.[4] Even if Skelton had been critical of the Army, Reimer deeply appreciated his core message about a growing gap between civilians and the military. Indeed, Skelton's speech hit upon some of the key problems that Army leaders wrestled with as they reshaped the force after the end of the Cold War. If downsizing inevitably put a strain on the Army's ability to carry out the increasingly broad range of missions it was tasked with, it also reopened a debate about exactly what sort of relationship it should have with civilian society and from where it should draw its soldiers.

This debate intersected in important ways with broader questions about the Army's post–Cold War identity and purpose, but if arguments over gender and sexuality and peacekeeping missions focused primarily on the soldier and only secondarily on the Army's relationship with civilian society, here the institution was grappling with a slightly different question where that order was reversed. When it came to recruiting and retention, Army leaders had to first and foremost think about the distance between the organisation and its pool of potential recruits, as well as the challenges that a strong economy posed to retention in a force being buffeted by a prolonged post–Cold War drawdown.

Three related trends meant that the gap between the Army and civilian society remained a subject of concern throughout the 1990s, despite widespread public admiration for the military. First, the drawdown saw the Army turn inwards to a degree, as it managed the shift from a force that was forward-deployed overseas to a smaller force primarily based in the continental United States on fewer but larger bases. As the Army's numbers fell and the overseas missions it deployed on increased, soldiers and their families suffered from the increase in operational tempo and the Army struggled to retain personnel, while this tempo and the diminished number of bases meant that they had less contact with the civilian world.

Second, by the end of the decade, the Army was failing to meet its recruiting targets, prompting widespread soul-searching about the strength of the All-Volunteer Force and its relationship with broader

---

[3] Skelton, 'Speaking on Issues Related to National Security', H2784.
[4] Dennis J. Reimer, 'Note to Ike Skelton', 25 May 1998, Denis J. Reimer Papers: General Management Correspondence Files: Box 11: May 1998 [2 of 2], AHEC.

American society. Policymakers, Army leaders and outside commentators all talked about the need for the Army to articulate its purpose more clearly in this new world, and many turned to nostalgic retellings of World War II to promote citizen-soldier ideals that might reinvigorate the connection between the Army and the American people. These appeals remained largely rhetorical though, with more radical proposals to rethink Army enlistment strategy and to focus on bringing in more college graduates for short-service tours largely falling on deaf ears.

The third and final way in which the Army's relationship with broader society was put under strain in this decade was the growing tension between the Army's leadership and its Reserve Component. These part-time soldiers were repeatedly celebrated as embodying the ideals of the citizen-soldier, yet they suffered heavily in the drawdown, and by the end of the decade many were questioning what sort of role the bulk of the Reserve Component might play in an expeditionary Army. Thus, the tensions between the twin ideals of the 'citizen-soldier' and the 'profession of arms' were heightened after the end of the Cold War, as the Army's leadership struggled to rethink the nature of military service while managing a large-scale drawdown from their 1980s peak.

4.1   Managing the Drawdown

Speaking to a group of NCOs at the Aberdeen Proving Ground in February 1997, Reimer talked about the changes wrought upon the Army by the end of the Cold War. After asking his audience how many of them were serving in the Army when the Berlin Wall came down, he reflected, 'I don't know about you, but I certainly underestimated the impact of that event, and we knew that something significant had changed. Something significant had happened, but I can tell you that I had no idea looking back on it, the significance, the total significance of that change.'[5] Certainly, the Army that Reimer now led was very different from the one in which he had served throughout the Cold War. Most fundamentally, it was a much smaller force: between 1990 and 1996, the Army lost 40 per cent of its budget and 35 per cent of its troop strength.[6] President George H. W. Bush had spoken about a 'peace dividend' at the end of the Cold War, given the reduction in global military tensions and the decreased need for military spending, and this slogan quickly became a

---

[5] Dennis J. Reimer, 'Speech at Aberdeen Proving Ground', 12 February 1997, Dennis J. Reimer Papers: 870-5f Organization Historical Files, VCSA, CGFORSCOM, CSA – Box 69 CSA, 12 February 1997, Drill Sergeants, Aberdeen Proving Ground, AHEC.

[6] David McCormick, *The Downsized Warrior: America's Army in Transition* (New York: NYU Press, 1997), 62–3.

bipartisan one.[7] Army leaders grudgingly accepted a series of cuts, beginning with the Bush administration's Base Force of 1989, and continuing the Clinton administration's 1993 Bottom-Up Review, with the cuts of the 1998 Quadrennial Defense Review yet to come. Between 1989 and 1996, the Active Component of the Army had gone from 769,741 to 491,000 soldiers while the strength of the Reserve Component, made up of both the Army National Guard and the Army Reserve, fell from 1,061,550 to 596,200.[8] By 1999, the Active Component had declined to 479,426 soldiers while the Reserve Component stood at 564,305.[9]

This decrease in numbers sparked unease within the Army about its trajectory. Speaking to a gathering at US Army Recruiting Command in 1992, Reimer, then the vice chief of staff, cautioned that 'that we must not gut our force and destroy our capability as we did in 1919, 1945, 1953, and 1972–3. Each of those retrenchments was paid for by the blood of our soldiers.'[10] Commentators warned about the need to prevent another 'Task Force Smith', referring to the poorly equipped and ill-fated task force rushed to Korea in 1950 to defend against Communist invasion. Writing in *Military Review*, retired Lieutenant General Johnny J. Johnston wrote that he wished to 'sound an alarm' and argued that T. R. Fehrenbach's history of Task Force Smith and the Korean War, *This Kind of War: A Study in Unpreparedness*, provided a template to understand what was happening with the post–Cold War drawdown.[11] Johnson's argument was an alarmist one and he claimed that 'the competition for government resources between a better life for the inner city versus trained and ready military forces is just beginning. A principal task that falls squarely on the shoulders of the Army's military and civilian leaders is to make sure, to make damned sure, that the condition of our forces never again approaches that of June 1950.'[12]

Apart from the occasional rhetorical allusion to Task Force Smith, the Army's leadership generally steered clear of this level of alarmism and

[7] Hobart Rowen, 'Making the "Peace Dividend" a Reality', *Washington Post*, 3 October 1991, www.washingtonpost.com/archive/opinions/1991/10/03/making-the-peace-dividend-a-reality/75d4ed2b-2f44-4830-ad87-3d1153913da6/.
[8] Connie L. Reeves, *Department of the Army Historical Summary: Fiscal Year 1996* (Washington, DC: Center of Military History, United States Army, 2002), 4; Vincent H. Demma, *Department of the Army Historical Summary: Fiscal Year 1989* (Washington, DC: Center of Military History, United States Army, 1998), 110, 141.
[9] Jeffrey A. Charlston, *Department of the Army Historical Summary: Fiscal Year 1999* (Washington, DC: Center of Military History, United States Army, 2006), 26.
[10] Dennis J. Reimer, 'VCS USAREC Remarks', 26 January 1992, Dennis J. Reimer Papers: 870-5f Organization Historical Files, VCSA, CGFORSCOM, CSA – 29 January 1992, USAREC Conference on Manpower and Recruiting Issues, AHEC.
[11] Johnny J. Johnson, 'Budgeting for Readiness', *Military Review* 73, no. 4 (April 1993): 28.
[12] Johnson, 29.

preferred instead to emphasise to the civilian leadership that the end of
the Cold War brought a level of geopolitical uncertainty that required
a strong standing army. Reimer's predecessor as chief of staff, General
Gordon R. Sullivan, had presided over many of those cuts and for Sullivan, as with the other service chiefs, the priority had been engaging
with the downsizing process to soften the blow as much as possible. For
all that military leaders complained in congressional testimony about
the extent of the cuts, they were aware that previous drawdowns had
been much more dramatic. To avoid bigger cuts, they needed to make
the case that geopolitical uncertainty meant that politicians should be
slow to take away capabilities that might be needed later. Major General
David Meade prepared talking points for Sullivan, arguing that 'we don't
know what "real" threats are and we're not going to know … you don't
want to peg the force based on the most likely threats only. We know
from our recent Panama and Persian Gulf experiences that major challenges can come unexpectedly.'[13] Indeed, for Sullivan, the key lesson of
the Gulf War was that 'we should not learn that victory was easy, and
we can now relax. The reverse is true … for in this uncertain world, we
can be sure of one thing: someday America will again call her Army and
expect us to fight and win. We must ensure that we are ready for that call
today and tomorrow.'[14]

The emphasis on uncertainty had two consequences for the Army's
force structure. First, it meant that Army leaders frequently referred to
the need for 'balance' in the force, and despite rhetoric about the possibilities of reshaping the armed forces for the twenty-first century, much
of the focus during the drawdown was on preserving the Army's existing
capabilities rather than building new ones. Writing to newly promoted
major generals in 1998, Reimer spoke about this need for balance and
argued that 'when you tinker with something as critical as the defense of
the United States of America you need to make sure you have it right.
When you try to convince a conservative organization like the U.S. Army
of the need to change, then you need to make sure you demonstrate that
change is better.'[15] Fundamentally, this meant that even as the Army
reduced in size from sixteen Active Component divisions to ten, the general mix of heavy and light forces stayed the same.

[13] David C. Meade, 'Aspin Dialogue', 12 February 1992, Gordon R. Sullivan Papers:
CSA Memorandums, February 1992, AHEC.
[14] Gordon R. Sullivan, 'Address to AUSA Winter Symposium, Orlando, Florida', 19
February 1992, Gordon R. Sullivan Papers: CSA Miscellaneous Papers, February
1992, AHEC.
[15] Dennis J. Reimer, 'Letter to Brig. Gen. John P. Abizaid', 10 May 1998, Dennis J.
Reimer Papers: 1mm Reading Files Box 6 May 1998 [1 of 2], AHEC.

The second consequence of uncertainty and the drawdown did, however, necessitate a change. The Army moved from being a forward-deployed force with significant numbers based in Europe to one based primarily in the United States that would deal in 'power projection' to get its forces overseas when it needed to. The US Army in Europe shrunk by 70 per cent between 1990 and 1999, going from 213,000 Army personnel to 62,000.[16] Sullivan reflected on how this changed his own role as chief of staff, arguing that prior to 1989 the Army chief of staff existed solely to supply troops to the Army in Europe, whereas after the Cold War the chief of staff's considerations were more global.[17] Despite the drawdown in Europe, the US Army in Europe's number of deployments dramatically increased. From 1945 to 1989, it had participated in only twenty-nine peacekeeping or humanitarian missions; however, from 1991 to 1999, it participated in over 100 such missions, marking a threefold increase in deployments with less than a third of the original number of personnel available to perform them.[18] Instead, units based in the United States were sent overseas to help fill the gaps. In many ways, the Army of the 1990s would be a smaller version of its Cold War self, but it was one that was being deployed from the continental United States on a diverse range of missions.

Given the decrease in the Army's strength and the increase in numbers of deployments, it was inevitable that the force would feel the strain of this new operational tempo. By the late 1990s, the *Army Times* and *Stars and Stripes* were referring to 'creeping hollowness' and running articles on how the Army's personnel shortage was placing the organisation under severe stress.[19] Units were capable of deploying overseas rapidly, but in order to do so they had to strip other units of their personnel in order to make up the numbers. One senior officer told an *Army Times* journalist that to send a brigade to Kuwait, the Army needed to divert inventory and personnel from a whole division and complained: 'I don't know how you can look at what's going on and say "Boy, I have 14 MP [Military Police] companies in Haiti, but it took 41 MP companies to keep them filled" ... I don't know you can say "boy, I put 20,000 guys in Bosnia for a year, but God, it took 60,000 guys to keep them there."' The 82nd

---

[16] Carl Castro and Amy Adler, 'OPTEMPO: Effects on Soldier and Unit Readiness', *Parameters: Journal of the US Army War College*, 29 (Autumn 1999): 86.

[17] Gordon R. Sullivan, 'Draft Letter to Brig. Gen. Harold W. Nelson', 10 March 1992, Gordon R. Sullivan Papers: CSA Letters, March 1992, AHEC.

[18] Castro and Adler, 'OPTEMPO', 86.

[19] Jon R. Anderson, 'Cohen Takes Aim at Readiness – Army Leaders Fear Return to Hollow Force Days', *Stars and Stripes – European Edition*, 5 May 1998; Sean D. Naylor, '"Creeping Hollowness": Is the Army Losing Its Edge?', *Army Times*, 3 February 1997.

Airborne Division had its training budget for 1997 cut by 20 per cent but elected to transfer the cuts to the barracks renovation budget rather than cut back on training. Speaking of the increased operational tempo, one colonel complained that '[o]ur attitude has always been, "We'll do the mission, even if it kills us" .... Well, it's beginning to kill us.'[20]

Reimer took issue with the findings of the *Army Times* article, particularly the use of the phrase 'hollow Army', which carried with it unwelcome connotations of the All-Volunteer Force's post-Vietnam nadir. In a memo to Chairman of the Joint Chiefs of Staff General Hugh Shelton, he argued, 'we understand the signs of a hollow Army and we are nowhere near that point at this time .... I have not and will not use that term'. Moreover, Reimer argued that those who complained to reporters may have given 'an accurate view from their perspective' but claimed that 'the risk we run is a prudent one' and that 'the Army is not overcommitted'. Reimer admitted that the tempo had increased for everyone and that 'battalion and brigade staffs are extremely busy' but argued that 'some of that is our own problem because we've never met a training event we didn't like. We're working hard to bring this in balance, but it will take us some time.'[21]

Congressional representatives and retired officers wrote to Reimer expressing their concern about the pace of deployments: retired Colonel Mason Young complained that one-sixth of soldiers were away from their families at Christmas on peacekeeping missions or 'feelgood' training missions, while Senator John McCain wrote to Reimer to express his concerns over readiness, arguing that the Army would struggle to respond to an unexpected threat.[22] Responding to McCain, Reimer was sympathetic to some of the congressional concern about the pace of operations, agreeing 'that today's forces are stretched and that we must take action now to address the emerging warning signs', but he still refused to accept a 'Hollow Force' narrative and argued that 'the Army is creating this demanding tempo' because of the need for 'tough, realistic training'.[23] For Reimer, to drop the training requirements that

---

[20] Naylor, '"Creeping Hollowness": Is the Army Losing Its Edge?'

[21] Dennis J. Reimer, 'Memorandum for the Chairman of the Joint Chiefs of Staff', 27 January 1997, Dennis J. Reimer Papers: General Management Correspondence Files – Box 8: January 1997, AHEC.

[22] Mason Young, 'Letter to Senator John Warner', 12 January 1998, Dennis J. Reimer Papers: 1mm Reading Files – Box 1: January 1997, AHEC; John S. McCain, 'Letter to General Dennis J. Reimer', 4 November 1998, Denis J. Reimer Papers: General Organization and Functions Correspondence Files – Box 15: August–December 1998, AHEC.

[23] Dennis J. Reimer, 'Letter to Senator John McCain', 2 December 1998, Denis J. Reimer Papers: General Organization and Functions Correspondence Files – Box 15: August–December 1998, AHEC.

were stressing an Army that had been reduced in strength by 34 per cent would be professional negligence.

That said, despite his frustrations at a discourse that compared the Army of the 1990s to that of the early 1970s, Reimer did recognise that the operational tempo had increased over the years and that personnel turbulence was proving a challenge amid the move from a forward-deployed force to one based in the continental United States. Speaking to defence writers later that year, he announced that he wanted to be able to guarantee deployed soldiers time at their home station and that the Army would give soldiers a month at home for every month they were deployed to places such as Bosnia.[24] Similarly, Army Vice Chief of Staff General Eric Shinseki acknowledged that the sheer volume of deployments influenced retention and attrition. Speaking at a conference on the Army's failure to meet its recruiting targets for 1998, Shinseki acknowledged the strain that these deployments put on soldiers and families, admitting that 'we move them around too much – they cannot have a "normal life"' and that 'because we are transitory, the community has no desire to meet our needs – we are not there long enough'.[25] Two years later, Commander of US Army Forces in Europe General Montgomery Meigs wrote to Shinseki, who was now Army chief of staff, about his concerns about balancing the needs of mission and family, reporting that soldiers complained that they didn't have enough time for kids, and that childcare was inadequate. He also noted that new family structures meant that Army spouses were no longer content to be homemakers and that the frequency of moves meant that a soldier's 'wife cannot find a job and with her credentials wants to be a breadwinner'. Meigs asked 'can we slow the pace down?' and noted that soldiers did not object to peacekeeping deployments per se but pointed out that 'they did not realize when they signed up that they would be gone so much when there was not a war in the offing'.[26]

In an Army where 62 per cent of active personnel were married and where soldiers were outnumbered by dependents, these family considerations were not inconsequential. When questioned about attrition rates, Secretary of the Army Louis Caldera repeated the Army's slogan – 'we

---

[24] George C. Wilson, 'Reimer: Guarantee Deployed Soldiers Time at Home Base', *Army Times*, 17 November 1997.

[25] Eric Shinseki, 'Brief, Senior Leaders' Conference on Recruiting, Attrition and Retention', 24 November 1998, Eric K. Shinseki Papers: Official Papers – Vice Army Chief of Staff, 18 September 1996 – 1 March 1999: Box 70, Folder 6, AHEC.

[26] Montgomery C. Meigs, 'Email to Eric Shinseki RE: West Point Graduate Separation Program Tasker #AEACG-3882', 7 April 2000, Eric K. Shinseki Papers: Official Correspondence – Army Chief of Staff, Electronic Mail Files, 19 February 2000–23 December 2000: Box 19, Folder 2, AHEC.

enlist soldiers, but we re-enlist families' – and acknowledged that spousal employment and education opportunities were crucial to retention efforts.[27] However, despite Caldera's insistence that the Army had put in place several family support programmes to address these issues, the problem was becoming harder, not easier.

In 1989, the Army counted 991,035 dependents, of which around 20 per cent lived in Europe. When it came to these families, the Army's primary policy concern was how to evacuate them in the event of war.[28] Units and commands continuously updated their non-combatant evacuation plans, and Army personnel were required to keep emergency provisions on hand and never let their car have less than half a tank of fuel. In the words of an Army historian, 'dependents were precious cargo to be whisked out of harm's way so their sponsors could focus on [wartime] responsibilities'. In a post–Cold War world families would be stateside and far from any conflict and so 'rather than an impediment to be cleared from the battlefield, families were now partners to be positively engaged with an eye toward sustaining the force'.[29] The key tool the Army had been using was the Family Support Group, a volunteer-run organisation that offered mutual support to the dependents of those deployed and that distributed command information to the family members of the unit. The Army's official history described them as 'miniature power projection platforms, capable of sustaining their members through the hardships of separation'.[30] Spousal training was a 'force multiplier' and elaborate departure procedures that involved briefings and town hall meetings accompanied each deployment. While these were mandatory for soldiers, their spouses were also strongly encouraged to attend. In this sense, Family Support Groups were not just about supporting Army families through deployments but ensuring that soldiers could deploy overseas with as few distractions from home life as possible.

As the historian Jennifer Mittelstadt has pointed out, though, these groups were marked by the effects of privatisation. In the wake of the Gulf War, the Army's after-action review praised Family Support Groups for playing a key role in sustaining families by providing up-to-date official information as well as social and emotional support. At the same time, the after-action review worried that these groups were creating

---

[27] Louis Caldera, 'Q&A, Fletcher Conference 2000 "National Strategies and Capabilities for a Changing World"', 15 November 2000, Louis Caldera Collection, Box 13, Folder 2, AHEC.

[28] John Sloan Brown, *Kevlar Legions: The Transformation of the United States Army 1989–2005* (Washington, DC: U.S. Army Center of Military History, 2012), 343.

[29] Brown, 343–4.

[30] Brown, 363.

unrealistic expectations, noting how wives expected the Army to help them to mow lawns and provide transportation, babysitting and grocery delivery services.[31] Thus, even as the pace of deployments increased, the Army began to emphasise self-reliance more and more. The Army Family Team Building programme was described as 'basic training for Army families', and made the case that support during deployments was not just an Army responsibility, but 'a process in which families must participate in order to reap benefits'.[32] Units began to think of family support programmes not just as part of the social compact of an organisation that required significant sacrifices on the part of family members but as a means of promoting military readiness among families.[33] By June 2000, the Army had relabelled Family Support Groups as Family Readiness Groups to make the philosophical shift clear. As Mittelstadt notes, the theme of self-reliance was made even more explicit when Army Morale, Welfare and Recreation officials modified the Army's slogan 'The Army Takes Care of Its Own' to 'The Army Takes Care of Its Own By Teaching Its Own to Take Care of Themselves'.[34] While less catchy than the original, the new motto made it clear that family members would need to be self-reliant in an era where deployments were a way of life, while also doing their part to sustain unit readiness throughout these overseas missions, even as the vast majority of deployments were now ones where soldiers travelled unaccompanied by their families.

The correspondence files of Dennis Reimer from his time as Army chief of staff are full of letters from soldiers or spouses complaining about the turbulence caused by the drawdown. Soldiers wrote to him detailing their divorces, their financial difficulties and their frustrations at being passed over for promotion in a more competitive environment. Some of Reimer's responses to these letters are quite instructive as to his priorities as chief of staff. To one Army officer complaining about an article in which Reimer had been (somewhat unfairly) quoted as describing those who were leaving the Army as 'quitters', he wrote, 'I understand your use of the term crisis in confidence, and I also understand a little bit about command climate' before reminiscing about his experience of the Vietnam War and his close friends who left the Army after they came back from Vietnam. Reimer claimed that he fully understood and respected 'those who chose another life' but that he had stayed in the Army because 'I loved the Army and knew we could do better'. For

---

[31] Jennifer Mittelstadt, *The Rise of the Military Welfare State* (Cambridge, MA: Harvard University Press, 2015), 172.
[32] Mittelstadt, 183.
[33] Mittelstadt, 186.
[34] Mittelstadt, 184.

Reimer, 'the memory of those who never came back will always be a part of me and I've dedicated my career to ensuring that we never again put soldiers in harm's way without making sure that they are properly trained for that mission'.[35] The priority, then, was readiness and training, and other considerations, such as family welfare, would take a back seat. In another letter, Reimer wrote to retired Lieutenant General Robert H. Forman about the plight of single-parent drill sergeants, who were struggling to balance the long hours required of their role and the demands of parenthood. Reimer wrote:

> You know, being in the military as a single parent is a tough life. The number of single parents is increasing, and we have to ensure they pull their load or else seek another profession. I've wrestled with this for some time because it seems like a hard-hearted decision. But ultimately, I go back to the purpose of the military and in so doing am convinced that this is the only fair and humane decision we can make for all.[36]

Reimer's comments speak to a frustration with the tension between the needs of the Army's training and deployment tempo and the realities of what historian Beth Bailey has described as 'the Army in the marketplace'.[37] In a world where the Army had to compete with other employers to recruit and retain personnel, the needs of soldiers and their families could not be an afterthought.

For some long-time critics of the All-Volunteer Force, such as Northwestern University sociologist Charles Moskos, the notion of the Army as an occupation rather than a vocation was at the root of the problem. Moskos argued that the All-Volunteer Force was 'over-married' and that while military spouses were once regarded as members of the military community, they were now much more likely to have employment outside of the home and that 'fewer and fewer of them … have either the time or the inclination to engage in the social life of military installations'.[38] Similarly, in an effort to retain junior enlisted personnel, barracks and individual dormitories were built to ensure greater privacy and Moskos claimed that 'to go into a modern barracks today, is like going into a Holiday Inn – one sees a long corridor with a lot of closed and

---

[35] Dennis J. Reimer, 'Letter to Major Brooke Janney', 1 March 1999, Dennis J. Reimer Papers: General Management Correspondence Files – Box 13: February–March 1999, AHEC.

[36] Dennis J. Reimer, 'Letter to Lieutenant General Robert H. Forman', 30 December 1997, Dennis J. Reimer Papers: 1mm Reading Files – Box 5: December 1997, AHEC.

[37] Beth Bailey, 'The Army in the Marketplace: Recruiting an All-Volunteer Force', *The Journal of American History* 94, no. 1 (2007): 47–74.

[38] Charles C. Moskos, 'Military Systems in the Twenty-First Century: Changes and Continuities', n.d., Moskos Papers.

locked doors'. This had a corrosive effect on unit cohesion as it meant that the NCO had 'become more of a shift boss than a person with broad leadership responsibilities'. Better pay for junior soldiers also had an insidious effect, according to Moskos, because it meant that recruits would see little lifestyle improvement as they looked up the promotion ladder. In an undated lecture, Moskos complained that 'we have today overpaid recruits, underpaid NCOs, and adequately paid officers'. He went on to 'categorically reject the proposition that every recruit deserves a decent wage comparable to what he or she might earn in civilian life', not because of the cost, 'but rather the consequences on military cohesion'.[39] For Moskos, the married All-Volunteer Force wasn't so much a warrior caste as it was an institution that was full of people who were too accustomed to treating their work as though it was just another job.

While Moskos' critique may have focused on the All-Volunteer Force and 'occupationalism', it was clear that the challenges of the drawdown went beyond questions relating to the stability of family life. A smaller Army meant not only compulsory redundancies but fewer opportunities for promotion for those who stayed. This inevitably created problems in the officer corps: given the intense competition for promotion, officers could not afford to make mistakes, and a 1995 Army Research Institute Command Climate Assessment, based on responses from more than 24,000 soldiers, claimed that the Army was becoming a 'zero defects' organisation that left no margin for error in which leaders could grow and learn. In an article sounding the alarm over this cultural shift, Reimer claimed the Command Climate Assessment demonstrated that 'the state of ethical conduct is abysmal. Few battalion commanders can afford integrity in a zero defects environment. Telling the truth ends careers quicker than making stupid mistakes or getting caught doing something wrong. I have seen many good officers slide into ethical compromise.' He worried that there was a 'return to … the ticket punching mentality of the 1960s and 1970s that nearly destroyed the officer corps'.[40]

The Army, like the Marine Corps, had long differentiated itself from the Air Force's and Navy's 'up or out' promotion policies and had only reluctantly agreed to the provisions of the 1980 Defense Officer Personnel Management Act and of the 1986 Goldwater–Nichols Act that provided for more rapid promotion and mandated an 'up or out' system across the armed services. One of the key tools for managing this transition was to the Selective Early Retirement Board (SERB), which would

---

[39] Charles C. Moskos, 'From Institution to Occupation', n.d., Moskos Papers.
[40] Dennis J. Reimer, 'Leadership for the Twenty-First Century: Empowerment, Environment and the Golden Rule', *Military Review* 76, no. 1 (February 1996): 5.

designate senior officers for mandatory retirement. As the Army shrank, the spectre of SERB loomed ever larger in the minds of senior officers who might be affected by it. A military psychiatry researcher for Walter Reed described the anguish it caused, reporting that 'resentment, anger, and frustration were commonly expressed feelings, especially by those reviewed or selected by the SERB'.[41] Even those who were in no immediate danger of being selected felt unnerved, as they complained of the Army breaking faith with them by not offering the longer careers that they had expected and of the frustration of having to move frequently, selling their house and uprooting their family, all the while fretting that they might be forced to retire within a year.[42]

In reality, though, while SERB had the effect of damaging morale among the colonels and lieutenant colonels who were most often targeted for mandatory retirement, it had little real impact on the promotion prospects for more junior ranks. One Army War College student complained that the Army was still promoting officers at slower and lower rates than the Navy and Air Force and that, amid a broader downsizing, simply not enough officers were being selected for early retirement.[43] Indeed, in 1995, a year where the Army was rapidly shedding numbers, only 409 officers were involuntarily separated by a SERB, while 2,069 voluntarily chose early retirement.[44] This reluctance to more extensively employ involuntary separation policies among senior officers had a marked effect on the makeup of the force. While the overall strength of the Active Duty Army of 1999 was only 62.28 per cent of what it had been in 1989, the Army retained 72 per cent of the officer strength of 1989 and fully 81.5 per cent of its colonels and 82 per cent of its lieutenant colonels.[45] Despite all of the unease caused by the threat of the SERB and the frustration of more junior officers at seemingly diminished opportunities, the Army at the end of the twentieth century was a much more top-heavy organisation than it had been at the Cold War's end.

This slowdown in promotions had a marked effect on junior officer morale. Echoing similar complaints from the 1970s and 1980s, one

---

[41] Mary Ann Evans, 'Human Dimensions of the SERB' (Washington, DC: Walter Reed Army Institute of Research, January 1994), 3.

[42] Evans, 5.

[43] Edwin W. Chamberlin, 'Officer Personnel Management – Changing the Paradigms', individual study project (Carlisle Barracks, PA: US Army War College, 1 April 1993), 7.

[44] John Sloan Brown, *Kevlar Legions: The Transformation of the United States Army 1989–2005* (Washington, DC: U.S. Army Center of Military History, 2012), 125.

[45] Vincent H. Demma, *Department of the Army Historical Summary: Fiscal Year 1989* (Washington, DC: Center of Military History, United States Army, 1998), 110; Jeffrey A. Charlston, *Department of the Army Historical Summary: Fiscal Year 1999* (Washington, DC: Center of Military History, United States Army, 2006), 26, 30.

study by a student at the School of Advanced Military Studies concluded that 'overall, an image of service does not permeate the U.S. Army officer corps; an image of success does .... Junior leaders view the senior leaders as self-focused and self-centered. They believe that commanders are more concerned with looking good on paper and looking good in motor pools instead of being functional and really addressing issues.'[46] These junior leaders complained that the officer-rating system bred cynicism and that officers had become 'so worried about their own careers that the survival instinct has been prevalent'.[47] The fixation with looking good meant that 'senior leadership is out of touch with the realities and challenges our soldiers face in the areas of training and maintenance'.[48]

Others argued that not only did decreased opportunities for promotion create a 'zero defects' environment that damaged cohesion and morale, but it nurtured anti-intellectualism within the Army as well. In *The Downsized Warrior*, a study based on hundreds of interviews with Army officers, former Army officer David McCormick noted that commanding a unit had become a crucial condition for promotion. This meant that there was far less time for pursuits such as graduate school and that any time spent away from the 'muddy boots' army would be punished by promotion boards. Thus, while Arabic-speaking officers used to be able to switch between Foreign Area Officer postings and roles in the field Army, such a diverse career path was now frowned upon.[49] One of McCormick's interviewees remarked to him that 'taking the time to go to grad school is now a bad thing. When you come back after two years, the attitude is "oh, you want to be a soldier again?"'[50] Even attendance at the School of Advanced Military Studies at Fort Leavenworth, a graduate programme celebrated for its production of the 'Jedi Knight' planning team that put together Operation Desert Storm, dipped as officers prioritised taking command appointments.[51] According to McCormick, the officer corps was divided into two cohorts: those with a graduate education who were focusing on making themselves marketable for a post-Army career, and 'the battalion commanders of the future' who were adhering 'more closely to a strictly muddy boots pattern'. This cohort would 'more likely have completed a master's degree in business

---

[46] Anneliese M. Steele, 'Are the Relationships between Junior and Senior Leaders in the U.S. Army Officer Corps Dysfunctional?' (Fort Leavenworth, KS: School of Advanced Military Studies, Command and General Staff College, 30 April 2001), 38, https://apps.dtic.mil/sti/citations/ADA394870.

[47] Steele, 39.

[48] Steele, 46.

[49] McCormick, *The Downsized Warrior*, 147.

[50] McCormick, 151.

[51] McCormick, 153.

by correspondence from Kennesaw State than a degree in engineering from Georgia Tech or in political science from Georgetown'.[52]

Thus, even as the Army found itself committed to a range of missions that went beyond 'warfighting' and that required soldier-scholars as much as warriors, the post–Cold War drawdown meant the Army's promotion system was pushing many of those with the relevant skill set and mindset out of the organisation and into the civilian world. For McCormick, downsizing the force was inadvertently promoting a cultural shift that elevated traditionalist 'warrior' officers focused on conventional warfare at the very time the world was becoming much more complex.

Despite the end of the Cold War and the United States' status as the sole remaining superpower, the drawdown caused the Army considerable problems as the decade wore on. The budget cuts, personnel reductions and base closures led to a smaller force based primarily in the continental United States, while the increased operational tempo of deployments led to significant personnel turbulence that put considerable strain on soldiers and their families. Frequent overseas missions, a less generous welfare system and a fiercely competitive promotion process meant that retention became an increasingly challenging problem. Speaking to the Army Adjutants General Association in 1997, Reimer complained that 'I think that people sometimes forget that we have taken almost half a million people out ... they forget that we've closed an awful lot of bases, they forget that we've changed a lot of flags .... They forget all those changes that have taken place and the human dimensions is so shaded with those changes.'[53]

The challenge would now be to adjust the All-Volunteer Force to cope with those changes. Army leaders recognised that the transition would be difficult, but they became especially concerned once they realised that recruiting enough soldiers to keep even this reduced force functioning would be a struggle as well.

4.2   'Recruiting Is Beginning to Crack': Debating Military Service

As early as 1993, Sullivan was warning congressional leaders that 'it is not preordained that the All-Volunteer Force will always work' and he pointed to a decreased advertising budget (down 70 per cent) and the negative publicity surrounding downsizing as threats to the Army's

---

[52] McCormick, 155.
[53] Dennis J. Reimer, 'Address to the Adjutant General Association. U.S.', 8 September 1998, Denis J. Reimer Papers: 870-5f Organization Historical Files – Box 89: January–February 1997, AHEC.

recruiting goals. In discussions with the Senate Armed Services Committee, he feared that 'recruiting is beginning to crack' and argued that recruiting propensity was down 30 per cent overall (Black recruiting propensity was down 45 per cent which was due, according to Sullivan's briefing notes, to 'negative rap music').[54] Asked by Senator John McCain to list risks to the force, Sullivan claimed that a reduced quality of recruit due to the decrease in funding for recruitment was one of greatest perils the Army faced that could lead to a return to a 'hollow force' by the end of the decade.[55] Sullivan's worries proved to be somewhat premature in that the Active Army met or exceeded its recruiting goals from 1993 to 1997. However, in 1998 it missed its goal of 72,500 by 801 recruits. Much more seriously, in 1999 it fell 6,290 short of its goal of 74,500, setting off renewed debate about the future of the All-Volunteer Force.[56] Amid a booming economy, the strongest the All-Volunteer Force had even seen, and recruitment targets that were increasing due to attrition, there were fears that the system that had served the Army for twenty-five years was no longer fit for purpose. Army Recruiting Command circulated a PowerPoint presentation that one of its authors described as 'doom and gloom', warning that 'current trends, coupled with growing accession missions, are now resulting in production failure'.[57] Newspapers ran articles with headlines such as 'The Bugle Sounds, but Fewer Answer' and the reintroduction of the draft was debated on television and in Congress.[58] An Army conference organised to discuss the recruiting crisis heard that the force now had an annual attrition rate of 37 per cent (up from 20 per cent at the end of the Cold War), which compared unfavourably with other large organisations such as McDonald's, which

---

[54] Gordon R. Sullivan, 'Talking Paper: It Is Not Preordained that the All-Volunteer Force (AVF) Will Always Work', 29 March 1993, Gordon R. Sullivan Papers: CSA Dr Hamre (PM, SASC), AHEC.

[55] Gordon R. Sullivan, 'Answers to Senator McCain's Questions on Defense Budget Cuts & Readiness', 3 June 1993, Gordon R. Sullivan Papers: CSA Senator McCain, AHEC. Given that the meeting took place during the debate over Don't Ask, Don't Tell, it is unsurprising to see that Sullivan also listed 'social experimentation as a risk factor', arguing that 'using the military for social experiments that do not contribute to enhanced readiness tends to degrade morale, readiness, and quality of life'.

[56] Matthew Morgan, 'Army Recruiting and the Civil-Military Gap', *Parameters: Journal of the US Army War College*, Summer 2001, 102.

[57] Greg Parlier, 'Memorandum for Professor Moskos Re: Possible Brief', 22 September 1999, Moskos Papers; Greg Parlier, 'Recruiting Research Consortium', 17 September 1999, Moskos Papers.

[58] Bradley Graham, 'The Bugle Sounds, but Fewer Answer: Services Rethink Recruiting as Ranks Thin', *Washington Post*, 13 March 1999; 'Being All They Can Be? US Army Recruiting Numbers Reach Low Levels', *PBS Newshour with Jim Lehrer*, 12 March 1999; 'House of Representatives – Daily Digest' (106th Congress, 1st Session: Congressional Record – vol. 145, no. 43 – Daily Edition, 18 March 1999), D304.

only lost 15 per cent of its personnel each year.[59] A study by the RAND Corporation suggested diverting Reserve Component soldiers into the Active Component pipeline in order to decrease the shortfall, and simultaneously only allowing lower-quality soldiers to serve one term in the Army, in order to minimise the damage that they would do to the force while serving.[60]

Given that the Army only significantly missed its target in one year (it would go on to meet its recruiting quota for 2000), this level of unease requires some explanation. The recruiting crisis of the late 1990s after all was nowhere near that which beset the force in the late 1970s and early 1980s, when the All-Volunteer Force genuinely seemed in danger of failing. Nonetheless, as historian Beth Bailey has noted, critics were again claiming that the All-Volunteer Force was in jeopardy, even if the current crisis was not of the same magnitude as that of the early years of recruiting without the draft.[61] Speaking to PBS, former Assistant Secretary of Defense for Manpower Lawrence Korb argued that there wasn't any reason for panic, arguing that the shortfall was mostly the result of the Army cutting back on advertising and recruiting during the downsizing, and that it would simply take some time before a new injection of advertising money and extra recruiters would pay off. He did, however, note that 'since the Cold War ended, the military and the country hasn't come up with a coherent message for what the military is all about'.[62] Others felt the lack of this message more acutely, which perhaps added more existential angst to fears about recruiting shortfalls. Indeed, Recruiting Command's 'doom and gloom' PowerPoint presentation closed somewhat melodramatically with a quote attributed to Sulla, speaking 'after the Romans completed their conquest of the known world' in 84 BC: 'now the universe offers us no more enemies, what may be the fate of the Republic?'[63]

The problem then was not so much missing recruiting targets but rather a broader sense of unease about the Army's place in society. Speaking in 2001, the then Vice Chief of Staff of the Army General Jack Keane argued that 'the absolute truth is that the American people ... do not look at the military option as a choice for their youngsters, [but] raising

---

[59] Shinseki, 'Brief, Senior Leaders' Conference on Recruiting, Attrition and Retention'.
[60] 'The Army Recruiting Picture: Short Term and Long Term Challenge', Rand Arroyo Center, 18 February 1999, Eric K. Shinseki Papers: Official Papers – Vice Army Chief of Staff, 18 September 1996 – 1 March 1999: Box 70, Folder 23, AHEC.
[61] Beth Bailey, *America's Army: Making the All-Volunteer Force* (Cambridge, MA: Harvard University Press, 2009), 234.
[62] 'Being All They Can Be? US Army Recruiting Numbers Reach Low Levels'.
[63] Parlier, 'Recruiting Research Consortium'.

and maintaining an army is a shared responsibility in which everyone has a stake'. Keane noted that with the recruiting shortfall, 'we did a lot of research and found that we were disconnected [from] the American youth'. He felt that young Americans 'do not see the military as a career or a way to get ahead' and were 'more likely to view enlistment in the military as a last resort'.[64] One speaker at the Association of the United States Army Winter Symposium in 2000 noted that the problem wasn't just the robust economy, it was 'the unmistakable lure of higher education' and that the Army's offer of up to $50,000 in tuition support wasn't working because 'money for college isn't the most important message for today's youth'.[65] The problem was that nobody was sure what the Army's message should be in this environment. When over 70 per cent of high school graduates were heading to college, the Army needed to be able to tell them a compelling story as to why they should serve in the military instead.

For Secretary of the Army Louis Caldera, that question of a compelling story was more important than financial incentives. Caldera – a former Army officer and West Point graduate who took office in 1998 just as the recruitment crisis was beginning to bite – argued that the most successful Army recruiters were those who spoke 'not just about the great incentives and opportunities we offer' but those who 'have also told young people that service to the nation is its own reward' and who 'reminded our young people that freedom isn't free and challenged them to consider whether they ... also have an obligation and step forward to be counted among those who are ready to defend our country and its principles'.[66] As Beth Bailey has argued, Caldera's appeal was based on patriotism and the notion that military service was an obligation of citizenship, 'one of the things that you ought to do and not just a great experience because you'll earn money for college or you'll get a skill, but because you'll grow as an American, to have had that opportunity to serve your country in uniform'.[67] He believed that the military served an important role in socialising the nation's youth and making them active citizens. Worried about the underrepresentation of Hispanic Americans in the ranks, Caldera argued that today 'too many of our young people

---

[64] Morgan, 'Army Recruiting and the Civil–Military Gap'.

[65] Patrick T. Henry, 'AUSA Winter Symposium Draft Presentation Remarks/Talking Points', 9 January 1998, Louis Caldera Collection, Box 12, Folder 5, AHEC.

[66] Louis Caldera, 'Proposed Remarks for the Honorable Louis Caldera at the Secretary of the Army Recruiter/Career Counselor of the Year Awards Ceremony, Room 2E715A, the Pentagon', 14 April 1999, Louis Caldera Collection, Box 12, Folder 5, AHEC.

[67] 'Being All They Can Be? US Army Recruiting Numbers Reach Low Levels'; Bailey, *America's Army*, 238.

are angry, confused, disheartened about what their place in the world is supposed to be'. Part of 'redeem[ing] the promise of opportunity for these young people' was service in the military as a way of 'giving something back'.[68]

Caldera's views fit comfortably within the mainstream of the Democratic Party: for instance, Senator John Glenn also worried that a decreasing propensity for military service was a sign of a broader societal malaise. Speaking at ceremony being held at Fort Meyer in his honour, he noted that he was concerned a little bit – not a little bit, a considerable bit about America's legendary "can do" spirit .... 'I am talking about an attack from within and talking about the cynicism so prevalent in America today, and especially among our young people.' Glenn worried that 'if we let cynicism towards our country, its democracy, its government rule, it will be suicidal'. This lack of civic engagement could precipitate a decline that would 'eventually be the end of this great experiment in democracy, or at least a lesser democracy than we could have for the future'.[69] Given these problems, Caldera, Glenn and other centrist Democrats such as Sam Nunn and Al Gore argued that while a return to the draft might not be wise, some form of national service for America's youth would certainly make sense. The problem with the All-Volunteer Force in its current form wasn't that it wasn't attracting enough recruits, but that the recruits that it was attracting were not demographically representative. Caldera worried that because only 15 per cent of adult males under the age of sixty-five had served in the military, parents were not encouraging their children to serve.[70] Writing in *Parameters*, Matthew Morgan argued that the downsizing had accentuated this problem and that fewer, larger military outposts meant that 'military bases, complete with their own schools, churches, stores, child care centers, and recreational areas, can be characterized as never-to-be-left islands of tranquillity removed from the seemingly chaotic, crime-ridden civilian environment outside the gates'. The service academies were full of cadets and midshipmen who were the children of career military personnel. Given these trends, the United States was

---

[68] Louis Caldera, 'Remarks for the Honorable Louis Caldera at the American GI Forum National Convention, Omaha, Nebraska', 31 July 1999, Louis Caldera Collection, Box 10, Folder 7, AHEC.

[69] John Glenn, 'Remarks by Defense Secretary William Cohen and Joint Chiefs Chairman General Henry Shelton, at Ceremony Honoring Sen. John Glenn (D-OH), Fort Myer, Virginia', 4 December 1998, Louis Caldera Collection, Box 4, Folder 3, AHEC.

[70] Louis Caldera, 'Do We Need a Draft? Challenging America's Youth to Serve in Uniform, Luncheon Speech at the National Press Club', 26 March 1999, Louis Caldera Collection, Box 4, Folder 2, AHEC.

creating a separate 'warrior caste', where an insulated military embodied different values to the society that it was meant to defend.[71]

Caldera was particularly concerned about the tension between going to college and serving in the military and focused much of his energy on challenging students from elite universities to consider military service. In a speech at Harvard, he argued that 'service to country should be one of the goals in life of anyone wishing to participate fully in, and contribute fully to, a democratic society'.[72] In his preparatory notes for the speech, Caldera noted that it wasn't 'just *noblesse oblige* about teaching those hicks how to be citizens' but an argument that graduates of Ivy League schools could absorb lessons from their less privileged fellow citizens.[73] He told his audience of students that 'by not serving in the Army, you are missing a chance to learn something about your fellow citizens. Our soldiers may not all be as well educated as you are, but you will be humbled by the things you will learn from them. You will be impressed by their courage, their kills, their tenacity, their resiliency, and their decency.'[74] Here, Caldera was appealing to the notion of the Army as a melting pot, and he hoped that his rhetorical appeals to elites could help infuse American youth with the ideals of service once again.

Part of this rhetorical appeal was clearly nostalgic; in preparation for his Harvard speech, Caldera's staff compiled lists of famous Americans who had served in the military during the draft era and took notes from memoirs that extolled the value of military service, even in experiences that were better remembered as national nightmares, such as the Vietnam War.[75] Above all else though, Caldera and those who argued for some form of national service tended to hark back to World War II. In his address where he worried about the waning of American 'can do' spirit, John Glenn had inevitably turned to the 'Greatest Generation' as an exemplar of what that spirit could achieve. Given that American cultural industries were then awash with products that celebrated the

---

[71] Morgan, 'Army Recruiting and the Civil–Military Gap'; David S. Sorenson, *Shutting Down the Cold War: The Politics of Military Base Closure* (New York: Palgrave Macmillan, 1998).

[72] Louis Caldera, '"Why Johnny Should Serve", Draft Remarks for an Address at the Harvard University Latino Law, Business and Public Policy Conference', 10 March 2000, Louis Caldera Collection, Box 10, Folder 7, AHEC.

[73] Louis Caldera, 'Harvard: Why Johnny Should Serve [Notes]', 10 March 2000, Louis Caldera Collection, Box 10, Folder 7, AHEC.

[74] Caldera, '"Why Johnny Should Serve", Draft Remarks for an Address at the Harvard University Latino Law, Business and Public Policy Conference'.

[75] Gregory Sieminski, 'Memorandum for the Secretary of the Army: Supplemental Material for NPC Speech', 24 March 1999, Louis Caldera Collection, Box 4, Folder 2, AHEC.

American role in World War II, from books such as Tom Brokaw's *The Greatest Generation* and Steven Ambrose's *Citizen Soldiers* to movies such as *The Thin Red Line* and *Saving Private Ryan*, it was not surprising to see the war invoked in the discourse on national service.[76] Historian Gary Gerstle has argued that the prevalence of these narratives indicates a liberal nationalist attempt to reclaim war from conservatives by rehabilitating the notion of a 'good war', and certainly the evidence from the speeches of senior Army leaders and internal Army correspondence supports that claim.[77] Caldera, for one, was attracted to the characters in *Saving Private Ryan* because they were simply 'ordinary citizen-soldiers who did not ask to be heroes, but who answered the nation's call' and in his call for broader representation in the ranks, he argued that 'we're experiencing shortfalls because we haven't challenged all our nation's young people to consider their obligation to be the Private Ryans – or more authentically – the Private Eugene Obregons and David Gonzales – of our day'.[78] He drew a direct line between the citizen-soldiers of that earlier war and contemporary soldiers, claiming that the peacekeepers deployed to Kosovo and the soldiers defending South Korea were 'the Captain Millers and Private Ryans of our time'.[79]

Army leaders were similarly taken by the comparison, organising special screenings of the movie for Congress, while the Department of Defense awarded Steven Spielberg, Tom Hanks and Matt Damon Distinguished Civilian Service Medals (Figure 4.1).[80] Individual units also organised screenings for their troops and in some cases, such as the screening organised by the 1st Infantry Division ('The Big Red One' that had played a central role in the Normandy landings), invited along World War II Medal of Honor recipients to talk with the troops

---

[76] Stephen E. Ambrose, *Citizen Soldiers: The U.S. Army From the Beaches of Normandy to the Surrender of Germany* (New York: Simon & Schuster, 1997); Tom Brokaw, *The Greatest Generation* (New York: Random House, 1998); *Saving Private Ryan*, 1998, www.imdb .com/title/tt0120815/; *The Thin Red Line*, 1999, www.imdb.com/title/tt0120863/.

[77] Gary Gerstle, 'In the Shadow of War: Liberal Nationalism and the Problem of War', in *Americanism: New Perspectives on the History of an Ideal*, ed. Michael Kazin and Joseph A. McCartin (Chapel Hill: The University of North Carolina Press, 2006), 128–52.

[78] Louis Caldera, 'Talking Points: Recruiting', n.d., Louis Caldera Collection, Box 9, Folder 2, AHEC.

[79] Louis Caldera, 'Remarks Delivered by the Honorable Louis Caldera, Greater Los Angeles Chapter, AUSA, Army Ball, Century City, CA', 4 June 1999, Louis Caldera Collection, Box 6, Folder 6, AHEC.; Denis J. Reimer and Louis Caldera, 'Letters to Steven Spielberg, Tom Hanks, and Matt Damon', 8 September 1998, Denis J. Reimer Papers: Reading Files, August 1998, AHEC.

[80] Caldera, 'Remarks Delivered by the Honorable Louis Caldera, Greater Los Angeles Chapter, AUSA, Army Ball, Century City, CA'.

Figure 4.1 Secretary of Defense William S. Cohen presents a framed citation accompanying the Department of Defense Medal for Distinguished Public Service to Steven Spielberg at a ceremony in the Pentagon, 1999

afterwards.[81] The imagery of the war was so prevalent in the Army that General Reimer consoled an officer who had been passed over for promotion and thus had had his career ended by inviting him to read Ambrose's *Citizen Soldiers* and reflect on its message about service.[82] In a speech where he presented the Distinguished Civilian Service Medal to Spielberg, Secretary of Defense William Cohen argued that the most important aspect of the film was its moral argument about the intrinsic virtue of citizen-soldiers. Despite the gruesome violence on display, the film was deeply sympathetic to soldiers and demonstrated that 'at the core, the citizen-soldier of the United States knew the difference between right and wrong. And they were unwilling to live in a world

---

[81] David L. Grange, 'Letter to Dennis Reimer', 27 August 1998, Dennis J. Reimer Papers: 1mm Reading Files – Box 93 September 1998 [2 of 2], AHEC.
[82] Dennis J. Reimer, 'Letter to Rudy T. Veit', 13 July 1998, Denis J. Reimer Papers: General Management Correspondence Files: Box 12: June 1998 [2 of 2], AHEC.

where wrong triumphed.'[83] Army leaders wanted to claim this moral mantle for all American soldiers, be they professionals or draftees.[84] The now-retired General Colin Powell made that connection when accepting an award at West Point by claiming that 'no group of Americans has a greater claim to the love, appreciation and respect of fellow citizens that the warriors of the nation'. Crucially for Powell, these warriors were not mercenaries but American citizens, 'they fight the nation's wars for us, not as strangers but as our very own. They are the pride of America – the best the nation has to offer. They are Private Ryans of America.'[85]

Others were more sceptical of the claim that the All-Volunteer Force really was composed of Private Ryans of the late twentieth century. Writing in *Parameters*, Eliot Cohen argued that there were several crucial differences. Noting the content of Powell's speech, he claimed that, *contra* Powell, 'the U.S. Army is no longer composed of Millers, Ryans, and Horvaths; it no longer faces the kind of desperate struggles that characterized Omaha beach; and its men (and now, women) no longer worry about overcoming an enemy in order to return to their normal lives – military service is their life'.[86] Cohen thought it was clear that contemporary soldiers, 'however admirable, are fighting no crusades', and, unlike Miller's melting pot platoon of ethnically and socially diverse GIs, they were far from being a cross-section of American society. For Cohen, the Army's acclamation of *Saving Private Ryan* was more about celebrating the myth of a 'citizen-soldier' that no longer existed rather than drawing authentic connections between World War II and the current era. Similarly, Charles Moskos thought it significant that one of the few contemporary films that offered a realistic portrayal of military service was one that had to be set fifty years ago. Surveying the other cinematic offerings of the 1990s, he noted that *Broken Arrow* and *The Rock* portrayed military officers going rogue and turning against American society, while *Forrest Gump* was a dignified Vietnam War hero but one who was 'Cat V' and thus should never have been allowed into the military.[87] Moskos noted

---

[83] William S. Cohen, 'Army Award to Steven Spielberg for "Saving Private Ryan", Ritz-Carlton Grand Ballroom, Arlington', 17 September 1998, Louis Caldera Collection, Box 6, Folder 6, AHEC.

[84] *Parameters* ran an extended review of the film that focused on its moral message. William J. Prior, "'We Aren't Here to Do the Decent Thing": Saving Private Ryan and the Morality of War', *Parameters: Journal of the US Army War College*, Autumn 2000, 138–45.

[85] Colin Powell, 'Remarks by General Colin Powell upon Receiving the Sylvanus Thayer Award, West Point', West Point Association of Graduates, 15 September 1998, www.westpointaog.org/page.aspx?pid=496.

[86] Eliot A. Cohen, 'Twilight of the Citizen-Soldier', *Parameters* 31, no. 2 (22 June 2001): 23.

[87] *Broken Arrow*, 1996, www.imdb.com/title/tt0115759/; *The Rock*, 1996, www.imdb.com/title/tt0117500/; *Forrest Gump*, 1994, www.imdb.com/title/tt0109830/.

that the difference between two military court-room dramas, *The Caine Mutiny* (1954) and *A Few Good Men* (1992), was that in the former film, the commander is shown in the end to be the hero, whereas in the latter, the commander is the villain and the lawyers are the heroes.[88] Moskos thought that these films were far more in keeping with elite American attitudes towards the military than the more sympathetic portrayal in *Saving Private Ryan* that Army leaders had been so eager to celebrate.

Moskos' own longstanding opposition to the All-Volunteer Force was itself based in part on nostalgia. He frequently recalled his own experience as a draftee in 1950s Germany in the correspondence, speeches and articles where he promoted an alternative vision of military service. For Moskos, it was significant that even as he served his time in the military, Elvis Presley was just 150 km down the road completing his own military service.[89] For Moskos, the 1950s-era draft represented something of a model; in his eyes, it was an institution that promoted egalitarianism, social mobility and patriotism, and while he accepted that a return to conscription was unlikely in the 1990s (although he frequently wrote op-eds in support of a draft), he was eager to push the military in that direction as much as possible. Moskos' thinking in many ways harked back to that of mid-century liberals, as he preferred to emphasise the obligations of citizenship rather than rights or the 'entitlements' which Clintonian Democrats and Republicans alike now railed against. For Moskos, military service was an essential part of being a male citizen, and much of his efforts to challenge the All-Volunteer Force were as much about citizenship as military efficacy.

In correspondence with Reimer, Moskos noted with some dismay that Army recruiting campaigns focused too much on existing markets. He complained that the advertising agencies contracted by the Army based their campaigns on interviews with serving soldiers rather than those demographics that had not previously been responsive to advertising. He was concerned that 'high socio-economic status' youth were not joining the Army and, in keeping with his opposition to generous benefits for junior enlisted soldiers, asked, 'do we want more young marrieds and single parents?'[90] He argued that, given the rising numbers of Americans who attended college, it would be 'much better to aim at the

[88] Charles C. Moskos, 'Commander-In-Chief (CINC) Conference: Social Issues', 1998, Moskos Papers; *The Caine Mutiny*, 1954, www.imdb.com/title/tt0046816/; *A Few Good Men*, 1993, www.imdb.com/title/tt0104257/.
[89] Brian McAllister Linn, *Elvis's Army: Cold War GIs and the Atomic Battlefield* (Cambridge, MA: Harvard University Press, 2016).
[90] Charles Moskos, 'Army Recruiting Woes: "It's Not the Economy, Stupid"', 2 February 1999, Moskos Papers.

broad middle and upper-middle classes of the American youth. This is the expanding youth pool.'[91] Moskos claimed that the sight of a Chelsea Clinton or a Jenna Bush enlisting, even for a short period of service, would be even more beneficial to the Army than tripling its advertising budget.[92] The 'halo effect' of attracting high-socioeconomic-status candidates would mean that the working class would want to follow them.[93] Not only would attracting more high-income candidates be a cost-efficient way to improve recruiting, but it could help to more effectively mobilise the country for war when required. Surveying the very low number of congressional representatives and senators who had children serving in the military, he argued that this explained a seeming aversion to casualties, claiming that 'only when the privileged classes perform military service does the country define the cause as worth young people's blood. Only when elite youth are on the firing line do war losses become more acceptable.'[94]

Unlike Caldera and the Army's leadership, however, Moskos' frustrations with this situation meant that he advocated more radical action. Whereas Caldera's strategy for increasing the elite participation in the military was largely a rhetorical one, focused on marketing and appeals at elite universities, Moskos wanted to fundamentally reshape recruitment and military service itself to make it more attractive to college students. Reacting to reports of the Army's 37 per cent attrition rate and a proposed $20,000 reenlistment bonus, he emailed a friend: 'my God, $20K requested as an enlistment bonus!! Anything not to have America's privileged youth serve.'[95] Moskos argued that the Department of Defense's entire recruiting logic was wrong and that their 'economic man' approach had misled them, claiming that 'a consequence of econometric analysis is to downplay the less-tangible noneconomic factors and value-derived aspects of military organizations ... it ignores the reality that the armed forces are not merely fluid collections of self-maximizing individuals but sets of social relations that include nonmaterialistic behavior'.[96] In response to claims that the booming economy was the

---

[91] Charles C. Moskos, 'Letter to General Dennis J. Reimer Re Army Recruiting', 18 February 1999, Louis Caldera Collection, Box 4, Folder 7, AHEC.
[92] David M. Halbfinger and Steven A. Holmes, 'Military Mirrors a Working-Class America', *New York Times*, 30 March 2003, www.nytimes.com/2003/03/30/us/a-nation-at-war-the-troops-military-mirrors-a-working-class-america.html.
[93] Moskos, 'Army Recruiting Woes: "It's Not the Economy, Stupid"'.
[94] Moskos, 'Military Systems in the Twenty-First Century: Changes and Continuities'.
[95] Charles C. Moskos, 'Email to Lisa Wright Re Re: National Guard Recruiting – Baltimore Sun 12/18/04', 22 December 2004, Moskos Papers.
[96] Charles C. Moskos, 'What Ails the All-Volunteer Force: An Institutional Perspective', *Parameters: Journal of the US Army War College*, Summer 2001, 29–47.

reason for missed recruiting goals, he argued that 'it's not the economy, stupid', and contended that a 'booming economy could be a godsend for non-materialist youth to join the service'.[97]

The solution was to offer a short-service enlistment of fifteen to eighteen months that would appeal to college students as something of a gap year between undergraduate and graduate studies. The opportunity to 'do something different for a short time' would attract a wholly different sort of recruit. Further, the argument was that shorter enlistments would inevitably mean a lower attrition rate, as soldiers were much more likely to fulfil their terms of service if those terms were significantly shorter, and that overseas deployments on peacekeeping missions would be welcome adventures for younger short-service soldiers, rather than the burden that they had become for married career soldiers with families.[98] Based on surveys of his own students at Northwestern University, Moskos estimated that this system could attract between 30,000 and 40,000 recruits a year – well over half of the Army's annual recruiting needs under the current system – and would create a new generation of citizen-soldiers, reinvigorating American democracy and the relationship between the Army and broader American society.[99]

Moskos vigorously promoted this concept all through the recruiting crisis of 1999. He was invited to appear before both the Senate and House Armed Services Committees, and Senator John Warner, the Republican Chair of the Senate Armed Services Committee, was enthusiastic about the idea, asking Reimer to have the Army study it.[100] Moskos acknowledged the high cost of training more recruits due to a shorter length of service but claimed that this would be more than offset by a decrease in attrition rates. Fundamentally though, his argument was not an economic one. He told the House Armed Services Committee that his scheme would bring significant benefits beyond financial saving, including reducing the attrition that was causing 'organizational heartburn' and creating a stream of 'failed service members' who brought 'a negative image of military life back to their communities'.[101]

Moskos was able to receive a relatively sympathetic hearing in Congress because his ideas recalled an older plan supported by the centrist Democratic Leadership Council. A National Service Bill along similar

---

[97] Moskos, 'Army Recruiting Woes: "It's Not the Economy, Stupid"'.

[98] Charles Moskos, 'From College to Kosovo', *Wall Street Journal*, 25 August 2000.

[99] Charles Moskos, cited in Peter Karsten, 'The US Citizen-Soldier's Past, Present, and Likely Future', *Parameters: Journal of the US Army War College*, Summer 2001, 6–73.

[100] John Warner, 'Letter to Charles Moskos', 16 March 1999, Moskos Papers.

[101] Charles C. Moskos, 'Letter to Representative Steve Buyer', 27 October 1999, Moskos Papers.

lines, supported by Moskos, had been introduced by Senators Sam Nunn and Barbara Mikulski in 1989 and a National Service Bill was part of Clinton's campaign platform in 1992.[102] Clinton's ambitions faltered in the face of Republican opposition, but he did manage to establish Americorps, a voluntary civil society initiative unconnected to the military that enrolled 20,000 high school graduates out of an eligible population of two million. Clinton himself understood the programme in somewhat militarised terms, telling *Newsweek* that 'I think all these kids doing drugs, shooting guns, dropping out of school, going to jail, changing the culture of life in a destructive way and losing their opportunity to have a good life – I see that as a national security issue'.[103] Even this rather small-scale initiative provoked a conservative backlash, with Speaker of the House Newt Gingrich critiquing what he called 'coerced volunteerism' and the Cato Institute declaring that national service proposals equated to those advanced by Chinese Communist leaders.[104] The Cato Institute also argued that the commitment of those undertaking national service would inevitably be less than that of 'true volunteers' and that such programmes would actively harm both charitable giving and the spirit of volunteerism in the United States.[105]

Despite this opposition, various national service proposals were floated throughout the decade. Even if he didn't fully support Moskos' short-service initiative, Louis Caldera did propose a form of national service that would either funnel new recruits into the military or civilian programmes such as Meals on Wheels.[106] These proposals found supporters in both political parties. The staff of Republican Senator Strom Thurmond let it be known to the media that he would support such an

---

[102] Jeffrey H Birnbaum, 'Sen. Nunn's Push for National Service Points up Use of Conventions for Causes', *Wall Street Journal*, 21 July 1988; Jill Lawrence, 'National Service Plans for Young Americans Scaled Back', *Associated Press*, 23 July 1989, https://newsok.com/article/2273538/national-service-plans-for-young-americans-scaled-back/; Democratic Leadership Council, *Citizenship and National Service: A Blueprint for Civic Enterprise* (Washington, DC: Democratic Leadership Council, 1988); Peter Maarten Van Bemmelen, *What You Can Do for Your Country: Report of the Commission on National and Community Service* (Washington, DC: DIANE Publishing, 1993); Will Marshall and Joel Berg, 'National Service and Student Aid: Myth and Reality' (Washington, DC: The Center for Civic Enterprise, 19 September 1989).

[103] Steve Waldman, '"Ask Not" – '90s Style', *Newsweek*, 20 September 1993, 51.

[104] John B. Judis, 'TRB from Washington: Citizen Soldiers', *The New Republic*, 28 June 1999; Doug Bandow, 'National Service: The Enduring Panacea', Cato Institute Policy Analysis (Washington, DC: Cato Institute, 22 March 1990).

[105] Doug Bandow, 'Testimony on the Corporation for National Service and Community Service' (Washington, DC, 21 May 1996), 104th Congress, 2nd Session, United States Senate Committee on Labor and Human Resources Oversight Hearing.

[106] Sig Christenson, 'Caldera Offers Compulsory Service Plan', *San Antonio Express-News*, 7 September 1999.

initiative, while former Democratic senator and presidential candidate Gary Hart publicly made the case for a return to the draft or some other form of compulsory military service in books such as *The Minuteman* and *The Patriot*.[107] Moskos also hoped that he might soon find more enthusiastic support for his proposals in the White House. An informal advisor to Al Gore's presidential campaign, he wrote to the vice-president to inform him of his plan and to argue that Gore's 'time as a common soldier' made him 'the only Presidential candidate that [had] credibility to address ... the serious national problem' of military recruitment.[108] Gore's service as an enlisted soldier in the Vietnam War was an example of the sort of citizen-soldier model that Moskos wanted to reinstate, and he hoped that the campaign might focus on his short-service proposal in their platform.

Partly in response to Moskos' plea for more attention to college graduates, and partly in response to economic conditions, the Army did introduce two recruiting programmes that appealed to previously neglected markets. The GED-Plus programme aimed at recruiting 6,000 non–high school graduates every year and then sponsoring them to complete their education, an initiative that Caldera hoped would attract more Hispanic candidates, while 'College First' would allow recruits to defer induction until after they had completed their education.[109] Moskos felt that these initiatives were too unambitious and were reflective of the 'economic-man mentality of civilians who manage personnel policies in the Defense Department'. He argued (truthfully) that there was bipartisan support for some form of citizen-soldier enhancement and national service. Moskos' goal went beyond fixing recruitment.[110] He argued that federal college aid needed to be linked to some form of national service, be it military or civilian. Returning to his target of high-income students, he claimed that the USA had 'created a GI Bill without the GI by offering federal aid to college students who do not serve their country'.[111]

---

[107] Gary Hart, *The Minuteman: Restoring an Army of the People* (New York: The Free Press, 1998); Gary Hart, *The Patriot: An Exhortation to Liberate America from the Barbarians* (New York: The Free Press, 1998). Hart was a longstanding member of the Military Reform movement, which critiqued wasteful Pentagon spending on expensive technology and called for a different military model based on cheap and plentiful weapons systems and a manoeuvre-based approach.

[108] Charles C. Moskos, 'Letter to Al Gore: Your Enlisted Army Days, Military Recruitment, and National Service', 14 August 1999, Moskos Papers.

[109] Louis Caldera, 'Remarks by the Honorable Louis Caldera Secretary of the Army on College First/GED Plus, Washington DC', 3 February 2000, Louis Caldera Collection, Box 9, Folder 2, AHEC.

[110] Charles C. Moskos, 'Letter to Richard J. Durbin', 20 November 2000, Moskos Papers.

[111] Moskos, 'Letter to Representative Steve Buyer', 27 October 1999; Moskos, 'Commander-In-Chief (CINC) Conference: Social Issues'.

Despite Moskos' enthusiastic lobbying and the work of some groups within the military (the US Military Academy had conducted a study along similar lines in 1998), the Army and the Department of Defense effectively rejected his proposals.[112] In response to Warner's prompting, Reimer had his staff examine the subject and they argued that training so many recruits who would go on to only serve a year after their initial training would both take up too much of the Army's energy and create too much personnel churn. Moreover, enlistments of fifteen to eighteen months were not long enough for soldiers to develop the technical skills vital to many roles within the Army.[113] Another major flaw was that current legislation mandated an eight-year mandatory service requirement after any enlistment, meaning that any short-service enlistees would have the possibility of being called back into service hanging over them long after their terms had expired.[114] Even if the military had been ambivalent about the All-Volunteer Force at its inception, they were now more than comfortable with it, and demonstrated no desire to change, even when faced with recruiting shortfalls. Moskos may have been right that there was considerable bipartisan support for his ideas and, based on his correspondence, he certainly had the support of influential senators on both sides of the aisle, but that support wasn't committed enough to overcome institutional inertia and the Army's vision of itself as a professional force whose ethos had been validated with victory in the Persian Gulf.

Even as Moskos campaigned for some form of return to the citizen-soldier ideal that he experienced as a draftee in the 1950s, other influential scholars of civil–military relations diagnosed similar problems with the All-Volunteer Force but were less optimistic about the ability to solve them by returning to earlier models, given the changed geopolitical and societal contexts. In October 2000, Elliott Abrams and Andrew Bacevich organised a symposium on citizenship and military service, the proceedings of which were published in *Parameters*. Bacevich and Abrams declared that 'the mythic tradition of the citizen-soldier is dead, its fate sealed by changes in modern war, in the aims of US national security strategy since the end of the Cold War, and in the aspirations and expectations of American citizens'. They argued that 'the federal government [had] effectively forfeited its ability to compel citizens to serve in the

---

[112] Office of Economic & Manpower Analysis, 'Presentation to LTG David H. Ohle: 18 Month Enlistments: The Junior Year Abroad' (Department of Social Sciences, United States Military Academy, 12 March 1999), Moskos Papers.

[113] Dennis J. Reimer, 'Letter to Senator John Warner, Encl. Information Paper on Short-Term Enlistment Proposal', 23 April 1999, Dennis J. Reimer Papers: General Organization and Functions Correspondence Files, Box 15, April–May 1999, AHEC.

[114] Thomas Bartow, 'Email to Charles Moskos Re 15 Month Enlistments', 23 January 2006, Moskos Papers.

military' and that it was now the individual, not the state, who would determine the terms under which they would serve.[115]

In their summary of the findings of the symposium, Bacevich and Abrams inadvertently highlighted the tensions and contradictions that were troubling the All-Volunteer Force at the close of the twentieth century. On the one hand, they recognised that combat was not about to disappear and that American soldiers would be 'required to manifest qualities not dissimilar from those of the soldiers who landed at Omaha Beach or went to war in the Ia Drang', while they worried that contemporary American society was 'in the grip of a consumerist mentality and postmodern values' and would thus 'find it increasingly difficult to sustain such an ethos in even a minority of its soldiery'. On the other hand, they claimed that:

The identity of the 'soldier as warrior' has become obsolete. It does not adequately describe the actual function – or, more accurately, the broader range of functions – of American military men and women in the aftermath of the Cold War. As such, it misleads citizens, creates false expectations among would-be recruits, and breeds cynicism among those already in uniform.[116]

Therefore, 'some more relevant identity, a refashioning of what it means to be an American soldier' was necessary. Bacevich and Abrams purported to want to extract the Army 'from the ongoing *Kulturkampf* in which they have become increasingly enmeshed since the end of the Cold War', but in reality their proposals fully embraced some of the themes of the culture wars.[117] While they argued that American military institutions should be neither fully insulated from American society nor used as 'sociological laboratories', they also argued that military service be promoted as 'a rite of passage to manhood'. They argued that in a society 'in which gender roles have blurred', the opportunities 'for the individual to demonstrate to himself that he is indeed a man' had dwindled. Thus, the 'rigor and purposefulness of military service' could 'offer just the opportunity to do a man's work'.[118]

One of the reasons for this emphasis on masculinity was the need to ensure that the combat arms could refight the Normandy landings if needs be, but it also related to the need for the 'force needed to perform the functions of a global constabulary … to be to the maximum extent possible, unencumbered by personal responsibilities and obligations'.[119]

---

[115] Elliott Abrams and Andrew Bacevich, 'A Symposium on Citizenship and Military Service', *Parameters*, Summer 2001, 19.
[116] Abrams and Bacevich.
[117] Abrams and Bacevich, 18.
[118] Abrams and Bacevich, 21.
[119] Abrams and Bacevich, 19.

Bacevich and Abrams wanted the services to adopt the Marine Corps' ill-fated and short-lived 1993 ban on married enlistees, as their ideal recruit was a 19- or 20-year-old single male.[120] Just as Army leaders such as Reimer were growing frustrated with the Army's obligations towards its married soldiers, and as the military welfare state was beginning to be rolled back, this group of scholars was suggesting that such a change was necessary to ensure that an expeditionary Army could fulfil its 'quasi-imperial' role.

While Bacevich and Abrams' summary of the conference's findings supported ideas such as Moskos' short-service enlistment (Moskos was, after all, an attendee at the conference and his paper was published in the special edition of *Parameters* that discussed the findings of the conference), they did not see his citizen-soldier ideal as either realistic or useful in the current climate. When discussing 'the refashioning of the identity of the American soldier', they instead wanted to turn to the historical experiences of 'bluejackets and blue-coated and khaki-clad soldiers of old' in order to persuade Americans of the importance of an activist role for the military in world affairs.[121] In his contribution to the symposium, Eliot Cohen argued that the 'citizen-soldier' ideal just could not fit the needs of contemporary geopolitics and that the constant invocation of that ideal by Private Ryan–loving generals was disingenuous at best. Cohen thought it was clear that for citizen-soldiers, military service was either an obligation imposed by the state or the result of mobilisation for a cause, and that for the volunteer of the 1990s, neither of those motivations applied. Further, the contemporary US military was not representative of broader society in any way (here, Cohen had some sympathy for Moskos' proposals), and that, in the case of the citizen-soldier, their identity remained fundamentally civilian, which was not the case with the Army of the 1990s. Even if citizen-soldiers served for years, they, like Tom Hanks' character Captain Miller in *Saving Private Ryan*, were still essentially citizens in uniform who would demobilise and go back to their previous lives as soon as the war was over. By contrast, for the contemporary soldier, the Army *was* their way of life, and even reservists were 'part-time professionals' rather than true citizen-soldiers.[122] This was the crucial difference that separated Cohen from Moskos. While the latter believed that changing the demographics of the force by bringing in more college graduates, short-service enlistees and unmarried soldiers

---

[120] For an account of the Marine Corps marriage ban, see John Worsencroft, 'A Family Affair: Military Service in the Postwar Era' (PhD dissertation, Philadelphia, Temple University, 2017), 239–59.

[121] Abrams and Bacevich, 'A Symposium on Citizenship and Military Service', 19.

[122] Cohen, 'Twilight of the Citizen-Soldier'.

would reinvigorate the ideal of the 'citizen-soldier' within the Army, the former thought that this change, while welcome, could never fully rehabilitate the citizen-soldier, given the very different needs of the Army in the post–Cold War world.

4.3   The End of the 'Weekend Warrior'? The Army's Reserve Component in an Era of Expeditionary Operations

The limits of citizen-soldier rhetoric could also be seen in the post–Cold War experiences of the Army's Reserve Component – the Army National Guard and the Army Reserve – which together made up 54 per cent of the Army's total strength. This figure was one that was invoked repeatedly by Army leaders whenever they addressed reservists, as was their commitment to making sure the Reserve Component was fully utilised in ongoing overseas operations.[123] Above all else though, these addresses tended to emphasise reservists' backgrounds as citizen-soldiers and their importance in connecting the Army to civilian communities. Writing in *The Officer*, the journal of the Reserve Officer Association of the United States, General Colin Powell declared that 'the men and women of the Guard and Reserve serve the nation as activist patriots'. One of their most important roles was to 'solidify the crucial roots of support among the American public for strong defenses'.[124] Similarly, Secretary Caldera highlighted the fact that the Reserve Component was a 'community-based force' that provided an 'essential link to our communities and thereby the grass roots support of our nation'. Caldera asked National Guard leaders to tell their friends and neighbours of the 'need for a strong Army, one prepared to fulfil all the missions the nation asks of it'.[125] The necessity for this link was highlighted by the experience of the Vietnam War and General Creighton Abrams' post-Vietnam Total Force reforms that ensured that when the Army went to war it was with its citizen-soldiers alongside the active forces.[126]

---

[123] Louis Caldera, 'Reserve Officers Association of the United States Annual National Convention, Anaheim, California', 25 June 1999, Louis Caldera Collection, Box 7, Folder 1, AHEC; Louis Caldera, 'National Guard Senior Leadership Conference, Washington, D.C.', 28 January 1999, Louis Caldera Collection, Box 2, Folder 1, AHEC; Dennis J. Reimer, 'VCSA EANGUS Speech (Draft)', 4 September 1991, Dennis J. Reimer Papers: 870-5f Organization Historical Files, VCSA, CGFORSCOM, CSA – Box 43 10 September 1991, EANGUS Conference, AHEC.

[124] Colin Powell, cited in James M. Perkins, 'The Citizen-Soldier in the Total Force', *Military Review* 73, no. 10 (October 1993): 26.

[125] Caldera, 'National Guard Senior Leadership Conference, Washington, D.C.'.

[126] Lewis Sorley, *Thunderbolt: General Creighton Abrams and the Army of His Times* (New York: Simon & Schuster, 1992).

Recent operational experience partly bore out the wisdom of those reforms, as over 145,000 members of the National Guard and the Army Reserve served in support of Operation Desert Storm, of which 75,000 deployed to South-west Asia, and by 1997 over 25 per cent of US Army forces in Bosnia were reservists.[127] So important were reservists in combat support roles that some specialties, such as public affairs, civil affairs and psychological operations, experienced a very high tempo of operations, with every single reserve civil affairs unit sending troops to Bosnia and some deploying to Haiti as well. Charles Cragin, Acting Assistant Secretary of Defense for Reserve Affairs, acknowledged that this pace of deployments effectively meant the demise of the concept of the 'weekend warrior' as the frequent absence of reservists from their civilian jobs placed a strain on relations with their employers, and Reserve Component units faced the same retention and recruitment challenges as their Active Component counterparts.[128]

These problems underlined some of the difficulties in Army leaders' approach to the Reserve Component. For much as they emphasised the importance of 'citizen-soldiers', their rhetoric also spoke about 'the profession of arms'. The Army's 'One Team, One Fight, One Future' white paper on the Reserve Component noted that 'we are a profession committed to unlimited and unrestrained service to the Nation, wherever and whenever America needs', a notion in obvious tension with the needs and abilities of part-time soldiers.[129] Looking to the future of a continental US-based 'power projection Army', General Gordon R. Sullivan had decided during his tenure as Army chief of staff that the structure of the Reserve Component would need some revision in the post–Cold War world. In a 1992 discussion with a RAND Corporation analyst, he suggested that the orientation of the Reserve and the Guard were nineteenth-century models and that the Army needed to break out of and develop models for the twenty-first century. Sullivan thought that the solution would be to move the National Guard and Army Reserve away from combat roles, which required too much in the way of training and readiness, and towards combat support and combat service support functions that would 'be

[127] William Joe Webb, *Department of the Army Historical Summary Fiscal Years 1990 and 1991* (Washington, DC: Center of Military History, United States Army, 1997), 43; *Department of the Army Historical Summary Fiscal Year 1997* (Washington, DC: Center of Military History, United States Army, 2005), 139.

[128] Charles Cragin, 'The Demise of the Weekend Warrior', *Bangor Daily News*, 27 May 1999, Louis Caldera Collection, Box 7, Folder 1, AHEC.

[129] *One Team, One Fight, One Future, Total Army Integration* (Washington, DC: Department of the Army, 1998), 3.

more relevant for contingency operations' and would help the Guard in their state missions.[130]

Sullivan's comments were made in the context of a growing rift between the National Guard and the Active Army, one caused by the experience of the Gulf War. While 62,000 members of the Guard did mobilise in support of Operation Desert Storm – a mobilisation that was declared a success by Army leaders – the Total Force did not function exactly as planned.[131] A central component of Reserve/Active Component integration was the concept of the 'roundout brigade', a combat brigade made up of National Guard troops attached to every Active Component division that would mobilise to augment that division in wartime. When it came to mobilisation for war though, three National Guard combat brigades slated to be deployed were not sent, their place filled by Active Component forces instead. In the case that received the most attention, the 48th Infantry Brigade of the Georgia National Guard, which was supposed to be part of the 24th Mechanized Division, was only mobilised in November 1990 and was sent to Fort Irwin, California for further training instead of being sent to Saudi Arabia. Army Chief of Staff General Carl Vuono argued that the Reserve combat brigades simply were not immediately available for deployment given that they would take time to be mobilised, and therefore, in the rush to make sure sufficient forces were in place in Saudi Arabia, it made sense to send full-time soldiers instead.[132] Critics pointed out that the 48th had passed its rotation at the NTC just the previous year and that in previous congressional testimony, the then Secretary of the Army John Marsh had declared that 'early deploying Reserve Component combat forces have been receiving equipment upgrades and adequate training .... These roundout units have a level of performance and proficiency that is quite high.'[133]

In contrast to this testimony, a pre–Desert Storm Pentagon briefing told the *Washington Post* that 'while the combat capability of the [Iraqi] Republican Guard is highly rated ... much of the regular Iraqi army is

[130] Gordon R. Sullivan, 'CSA Luncheon with Mr Steven Dressner, Rand Corporation', 7 February 1992, Gordon R. Sullivan Papers: CSA Memorandums, February 1992, AHEC.

[131] Michael D Doubler, *I Am the Guard: A History of the Army National Guard, 1636–2000* (Washington, DC: Department of the Army, 2001), 264.

[132] A subsequent Government Accountability Office report supported Vuono's views. US Government Accountability Office, 'Army Training: Replacement Brigades Were More Proficient than Guard Roundout Brigades', no. NSIAD-93-4 (6 January 1993), www.gao.gov/products/NSIAD-93-4.

[133] Craig S. Chapman, 'Gulf War: Nondeployed Roundouts', *Military Review* 72, no. 9 (September 1992): 20–35.

roughly equal in combat readiness to National Guard troops'.[134] This comparison to the Iraqi Army infuriated the National Guard, as did the overall failure of the roundout unit concept. One officer of the 48th told the *New York Times* that the unit had been treated 'like the Army's red-headed stepchild'.[135] The affair was relitigated several times in the pages of *Military Review* after the war, where one observer argued that the Army's decision not to deploy the National Guard's combat brigades was as much about the politics of the post–Cold War drawdown as it was the needs of the war in the Gulf.[136] Here the duelling rhetoric of the 'citizen-soldier' and the 'profession of arms' was laid bare, as the Army fundamentally did not trust the Guard's professionalism in combat and moved to make sure that reserve units would make up a much smaller percentage of combat forces after the drawdown.[137] The editor of *Military Review* recognised the challenges that these exchanges posed for Active– Reserve Component relationships, maintaining that 'if this perception of bad faith is widespread among National Guard and Army Reserve soldiers, it has significant implications for the process of change, because change at every echelon must then tackle not only missions, organisa- tions and training systems but personal opinions as well'.[138] This depth of feeling was evidenced by the letter sent by Brigadier General Joseph F. Conlon of the Army Reserve to Sullivan during his tenure as chief of staff. Conlon wrote to Sullivan to reject an official history of Operation Desert Storm because it was 'a slap in the face' to the reservists of the 500th Military Police Brigade who had served in the Gulf and not gotten sufficient credit for their work.[139] That a serving brigadier general saw fit to write to the chief of staff of the Army with such sentiments speaks to how deeply some of the failures of the Gulf War rankled with National Guard and Reserve leaders, even as the Army's leadership declared the operation a great vindication of the Total Force. These senior reservists understood that if their units were not trusted to take part in combat

---

[134] Bruce Jacobs, 'Tensions between the Army National Guard and the Regular Army', *Military Review* 73, no. 10 (October 1993): 16.

[135] Peter Applebome, 'Guardsmen Return from War They Didn't Fight', *New York Times*, 27 March 1991, www.nytimes.com/1991/03/27/us/guardsmen-return-from-war-they-didn-t-fight.html.

[136] Kris P. Thompson, 'ARNG Unfairly Slammed', *Military Review* 73, no. 10 (October 1993): 3.

[137] Jacobs, 'Tensions between the Army National Guard and the Regular Army'; Chapman, 'Gulf War: Nondeployed Roundouts'; Richard L. Stouder, 'Roundout Brigades: Ready or Not?' *Military Review* 73, no. 6 (June 1993): 38–49.

[138] John W. Reitz, 'From the Editor', *Military Review* 73, no. 10 (October 1993).

[139] Joseph F. Conlon, 'Letter to Gordon R. Sullivan', 19 October 1993, Gordon R. Sullivan Papers: CSA Correspondence Files October 1993, AHEC.

operations, then they would slip further down the social hierarchy of an organisation that valorised the experience of combat above all else.

Certainly, the roundout brigade affair was a harbinger of the difficulties to come in the relationship between the Army and the National Guard. As part of the drawdown, the Army eliminated the National Guard's roundout brigades, instead creating fifteen 'enhanced separate brigades' that would not be deployed until ninety days into a conflict. Further, the Guard lost the equivalent of two divisions and eleven combat brigades and eliminated 64,000 positions.[140] Michael Doubler's official history of the National Guard claims that the stress of the drawdown 'caused the most serious deterioration in Army-Guard relations since the mobilization of 1940–1941', when several long-serving Guard division commanders had been relieved of command rather than being allowed to lead their troops into combat during World War II.[141] By 1997, the National Guard Association was complaining that the Guard had unfairly borne the brunt of budget cuts and that the Army's post–Gulf War retreat from the roundout brigade concept was an attempt to secure more funding for the Active Component. In a position paper, the association pointedly noted that it had the support of both the Senate and state governors in its advocacy and argued that after the way the drawdown had been handled thus far, they 'had reason not to trust the Army'. Remarkably, they also equated the National Guard with the people as a whole, claiming that 'the Army has never trusted the American people', making reference to previous crises in relations between the Guard and the Army.[142] The move to convert National Guard combat formations into support units was particularly controversial, and members of the Guard penned articles in the Army's professional journals to warn of the dangers in cutting back on the Reserve Component's combat capabilities. If reservists were now only required to serve in support roles, there was a real danger that the Army would not be able to raise combat forces quickly enough in the event of a crisis, as all of those tankers who had been converted to truck drivers could not revert back to their previous roles quickly and it would take the Army at least two years to recruit, train and equip a combat division from scratch.[143]

Similarly, the Army Reserve was suffering. While the National Guard still retained some combat units after the drawdown, the Reserve lost

[140] Doubler, *I Am the Guard*, 299.
[141] Doubler, 311.
[142] National Guard Association of the United States, 'The Five Issues Most Important to the National Guard in December 1997', 9 January 1998, Louis Caldera Collection, Box 2, Folder 1, AHEC.
[143] George D. Schull, 'Correcting the Force Structure Mismatch', *Military Review* 80, no. 3 (June 2000): 31–9.

all its combat capability and was converted entirely to combat support and combat service support roles. Because soldiers in the Army Reserve were often in high-demand areas, they quickly found themselves to be overworked and underappreciated. One veteran sent Reimer a manuscript authored by a group of reservist officers who were leaving the service and threatening to send their complaints to the media.[144] The authors complained that 'the tragic truth which nobody in Washington wants to talk about is that although the elite echelons of the U.S. Army are continuously praising its reserve solders and expressing how important they are to the "Total Army" team concept, these very same reserve soldiers have been and still are being treated as "Third Class" soldiers when it comes to promotions in rank and in total compensation'.[145] Reimer's correspondent, who had persuaded them not to leak the manuscript to the press, agreed with them and argued that 'soldiers in the Army Reserve are some of our most loyal and dedicated professionals in uniform', but that they were also grossly 'overworked, underpaid and receive third rate treatment by the Army when compared to their full-time counterparts'.[146]

If the National Guard and Army Reserve were vocal in their complaints about changes to the Army's structure, their Active Component counterparts were equally suspicious of the motivations of reservists and repeatedly complained about their perceived lack of professionalism in a variety of fora. Writing in *Parameters*, one author praised both the Active Army and the Army Reserve for their ability to rapidly deploy overseas but complained that 'because of the Guard's constitutional link to the individual states, it is practically inaccessible to the Active Army to meet immediate deployment requirements'. Further, because the Guard had kept a few of its combat formations, it was 'less combat ready precisely because it possesses the largest percentage of combat forces (the toughest arm to keep ready)' and it was less relevant in the overall force structure because such units were less central to the needs of contingency operations. Further, these contingency operations did not fit with the expectations of citizens who had joined the Guard or Reserve in the belief 'that they were volunteering to serve part-time in a force whose object was to prepare them to fight the nation's next war or to meet national

[144] John J. Green, 'Letter to Dennis Reimer', 25 June 1998, Dennis J. Reimer Papers: General Organization and Functions Correspondence Files, Box 15, June–July 1998, AHEC.

[145] Anonymous, 'Third Class Soldiers: How the US Army Short-Changes Reservists', 25 June 1998, Dennis J. Reimer Papers: General Organization and Functions Correspondence Files, Box 15, June–July 1998, AHEC.

[146] Green, 'Letter to Dennis Reimer', 25 June 1998.

emergencies when called up'.[147] Frequent overseas deployments in situations short of war or a national emergency did not fit with these traditional conceptions of part-time service.

Other authors noted similar problems. Citing the increasingly heavy requirements of professional military education along with unit training, one recently retired lieutenant general argued that 'the uncompromising intensity imposed by the Regular Army ... can drive out many young leaders striving to succeed both in the Army and in the IBMs and Motorolas of competitive industry'.[148] The same author argued that the Guard's combat formations simply were not good enough for the strains of contemporary war and noted that such formations would be 'subject to heavy, highly localized losses in the event of hard combat' and thus those 'losses become a tragedy for the home town and a media disaster in any sensitive contingency situation'.[149] Some even questioned the Reserve Component's ability to effectively fulfil a logistical role on the future battlefield, claiming that the Army Reserve would not be able to mobilise quickly enough and that their job could be done better by civilian contractors.[150] Daniel Bolger effectively distilled the essence of these complaints in his 1992 article in *Parameters*, where he argued that 'power projection must be a way of life for full-time warriors, not an avocation for part-time soldiers who also carry a full-time civilian job, no matter how patriotic or dedicated these soldiers are'. Contemporary combat demanded 'an extraordinary degree of battle readiness', which meant that 'technically astute, tactically aware expeditionary soldiers and units must be ready to go now'. Maintaining these standards would inevitably 'require total professional commitment', a commitment far beyond what Reserve Component units could be reasonably asked to give.[151]

The end result of these tensions between the Active and Reserve Components was not only a significant amount of bitter feelings on both sides, but also an uneasy compromise where Army leaders carried out their promised cuts but also championed slogans such as 'One Team, One Fight' and sought to further integrate Active and Reserve Component units through such initiatives as creating more multicomponent units and having soldiers from both components serve rotations in each

[147] David T. Fautua, 'How the Guard and Reserve Will Fight in 2025', *Parameters: Journal of the US Army War College*. 29, no. 1 (Spring 1999): 127–49.
[148] Frederic J. Brown, 'Reserve Forces: Army Challenge of the 1990s', *Military Review* 71, no. 8 (August 1991): 7.
[149] Brown, 14.
[150] David T. Fautua, 'Transforming the Reserve Components', *Military Review* 80, no. 5 (October 2000): 57–67.
[151] Daniel P. Bolger, 'A Power Projection Force: Some Concrete Proposals', *Parameters: Journal of the US Army War College*, Winter 1992–3, 54.

other's formations. These initiatives were generally welcomed but did not manage to resolve the tension between the ideal of the citizen-soldier and the perceived professional requirements of contemporary contingency operations.

Despite the 'citizen-soldier' rhetoric of the Army leadership, they were no closer to solving this problem at the end of the decade than they had been in the aftermath of the Gulf War. Indeed, some civilian interlocutors picked up on the limits of the Army's citizen-soldier discourse. In a memo that otherwise offered praise of the Army's 1998 'One Team, One Fight' white paper that outlined some of their integration efforts, National Security Council staffer Robert Bell queried what the Army really meant by 'citizen-soldiers'. Writing to Reimer, he said: 'I know the Army Guard and Army Reserve fit the classic definition of "citizen-soldiers" but I am not clear reading this text whether you are arguing that the Active Army are citizen-soldiers too or whether the Total Force has a citizen-soldier quality because of the inclusion of the Reserve Components'.[152] This query, even if it was an offhand one, got at the heart of the Army's problems with the concept. Even if they believed their own rhetoric, Army leaders' conception of what it meant to be a 'citizen-soldier' was vague enough to be meaningless, while the realities of Reserve service in the era of a 'power projection' Army were very far removed from the sort of ideals that the Army loved to celebrate in *Saving Private Ryan*.

4.4   Conclusion

In a 1998 address to the four-star commanders-in-chief who ran the US Combatant Commands that stretched across the globe, Moskos reflected on the future of the Army's relationship with society. He saw three possible paths forward: the first was what he called a 'From Here to Eternity military' (a reference to the 1953 film examining the pre-Pearl Harbor peacetime Army) that was essentially closed off from broader society; the second, a 'postmodern military' that was 'subject to all the fashions and trends of the civilian society', including 'women in ground combat, open gays in the military, suing commanders, an occupational ethos, [and] emphasizing multiculturalism'. The third and final path was a 'Civic Army ... broadly representative of America with service as an ideal aspect of citizenship'. Moskos called for a 'return to the GI Bill principle of vocational and higher education funding as a recognition of

---

[152] Robert G. Bell, 'Memorandum for General Dennis Reimer RE: "One Team, One Fight, One Future"', 3 April 1998, Dennis J. Reimer Papers: 1mm Reading Files – Box 6: April 1998, AHEC.

citizenship service' and argued that 'the need is for continuing reinvigoration of the citizen-soldier for the good of both the armed forces and the larger American society'.[153] The turmoil caused by the post–Cold War drawdown and subsequent increase in deployments along with widespread worry over the recruiting crisis of the late 1990s may have given Moskos some hope about the possibility of a 'Civic Army' but ultimately the Army's refusal to do more than rhetorically celebrate the citizen-soldier firmly closed off that path forward. To use Moskos' typology, was unclear whether the military of the near future would be a 'postmodern' one or one more isolated from broader society in terms of its values and demographics, but it would certainly not be one that looked anything like the Army of *Saving Private Ryan* or *The Greatest Generation*, an ideal type celebrated so much by Moskos and others.

The Army's actions throughout the drawdown showed that while senior leaders had some sympathy for Moskos' concerns – indeed, many may have been attracted to his vision of a force primarily made up of 19–21-year-old unmarried middle-class young men – the citizen-soldier ideal was ultimately not one that was a high priority for them. No senior leaders were willing to change the Army's recruiting priorities or service model to achieve Moskos' vision, and even those who broadly shared his concern about the civil–military gap, such as Secretary Caldera, were not ready to make the trade-off between socioeconomic diversity in the ranks and the perceived loss of readiness that would be caused by such a change. The experience of the Reserve Component, celebrated as citizen-soldiers and patriots by virtually every senior leader who spoke about them, but also seen as unready for the rigours of contemporary combat, further underlined the extent to which Army leaders prioritised the notion of the 'profession of arms' over that of the citizen-soldier.

[153] Moskos, 'Commander-In-Chief (CINC) Conference: Social Issues'.

5   Technological Transformation and the American Soldier

In early March 1995, Army Chief of Staff General Gordon R. Sullivan received a somewhat unusual item in his reading file: a review essay on Robert Heinlein's 1959 sci-fi novel, *Starship Troopers*.[1] The essay, seemingly authored by a staff officer at Sullivan's request, didn't focus on themes frequently highlighted by literary scholars, such as the novel's celebration of militarism, its critique of the moral decline of western society or its depiction of an essentially fascist society, but instead discussed its portrayals of military technology and the future battlefield.[2] The author spoke of Heinlein offering a 'window into the future' and talked about how the novel anticipated 'telemedicine, simulated and virtual training exercises, complete situational awareness, a heads-up display, remote sensors, terminally guided munitions, fire-and-forget brilliant munitions, and voice-activated weapons'.[3] On this future battlefield, each soldier was 'an integrated weapon system with a wide variety of options to identify, discriminate, and attack targets', all while 'assimilating vast amounts of data while maintaining complete situational awareness'. Essentially, *Starship Troopers* offered a 'glimpse of the present through the lens of a man from the 50s'.

The only critique the author had of Heinlein was that 'his timetable was wrong', and he argued that 'what was science fiction in 1959 is reality today. Perhaps we need to think about the next forty years much the same way Heinlein did in 1959, letting our minds imagine what could be.'[4]

---

[1] LTC Moore, '"Review Essay: Starship Troopers by Robert A. Heinlein", in Memorandum from Michael V. Harper to Various Regarding CSA Staff Group Weekly Update', 10 March 1995, Gordon R. Sullivan Papers, Box 254, Folder 3, CSA Correspondence, 1995, AHEC.

[2] Robert A Heinlein, *Starship Troopers* (New York: Putnam, 1959); H. Bruce Franklin, *Robert A. Heinlein: America as Science Fiction* (New York: Oxford University Press, 1980); Jeffrey Cass, 'SS Troopers: Cybernostalgia and Paul Verhoeven's Fascist Flirtation', *Studies in Popular Culture* 21, no. 3 (1999): 51–63.

[3] Moore, '"Review Essay: Starship Troopers by Robert A. Heinlein", in Memorandum from Michael V. Harper to Various Regarding CSA Staff Group Weekly Update'.

[4] Moore.

On this point, Sullivan noted his agreement, underlining the text and scrawling 'I believe [Chief of Military History] BG [Brigadier General Harold] Nelson is trying to do this'.[5] Sure enough, three days later, Nelson, a close confidant of Sullivan, followed up on a conversation and faxed him an *Army Aviation* magazine article with the subject line 'Starship Troopers' on the cover sheet, noting that it depicted a 'near-future scenario' that could help 'get the word out' on the fundamentals of the Army's digital transformation.[6] This article described a fictional scenario in which an Army aviation brigade was able to communicate and coordinate seamlessly on the battlefield using new digital technology while they destroyed an enemy motorised division without loss.[7] Despite the futurism of the *Army Aviation* piece, Nelson was possibly overreaching when comparing it to Heinlein's bestseller and hoping that it might help 'get the word out' on Sullivan's initiatives. The prose was leaden, highly technical and jargon-filled, and the dry language of procurement and software development was a world away from *Starship Troopers'* depictions of nuclear battle against arachnid enemies on alien planets. Nonetheless, it is telling that Nelson chose to draw a line between these different renditions of the future and that the language of science fiction was being spoken in the Army's corridors of the Pentagon in this era.

While previous chapters have shown how the Army as an institution struggled to adapt to changing geopolitical, demographic and cultural circumstances, Army leaders were doing more than just reacting to contingencies and events in this period. Indeed, both they and the service as a whole spent a considerable portion of their time preoccupied by questions about what the future might look like and how the Army could position itself to get ahead of technological trends and reform itself rapidly. The visions offered by different factions differed in detail but virtually all the Army's imagined futures centred on iterations of high-tech conventional war. Many agreed that the Army should focus on skipping a generation of technological development by embracing 'leap-forward' digital technologies that would produce a networked and essentially frictionless battlefield on which American soldiers would rapidly triumph.

---

[5] Moore.

[6] Hal Nelson, 'Fax from Brigadier General Hal Nelson to General Gordon R. Sullivan Regarding Starship Trooper', 13 March 1995, Gordon R. Sullivan Papers; Box 204A, Folder 10 CSA General Officer Files 95 March [part 2 of 2], AHEC.

[7] Peter M. Bartosch and Robert A. Leutwyler, 'The Army Aviation Information Processing Facility', *Army Aviation*, 28 February 1995, Gordon R. Sullivan Papers; Box 204A, Folder 10 CSA General Officer Files 95 March [part 2 of 2], AHEC.

To arrive at this future, the Army would need highly professional and technology-literate soldiers, who were, in the words of one senior figure, 'hyper-proficient' at their job. Army exercises and experiments throughout the digitisation process highlighted the dangers of cognitive overload caused by the sheer amount of raw information provided by the new digital systems, and the Army had to invest heavily in training and software to help combat this overload. This move precluded any return to the sort of short-service 'citizen's army' that advocates such as Charles Moskos had been pushing for.[8] Not only that, but the cost of these new systems made it very difficult for the Army to resist cuts to its numbers to pay for digitisation.

Part of the solution to this problem of numbers was to tap into another 1990s-era development: privatisation. While the 'iron mountain' of supplies that the Army required to sustain itself on operations could be reduced somewhat by adapting 'just-in-time' logistics innovations from the civilian sector, the Army also moved to privatise large chunks of its logistics and support chain. Doing so allowed them to have a better 'tooth-to-tail' ratio where more soldiers were dedicated to combat and combat-adjacent activities, while contractors took on what had previously been core military functions in sustainment. Contractors would also be vital for servicing the new technology being brought into the Army. Some systems, especially communications networks, simply couldn't function without contractors from private industry there to troubleshoot. Thus, the digital transformation might have demanded more of American soldiers, but it also required the heavy usage of civilian specialists to make future war feasible.

As the force became more technology-focused and more reliant on contractors, it also had to adapt to become more expeditionary. While Army leaders looked to science fiction, they also spent time reading their history and frequently worried about the nightmare scenario of another 'Task Force Smith', the cobbled-together, underequipped and poorly trained outfit that had been rushed to Korea at the outbreak of war there in July 1950 and badly mauled by North Korean forces. The Army of the 1990s would primarily be based in the continental United States and concentrated on a few mega-bases, and would therefore need to be able to rapidly deploy anywhere in the world on short notice, while arriving at their destination capable of winning the first battle. To do this would require new, lighter and more lethal equipment, but also a change in mindset by creating an 'expeditionary' culture. Inevitably, rhetoric that emphasised the Army's expeditionary future ran up against a Marine Corps aggrieved at another service moving in on their territory. Squabbles between Army

---

[8] For more on this, see Chapter 4, but also Charles Moskos, 'From Citizens' Army to Social Laboratory', *The Wilson Quarterly* 17, no. 1 (1993): 83–94.

and Marine leaders focused on doctrinal distinctions between 'contingency' and 'expeditionary' forces, but the deeper conflict seemed to be about which service should be designated as the 'first responders' in an international crisis. In a world where high-tech American forces could be expected to win quickly and comprehensively, how could large numbers of seemingly redundant ground forces be justified?

5.1   A Revolution in Military Affairs?

Victory in the Gulf War left many Army leaders with an uneasy feeling. On the one hand, the conflict seemed to be a resounding vindication of the Army's post-Vietnam reforms in general and Air-Land battle doctrine in particular.[9] On the other, the apparently decisive role played by airpower and precision bombing raised the question of whether the Army could expect to merely be a secondary actor in future wars, relegated to guarding airfields and occupying ground that had effectively been cleared by air-power first.[10] While the Gulf War had seemingly been a model of the use of precision-guided munitions, new GPS technology and communications systems, many defence intellectuals argued that this was just the start and that the 1990s would see a 'Revolution in Military Affairs' (RMA) to rival the gunpowder revolution.[11] The use of electronics, smart sensors and 'networked' weapons systems would profoundly transform war.[12]

While the Air Force and Navy were predictably enthusiastic about a mode of warfare that emphasised weapons systems rather than manpower, the Army was considerably more ambivalent about what became known as 'transformation'. Sullivan later decried 'the easy but erroneous conclusion that by spending hundreds of billions of dollars weaponizing space, developing national missile defence, and buying long-range precision weapons, we can avoid the ugly realities of conflict'.[13] Another Army critic complained that transformation enthusiasts were advocating

[9] Robert H. Scales, *Certain Victory: The U.S. Army in the Gulf War* (Washington, DC: Potomac Books, Inc., 1998); Tom Clancy and Fred Franks, *Into the Storm: A Study in Command* (New York: Putnam, 1998).
[10] Eliot A. Cohen and Thomas A. Keaney, *Gulf War Air Power Survey* (Washington, DC: Office of the Secretary of the Air Force, 1993).
[11] For historiographical sketch of the development of this debate, see Macgregor Knox and Williamson Murray, *The Dynamics of Military Revolution, 1300–2050* (Cambridge: Cambridge University Press, 2001), 1–14.
[12] Arthur K. Cebrowski and John H. Gartksa, 'Network-Centric Warfare – Its Origin and Future', *Proceedings, United States Naval Institute* 124, no. 1 (January 1998), www.usni.org/magazines/proceedings/1998/january/network-centric-warfare-its-origin-and-future.
[13] James Kitfield, 'Army Shell-Shocked in Face of Rumsfeld Reforms', *National Journal*, 11 June 2001, www.govexec.com/defense/2001/06/army-shell-shocked-in-face-of-rumsfeld-reforms/9300/.

an unrealistic form of '"immaculate warfare" whereby the United States can stand secure behind high-tech missile defences and space systems and smite enemies from afar without fear of suffering casualties'.[14] While other services fully embraced the RMA, Army leaders wondered how to adapt to this new world. In his memoirs, Sullivan quoted a letter from Army historian Roger Spiller that described this period as an 'age of anxiety', where far from feeling 'calm and confident in the future when the Cold War was finally over', Army officers of all ranks were struggling to make sense of the times in which they lived.[15]

For Sullivan, the solution was to take advantage of the absence of major geopolitical threats to embrace new technologies that would allow the Army to 'leap ahead' and skip a generation of development to produce a force that could meet whatever challenges the unknown future posed. While the Army never wholeheartedly embraced the RMA in the way that other services did, Sullivan and his successors did invest heavily in digitisation and in a series of initiatives that sought to overhaul and ultimately transform the force. As the decade wore on, modernisation efforts became more and more ambitious. Sullivan launched Force XXI, which effectively sought to digitise existing formations. In 1996, Reimer commissioned the 'Army After Next' study, which sought to push beyond digitisation to create a more nimble and 'flat' organisation, with fewer layers of bureaucracy. Shinseki pushed beyond this again, embracing a broader vision of 'Army Transformation' (a phrase which he insisted on capitalising) as a key objective during his tenure as chief of staff.[16]

Advocates of transformation within the Army argued that the force needed to completely reimagine itself in the post–Cold War world. Major General James Dubik, who headed Shinseki's Transformation effort, reached for the language of scientific revolutions when he likened the current situation to the transformation wrought by Galileo or Einstein. In each case, adherents of the pre-revolutionary worldview tried to rationalise their difficulties as mere anomalies, and, when the anomalies multiplied, they unsuccessfully tried to 'tweak' the prevailing view until suddenly that prevailing view gave way to a new scientific theory that amounted to a 'transformation of vision'.[17] So it was

---

[14] Kitfield.
[15] Gordon R. Sullivan and Michael V. Harper, *Hope Is Not a Method: What Business Leaders Can Learn from America's Army* (New York: Broadway Books, 1997), 167.
[16] For comprehensive histories of the Army's modernisation efforts, see John Sloan Brown, *Kevlar Legions: The Transformation of the United States Army 1989–2005* (Washington, DC: U.S. Army Center of Military History, 2012); Thomas K. Adams, *The Army after Next: The First Postindustrial Army* (Stanford: Stanford University Press, 2008).
[17] James Dubik, 'Speech to Center of Naval Analysis on Principles of War', n.d., James M. Dubik Papers, Box 32, Folder 6, AHEC.

with the Cold War. Dubik claimed that 'the way we raised, organ-ised, acquired, equipped, deployed, based, employed, sustained, pro-grammed, and funded our armed forces to succeed in the Cold War by using industrial age tools and processes cannot be "tweaked" to succeed in our current and future realities'.[18] What was required, then, was a completely new vision.

To the extent that any one individual offered a compelling story about what a transformed army would look like, it was Lieutenant Colonel Douglas Macgregor. In his 1997 book *Breaking the Phalanx: A New Design for Landpower in the Twenty-First Century*, Macgregor both offered a provocative vision of a smaller, lighter, more modular and more agile force and a scathing critique of Army efforts to embrace the RMA to date.[19] Macgregor argued that the heavy armoured forces of the Cold War era were the equivalent of the Macedonian Phalanx, a force that had been shattered by the lighter and more nimble Roman Legions. In Macgregor's mind, the Roman Legion offered an ideal model for the twenty-first-century Army because 'the same legions who routed the enemy in battle, could handle disarmament control, police patrols and general administrative supervision'.[20] Much as the 'arrival of a Roman Legion on foreign soil was synonymous with the presence of order, stability and civilization', 'reorganizing the Army into mobile combat groups positioned on the frontiers of American security, ready to act quickly and decisively, primed to move with a minimum of prep-aration' would ensure that the *Pax Americana* extended well into the twenty-first century.[21]

In practical terms, this meant creating smaller combined arms forma-tions that could take advantage of increasingly lethal weapons systems and the enhanced surveillance capabilities provided by unmanned aerial vehicles, airborne radars and satellites to dominate larger areas. Instead of moving to contact, these units would 'electronically search and then destroy the enemy on the battlefield'.[22] These formations would be more dispersed than in the past and much more mobile too, capable of self-synchronising and manoeuvring 'like irregular swarms spaced in breadth and echeloned in depth, moving to gaps and weaknesses revealed or cre-ated by organic armed air-ground reconnaissance and indirect fires'.[23]

---

[18] Dubik.
[19] Douglas A. Macgregor, *Breaking the Phalanx: A New Design for Landpower in the Twenty-First Century* (Praeger Paperback, 1997).
[20] Macgregor, 2.
[21] Macgregor, 4.
[22] Macgregor, 49.
[23] Macgregor, 146.

They would rely heavily on advanced communications equipment to maintain command and control but also on 'subordinate officers' and soldiers' judgment, intelligence and character'.[24]

Most controversially, Macgregor proposed that these smaller, brigade-sized all-arms units would mean that the entire division-level layer of command could be abolished. He claimed that 'current Army echelons of command and control with their origins in the age of Napoleon' could surely be eliminated in this new age and drew on the example of Microsoft's success to argue that 'flat', horizontal organisational structures allowed for the smooth flow of information.[25] Ultimately, Macgregor's argument was an optimistic, even utopian vision that wondered why 'advances in microcircuitry and weapons technology' couldn't assist in abolishing unnecessary echelons and asked 'why can't new technology extend human potential in new, more economical and efficient ways that are within reach today'.[26] He believed that the lessons of both the Gulf War and the ongoing tech boom in the American economy indicated that they almost certainly could.

Macgregor's book, first published internally as the Army War College Fellowship Research Project in 1996 and then commercially by Praeger the following year, found a wide readership both inside and outside the Army.[27] Newt Gingrich, Speaker of the House and a long-time participant in the Military Reform movement that had critiqued the Pentagon's unwillingness to embrace change, was reported to be a fan and Reimer, who had then taken over as chief of staff from Sullivan, emailed his subordinates to say that Breaking the Phalanx was 'thought-provoking' and 'worth reading'.[28] Reimer had been attending Army warfighting experiments in the California desert and believed that the Army did indeed have an opportunity to follow Macgregor's advice to 'reduce the size and enhance the capabilities'. Reimer told his generals that 'it behoves

---

[24] Macgregor, 5.

[25] Macgregor, 34.

[26] Macgregor, 69.

[27] For the original version of the report, see Douglas A. Macgregor, 'Breaking the Phalanx: A New Design for Landpower in the Twenty-First Century', Fellowship Research Project (Carlisle, PA: US Army War College, 20 May 1996), https://apps.dtic.mil/sti/citations/ADA310904.

[28] Douglas Macgregor, Warrior's Rage: The Great Tank Battle of 73 Easting (Annapolis, MD: Naval Institute Press, 2001), 2; Dennis J. Reimer, 'CSA 97-05 Random Thoughts While Running', 1 April 1997, Frederic J. Brown III Papers; Box 165A; Folder 11, Miscellaneous Correspondence and Other Documents Pertaining to Force XXI Advanced Warfighting Experiment, circa 1997, AHEC. For an excellent intellectual history of the Military Reform movement, see Michael W. Hankins, Flying Camelot: The F-15, the F-16, and the Weaponization of Fighter Pilot Nostalgia (Ithaca, NY: Cornell University Press, 2021).

us to look at the concepts proposed in *Breaking the Phalanx* and decide what makes sense and what we can discard' and commissioned a formal analysis of the concepts it proposed.[29]

Reimer's openness to exploring these ideas did not go down well across the Army and drew a sharp response from retired General Don A. Starry, a revered figure who had both revamped Army training in the early 1980s and been the primary architect of the Air-Land battle doctrine that had succeeded so well in the Persian Gulf. Starry claimed that 'the whole book, briefing, is terribly sophomoric. From a prof who knows his business, the best the author could hope for would be a "D-."' He told Reimer not to 'waste [his] precious time reading the book' and to 'learn and revise judgements about whomever Macgregor may have shown *Phalanx* to before they asked to bother you with it'.[30] There were two reasons for Starry's ire. First, Macgregor was proposing a radical reorganisation of the Army in the absence of any clear vision of who the Army's future foes might be and what threats it might face. Second, the whole proposal reminded him of the Army's ill-fated 'Pentomic Division' experiment from the 1950s, where a service worried by fears of irrelevance in a nuclear war embraced a dramatic restructuring of its combat formations that created smaller and more nimble units that could quickly converge and then disperse before they became vulnerable to tactical nuclear strikes, a structure that bore close resemblance to that proposed by Macgregor.[31] In the case of the Pentomic Division, the Army's communications technology could not keep up, and it became virtually impossible for these smaller units to coordinate across a larger and more dispersed battlefield. These flaws became quickly apparent to Army leaders, and the Army chief of staff commissioned a study on replacing the Pentomic Division only three years after its inception. For Starry and other critics of *Breaking the Phalanx*, the expensive failure

[29] Reimer, 'CSA 97-05 Random Thoughts While Running'.
[30] Don A. Starry, 'Letter to Dennis Reimer', 19 March 1997, Dennis J. Reimer Papers: General Management Correspondence Files, Box 8: March 1997, AHEC. For an account of Starry's role in developing Air-Land Battle, see John L. Romjue, 'From Active Defense to AirLand Battle: The Development of Army Doctrine from 1973 to 1982', TRADOC Historical Monograph Series (Fort Monroe, VA: Historical Office, US Army Training and Doctrine Command, 1984).
[31] Brian McAllister Linn, *Elvis's Army: Cold War GIs and the Atomic Battlefield* (Cambridge, MA: Harvard University Press, 2016); Andrew J. Bacevich, *The Pentomic Era: The U.S. Army Between Korea and Vietnam* (Washington, DC: National Defense University Press, 1986); Kalev I. Sepp, 'The Pentomic Puzzle: The Influence of Personality and Nuclear Weapons on U.S. Army Organization 1952–1958', *Army History*, no. 51 (2001): 1–13; Ingo Trauschweizer, *The Cold War U.S. Army: Building Deterrence for Limited War* (Lawrence: University Press of Kansas, 2008).

of the Pentomic concept demonstrated that technology could not be a panacea in the chaos of the battlefield.[32]

Even advocates of transformation acknowledged that technology alone would not be enough to revolutionise warfare. Dubik noted that the Gulf War had highlighted the potential of 'high speed computers, artificial intelligence, satellite communications and [a] host of other technological advances', but that the Army's staff system of synchronisation, 'using chart, pen, and acetate', was simply too primitive to take full advantage of the possibilities afforded by these technologies.[33] Major Donald Vandergriff, another self-described reformer, noted that the sort of synchronisation the Army was emphasising was a 'methodical, top-down thinking process that assumes that a top-level commander can observe and orient himself to all details on the entire battlefield', which effectively meant further centralising decision-making.[34] The response to an 'explosion of information fuelled by the quest for a perfect picture' would not be empowered subordinates but rather a reliance on mechanistic filtering procedures to synthesise the flood of observations coming from battlefield sensors.[35] This meant that commanders would be forced to use rigid internal procedures, matrices and templates to make sense of what was going on around them.[36]

The same warfighting experiments that had encouraged Reimer about the potential of digitisation highlighted many of the same issues. The Army deployed a 'digitised' tank battalion to the NTC in April 1994, but a General Accounting Office report found that this digitised force performed no better than the seven non-digitised units that were at the NTC at the same time.[37] Reports found that some leaders felt 'tied' to their digital screens and were overloaded by information, at times failing just to get their heads up and look around them.[38] Similarly, tank

---

[32] See also Dale A. Jones, 'The Past Revisited: Comparing and Contrasting the Army after Next's Battle Force to the Pentomic Division' (Fort Leavenworth, KS: School of Advanced Military Studies, Command and General Staff College, 27 May 1999), https://apps.dtic.mil/sti/citations/ADA366232.

[33] James Dubik, 'Memorandum for the Record (a Thought Piece): What Are the Roots of the Army of 2015?', n.d., 7, James M. Dubik Papers, Box 26, Folder 7, AHEC.

[34] Donald Vandergriff, *The Path to Victory: America's Army and the Revolution in Human Affairs* (Novato, CA: Presidio Press, 2002), 9.

[35] Vandergriff, 10.

[36] For an account of how contemporary western headquarters have adapted to these issues, see Anthony King, *Command: The Twenty-First Century General* (Cambridge: Cambridge University Press, 2019).

[37] United States General Accounting Office, 'Battlefield Automation: Army's Digital Battlefield Plan Lacks Specific Measurable Goals' (Washington, DC: General Accounting Office, 29 November 1995), 7, www.gao.gov/assets/nsiad-96-25.pdf.

[38] Walter N. Anderson, 'Memorandum from Walter N. Anderson to Commander, Operations Group Regarding Status of TF-1-70 AR Digital Systems (as of 08 1600 Apr

commanders were overloaded by the 'visual, auditory, motor, and cognitive tasks' that were occurring simultaneously during an engagement, and many actually turned off their digitised equipment to reduce their visual overload.[39] Researchers found that the digitised version of the Bradley Fighting Vehicle – the M2A3 – required that the crew learn over eighty separate tasks to operate the vehicle. Thirty-seven of these tasks were entirely new and eighteen were significantly modified from tasks required on earlier versions of the vehicle.[40]

By 1997, experimental digitised units were still struggling to integrate their new communications systems, while digital traffic flowed too slowly and computers broke down under the harsh conditions of the Mojave Desert. Again, a report found that 'leaders did not trust the information and too often soldiers relied on digital readouts and displays rather than simply looking around' (Figure 5.1).[41] Others noted that information overload not only led to leaders ignoring information that led to serious errors, but that the overload fed on itself, since 'the typical means of blowing off excessive incoming traffic is to forward to more people, frequently the wrong ones, which in turn increases their information overload'.[42] Evaluators of these experiments emphasised the need to make managing information flow both 'seamless' and 'an integral part of soldiers' functions'.[43] This would require not only well-designed and robust systems but increased training, precision and discipline on the battlefield. Leaders would have to be trained in how to understand digital systems' 'architecture, capabilities, and limitations' in addition to all of their combat tasks.[44]

94)', 8 April 1994, Frederic J. Brown Papers; Box 57, Folder 1, Documents pertaining to 1/70 Armor at Fort Irwin, circa 1994, AHEC.

[39] Theodore G. Stroup, 'Memorandum from Lieutenant General Theodore G. Stroup, Jr. to VCSA Regarding ARL Report on Information Overload', 16 February 1995, Theodore G. Stroup Papers; Box 50, Folder 9, Force Structure Changes [part 1 of 5], January 1995-May 1996, AHEC.

[40] Adams, *The Army after Next*, 238.

[41] Adams, 41.

[42] William B. Cunningham, 'Email to Paul Berenson Jr. Re: Your Slides', 11 December 1997, Paul Berenson Papers; Box 1A, Folder 11, Thoughts on Leadership: A Treasury of Quotations [part 3 of 9], AHEC.

[43] Walter N. Anderson, 'Memorandum for BG Maggart Re: Rotation 94-07 – TRADOC Commander Talking Points', 20 April 1994, Frederic J. Brown Papers; Box 57, Folder 1, Documents pertaining to 1/70 Armor at Fort Irwin, circa 1994, AHEC.

[44] Paul Berenson, 'Presentation Slides: Division Army Warfighting Experiment Leadership/ Leader Development Findings – Implications for the Army After Next', n.d., Paul Berenson Papers: Box 2B; Folder 15, U.S. Army Research Institute, Human and Organizational Issues for Army After Next, DCSPER and DCSDOC, HQ TRADOC, Leesburg, Virginia [part 5 of 7], November 1997-June 1998, AHEC.

Figure 5.1 A soldier testing the Dismounted Soldier System Unit during the Advanced Warfighting Experiment at the NTC, Fort Irwin, California, 1997

The results of these experiments made it clear that soldiers would not be able to adapt to the battlefield without significant amounts of complex training. Reporting on what he had seen at the JRTC at Fort Polk, Louisiana, Reimer exulted that the Army was 'moving from the industrial age to the information age' but also noted that these sorts of operations were 'PhD-level work'.[45] In response to the problems thrown up by exercises, Army researchers launched a project to explore how they could 'cognitively engineer' the 'digital battlefield'. Their report noted that 'a gap is developing between the Army's ability to generate and distribute megabytes of data across the battlefield and the soldiers' ability to cognitively assimilate and translate this data into situation awareness, a common

---

[45] Dennis J. Reimer, 'CSA 99-06 Random Thoughts While Running (JRTC and NTC – What I Saw Was an Army Transforming Itself)', 22 March 1999, 99-, James M. Dubik Papers, Box 32, Folder 7, AHEC.

relevant picture, and effective decision making'.[46] Their proposed solution to this problem involved a mixture of enhanced training methods and improved software to aid decision-making.

While the enthusiasm for software-based solutions seemed to validate Vandergriff's fear of templates and rigid procedures, all agreed that developing better leaders would be vital on the digital battlefield. The Army Science Board recommended 'imbuing technology values in the ethos of the officer corps', creating a 'technologist officer' career track and assigning PhD graduate technologist officers to most three- and four-star generals.[47] Further, they recommended that all officers complete eight courses of maths and computer science before they enter the Army, and that 50 per cent of West Point scholarship students study for STEM degrees.[48] While the study's authors denied that they were recommending 'draconian measures that will destabilise the Army' or turn its warriors into 'techno-geeks', they emphasised that the Army was far behind the civilian world in understanding what 'the microchip age means'.[49] While they may not have intended to destabilise the notion of what a soldier was, the Army Science Board's recommendations inevitably involved making trade-offs with limited time and resources and tentatively pointed to a future where traditional masculine attributes such as physical fitness might matter less than technological know-how.

Frederic Brown, the retired lieutenant general heading the Army Knowledge Management project, was optimistic about this future and believed that the Army could take advantage of science to develop not just proficient leaders for the digital battlefield but 'hyper-proficient' teams 'possessing extraordinary levels of personal and team proficiency across both echelon and function'. In order to illustrate the sort of tactical proficiency he thought was achievable, he quoted Tom Clancy's

---

[46] 'STO Nomination Factsheet: Cognitive Engineering of the Digital Battlefield, IV.N.ARL-13', n.d., Frederic J. Brown III Papers; Box 174B, Folder 7, Technical Report: Documents from Fort Leavenworth on Training and Simulations, circa 1998, AHEC.

[47] 'Presentation: Ad Hoc Study, Military Officers for the High Tech Army of Today and Tomorrow', 5 January 1995, Frederic J. Brown III Papers; Box 51A, Folder 9, Briefing Material: Army Science Board Study, Military Officers for the High Tech Army, circa 1995, AHEC. The study received some pushback on the question of ethos, with one staff officer sarcastically reworking Douglas MacArthur's famous line into 'duty, honor, country, technology' and asking: 'do we really want to do this?'

[48] 'Presentation: Ad Hoc Study, Military Officers for the High Tech Army of Today and Tomorrow'.

[49] Edwin H. Burba, 'Correspondence from General Edwin H. Burba to General Gordon R. Sullivan Regarding BCTP Rotations', 28 March 1995, Gordon R. Sullivan Papers, Box 204A, Folder 3, CSA Correspondence Files 95 March [part 3 of 3], AHEC.

techno-thriller novel *Rainbow Six*'s description of Delta Force training: 'every member knew how every other member thought, and so, on exercises where the actual scenario was different from the tactical intelligence they'd been given going in, somehow the team members just adapted, sometimes without words, every trooper knowing what his partner and the others in the team would do, as if they'd communicated by – telepathy'.[50] To achieve this future, Brown suggested looking to psychochemical solutions: he noted that Walter Reed hospital had been exploring the use of drugs to overcome sleepiness and that 'the chemistry of learning and memory formation has witnessed technical breakthroughs over recent years that remain to be applied to practical needs'.[51] On top of this, he recommended working with the Defense Advanced Research Projects Agency (DARPA) to take advantage of advances in computer technologies to create better learning environments, using virtual reality programmes for immersive training and paying attention to research on magnetic resonance imaging to better understand how the brain processed information. Put together, Brown thought that this would lead to an environment where ad hoc teams could assemble and meet Delta Force levels of proficiency within 72–96 hours of meeting each other.[52]

Those in the Military Reform movement were more focused on what current Army training and education got wrong. Macgregor wanted more rigour in professional military education and argued that the services should pool their resources and create one exceptional War College that would produce imaginative and creative leaders capable of thinking outside of service or branch silos.[53] Vandergriff wanted more open-ended training exercises that made use of unorthodox opponents. He suggested that a 'young former gang member from Los Angeles can teach more about 4th generation warfare in an urban environment than most might want to admit'.[54] He proposed finding the funding for these exercises by slashing the 'bloated officer corps in the middle and senior grades'.[55] Vandergriff blamed this state of affairs on the need to retain highly trained personnel to service increasingly advanced weapons systems, a concern which he shared with the Army Science Board. Macgregor argued that better equipment and more training opportunities simply

---

[50] Frederic J. Brown, 'Regarding Military Performance', n.d., 1, Frederic J. Brown III Papers; Box 188C, Folder 4, documents pertaining to man print, digital training models etc, circa 1998–1999, AHEC.

[51] Brown, 2.

[52] Brown, 'Regarding Military Performance'.

[53] Macgregor, *Breaking the Phalanx*, 1997, 163.

[54] Vandergriff, *The Path to Victory*, 258.

[55] Vandergriff, 121.

would not be enough for success, no matter how much DARPA studied the issue and how many technological officers the Army employed. In his telling, leadership in wartime was an ineffable art, and it should be the goal of the military education system to produce inventive and intelligent risk takers, not officers with a 'perfect file' 'who "goes along" and never questions his superior's opinions or directives'.[56] In essence, then, these critics had a much more heroic and romantic view of twenty-first-century warfare than the Army writ large.

Popular treatments of modern war tended to emphasise both the romantic and technological views at the same time. When novelist Tom Clancy and John McKiernan, director of *Die Hard* and *The Hunt for the Red October*, signed on to make a film about the Gulf War's Battle of 73 Easting, the celebrated tank engagement where a single Armoured Cavalry Squadron destroyed two Iraqi armoured brigades without taking any casualties of its own, they pitched it as the 'true story of the Army's Top Gun, Captain H.R. McMaster, the one frontline soldier most responsible for the victory of the Desert Storm ground war'.[57] Clancy and McKiernan, who were enthusiastically supported by the Army in their ultimately unsuccessful effort to put together the film, saw it as a story about intergenerational conflict between older officers made cautious by the shadow of Vietnam and the 'young West Point graduates who were not alive during the Vietnam War who believe in their high-tech weaponry'.[58] The movie was to be 'a real-world techno thriller. American soldiers, fighting for their lives in the desert, use hi-tech systems to win.' These systems included 'depleted uranium and superb ATGM [anti-tank guided missile] weapons, computer and laser-based fire control systems featuring thermal sights and wind sensors, data linked artillery locating radars and powerful rocket launcher fire support'.[59] McMaster, the captain who had commanded Eagle Troop, which bore the brunt of the battle and destroyed an entire Iraqi brigade on its own, was to be depicted as 'a true maverick'. The screenplay began in West Point's Beast Barracks, where McMaster struggled to adhere to cautious Army tactical doctrine, before moving to Fort Knox where he and his peers trained on their tanks and realised that technological advances would allow them to adopt far more offensive tactics than 'timid' military

[56] Macgregor, *Breaking the Phalanx*, 1997, 168.
[57] 'Screenplay: "73 Easting"', n.d., 1, Frederic J. Brown III Papers; Box 28A, Folder 10, documents pertaining to television productions during Desert Shield/Storm, circa 1990–1991, AHEC.
[58] Robert W. Welkos, 'Clancy, McTiernan Team for Film on Gulf War: Movies – The Novelist and Director Are Reuniting after Their Success with "The Hunt for Red October". "73 Easting" Will Be Clancy's First Original Screenplay', *Los Angeles Times*, 4 April 1992, www.latimes.com/archives/la-xpm-1992-04-04-ca-177-story.html.
[59] 'Screenplay: "73 Easting"', 7.

doctrinal concepts would allow.[60] Finally, when deployed to the Iraqi desert, McMaster disregarded an order to halt his advance and pressed on, destroying the enemy brigade with his superior equipment even when outnumbered by five-to-one. In this telling, heroic officers made use of a generation's worth of technological development to act decisively and independently. Although he was not mentioned in the screenplay, it was no coincidence that Douglas Macgregor had also participated in the battle as squadron operations officer.[61]

The Army's strong support for the film was not in any way dented by its depiction of intergenerational conflict and its critique of the conservatism of senior officers. While senior officers may have baulked at the screenplay's claim that 'the initiative and valour of the Army's Top Gun, H.R. McMaster, was the decisive act of the ground war', the allure of having a film do for them what *Top Gun* and *The Hunt for Red October* did for the Navy was too great.[62] The Army was very conscious that modernisation money tended to flow towards the Air Force and Navy. As the Army's official history of transformation put it: 'if infallible sensors could invariably detect all relevant targets, digital command and control could perfectly match them up with appropriate "shooters," and precision-guided munitions could flawlessly dispatch them on a one-for-one basis, why not let the Air Force do the job?'[63] As budgets came under pressure, and the full cost of training soldiers for the digital battlefield became apparent, it seemed as though too heavy an emphasis on technology might put the Army's strength at risk.

When discussing long-term strategy with the Secretary of Defense and the joint chiefs, Reimer cautioned against 'pursuing a modernization bogey that, while it has merit, is only loosely linked to our defence strategy and has yet to be precisely defined'. Pointing to deployments around the world, he argued that 'moving personnel dollars into modernization accounts is a shell game with few winners'.[64] Reimer, like Sullivan before him, did realise that a successful transformation effort might allow the Army to do more with fewer personnel, but he advised 'that we not harvest potential savings until we've proven the technologies and our soldiers and leaders are comfortable with them'.[65] The Army was paying for

---

[60] 'Screenplay: "73 Easting"', 3.
[61] Macgregor later published his own account of the battle. Macgregor, *Warrior's Rage*.
[62] 'Screenplay: "73 Easting"', 9.
[63] Brown, *Kevlar Legions*, 164.
[64] Dennis J. Reimer, 'Memorandum for John M. Shalikashvili', 31 March 1997, Dennis J. Reimer Papers: General Management Correspondence Files – Box 9: March 1997, AHEC.
[65] Reimer.

its modernisation efforts with the savings from base closures and reduced manpower, but it still only accounted for 8 per cent of the Department of Defense's overall expenditure on modernisation.[66] Analysts in the Office of the Secretary for Defense (OSD) believed that the Army needed to increase its modernisation spending by shedding more personnel. Even in the aftermath of the invasion of Iraq in 2003, the OSD, now led by transformation enthusiast Donald Rumsfeld, was arguing that the Army was overstrength and should be reduced from ten divisions to eight.[67] So ingrained was the drive to reduce personnel costs to fund new technology that when Congress recommended increasing the size of the active duty military for the first time in sixteen years in May 2004, as the occupation of Iraq showed no signs of winding down any time soon, OSD resisted, because some of this increase would be paid for by cutting back on long-term transformation programmes.[68] Some analysts even argued that permanently increasing the number of soldiers in the Army would create a new 'hollow Army' by making it harder to modernise and transform the force.[69] In this vision of the future, only partially embraced by Army leaders at best, there would be far fewer American soldiers, but they would be well equipped, agile and capable of operating as part of a joint force that was able to do miraculous things on the battlefield.

5.2   Contractors on the Battlefield

As modernisation became an overriding priority for the organisation, all parts of the Army began to produce plans for how they would implement transformation. In its 1995 'Warrior XXI Vision of Army Training', TRADOC outlined a scenario 'in the far or not so far distant future', where a tank commander 'traverses digital terrain which exactly duplicates an upcoming mission'. Using the simulation tool, this commander engages numerous targets that have 'been replicated to mimic the capabilities of the threat'.[70] This rehearsal would develop the 'electronic choreography of the battlefield' and provide a template for the actual mission. Remarkably, while this commander was working out avenues of approach and attack plans, artificial intelligence would provide an assessment of the

---

[66] Macgregor, *Breaking the Phalanx*, 1997, 166.
[67] Adams, *The Army after Next*, 164.
[68] Adams, 167.
[69] Adams, 189.
[70] Headquarters, United States Army Training and Doctrine Command, 'Warrior XXI: A Vision for Army Training', July 1995, 8, Frederic J. Brown III Papers; Box 180A, Folder 8, Draft TRADOC Warrior XXI campaign plan [part 1 of 2], circa 1995, AHEC.

logistical requirements for the proposed mission. Without even needing to think about supply issues, the commander would be provided with answers by the software. Eventually, the template developed in these simulations would form the foundation for the integration of robotic tactical vehicles into the formation. In the most optimistic version of this future, automation would take over large chunks of battlefield tasks.

The inspiration for these sorts of visions came from the private sector. Military leaders watched as the rollout of the World Wide Web heralded a tech boom and a related surge of business books celebrating the supply chain revolution, new management paradigms and flatter organisations. The crossover between military and corporate concerns seemed obvious.

Marine Corps Commandant General Charles Krulak sent his senior officers to the New York Stock Exchange in December 1995 to learn from Wall Street traders about how to make speedy decisions.[71] Some Army leaders even contributed to this burgeoning literature themselves. On retirement, Sullivan co-authored *Hope Is Not a Method: What Business Leaders Can Learn from America's Army*, a how-to book arguing that the Army's experience of restructuring and downsizing offered valuable lessons for the private sector.[72] Sullivan drew parallels between the post–Cold War drawdown and the challenges of 'disruptive innovation', claiming that, for Army leaders, the fall of the Berlin Wall 'was as if we were IBM contemplating the first Apple computer, or General Motors the first Volkswagen or Toyota'.[73]

Sullivan also argued that the Gulf War highlighted not only the quality of the Army's combat forces but the lack of agility in its logistics base. The Army had to build a huge 'iron mountain' of supplies, consisting of huge depots and large inventories, before it moved to the offensive.[74] Over 40,000 containers were shipped to the Gulf but couldn't be tracked properly, so workers had to open them just to see what was inside.[75] High-priority requisitions from the United States were lost or misplaced. Sullivan believed that reforming this system was one of the most important things that he could do with his tenure as chief of staff. For him, the 'real reengineering story is not in the fighting part of the Army so much as in its sustaining base, the more bureaucratic and industrial part of the army'. Army Materiel Command, the Medical Command and

---

[71] Macgregor, *Breaking the Phalanx*, 1997, 47.
[72] Sullivan and Harper, *Hope Is Not a Method*.
[73] Sullivan and Harper, 3.
[74] The Gulf War logistics operation produced its own how-to business book in the form of William G. Pagonis and Jeffrey L. Cruikshank, *Moving Mountains: Lessons in Leadership and Logistics from the Gulf War* (Cambridge, MA: Harvard Business Review Press, 1992).
[75] Sullivan and Harper, *Hope Is Not a Method*, 7, 180.

TRADOC were all 'the unsung heroes of the Army's transformation'.[76] Critics of the Army's pace of change, such as Macgregor, agreed with Sullivan. Macgregor argued that the Army needed to embrace concepts such as 'just-in-time logistics', 'velocity management' and 'total asset visibility' to help solve its logistics problems. Further, combat forces needed to place fewer demands on the logistics system, a change that could be made by embracing a 'culture of leanness and privatization'.[77]

All these phrases soon became part of the Army leadership lexicon. As the Army faced budget cuts and manpower reductions, it, along with the other services, looked for ways to become more efficient and 'leaner' to preserve as many of its capabilities as possible. All of this took place alongside a broader bipartisan attempt to 're-engineer government' by changing management structures and outsourcing some of its functions.[78] From 1995 onwards, the Department of Defense aggressively attempted to pursue savings by contracting with private companies for commercial activities rather than relying on government employees to provide them.[79] In general terms, the principle that the government should only carry out a commercial activity if it couldn't procure that service or product from the private sector had been around since the Eisenhower era, but civilian officials and Army leaders alike now began to look in much more detail at which parts of the organisation could be usefully privatised. Advocates for privatisation, such as retired General William Tuttle, president of the Logistics Management Institute, claimed that the Army could cut logistics costs by up to 20 per cent by using civilian contractors, potential savings that couldn't be ignored while the Army was seeking both to reduce its size and invest in modernisation.[80]

Outsourcing certainly affected the Army's uniformed manpower, but the real burden of these cuts fell on its civilian workforce. The number of civilians working for the Department of the Army dropped from 487,852 in 1989 to 224,900 in 1999.[81] In a world where the Army was focusing on preserving its 'core' functions and privatising those that were 'non-core', it was apparent that the civilians who carried out less glamorous functions such as base housing maintenance, vehicle repair or warehouse management would be the first to go. In correspondence with the Secretary

[76] Sullivan and Harper, 245.
[77] Macgregor, *Breaking the Phalanx*, 1997, 216.
[78] Gary Gerstle, *The Rise and Fall of the Neoliberal Order: America and the World in the Free Market Era* (New York: Oxford University Press, USA, 2022), 162–4.
[79] Brown, *Kevlar Legions*, 172.
[80] Christopher D. Croft, 'Contractors on the Battlefield: Has the Military Accepted Too Much Risk?' (School of Advanced Military Studies, Command and General Staff College, 1 May 2001), 9, https://apps.dtic.mil/sti/citations/ADA406068.
[81] Brown, *Kevlar Legions*, 173.

of Defense on budget cut proposals in 1997, Reimer proposed that 'the Army would outsource or privatise logistics storage, maintenance and supply functions; consolidate overhead functions; centralize operational and developmental testing and evaluation; and consolidate research, development and engineering activities into a single command'.[82] Tellingly, this proposal would reduce the Army's structure by approximately 2,700 Active Component military personnel, but by over 38,000 civilians. It was also revealing that the logic Reimer offered for this plan was a business one, as he claimed that 'we must benchmark the best business practices of American industry – the finest in the world – to streamline, downsize, outsource, and otherwise ensure the best possible return on our investments'.[83] Much as Army leaders hoped to harness private sector innovations such as radio frequency inventory tracking and automation, they also fully embraced the tenets of privatisation and outsourcing.

However, it was not clear that using contractors was easier than civilian government employees, at least in the short term. The Army's official history noted that the real savings would come in the long run, when the Department of Defense would have 'reduced commitments to pensions, medical benefits, and the like'.[84] Contracts were also difficult to change if they were poorly written, and 'the relative ease of redirecting the energies of soldiers and civil servants was no longer there. Contractors could be patriots, but inevitably they were businessmen. To succeed they had to turn a profit, and this imperative could trump commitment to a mission per se.'[85] A TRADOC assessment also noted that many of those who were frustrated in their dealings with contractors simply hadn't adequately spelled out their needs in a precise statement of work.[86] Learning to deal with the private entrepreneurs now embedded within the Army's logistics chain proved to be a steep learning curve.

More broadly, embracing contractors did not actually seem to substantially reduce the Army's logistics burden. Historically, the logistical requirements of warfare have only increased, not decreased, and none of the Army's reforms of the 1990s fundamentally altered that trajectory.[87]

---

[82] Dennis J. Reimer, 'Memorandum for the Secretary of Defense: Quadrennial Defense Review Alternatives', 9 April 1997, 7, Dennis J. Reimer Papers: General Management Correspondence Files, Box 9: April 1997, AHEC.

[83] Reimer, 4.

[84] Brown, *Kevlar Legions*, 177.

[85] Brown, 177.

[86] Headquarters, United States Army Training and Doctrine Command, 'Warrior XXI: A Vision for Army Training', 28.

[87] The classic account of military logistics is still Martin van Creveld, *Supplying War: Logistics from Wallenstein to Patton* (Cambridge: Cambridge University Press, 1977). See

Supply chains certainly ran more smoothly, and inventory management improved, but new technology also brought with it new maintenance, fuel and power requirements. Much of this new technology also required highly specialised contractors to keep it running. The Army's modernisation plans involved heavy investments in missiles, communications equipment, electronics, and research and development in general.[88] All these areas were heavily dependent on contractor support to function. Even the purported TRADOC command simulator of the future, which would allow the commander to rehearse a mission in great detail and provide artificial intelligence–supplied logistics plans to support that mission, would inevitably need specialist maintenance provided by civilians.

If digitisation and outsourcing would not actually decrease the material demands on the logistics chain, it certainly seemed as though the latter might make it cheaper to operate the digitised force. The Army's logistics after-action report after the Gulf War had concluded that 'there is a role for contractors on the battlefield, particularly when the tasks ... are so complex that it is not economically beneficial for the Army to maintain needed capability within the force'.[89] As one Air Force officer noted, 'continual and rapid technological change has made it uneconomical to keep soldiers technologically capable of maintaining, troubleshooting, and in some cases, employing sophisticated weapons'.[90] It seemed to be far cheaper to hire contractors on a short-term basis rather than trying to keep long-service military personnel current with every aspect of weapons systems maintenance. The Army would either need to use contractors to maintain these systems or give soldiers increased salaries so that they would stay in the Army long enough to become master technicians, which could take up to fifteen years for some of the more complex systems.[91]

The extent to which a digitised Army would be reliant on contractors became clear as experimental units went through evaluation exercises. In March 1997, 5,000 soldiers from 1st Brigade, 4th Infantry Division, the Army's testbed 'digital' brigade, rotated into the NTC accompanied by

also John A. Lynn, *Feeding Mars: Logistics in Western Warfare from the Middle Ages to the Present* (London: Routledge, 2019).

[88] Brown, *Kevlar Legions*, 175.

[89] George B. Dibble, Charles L. Horne, III and William E. Lindsay, 'Army Contractor and Civilian Maintenance, Supply, and Transportation Support during Operations Desert Shield and Desert Storm. Volume 1: Study Report' (Bethesda, MD: Logistics Management Institute, 1 June 1993), G-6, https://apps.dtic.mil/sti/citations/ADA272250.

[90] Steven J. Zamparelli, 'Contractors on the Battlefield: What Have We Signed up For?', *Air Force Journal of Logistics* 23, no. 3 (Fall 1999): 14.

[91] Croft, 'Contractors on the Battlefield', 2.

Figure 5.2 A civilian electronics technician inspecting and testing the installation of a computer in an armored personnel carrier during the Advanced Warfighting Experiment at the NTC, Fort Irwin, California, 1997

no fewer than 1,200 civilian contractors.[92] This may have been an outlier, given the sheer volume of equipment being tested, but it did point to how deeply embedded contractors now were, even at the tactical level. One major reported that he had been involved in the fielding of several new vehicles, and that 'each of these fieldings was totally dependent upon contractors for each step of the execution process to include operator and maintainer field testing and training'. The contractors 'set the tone for the issuance of the equipment, established the fielding schedule, and enforced the timeline with the tactical unit'.[93] Simply put, this new equipment would not work without contractors there to maintain it (Figure 5.2).

[92] Mark Hanna, 'Task Force XXI: The Army's Digital Experiment' (Washington, DC: National Defense University Strategic Forum, 1 July 1997), 4, https://apps.dtic.mil/sti/citations/ADA394389.

[93] Michael T. McBride, 'The Proliferation of Contractors on the Battlefield a Changing Dynamic that Necessitates a Strategic Review', Strategy Research Project (Carlisle, PA: Army War College, 7 April 2003), 9, https://apps.dtic.mil/sti/citations/ADA415747.

The experience of seeing 'swarms' of contractors on the simulated battlefields of the Army's warfighting experiments led the Army Science Board to examine the issue. They expressed the hope that this phenomenon was one that would just be confined to the transition phase from an analogue to a digitised force. They did, though, caution that the operation and maintenance of the digitised equipment had to 'be simple and straightforward so as not to require operators and maintainers of a level of skill beyond that able to be provided by the Army personnel recruiting, training, and retention systems'.[94] Given that the Army was struggling with recruitment and retention, though, and that the Army Science Board itself had called for the Army to do more to train and retain technical personnel, this was easier said than done. Even as they were sanguine about the long-term balance between soldiers and contractors, the report's authors admitted that 'some unique understanding of individual systems may best be provided by knowledgeable civilian contractors (perhaps in major numbers)' and that commanders should 'expect contractors on local test ranges'.[95]

It was clear, though, that contractors weren't just going to be involved with the fielding of new equipment. The digitised force used vastly more bandwidth than its predecessor and required an extensive and sophisticated communications network serviced by information technology contractors. To put it in perspective, the unmanned aerial vehicles used in the early years of the war in Afghanistan consumed about 48 mbps of bandwidth per aircraft, which was half the bandwidth used during the Gulf War to support 500,000 troops.[96] Given the number of job openings in the civilian tech sector, the Army would have struggled to develop the internal capacity to maintain these systems even if it had wanted to. 'Technologically literate field soldiers' were in short supply, and Edwin Burba, the retired general who had consulted on the Army Science Board's study on technical training for Army officers, reported that 'we are on the verge of losing many of our warrior-technologists', telling Sullivan that he had increasingly come across mid-ranking technologist officers with a wealth of education and experience who were leaving for the

---

[94] '"Civilian Contractors on the Battlefield": Army Science Board Independent Assessment: Interim Progress Report', 10 July 1998, Paul J. Kern Papers; Box 26B, Folder 25, Winter AUSA Symposium [part 2 of 3], AHEC.

[95] '"Civilian Contractors on the Battlefield": Army Science Board Independent Assessment: Interim Progress Report'.

[96] Timothy Coffin, 'Is There Space for the Objective Force?' Strategy Research Project (Carlisle, PA: US Army War College, 7 April 2003), 7.

private sector.[97] This meant that when the Army deployed, it did so with contractors filling crucial IT positions. For instance, the 4th Infantry Division, the force designated as the first 'digital' Division in the Army, rolled into Iraq in April 2003 with sixty civilian contractors deploying with it to maintain its command and control systems.[98] There were no military personnel trained for the job.

The need to maintain specialist equipment was not the only reason contractors accompanied American soldiers overseas. Where Congress had mandated caps on the numbers of soldiers on deployments, contractors could help ensure that soldiers were freed up from support duties to fill other roles. In an article for *Army Logistician* entitled 'More Tooth, Less Tail', Colonel Herman T. Palmer relayed his experiences as logistics officer for Task Force Eagle in Bosnia to argue that contractors had been a valuable 'force multiplier'. He told the story of American soldiers seizing control of a hilltop transmission tower in September 1997 and digging in to secure it. Just thirty minutes after the arrival of the last infantryman, 'military vehicles loaded with contingency supplies of sandbags, plywood, barbed wire, and pickets, roared to a stop on the hilltop. The troops were surprised at its arrival, and even more surprised when civilians jumped from the vehicles and began preparing to drop its cargo.'[99] While the presence of contractors so close to the front lines was indicative of a relatively benign security situation, it was also due to the fact that the Army was trying to reduce its footprint in the Balkans and saw transferring some logistics functions to contractors as a relatively straightforward way to do so.

The Army's mission in Bosnia was a showcase for privatisation. In the words of one veteran of the campaign, contractors provided everything 'from LifeCycle treadmills to helicopter maintenance by Bell and Boeing'.[100] In total, over fifty-two contractors supported the US mission there.[101] Brown & Root Services Corporation operated the dining facilities and laundry service, and provided water, petroleum, oil and lubricants. Raytheon, Lockheed-Martin, Bell and United Defense provided maintenance support for ground vehicles and helicopters, AT&T and Sprint supported communications systems, and BDM International supplied most of the force's interpreters.[102] By law, contractors

---

[97] Burba, 'Correspondence from General Edwin H. Burba to General Gordon R. Sullivan Regarding BCTP Rotations'.

[98] Adams, *The Army after Next*, 238.

[99] Herman T. Palmer, 'More Tooth, Less Tail: Contactors in Bosnia', *Army Logistician* 31, no. 5 (October 1999): 6.

[100] Croft, 'Contractors on the Battlefield', 2.

[101] Palmer, 'More Tooth, Less Tail: Contactors in Bosnia', 7.

[102] Palmer, 7.

could fulfil all but three military functions: armed combat, command and control of US military and civilian personnel, and the actual process of contracting itself. Except for these limitations, contractors could perform any hitherto military function, and Army logistics officers eager to find savings enthusiastically looked for opportunities to outsource support services.[103] At one point, planners calculated that it would be cheaper to replace a reservist truck unit with contractors, so the truck company's mission was absorbed into the Brown & Root contract. Brown & Root hired American civilian drivers but actually used trucks and equipment furnished by the departing reservist unit.[104] Such practices meant that the Bosnia mission saw an unprecedented number of civilians deployed. Whereas one in fifty Americans deployed for the Persian Gulf War was a civilian, that ratio was one in ten in Bosnia.[105] When non-American contractors were included, the military–civilian ratio in Bosnia was nearly one to one.[106]

Outside of Bosnia, the Army relied on ITT Corporation to maintain their prepositioned brigade equipment set at Camp Doha in Kuwait and to issue equipment to incoming units, while OshKosh Truck maintained US Army Europe's heavy equipment transporters.[107] When the Army deployed Task Force Hawk to Albania during the Kosovo conflict, a reconnaissance party was sent ahead to Tirana Airport. Among the first on the ground were an Army contracting officer, a representative from Brown & Root and a civilian real estate expert.[108] For senior logistics officers such as Palmer, the benefits of these arrangements were obvious. He noted that local national contractors were vastly cheaper than their US military counterparts and that, in general, 'civilian contractors do not require the same levels of mail support, off-the-job medical care, and other support furnished to their soldier, sailor, airman, and marine counterparts'.[109] Contractors could also provide their own transport into theatre, easing the burden on military transport. These budget savings could both allow soldiers to focus on more purely military tasks and help provide the funds needed for modernisation.

---

[103] Ronda G. Urey, 'Civilian Contractors on the Battlefield', Strategy Research Project (Carlisle, PA: US Army War College, 18 March 2005), 8, https://apps.dtic.mil/sti/citations/ADA431808.
[104] Palmer, 'More Tooth, Less Tail: Contactors in Bosnia', 7.
[105] Zamparelli, 'Competitive Sourcing and Privatization', 12–13.
[106] McBride, 'The Proliferation of Contractors on the Battlefield a Changing Dynamic that Necessitates a Strategic Review', 6.
[107] Norman E. Williams and Jon M. Schandelmeier, 'Civilian Contractors on the Battlefield', *Army*, January 1999, 35.
[108] Brown, *Kevlar Legions*, 175.
[109] Palmer, 'More Tooth, Less Tail: Contactors in Bosnia', 9.

Even those who largely embraced these changes worried about their risks, though. Major General Norman E. Williams, chief of staff of Army Materiel Command, was broadly supportive of the use of contractors, calling them a 'true combat service support force multiplier', but admitted that there were 'unanswered questions and challenges regarding contractors on the battlefield'.[110] Among them were the fact that non-combatants would require more force protection resources since, unlike Army personnel, they couldn't defend themselves or conduct rear-area security missions. These contractors would not be subject to military discipline, and the applicability of the Geneva Conventions and local Status of Forces Agreements were also unclear. Most fundamentally, there was no legal way to compel contractors to remain in place if hostilities broke out. This problem had been flagged by the DoD inspector general in 1991 and remained unsolved.[111] One Army critic noted that 'our logistics infrastructure is currently inundated with contract personnel who routinely perform critical sustainment functions in support of our Combatant Commanders in our most forward active theaters of operation' and that 'many of these critical support functions have virtually no uniformed redundancy or back-up'.[112] Williams also worried that 'non-combatants are not trained for the emotional and physical hardships of the wartime environment'.[113] Certainly, there was the danger of culture shock. Eric Carpenter, an Army civilian who deployed to Bosnia, reported that his appearance drew unwanted attention: 'they'd ask me what my unit was because I didn't have the military hairdo. A couple of times I was asked why I didn't salute.'[114] Military personnel were used to working long hours with little privacy or free time, and this could be a shock to civilians working alongside them.

These worries could be overstated though. Many American contractors were in fact retired military personnel who needed little time to culturally acclimatise. As Army historian John Sloan Brown puts it, 'an iconic figure of the time was the civilian, soldier, or non-commissioned officer who terminated his government employment one day and came back to the same position as a contractor the next'.[115] Often contractors,

---

[110] Williams and Schandelmeier, 'Civilian Contractors on the Battlefield', 35.
[111] Robert M. Friedman, 'Civilian Contractors on the Battlefield: A Partnership With Commercial Industry or Recipe for Failure?', Strategy Research Project (Carlisle, PA: US Army War College, 9 April 2002), 10, https://apps.dtic.mil/sti/citations/ADA404511.
[112] McBride, 'The Proliferation of Contractors on the Battlefield a Changing Dynamic that Necessitates a Strategic Review', 2.
[113] Williams and Schandelmeier, 'Civilian Contractors on the Battlefield', 35.
[114] Katherine McIntire Peters, 'Civilians at War', Government Executive, 1 July 1996, www.govexec.com/magazine/1996/07/civilians-at-war/348/.
[115] Brown, Kevlar Legions, 173.

veteran or not, had steady and habitual relationships with the soldiers they worked alongside. Far from there being a culture clash, contractors became deeply ingrained into the Army's structures and were present at virtually all levels, including in the service support elements of combat units. When Army leaders offered visions of the Army of the future, whether via Force XXI, the Army After Next or the Army Transformation programme, those visions focused on highly trained, networked soldiers making use of high-tech weaponry and surveillance equipment. The less exciting figure of the civilian contractor was absent from these visions, but they were no less central to them in reality.

5.3   Creating the Expeditionary Soldier

One of the objectives in outsourcing so many parts of the Army's logistics infrastructure was to free up more soldiers for deployments. Given the reality of increased deployments, Army leaders hoped that the combination of technology and privatisation could deliver lighter, 'leaner' units that could rapidly deploy overseas. Army units were increasingly clustered on a smaller number of 'mega-bases', a move driven by budgetary constraints, but one that leaders hoped would mean that soldiers would have to move around less than during the Cold War, and would have more opportunities to build careers and social support networks.[116] The intent was to follow the Navy's model of 'homesteading', where families remained in one place while service members deployed and moved through different career positions.[117] The drawdown from Europe, where the Army cut its numbers from 200,000 in 1989 to 65,000 in 1995, meant that installations that survived the Base Realignment and Closure process thrived, as units previously stationed overseas found new homes on the continental United States.[118] Congressional allies ensured that money for improved deployment infrastructure poured into these posts, as railheads, airfields and ports were upgraded to handle the increased number of units being sent overseas from American home stations.[119]

This move to upgrade deployment-related infrastructure at stateside locations was driven in part by the failures of Operation Desert Shield. Shinseki later claimed that 'we were lucky in the Gulf. We deployed quickly, but it was six months later before we had a decisive combat force there to deal with the Iraqi threat. We will not have six months in

---

[116] David S. Sorenson, *Shutting Down the Cold War: The Politics of Military Base Closure* (New York: Palgrave Macmillan, 1998).
[117] Brown, *Kevlar Legions*, 158.
[118] Brown, 93.
[119] Brown, 94.

the future. Our potential enemies have studied the way we deploy, and they know what we need.'[120] The 82nd Airborne Division had deployed quickly but 'dug in with not much in the way of lethality of anti-tank capability or artillery ... It's not a battle that we would have designed. Heavy mechanized forces were coming up against light infantry, and frankly, we held our breath.' Had Saddam Hussein's forces continued their advance south from Kuwait, disaster – even another Task Force Smith – might have ensued. Shinseki believed that the Army had not fixed this problem in the intervening years, arguing that 'if we had the same situation [now] ... our move would be with the light infantry and primarily the 82nd Airborne Division again'. Once these light forces had deployed, 'we'd wait for the heavy divisions to arrive, which would be a number of weeks ... that's an operational shortfall'.[121]

Evidence from more recent deployments made it clear that the Army had not adapted. The abysmal performance of Task Force Hawk, a brigade-sized force with twenty-four AH-64 Apache attack helicopters that was assembled to provide support for NATO's 1999 air campaign against Yugoslavia, illustrated the point well. It took over a month to deploy this force to Albania and it never managed to launch a single combat mission, which meant that while Air Force and Navy jets were busy over Kosovo and Serbia, the Army essentially missed the entire operation.[122] While the Army originally planned on a 2,000-strong task force, force protection and unexpected logistics requirements meant that it would take over 5,000 personnel to support the Apache deployment.[123] While it got less media attention, the Army had also struggled to move its heavy equipment into Bosnia and Haiti, with tracked Bradley Infantry Fighting Vehicles unable to make it more than two blocks from their disembarkation points in Cap-Haïtien, and mechanised infantry brigades finding it very difficult to move on Bosnia's poor road network.[124] Shinseki, who had commanded US forces in Bosnia, reported that 'most of our heavy equipment, in a country

---

[120] Eric Shinseki, PBS Frontline: the future of war, 24 October 2000, www.pbs.org/wgbh/pages/frontline/shows/future/interviews/shinseki.html.

[121] Shinseki.

[122] Given the impetus it gave Army leaders to push for greater mobility, Task Force Hawk is relatively understudied. John Gordon, Bruce Nardulli and Walter L. Perry, 'The Operational Challenges of Task Force Hawk', *Joint Forces Quarterly*, Autumn/Winter 2001, 52–7; Cynthia M. Womble, 'Task Force Hawk: Operational Mobility Lessons for the Joint Force Commander' (Newport, RI: Naval War College, 5 February 2001), https://rosap.ntl.bts.gov/view/dot/2113.

[123] William J. Clinton, 'Letter from the President to the Speaker of the House of Representatives and the President of the Senate', 5 April 1999, https://1997-2001.state.gov/www/regions/eur/990404_clinton_ksvoletter.html.

[124] Peter J. Boyer, 'A Different War', *New Yorker*, 23 June 2002, www.newyorker.com/magazine/2002/07/01/a-different-war.

that was wrestling to re-establish itself economically, tore their roads up so badly that commerce could not get through. And then we had to come back in and repair those roads.'[125] This meant that Army units in Bosnia preferred to patrol in much lighter wheeled vehicles, such as Humvees, that were much more vulnerable to potential enemy fire.

If the conundrum was that the Army's heavy forces were too slow to deploy and too dependent on an extensive logistics chain, and that the Army's light forces didn't have enough firepower or armour to protect themselves, then the solution would be to come up with something in the middle. In October 1999, Shinseki announced that he wanted the Army to be able to field a combat-ready brigade anywhere in the world in ninety-six hours, a division in 120 hours and five divisions in thirty days.[126] To achieve this, the Army would work towards what he called the Objective Force, and would replace existing armoured vehicles with smaller, lighter equivalents that could be air-transported more easily. In the long term, the M1 Abrams and Bradley Fighting Vehicles would be replaced by the as-yet undeveloped Future Combat System that would be approximately 70 per cent lighter than the Abrams.[127] In the interim, the Army would immediately purchase already-available equipment to create Interim Brigade Combat Teams (IBCTs) that would bridge the gap between heavy and light forces by using lighter wheeled armoured vehicles and taking advantage of all of the advances in sensors and communication equipment that had taken place under the Army's digitisation efforts. Major General James Dubik, who had been appointed by Shinseki to run the Army's transformation efforts, noted that much as the radio allowed militaries to more effectively synchronise different combat elements during World War II, 'the internet will allow even more combat power at the point of battle', devolving more capabilities to junior leaders.[128] Not only that but, rather than relying on large stockpiles of materiel close at hand, 'because of its internet capabilities, this brigade can get stocks that are in the intermediate staging base 100 kilometres behind. It can get stocks in-theatre, in-region or all the way back to the United States, so the number of logistics layers required for this brigade is much reduced from the current brigades.'[129] These advances meant that both the interim brigade and its Objective Force successor would not sacrifice much combat power, despite its lightness.

---

[125] Shinseki, PBS Frontline: the future of war.
[126] Brown, *Kevlar Legions*, 197.
[127] Brown, 198.
[128] James Dubik, 'PBS Frontline: The Future of War', 24 October 2000, www.pbs.org/wgbh/pages/frontline/shows/future/interviews/dubik.html.
[129] Dubik.

Looking a lot like the sort of independent 'units of action' recommended by MacGregor in *Breaking the Phalanx*, these brigades
would be capable of taking on the 'full spectrum' of operations, from
battle with near-peer competitors to peacekeeping and humanitarian assistance. Shinseki believed that these medium-weight brigades
could become the standard template for all Army combat units in
the future. He noted that 'the missions that we're asked to perform
run from humanitarian assistance, fire-fighting, and non-combatant
evacuation from the most remote corners of the world', and that the
challenge was 'to understand how to organise your limited forces
to do all of those things'.[130] In the contemporary environment, the
Army could not afford to 'fall into the trap of organising ourselves for
specific missions, and then not being able to perform other missions
when the conditions change very quickly – as they can in places like
Kosovo – in 20 minutes'. Indeed, the very speed with which the Army
could deploy these capable units would help solve problems in and of
itself. Shinseki believed that if the Army could quickly deploy combat capability on the ground, then it would be 'able to stabilize the
situation and not have to go to war fighting. Just the fact that you've
got early deploying combat capability allows you then to shape the
outcome of a crisis.'[131]

Others were more cautious about these claims, particularly after the
Bush administration came to office in early 2001. Writing to Shinseki
after a field trip to Fort Lewis to check in on progress on the IBCT,
Undersecretary of the Army Gregory Dahlberg reported that he had
'become concerned in recent weeks that with the change in Administra-
tions and a new Congress, our message, as it is currently framed, may
increasingly fall on deaf ears'. He argued that Army retirees, Department
of Defence budget managers and congressional staffs were beginning
to think that the IBCT was 'moving the Army away from its traditional
warfighting mission in favour of a force more suitable for peacekeeping' and cautioned that 'this obviously will not play well with the new
Administration if we don't better explain the IBCT concept in warfighting terms'.[132] Along a similar vein, Army Vice Chief of Staff Jack
Keane asked the chief of military history to commission a 'think piece',

[130] Shinseki, 'PBS Frontline: The Future of War'.
[131] Shinseki.
[132] Gregory Dahlberg, 'Memorandum for the Chief of Staff, Army: Thoughts from My
Trip to Fort Lewis, Washington, and Fort Leavenworth, Kansas, 8–10 January 2001',
19 January 2001, Eric K. Shinseki Papers; Box 21, Folder 7, Official Correspondence,
AC of S, incoming and outgoing, 18–22 January 2001, AHEC.

examining what might have happened if an IBCT had been available to the Allies for their ill-fated Operation Market Garden offensive in 1944.[133] By imagining a rerun of a famous defeat that could have turned out differently had this revolutionary formation been available, Keane was trying to make the case that the IBCT was perfectly suited to high-tempo conventional war.

The reaction to Shinseki's plan was certainly mixed. In the first instance, because Shinseki had emphasised in his October 1999 speech that he saw the Army's future combat vehicle fleet as lighter and all wheeled, many within the Army's armour branch saw medium-weight brigades as a threat to their very existence. Heavy armoured and mecha-nised forces had just won the Gulf War, had been the lynchpin of the Army's Cold War–era strategy in Europe and Korea and had played the lead role in the advance from Normandy to Germany during World War II, and so had broadly been the dominant culture within the Army for over fifty years. Now Shinseki was proposing to fundamentally down-grade their importance. Anonymous sources briefed the *Washington Times* that they felt that these changes would produce 'too flimsy an army to fight a great land war' with North Korea or Russia. As one critic put it, 'I don't want to be stuck with wheeled vehicles and light armour tracked vehicles to slug it out with these guys'.[134] The same critic argued that the Clinton administration was so enamoured with air power that they didn't understand the need for ground forces to pack a heavy punch of their own. Another retired general complained that the Future Com-bat System that would provide the backbone for the Army of the future simply wasn't feasible, claiming that 'I don't think there is any way by 2010 you can create a [light tank] that weighs 20 tons that has the same lethality of existing combat systems on the field'.[135] For these critics, the promise that lighter, more mobile units employing precision munitions and enabled by advanced communication and sensor networks could be as resilient as heavy armoured units built around tracked vehicles was a false one that was the product of overoptimistic thinking by both civilian and military acolytes of the RMA.

While some of these debates may have seemed esoteric to outsiders, they touched on real cultural schisms within the Army: the heavy–light divide between the mechanised forces that had been the mainstay of the Cold War Army in Europe, and the light infantry that had been tasked

[133] Brown, *Kevlar Legions*, 208.
[134] Rowan Scarborough, 'Generals Not Fans of Lighter Army', *Washington Times*, 30 May 2000, www.washingtontimes.com/news/2000/may/30/20000530-011414-8592r/.
[135] Rowan Scarborough, 'Generals Not Fans of Lighter Army', *Washington Times*, 30 May 2000, www.washingtontimes.com/news/2000/may/30/20000530-011414-8592r/.

with so many short-notice interventions. As Army historian John Sloan Brown put it, both sides had prejudices that affected how they thought about each other: 'paratrooper banter stereotyped tankers as corpulent dwarves, strong enough in the shoulders to sling ammunition and break track, short enough to get around in the confines of their turrets and fattened by their aversion to running – or even walking – and by a diet dominated by Bier and Bratwurst'. Meanwhile, heavy mechanised troops 'envisioned paratroopers as equivalent to the Eloi of H. G. Wells' *The Time Machine*, prancing around in the great outdoors but never doing the real work of logistics, maintenance, and motor pools'.[136] Attempting to bridge this divide by merging both cultures into new medium-weight formations would be a tall order for any leader.

Others noted that the whole debate over wheels versus tracks meant that key questions about organisation, doctrine and training were being skipped over. As one analyst put it, 'right now, we're very focused on what the new piece of equipment is – what's the new tank, is it wheels or is it tracks? Does it have a big gun, does it have a small gun? Is it long range, is it short range, is it stealthy? ... 90 percent of the energy in this transformation effort is focused on that.'[137] There had been such an emphasis on 'solving the Task Force Hawk problem' that few involved in the debate had stopped to think about what medium-weight forces might be expected to accomplish once they had deployed. Indeed, another analyst argued that the medium-weight brigades wouldn't even solve that particular problem, since the major issues with Task Force Hawk had stemmed from the fact that planners had cobbled it together with personnel from several different units at the last minute.[138] Absent a rethinking of Army personnel policy that would ensure that units stayed together long enough to deploy as a cohesive team, lighter and more mobile armour wouldn't make much of a difference when it came to their performance in the field, even if that armour came with sophisticated sensor and communications equipment.

Certainly, as the Army moved to create these new brigades, it was clear that it would have to rethink what it would require of its personnel. The critics were right that much of the discussion about the Army's future had centred on technology. The Army's Objective Force White Paper, which laid out its vision for the future, made very little mention of personnel. It declared that 'the human dimension of warfare will

---

[136] Brown, *Kevlar Legions*, 99.
[137] John Hillen, 'PBS Frontline: The Future of War', 24 October 2000, www.pbs.org/wgbh/pages/frontline/shows/future/interviews/hillen.html.
[138] Chuck Spinney, 'PBS Fronline: The Future of War', 24 October 2000, www.pbs.org/wgbh/pages/frontline/shows/future/interviews/spinney.html.

always remain pre-eminent' and that 'technology is not a panacea', but spent more time discussing satellites and space communications than it did training needs.[139] Writing in *Military Review*, the brigade commander and brigade command sergeant major of one of the new IBCTs, now named Stryker Brigades, argued that the Army would have to do more to 'develop soldiers' agility and adaptability' to cope with the difficult environments that they would face.[140] In the Stryker Brigade, combined arms tactics, which had been the remit of battalions, brigades and divisions in World War II, were now being practised at the platoon level, which would put huge demands on junior leaders, especially those that were used to being micromanaged in a garrison environment.[141]

These leaders would be further challenged by the Army's focus on creating modular, interchangeable units and headquarters.[142] Army planners had noted that, in a post–Cold War world, 'the Army could probably never again expect to conduct major operations on its own'.[143] This meant that Army command elements would likely have to be prepared to serve as combined headquarters, encompassing the command of other US military branches as well as foreign militaries. Meanwhile, they would likely be expected to coordinate with nongovernmental agencies as well. This would mean that standardised headquarters would need to be infinitely adaptable and, in the parlance of the tech industry from which many of these reforms were drawn, be ready to 'plug and play' with other elements as required. In theory, technology would allow fewer personnel to handle this increased workload, but in reality modular forces would need more leaders of all ranks in order to be able to coordinate the disparate elements that some missions would entail. Thus, in headquarters as much as in combat formations, soldiers and officers at every level would have to be prepared to assume greater responsibilities than those ordinarily associated with their positions.[144]

---

[139] 'US Army White Paper – Concepts for the Objective Force' (United States Department of the Army, 2002), 19, www.hsdl.org/?abstract&did=457911.

[140] Robert B. Brown and Carlton E. Dedrich, 'The SBCT: Developing Agile, Adaptive Soldiers', *Military Review* 83, no. 3 (June 2003): 33.

[141] Brown and Dedrich, 36, 39.

[142] In 2004, the Army made the modular Brigade Combat Team its primary unit of action. This decision was reversed in 2014 and the division reinstated as the primary combat unit, as experience in Iraq and Afghanistan demonstrated that the brigade headquarters was too small to handle the challenges of modern command, even when augmented. William M. Donnelly, *Transforming an Army at War: Designing the Modular Force, 1991–2005* (Washington, DC: Center of Military History, 2007); King, *Command*, 29–31.

[143] Donnelly, *Transforming an Army at War*, 7.

[144] Donnelly, 9.

Similarly, an Army War College student paper noted that 'full spectrum operations with rapid deployment timelines require soldiers with greater knowledge of operations, from humanitarian assistance to major theatre war', and argued that the fact that these operations would often involve dispersed units would require soldiers with sound judgement, as they would often be isolated and faced with making major decisions on their own.[145] Given that these brigades would likely deploy independently, perhaps without a division- or corps-level logistics echelon to support them, soldiers would have to be multifunctional and adaptable, capable of performing roles such as driver or weapons systems operator that might previously have been the job of two or more soldiers.[146] A study carried out by Booz Allen Hamilton for the Army Research Institute recommended that the Army fully define and embrace a 'multi-skilled soldier' concept that would begin cross-training soldiers in different specialities at basic training and then continue throughout their career.[147]

The range of missions that these units could expect to face meant that 'all ... operational units will need to be at a level of readiness common only to elite units today'.[148] The authors of the Army's Objective Force White Paper agreed with this sentiment and claimed that the Army was 'erasing the distinctions between heavy and light forces and are training conventional units using special operations techniques'. This meant creating a new culture that took from heavy forces 'speed, overwhelming firepower, and combined operations', from light forces a culture of 'highly versatile soldiers who bring a rapid deployment mentality – rucks packed and ready to deploy worldwide on a few hours' notice', and from the Special Operations community a specialisation in close combat and urban and night operations. All of this meant that the Army had 'an opportunity to combine what is best from each community, to transcend the differences between the three as we create a Warrior culture for The Objective Force'.[149] For this concept to succeed, the soldiers of the high-technology expeditionary Army would have to be capable of operating in austere environments and so needed to be as flexible and as adaptable as their vehicles.

---

[145] Christian de Graff, 'Transforming Initial Entry Training to Produce the Objective Force Soldier', Strategy Research Project (Carlisle, PA: US Army War College, 23 April 2003), 1, https://apps.dtic.mil/sti/citations/ADA414927.

[146] De Graff, 4.

[147] John T. Nelsen and Allan Akman, 'The Multi-Skilled Soldier Concept: Considerations for Army Implementation' (Alexandria, VA: Army Research Institute for the Behavioral and Social Sciences, 1 April 2002), https://apps.dtic.mil/sti/citations/ADA402901.

[148] De Graff, 'Transforming Initial Entry Training to Produce the Objective Force Soldier', 3.

[149] 'US Army White Paper – Concepts for the Objective Force', 20.

That the expeditionary Army of the future sounded in many ways like the Marine Corps of the present did not go unnoticed. Indeed, it was telling that when the Army selected the wheeled armoured fighting vehicle that would equip its IBCT, they chose the Canadian LAV III, an updated version of a vehicle that had been in service with the Marine Corps since 1983.[150] One Army colonel thought that the Army was too closely following the Marine model, and argued that 'our national security strategy would be better served if the IBCT were a Marine unit. The Marine focus would be purely on forced and unassisted entry while the Army focus would be on assisted entry and counterattack forces that would decisively conclude the conflict.' Envisioning a clear division of labour, he believed that the ideal state of affairs would be when 'the Marines kick the door down and the Army takes down the building!'[151]

Even before Shinseki announced his plans for a rapidly deployable force, though, the Army was working on ways to make sure that they got to the door first. In the wake of the Gulf War, Army logisticians not only enhanced their stockpiles of prepositioned equipment in Europe and Korea and positioned an extensive set of war materiel in Kuwait and Qatar, but invested in a new capability: a fleet of eight new ships carrying a heavy brigade's worth of equipment that could deploy anywhere in the world.[152] The 'Army Prepositioned Afloat' programme planned to have these ships loiter near potential flashpoints where they could move to unload their equipment at pre-designated ports with only four hours' notice.[153] This gave the Army the sort of rapid response capability that the Marine Corps prided themselves on. Surveying these developments, the commandant of the Marine Corps warned other services against any attempt to trespass on the role of expeditionary force, claiming 'there is no way that the entire armed forces of the United States can fit into the tip of the spear'.[154]

For its part, the Army looked askance at the Marine Corps' successful efforts to have Congress transfer eighty-four new M1A1 Abrams tanks

---

[150] Thomas E. Ricks, 'Light Armored Vehicles Key to New Army Units', *Washington Post*, 18 November 2000, www.washingtonpost.com/archive/politics/2000/11/18/light-armored-vehicles-key-to-new-army-units/5fdae3a7-52a2-46c8-8c1c-33d8de280f96/.

[151] Michael J. Corley, 'The Future of Power Projection', Strategy Research Project (Carlisle, PA: US Army War College, 1 January 2002), 15, https://apps.dtic.mil/sti/citations/ADA404513.

[152] Michael G. Bettez, 'Army Pre-positioned Stocks: The Key to Our Rapid Force Projection Strategy', Strategy Research Project (Carlisle, PA: US Army War College, 10 April 2000), 6, https://apps.dtic.mil/sti/citations/ADA378024.

[153] Michael S. Tucker, 'Army Pre-positioned Stocks', *Military Review* 80, no. 3 (June 2000): 54.

[154] Adams, *The Army after Next*, 71.

from the Army National Guard to the Marines and at Marine Corps doctrine that now defined 'littoral' operations taking place hundreds of miles inland.[155] Clearly, the lines between the two services were blurring as they both grappled in their own way with what their roles should be in the post–Cold War world. This entangling of missions had already been made clear earlier in the decade, when the 1994 National Defense Authorization Act mandated the creation of a Department of Defense Commission on Roles and Missions of the Armed Forces. This commission was to assess areas of overlap and make recommendations about streamlining unnecessarily duplicative capabilities.[156] Immediately, there were points of tension between the Army and the Marine Corps. Much of the debate was over the distinction between 'contingency' forces, something that the Army claimed to provide, and 'expeditionary' forces, a Marine Corps speciality.[157] It was clear to all involved that, despite Army and Marine defensiveness over these terms and many, many memoranda seeking to define them, they did not describe significantly different concepts.

One Army staffer admitted that the fundamental problem was that 'at their root, Marine Divisions, Airborne Divisions, Air Assault Divisions, Light Infantry Divisions and Infantry Divisions are essentially the same'. All of them had the primary role of ground combat featuring infantry, none had much of an organic lift capability and all were essentially restricted to moving at about 2.5 miles per hour once they were inserted via their respective specialised transport.[158] If it was that case that 'when the people of the United States … think of rapid reaction, they think Marines … you may begin to wonder why the Army has any non-mechanized infantry rapid reaction forces of division size'.[159] The flip side of this was that the Marine Corps traditionally did not have the same sort of logistics support that the Army had and therefore could not be expected to sustain operations in the same way, which meant that it was only the commitment of Army forces to

---

[155] John H. Cushman, 'Time to Knock It Off', 20 November 1994, Army Roles and Missions collection; Box 2B, Folder 16, Marine Corps [part 2 of 5], AHEC.

[156] 'H.R.2401 – National Defense Authorization Act for Fiscal Year 1994', Pub. L. No. 103–160, § Subtitle E – Commission on Roles and Missions of the Armed Forces (1993).

[157] J. H. Binford Peay, 'Memorandum for the Director of the Joint Staff: Final Draft Report, "Roles, Missions, and Functions of the Armed Forces of the United States"', 28 January 1993, Army Roles and Missions collection; Box 41A, Folder 11, Information Memoranda [part 1 of 5], 1993, AHEC.

[158] 'Army/USMC Redundancy: A Staffer's Stream of Unconsciousness', 4 October 1994, 1, Army Roles and Missions collection; Box 2B, Folder 15, Marine Corps [part 1 of 5], AHEC.

[159] 'Army/USMC Redundancy: A Staffer's Stream of Unconsciousness', 2.

a crisis that could be 'used to signal an intent to stay, a long term, vital national interest'.[160]

At the echelons of corps and above, the Army possessed a huge and diverse array of engineering, medical, civil affairs, psychological operations and administrative capabilities that could not be matched by any other service. Ironically, the move towards IBCTs meant that in the future, Army combat units would, initially at least, deploy without these extensive capabilities in tow. A medium-weight brigade equipped with wheeled vehicles, enabled by sophisticated communications and surveillance equipment, and supported by private contractors would deploy quickly and be able to take on the full panoply of missions that ground forces might be expected to face, but its lighter footprint meant that it would not bring with it the sort of heavy logistics tail that denoted a long-term commitment. This, then, was the perverse outcome of the Army's digitisation process and its somewhat reluctant embrace of the concept of an RMA. The Army would need, in its combat units at least, soldiers that were very similar to Marines, a culture that, while hardly technophobic, was much more austere in its outlook than the more technician-focused cultures of the Navy or Air Force. In the immediate term, then, the Army's embrace of technological transformation combined with its push for a great expeditionary capability didn't so much produce a generation of 'warrior geeks' as it did a need for soldiers who were comfortable with deploying anywhere in the world at short notice and doing so with the expectation that they would be ready to fight on arrival.

5.4   Conclusion

Conversations about overlaps with the Marine Corps and the need for a more expeditionary ethos within the Army should not be taken as evidence that the intellectual energy surrounding the RMA and transformation was also producing a serious reckoning with questions of institutional culture and priorities. Certainly, Shinseki recognised that something needed to change and, as we will see in Chapter 6, began to put in place measures to force such a rethink towards the end of his tenure as chief of staff, but the vast majority of discussions about transformation focused on technology and equipment. Even with Shinseki's Stryker Brigade initiative, a move that offered a vision of a very different Army, the central

---

[160] Birger Bergesen and John McDonald, 'Assessment of Contingency and Expeditionary Force Capabilities' (Science Applications International Corporation, 26 January 1994), 12, Army Roles and Missions collection; Box 36A; folder 7, logistics, 1994, AHEC.

point of the debate was over whether or not the formations of the future should be equipped with wheeled rather than tracked vehicles, without much in the way of clarity about what the soldiers of these formations might be expected to do once they were employed overseas.

The tone of the discussion on technology in the Army was fundamentally optimistic. While Army officers never fully embraced the visions of clean, virtually cost-free warfare promulgated by their counterparts in the Air Force and Navy, there was a sense that once well-equipped and networked American forces deployed quickly overseas, they would surely be able to handle anything facing them. Some of that optimism no doubt derived from recent experiences in the Persian Gulf, but the more enthusiastic proponents of change clearly drew on the success of Silicon Valley for their inspiration. The tech boom of the 1990s and the increasing importance of the internet seemed, to those who believed in transformation, to offer extraordinary opportunities for the Army to become lighter and more lethal at the same time, a move that would allow it to perform well across the full spectrum of possible operations, from peacekeeping to conventional war.

Ironically, even as these reformers looked to the civilian world for inspiration, the implication of their vision was that the transformed Army would have to stand further apart from broader American society. While there was a large influx of civilian contractors brought both to help digitise the Army and to produce savings that could be invested in transformation, the sort of specialised skills required by soldiers of the future would mean both longer and more expensive training and would give the Army more incentive to work harder to retain these expensively trained troops. Working in an organisation that had fewer troops and more deployments, these highly skilled soldiers would inevitably be further removed from civilian society than ever, given that much of their time would inevitably be spent either on deployment or training for a deployment. Even if this widening gap was not what transformation advocates had intended, it was clear that this would be one of the consequences if they succeeded in their initiative.

6   The Warrior Ethos

When briefing various audiences on the future direction of the force, Army Chief of Staff General Gordon R. Sullivan had a standard set of slides that he would rely on. These presentations largely focused on the hard numerical realities of the Army's post–Cold War drawdown – the number of bases closed, units disbanded and personnel reduced – and brighter discussions of the new doctrine, equipment and technology that would keep the Army's edge sharp. The length of the briefing varied by audience: a senior commander's seminar would get the full version whereas a speech to the troops in an Army base would get a much abridged account of Sullivan's vision of the Army's future. In every presentation, though, Sullivan made a point of briefly highlighting anxieties within the force relating to missions, training, pay and family support, before turning to a more triumphant note. He quoted the military historian John Shy's criticism from *America's First Battles* that historically 'headquarters in the U.S. Army habitually expend their time and energies on routine administration, seldom pushing, training, and testing themselves as they push, train, and test their troops', but then claimed that the Army's senior leadership had learned their lesson and had 'broken the mold' in this post-war period by focusing on revamping the organisation's capabilities.[1]

Part of the evidence Sullivan offered for this claim was the prevalence of the phrase 'Hooah!' throughout the Army. Army doctrine in subsequent years defined it as 'an informal but always understood sound [that] is less a word than an audible affirmation of the warrior ethos'.[2] Sullivan gave his audience a potted history of the term, noting its supposed origins in the Seminole campaigns of the 1840s and its modern-day usage

---

[1] Gordon R. Sullivan, '[Presentation] The Main Effort', n.d., Gordon R. Sullivan Papers; Box 234, Folder 8, Force XXI, AHEC; Gordon R. Sullivan, 'Letter to Army's General Officers Regarding "Ooah!"', 4 February 1994, Gordon R. Sullivan Papers; Box 73, Folder 2, CSA Collected Works, parts III–IV [part 2 of 5], circa 1993–1994, AHEC.

[2] *Field Manual 7-21.13* (Washington, DC: Department of the Army, 2003), 4–27.

among Army Rangers before arguing that 'how it is spelled, who started saying it, when or where it may have arisen all provide good conversation topics, but none of those concerns really capture the core issue. What is important about "Hooah!" involves the thought behind this word. It means that we have kept our fighting edge, that we believe in the spirit that brings victory in battle.' For Sullivan, 'Hooah' meant 'look at us. We are trained. We are ready. We are proud to be soldiers in America's Army. We have the warrior ethos. Count on us!'[3] Sullivan believed that when he heard soldiers utter that sound that it was evidence that the Army had 'internalized the warrior ethos' and that, far from floundering, the force was adapting in such a way that made it clear that it was not 'business as usual' during what amounted to another post-war epoch.

In the aftermath of Sullivan's tenure as chief, though, it was far from clear that this optimistic sentiment was universal. By the end of the decade, a surge of articles decried the absence of the warrior ethos in the Army, the very thing that Sullivan took the cry of 'Hooah' to exemplify, and commentators both within and outside the Army focused with increasing rancour on the organisation's ongoing identity crisis. Here, optimism about technological transformation and future war was nowhere to be found, as uncertainty over missions, discomfort with technocentric promises about the clean future battlefield and cultural objections to changing gender norms combined to produce critiques claiming that something was deeply amiss in the Army's culture. In a typical piece, John Hillen, an Army veteran and future assistant secretary of state for political-military affairs, argued that the US military as a whole was 'under threat from several different directions, all from within America itself'.[4] Quoting John Keegan's *A History of Warfare*, he argued that 'soldiers are not as other men' and that attempts to create an 'ungendered military' threatened to undermine the military's success in the 1980s in reinculcating 'the warrior culture in a military deprived of victory in Vietnam'.[5] The lesson of Vietnam had been that the bloodless and technocratic managerial culture of the American military 'could not prevail over the warriors who fought America in that unhappy land'.[6]

Hillen's article was virtually identical in form to similar complaints from within the military. As anxiety about the future failed to abate, more and more officers published articles and wrote research papers that emphasised the need to maintain a 'warrior ethos' or 'warrior spirit' in the contemporary Army. While these critiques were far from uniform

---

[3] Sullivan, 'Letter to Army's General Officers Regarding "Ooah!"'.
[4] John Hillen, 'The Military Ethos', *The World & I*, July 1997, 34.
[5] Hillen, 36, 38.
[6] Hillen, 38.

in their approach, and while some explicitly rejected the sort of conservative politics that Hillen espoused, virtually all of them concluded that, in some sense, a warrior ethos was indeed missing from the Army, and none echoed Sullivan's optimism about a force that was poised to handle any challenge thrown at it. In response both to this general feeling of malaise and to the drumbeat of external criticism that had become steady by the end of the decade, Army leaders attempted to explicitly address concerns about cultural drift by making changes to symbols and language, along with training and doctrine to try and give the force a greater sense of unity of purpose.

Although much of his tenure as Army chief of staff was taken up with pursuing a transformation agenda, General Eric K. Shinseki was equally concerned with these cultural issues. Among his most controversial moves was his decision to mandate that soldiers across the Army adopt berets, which had previously been reserved for Special Forces and airborne units, as their working headdress. Shinseki hoped that this uniform change would provide a psychological jolt to the force and convey the message that the Army was transforming into a more agile and lethal force, but the blowback he received instead emphasised the same tropes about the lack of a 'warrior spirit' that had been concerning him. Critics argued that the move was a further sign of a 'demasculinising' Army in which standards were dropping. More consequentially, Shinseki used his last few months in office to launch the 'warrior ethos' programme, an initiative that seemed to directly respond to external criticism by formally enshrining the warrior ethos into Army doctrine and training. Much as his less popular beret policy did, the programme attempted to psychologically orientate all soldiers, regardless of branch or speciality, towards combat. This move, made in the immediate aftermath of the invasion of Iraq and continued by Shinseki's successor, General Peter Schoomaker, would have long-lasting consequences for Army culture, especially when it came to the fears of a warrior caste separated from civilian society. That said, even as Army leaders embraced and promoted a 'warrior ethos', the gap between what outside critics and Army senior leadership meant when they said 'warrior' was as broad as ever. This ambiguity may have helped ease tensions in the short run, but it meant that questions about who American soldiers were and what they were for were ultimately left unresolved.

6.1   Searching for the Warrior Spirit

Throughout Sullivan's tenure as chief of staff, he kept two books on his desk: Robert Doughty's *The Seeds of Disaster*, a study of the interwar French military, and *America's First Battles, 1776–1965*, an edited collection that demonstrated how the Army often struggled to field an effective force in the early days of conflict.[7] Similarly, on assuming the role of Army chief of staff, Shinseki made a point of sending ten copies of *America's First Battles* to every member of the Senate Armed Services Committee.[8] The message from both was obvious: for the Army to suffer a similar fate in a contemporary war was unthinkable, and virtually all senior leaders and external critics alike made a point of arguing that the Army had to be prepared to decisively win the first battle of any war that it was involved in. The historical analogy that dominated in this form of analysis was the ill-fated Task Force Smith, the unit hastily thrown into action in the first days of the Korean War and badly defeated by its better-equipped and better-trained North Korean adversary. The phrase 'no more Task Force Smiths' was one that could be easily found in professional journals, student essays and senior leader speeches throughout the 1990s.[9]

However, critics of the Army tended to draw on a particular line of analysis to explain that defeat. Rather than the deficiencies in equipment and training emphasised by senior leaders, critics argued that the defeat of Task Force Smith was as much about culture as anything else. The source for this argument was often T. R. Fehrenbach's *This Kind of War: A Study in Unpreparedness*.[10] In lines that modern-day critics loved to quote, Fehrenbach pinned the blame for the defeat on liberal society in general and on the 1946 Doolittle Report, which had called for an elimination of differences in living conditions and privileges between officers and enlisted soldiers. He wrote that 'liberal society, in its heart, wants not only domination of the military, but acquiescence of the military toward the liberal view of life …. But acquiescence society may not have, if it wants an army worth a damn …. Society's purpose is to live; the military's is to stand ready, if need be, to die.'[11] If this maxim was ignored then, in Fehrenbach's telling, the lessons of history were clear: 'when Greek culture became so sophisticated that its common men would no longer fight to the death … a horde of Roman farm boys overran them …

---

[7] John Sloan Brown, *Kevlar Legions: The Transformation of the United States Army 1989–2005* (Washington, DC: U.S. Army Center of Military History, 2012), 185.

[8] Eric Shinseki, 'PBS Frontline: The Future of War', 24 October 2000, www.pbs.org/wgbh/pages/frontline/shows/future/interviews/shinseki.html.

[9] Gordon R. Sullivan, 'No More Task Force Smiths', *Army Magazine*, January 1992; Arthur Connor, 'The Armor Debacle in Korea, 1950: Implications for Today', *The US Army War College Quarterly: Parameters* 22, no. 1 (4 July 1992), https://doi.org/10.55540/0031-1723.1620; John Garrett, 'Task Force Smith: The Lesson Never Learned' (Fort Leavenworth, KS: School of Advanced Military Studies, Command and General Staff College, 1 January 2000), https://apps.dtic.mil/sti/citations/ADA381834.

[10] T. R. Fehrenbach, *This Kind of War: The Classic Korean War History – Fiftieth Anniversary Edition* (Washington, DC: Potomac Books, Inc., 2000).

[11] Fehrenbach, 292.

the descendants of Macedonians, who had slaughtered Asians till they could no longer lift their arms, went pale and sick at the sight of the havoc wrought by the Roman *gladius Hispanicus* as it carved its way toward Hellas'.[12] A society that lost sight of military virtues was one that ultimately would not survive.

Among those citing Fehrenbach's ode to warrior societies was John Hillen. He argued that 'we always realize we are not prepared when it is too late – after a Pearl Harbor, a Kasserine Pass, a Task Force Smith, a Desert One, or some other military tragedy', and that the advocates of an 'ungendered military' would precipitate another military defeat. The only saving grace in this scenario was that 'it often takes a disaster of some sort to bring the social fictions of these various movements in the light of day'.[13] For Hillen and other critics, the issue was not, as Charles Moskos and others had argued, that the civil–military gap was getting too wide; it was that it was not wide enough. Hillen claimed that the 'the values and social mores of 1990s America – narcissistic, morally relativist, self-indulgent, hedonistic, consumerist, individualis-tic, victim-centered, nihilistic, and soft – seem hopelessly at odds with those of traditional military culture'.[14] He argued that traits such as 'duty, honor, country, courage and commitment' were unique to the military due to its responsibility to prepare for the 'unnatural stresses of war'.[15] Similarly, other critics claimed that military culture had to be oriented not around good relations with civilians but around 'the critical task of nurturing and preparing the single instrument capable of meeting the standard and the horror of the primary mission – the warrior'.[16]

For some, the roots of this malaise were in the Army's efforts to fur-ther integrate women into the ranks. We can see these sentiments in the typical venue for discussion of Army policy: the strategy research project papers at the Army War College where senior officers used their time away from their typical duties to tackle the most important issues of the day. Several War College students wrote papers critiquing 'the kinder, gentler military', a phrase drawn from the title of journalist Stephanie Gutmann's 2000 book, *The Kinder, Gentler Military: Can*

---

[12] Fehrenbach, 302.
[13] Hillen, 'The Military Ethos', 39.
[14] John Hillen, 'Must U.S. Military Culture Reform?', *Orbis* 43, no. 1 (1 December 1999): 53.
[15] John Hillen, 'Teaching Values to Beavis and Butthead', *Navy Times*, 15 December 1997.
[16] Wanda L. Good, 'The Damascus Paradox the Code of the Warrior – The Kinder, Gentler Army', Strategy Research Project (US Army War College, 2 April 2001), 20, https://apps.dtic.mil/sti/citations/ADA391843.

America's Gender-Neutral Fighting Force Still Win Wars?, which made the case against gender integration and 'political correctness' in the armed forces.[17] Gutmann's book was widely cited in these debates and drew praise from no less a figure than Francis Fukuyama, who reviewed it in *Commentary*, where he deplored the fact that 'the military has become one of the most politically correct of all American institutions' and claimed that it had adopted the 'pervasively therapeutic ethos of contemporary America'.[18] For Fukuyama, it had been a good thing that 'the military was one of the few American institutions in which, to put it bluntly, it was still legitimate to talk about ripping the lungs out of another human being'. Now, 'absent the male bonding rituals and warrior culture that seem so absurd to outsiders, the armed forces have become just another workplace, with worse hours and lower pay than the civilian competition'.[19]

Another military critic (this one at Air University) argued that the Army had bowed to the 'battle cries of American liberalism in the politically correct era' by emphasising values such as diversity, inclusion and sensitivity. These values inherently contradicted the military services' mission and focus. Diversity and inclusion would undermine unit cohesion while 'because a warrior's principal purpose is killing people, much of the sensitivity must be stripped away'.[20] One retired major general complained in the pages of the *Wall Street Journal* that military leaders believed that 'anyone can be a warrior if standards are lowered enough, and silver-bullet technology turns warfare into just another video game anyone can "play."' Training standards had been lowered 'so as to accommodate women' and 'warriors' were leaving because 'their leaders have created an environment that doesn't appreciate them as special – as an elite that is not open to everyone'. All of this meant that 'the ethos of being a warrior is disappearing' and that 'unit esprit built around "bonding" between warriors is now disparaged as an irrelevant concept

---

[17] Philip Calahan, 'The Code of the Warrior, the Kinder, Gentler Military and Marksmanship: Changing a Culture', Strategy Research Project (Carlisle Barracks, PA: US Army War College, 2002); Mark J. Eshelman, 'The Code of the Warrior and the "Kinder, Gentler Army"', Strategy Research Project (Carlisle, PA: US Army War College, 7 March 2001), https://apps.dtic.mil/sti/citations/ADA390609; Good, 'The Damascus Paradox the Code of the Warrior – The Kinder, Gentler Army'; Gutman, *The Kinder, Gentler Military*.

[18] Francis Fukuyama, 'The Kinder, Gentler Military by Stephanie Gutmann', *Commentary Magazine*, February 2000, www.commentary.org/articles/francis-fukuyama-2/the-kinder-gentler-military-by-stephanie-gutmann/.

[19] Fukuyama.

[20] Hugh S. Vest, 'Employee Warriors and the Future of the American Fighting Force', Fairchild Paper (Maxwell AFB, AL: Air University, 1 June 2002), 42, https://apps.dtic.mil/sti/citations/ADA420759.

and one that only serves to rationalize politically incorrect behaviour and policies'.[21]

As one Army War College student put it, though, it could not be the case that women were 'the root cause of kinder, gentler army of today' because the 'slow erosion of the military culture and a dimming of the warrior ethos' had begun in the 1940s with the adoption of the Doolittle Report and the beginning of a process of 'democratizing' the force.[22] This tendency accelerated, not because of any reluctant moves towards gender integration, but rather because of the adoption of a 'business-scientific/ management professional culture' on the part of the Army's officer corps. The ability of officers to speak the language of 'participatory management, management by objectives (MBO), scientific management, professionalism, total quality management (TQM), and operational risk management' may have made the organisation more efficient and enhanced its ability to communicate with the civilian world, but it also fundamentally undermined traditional warrior values.[23] A culture that sought to mimic that of the contemporary American corporation was one that would be ill-equipped to retain its warriors and win in war. For all that the 'microchip revolution' had enabled an RMA that paralleled the revolution in the world of business, the Army should not lose sight of how fundamentally different its mission was compared to that of any civilian counterpart.

Even War College students who wanted a broader definition of the military ethos echoed elements of this critique. One officer who thought that the officer corps of the twenty-first century had 'to reconcile the distinctiveness of soldier's calling with changing social norms' argued that 'technological advances will not alter the fundamental features of war: fear, uncertainty, and ambiguity', and that 'the officer corps will likely confront wars more akin to Vietnam than Starship Troopers in the coming decades'.[24] This would require an extraordinary degree of mental flexibility to 'adjust to rapidly changing conditions, to switch from one form of warfare to another, and to improvise'.[25] In Vietnam, as in Afghanistan, Chechnya and Palestine, 'technological superiority failed to produce quick, decisive results', and success came to those who 'stress[ed] the enduring power of man over machine'.[26] To succeed

---

[21] William C. Moore, 'The Military Must Revive Its Warrior Spirit', *Wall Street Journal*, 27 October 1998, www.wsj.com/articles/SB90944359798194500.

[22] Good, 'The Damascus Paradox the Code of the Warrior – The Kinder, Gentler Army', 19.

[23] Vest, 'Employee Warriors and the Future of the American Fighting Force', 3–4.

[24] David R. Gray, 'New Age Military Progressives: U.S. Army Officer Professionalism in the Information Age', Strategy Research Project (Carlisle, PA: US Army War College, 8 March 2001), 7, 10, https://apps.dtic.mil/sti/citations/ADA389799.

[25] Gray, 19.

[26] Gray, 10.

in this environment would require successfully fusing a warrior ethos with technological ability and sophisticated political understanding. This analysis drew on notions of 'Fourth Generation Warfare', which had been animating thinking within the Marine Corps since 1989.[27] Unlike the sort of techno optimism that permeated the Army leadership for much of the 1990s, Fourth Generation Warfare posited that global demographic and economic trends meant that sophisticated, high-tech, transnational insurgencies would pose a significant challenge to conventional militaries.

For those who subscribed to versions of this theory, then, the laments about the decline of the warrior ethos came not only from an assessment of internal weakness but from a sense that there was a growing, if inchoate, external threat that mirrored this internal weakness.[28] Journalists such as Robert Kaplan, author of influential works such as *Balkan Ghosts* and 'The Coming Anarchy', argued that the end of the Cold War had spurred 'the rise of new warrior classes as cruel as ever, and better-armed'.[29] This new warrior class included 'murderous teenagers in West Africa; Russian and Albanian Mafiosi; Latin American drug kingpins; West Bank suicide bombers; and associates of Osama bin Laden who communicate by e-mail'. Kaplan believed that globalisation was a 'Darwinian' process where dynamic and disciplined groups would 'float to the top, while cultures that do not compete well technologically will produce an inordinate number of warriors'. These warriors were only motivated by the basest of instincts, for 'like Achilles and the ancient Greeks harassing Troy, the thrill of violence substitutes for the joys of domesticity and feasting'.[30]

Kaplan's analysis was informed by his own reporting but also the ideas of Army intelligence officer Lieutenant Colonel Ralph Peters, who was making similar arguments in the pages of *Parameters* and in Pentagon briefings.[31] Peters took this dark worldview and attempted to translate it into a direct challenge to Army doctrine and culture. In his article, 'The

---

[27] William Lind et al., 'The Changing Face of War: Into the Fourth Generation', *Marine Corps Gazette*, October 1989, 22–5, https://doi.org/10.4324/9780203089279-8; Hammes, 'The Evolution of War: The Fourth Generation'.

[28] The best account of this school of thought is Ian Roxborough, 'The New American Warriors', *Theoria: A Journal of Social and Political Theory*, no. 109 (2006): 49–78.

[29] Robert D. Kaplan, 'The World of Achilles: Ancient Soldiers, Modern Warriors', *The National Interest*, no. 66 (2001): 39; Robert D. Kaplan, *Balkan Ghosts: A Journey Through History* (New York: St. Martin's Press, 1993); Robert D. Kaplan, 'The Coming Anarchy', *The Atlantic*, February 1994, www.theatlantic.com/magazine/archive/1994/02/the-coming-anarchy/304670/.

[30] Kaplan, 'The World of Achilles', 39.

[31] Ralph Peters, 'The New Warrior Class', *Parameters: Journal of the US Army War College*, Summer 1994, 16–26; Ralph Peters, '[Presentation] The New Warrior Class', 18 May

New Warrior Class', which he also briefed to the Army Staff to favourable reviews, he argued that although 'the soldiers of the United States Army are brilliantly prepared to defeat other soldiers', 'the enemies we are likely to face through the rest of this decade and beyond will not be "soldiers," with the disciplined modernity that term conveys in Euro-America, but "warriors" – erratic primitives of shifting allegiance, habituated to violence, with no stake in civil order'.[32] Where soldiers were oriented towards sacrifice, discipline, loyalty and the maintenance and restoration of order, warriors were undisciplined, individualist, fickle in their loyalties and invested in destroying order for their own personal gain. In lurid prose, Peters described a character that 'with gun in hand and the spittle of nationalist ideology dripping from his mouth ... [who] murders those who once slighted him, seizes the women who avoided him, and plunders that which he would never otherwise have possessed'.[33] Crucially, these new warriors could not be reasoned with, as, for them, 'the end of fighting means the end of the good times', and so they had no incentive to stop. For Peters, as with Kaplan, the roots of this violence could be found in the churn of globalisation, but also in the fundamentals of human nature. Peters asked, in a clearly rhetorical fashion:

Are we really the children of Rousseau and of Benetton ads, waiting only for evil governments to collapse so that our peaceable, cotton-candy natures can reveal themselves? Or are we killing animals self-organized into the disciplinary structures of civilization because the alternative is mutual, anarchic annihilation.[34]

Much as Kaplan drew on ancient Greek history to argue that warriors were a transhistorical phenomenon that needed to be reckoned with, Peters used a rudimentary understanding of political theory to make the case that the US Army needed to be prepared for a very ugly form of war.

1994, U.S. Army Dental Corps History Collection; Box 55A, Folder 7, Colonel Harper [part 4 of 6], June 1994, AHEC.

[32] Peters, 'The New Warrior Class'. The weekly staff update for the Army Staff described Peters' briefing as 'excellent' and recommended that he be invited to give it again at professional development sessions. Michael V. Harper, 'Memorandum for General Sullivan. Subject: Staff Group (SG) Weekly Update for 14–20 May 1994', 20 May 1994, Gordon R. Sullivan Papers; Box 253, Folder 4, Staff Group Weekly Update for 30 April–27 May 1994, AHEC. Peters also flew to Europe to brief 500 officers on the topic and reported that UNESCO was adopting some of his findings. John J. Madigan, 'Memorandum to Commandant Regarding Autumn 1994 Issue of Parameters', 22 July 1994, Lloyd Matthews Papers; Box 1B, Folder 14, notes for 'The Early Struggle, The Later Success' by Colonel Lloyd J. Matthews, 2nd binder [part 8 of 9], AHEC.

[33] Peters, 'The New Warrior Class'.

[34] Peters.

Kaplan and Peters differed somewhat in their diagnoses of how to deal with this new warrior class. Kaplan put more faith in technology, hoping that precision-guided munitions would make it possible to target individual perpetrators with pinpoint accuracy. Ironically, Kaplan termed this a reinvention of 'ancient war', with a focus on personalities and individuals.[35] Peters was much less sanguine on this front. In his briefing to the Army Staff, he warned that warriors were 'highly emotional, even animal-like' and 'shouldn't be backed into a corner'.[36] This meant that 'you cannot bargain or compromise with warriors. You cannot "teach them a lesson" .... You either win or you lose. This kind of warfare is a zero-sum game. And it takes guts to play.' Peters believed that the Army needed to dedicate much more training time to 'combatting the warrior threat' and ultimately 'move away from the highly stylized, ritualized form of warfare, with both written and customary rules' that it was used to, in order to employ 'irresistible violence' against the warrior class.[37]

When Peters talked about 'irresistible violence', he was not thinking about long-range, precision-guided munitions. This sort of warfare would require infantry skills and the ability to kill up close. The promise of technological transformation would not obviate the need for traditional skills, and indeed some of the Army's more ambiguous missions overseas might require more of them. As an author in *Infantry Magazine* put it, 'wherever we fight the next war, chances are it will be a close-range proposition ... every soldier must be able to hit those targets that appear unexpectedly and close in'.[38] One Army War College student made the case that this meant that the route to an effective 'warrior culture' in the Army lay in marksmanship training. The author hoped that with an increased emphasis on marksmanship across the Army, the tension between the 'warrior ethos' and the 'kinder, gentler Army' would be 'become moot' because 'the enemy is just as dead no matter the gender nor temperament of the soldier who squeezed the trigger'.[39] As the author put it, 'if a female transportation specialist routinely fires expert with her weapon, very few soldiers who consider themselves "warriors" could convince an audience that this female soldier had denigrated the Army's ability to destroy the enemy'.[40]

He complained that the contemporary Army was nowhere near achieving this standard because it wasting too much time on non-essential tasks

---

[35] Kaplan, 'The World of Achilles', 40–1.
[36] Peters, '[Presentation] The New Warrior Class'.
[37] Peters, 'The New Warrior Class'.
[38] Russell A. Eno, 'From the Editor: It's Going to Be a Close One', *Infantry*, August 2000, 52.
[39] Calahan, 'The Code of the Warrior, the Kinder, Gentler Military and Marksmanship', iii.
[40] Calahan, 18.

such as non-combat-related physical training, paperwork and 'consideration of others' lectures.[41] Moreover, those outside of combat units were not spending close to enough time on the range, with mechanics only required to fire their assigned weapons once in a twelve-month period and Pentagon staff officers not even allowed to fire a weapon during their entire tour there.[42] Active Component infantrymen were assigned eight times the amount of live ammunition as their support unit counterparts, while these Active Component support troops received 3.75 times more training ammunition than their Reserve Component equivalents did. In an environment where support units could easily find themselves in a firefight, it was imperative to train everyone to fight as infantry.[43] To free up training time for this, sexual harassment, equal opportunity and consideration of others training could be conducted as concurrent training on rifle ranges, where soldiers could receive these lectures while waiting their turn on the firing line. Similarly, the Army needed to look at its regulations that restricted the presence of privately owned firearms on its installations. While soldiers were encouraged to take part in all sorts of sports in their free time, those who wanted to pursue shooting sports were disadvantaged by the need to register their weapons with the provost marshal.[44]

This paper was indicative of a broader movement towards emphasising close combat skills. We need only look to the popularity of Lieutenant Colonel David Grossman's 1996 book, *On Killing: The Psychological Cost of Learning to Kill in War and Society*, to see how links between marksmanship and a warrior ethos were being developed.[45] Grossman, then a psychology professor at West Point, drew on S. L. A. Marshall's World War II–era work that purported to show that few soldiers in combat actually fired their weapons because of an innate resistance to killing, and discussed both the psychological barriers to killing and the training regimes that could be used to overcome it.[46] Grossman credited the modern military with having solved this problem, as he claimed that the rate of soldiers who fired their weapons in combat jumped

---

[41] Calahan, 6.

[42] Calahan, 7.

[43] Calahan, 15.

[44] Calahan, 7–8.

[45] Dave Grossman, *On Killing: The Psychological Cost of Learning to Kill in War and Society* (New York: Back Bay Books, 1996). Grossman's stated objective was to uncover how humans had had their 'psychological safety catch' taken off and to understand how to put it back on, in other words, how the desensitisation that allows soldiers to kill in wartime (an act he ultimately sees as honourable) had been transported to the civilian world, and was promoting a new and dangerous cult of violence there.

[46] S. L. A. Marshall, *Men against Fire: The Problem of Battle Command in Future War* (Oxford: The Infantry Journal Press, 1947).

from 15–20 per cent in World War II to 90–95 per cent in the Vietnam War.[47] The book sold over half a million copies and, upon retirement, Grossman was invited to give dozens of seminars and training events to different military units, where he argued the soldiers needed to develop a 'warrior mindset' and a healthy emotional reaction to killing in order to both avoid post-traumatic stress disorder and be able to do their jobs effectively.[48] He argued that it was possible to promote this mindset via effective training and divided society into three groups: the non-violent majority, who he called 'sheep'; the 'wolves', who had a capacity for violence and no empathy for fellow citizens; and the 'sheepdogs', who protected the former from the latter.[49] He defined 'sheepdogs' as having 'a capacity for violence and a deep love for [their] fellow citizens … a warrior, someone who is walking the hero's path. Someone who can walk into the heart of darkness, into the universal human phobia, and walk out unscathed.'[50]

Not everyone bought into the Peters-inspired vision of the warrior ethos, though. While many of the Army War College strategy research projects on the warrior ethos and the 'kinder, gentler army' decried a slippage in standards and a feminisation of the military, some authors believed that the solution could not be to mimic the ethos of the 'warrior class' that Peters and Kaplan described. Lieutenant Colonel Mark Eshelman argued that, far from something that should be relegated to a brief lesson to be crammed into downtime on the firing range, consideration of others was fundamental to the functioning of an effective military because it was 'what motivates soldiers risk their lives for their fellow soldier'.[51] In this version of the warrior ethos, it had 'less to do with unleashing the violence and passions of war than it does with restraining, controlling, concentrating, and focusing those passions'. Twenty-first-century

[47] Grossman, *On Killing*, 132.

[48] David Grossman, 'Full CV', www.killology.com/vitae.

[49] Grossman later became highly influential (and highly controversial) when he taught these training methods to hundreds of local police departments across the United States. Jasper Craven, 'The Police's "Sheepdog" Problem', *New Republic*, 11 June 2020, https://newrepublic.com/article/158136/military-veterans-police-sheepdog-problem; Michael Cummings and Eric Cummings, 'The Surprising History of American Sniper's "Wolves, Sheep, and Sheepdogs" Speech', *Slate*, 21 January 2015, https://slate.com/culture/2015/01/american-snipers-wolves-sheep-and-sheepdogs-speech-has-a-surprising-history-with-conservatives-and-the-right-wing.html; 'The Police Trainer Who Teaches Cops to Kill', *New Yorker*, 2017, www.youtube.com/watch?v=ETf7NJOMS6Y; Bryan Schatz, '"Are You Prepared to Kill Somebody?" A Day with One of America's Most Popular Police Trainers', *Mother Jones* (blog), n.d., www.motherjones.com/politics/2017/02/dave-grossman-training-police-militarization/.

[50] Dave Grossman and Loren W. Christensen, *On Combat: The Psychology and Physiology of Deadly Conflict in War and in Peace* (Millstadt, IL: Warrior Science Publications, 2008).

[51] Eshelman, 'The Code of the Warrior and the "Kinder, Gentler Army"', 1.

warriors needed to be both compassionate and mindful of how fragile these virtues could be under the extreme stresses of combat. Eshelman took external critics of the Army such as Stephanie Gutmann and Brian Mitchell to task when he noted that their complaints that drill sergeants were forbidden to belittle recruits implied that 'at least some degree of abuse is good'.[52] While he was somewhat sympathetic to Grossman's arguments about the need to desensitise soldiers to the realities of combat, he thought it was no bad thing that the Army of the 1990s did not seek to dehumanise its enemies the way the Army did in Vietnam and in the Pacific Theatre during World War II.[53] Ultimately, for Eshelman, the notion that 'today's Kinder, Gentler Army erodes the warrior spirit' and the 'belief that the American soldier will not fare well when faced with the modern-day equivalent of the berserker' were wrongheaded.[54] American soldiers would defeat these enemies, not because they were more violent than them, but because they could apply that violence in a controlled and measured way. This discipline was the difference between the soldier and the barbarian.

One of the authors of the influential 1970 Army War College study on military professionalism, Walter Ulmer, chimed in on this debate in the pages of *Parameters*. Ulmer, now a retired lieutenant general, thought that the 'warrior ethic' was 'essential, but potentially disruptive' in the modern military. Like Eshelman, Ulmer believed that the concept of self-sacrifice was at the heart of the Army's professional tradition, but that an overly aggressive 'warrior spirit' could produce leaders who couldn't embrace 'change, agility, creativity, and self-awareness when the need for those attributes is paramount'.[55] Thus, this warrior spirit had to be channelled in ways that were situationally appropriate. Unlike some critics, he wasn't overly worried about its decline, noting that it 'has somehow survived the influx from a supposedly self-centred generation' and that 'West Point cadets still compete for assignments in the combat arms', but he still believed that the Army did need to reconsider

---

[52] Eshelman, 22; Gutman, *The Kinder, Gentler Military*; Mitchell, *Women in the Military*.

[53] Eshelman, 'The Code of the Warrior and the "Kinder, Gentler Army"', 52; John Dower, *War without Mercy: Race and Power in the Pacific War* (New York: Pantheon Books, 1986); Craig M. Cameron, *American Samurai: Myth and Imagination in the Conduct of Battle in the First Marine Division 1941–1951*, (Cambridge and New York: Cambridge University Press, 1994), 89–129; Gregory A. Daddis, *Pulp Vietnam: War and Gender in Cold War Men's Adventure Magazines* (New York: Cambridge University Press, 2020).

[54] Eshelman, 'The Code of the Warrior and the "Kinder, Gentler Army"', 19.

[55] Walter Ulmer, 'Military Leadership into the Twenty-First Century: Another "Bridge Too Far?"', *The US Army War College Quarterly: Parameters* 28, no. 1 (17 February 1998): 4–25.

its overall culture. Given all the strains on the force throughout the 1990s, the fact that the Army accomplished all of its assigned missions 'represents one of the finest examples of institutional stamina, commitment, and versatility in military history'.[56] This success could not be taken for granted, though, and Ulmer noted that Army leaders were far more interested in technology and doctrine than they were in morale and organisational culture. He decried the 'relatively cavalier coverage of human dynamics ... typical of brochures describing the Army After Next and the Revolution in Military Affairs' and complained that there 'appears to be no strategic design for how to change Army culture'. The various immediate crises facing the Army, along 'with a mixed appreciation of the need for "cultural change" among serving Army general officers, seem to have colluded to put non-technical macro issues on the back burner'.[57]

The Army's own studies confirmed some of these complaints. In 2000, over 750 students, mostly majors, at the Command and General Staff College took part in the Chief of Staff of the Army's Leadership Survey and delivered a scathing verdict about both Army senior leadership and Army culture in general.[58] Amid familiar complaints about careerism, micromanagement, a box-ticking 'zero defects' culture and excessive operational tempo combined with poor quality of life for military families, the responses overwhelmingly indicated that the job was no longer 'fun', and that absent that job satisfaction, it was it very difficult to retain junior officers.[59] When pressed to elaborate on what 'fun' meant, some participants argued that there was 'too much focus on managing careers and not enough on building warriors'. Others claimed that 'we need to be fair and considerate, but we need to be warriors first, not social workers'.[60] They complained about a culture of risk aversion, that the Army didn't provide enough resources for tough, realistic training, and that it had lost sight of the fact that 'everyone's a warrior. Combat training shouldn't be limited to combat arms.' The researchers summarising the survey results believed that this sense of alienation had geopolitical roots as the 'loss of [a] full time enemy within the careers of majors has caused disillusionment with why they are here'. They wanted to know, 'do we do war

[56] Ulmer.
[57] Ulmer.
[58] Thomas E. Ricks, 'Younger Officers Quit Army at Fast Clip', *Washington Post*, 17 April 2000, www.washingtonpost.com/archive/politics/2000/04/17/younger-officers-quit-army-at-fast-clip/5290a8e6-eab6-4bfa-94b8-473e0868bdee/.
[59] 'Army Leadership Survey Comments', D-N-I.net, archived at the Wayback Machine, 21 May 2008, https://web.archive.org/web/20080521012809/http://www.d-n-i.net/fcs/leadership_comments.htm.
[60] 'Army Leadership Survey Comments'.

(train for combat)? Or do we spread peace and love (and the occasional foodstuff) all over the world?'[61] Ultimately, this resulted in the familiar complaint that the 'warrior ethos' was disappearing, due to too many peacekeeping missions, the use of soldiers as 'diplomatic police' and too much of a focus on technology rather than on soldiers and leaders.

Following the results of this survey, Army Chief of Staff General Eric K. Shinseki commissioned a large-scale Army Training and Leadership Development Panel (ATLDP) to get a sense of the concerns of the broader institution. Based on interviews with 13,500 Army leaders and their spouses, this panel also found that an excessive operational pace was eroding both morale and institutional culture.[62] Crucially, they found that 'the warrior ethos for lieutenants diminishes when confronted by an often too-brief experience as a platoon leader or other small-unit leader to fill staff positions left vacant by our shortage of captains' and that training frequently wasn't conducted in accordance with Army doctrine 'due to resource constraints and the undisciplined application of our training doctrine'.[63] These problems were mirrored at higher levels. Major Donald Vandergriff complained that officers tended to leave company command in their fifth or sixth year of service without returning to line duty for five years and then as a major for only year if they were lucky.[64] Indeed, the Chief of Staff's Leadership Survey had echoed complaints about 'too many back-to-back non-troop assignments', citing the case of an infantry officer due to go on his third consecutive non-troop deployment after graduating from the Command and General Staff College (CGSC), a situation that was causing him to consider leaving the Army altogether.[65] Given the scale of discontent apparent in so many venues – from War College student research papers, to surveys of mid-ranking officers at the CGSC, to the large-scale ATLDP study – it was clear that something was amiss. Seemingly, many within the Army were now lamenting the absence of a 'warrior ethos', although what they meant by that wasn't always clear. While many appeared to use 'warrior' as a synonym for aggression and martial masculinity, others saw warriors as an external threat that would need to be combatted by disciplined and professional soldiers.

---

[61] 'Army Leadership Survey Comments'.
[62] William M. Steele and Robert P. Walters, 'Training and Developing Army Leaders', *Military Review* 81, no. 4 (August 2001): 5.
[63] William M. Steele and Robert P. Walters, 'Training and Developing Leaders in a Transforming Army', *Military Review* 81, no. 5 (October 2001): 3.
[64] Donald Vandergriff, *The Path to Victory: America's Army and the Revolution in Human Affairs* (Novato, CA: Presidio Press, 2002), 157.
[65] 'Army Leadership Survey Comments'.

6.2   The Black Beret and the 'Army of One'

By the time Shinseki took over as Army chief of staff in June 1999, any claim that the institution was permeated by a 'Hooah' spirit would have been hard to make. At this stage, the Army was facing the height of its recruiting crisis, had been attempting to navigate the aftermath of the controversies unleashed by the Aberdeen Proving Grounds scandal for nearly three years and was in the midst of a budgetary battles with the Office of the Secretary of Defense as to how to fund its transformation efforts. Along with his focus on transformation, Shinseki wanted to bring about a cultural change. He emphasised the need for such a shift repeatedly in briefings with senior leaders and in meetings with junior troops. He felt, however, that talk of a cultural shift would not be enough, and that the Army would have to do something to dramatise the important changes taking place. Shinseki's answer was to focus on headdress, a seemingly trivial issue, but one that ended up provoking passionate debate across the Army. Regular Army troops had been wearing their functional patrol caps since 1981. To symbolise the shift from a Cold War Army to an expeditionary Army, Shinseki thought a uniform change was needed to make clear the break with the past. On 11 November 2000, while the rest of the country obsessed over the contested Florida recount in the presidential election, Shinseki formally announced that effective from the Army's birthday on 14 June 2001, all soldiers would wear berets as their working headdress, something previously reserved for Special Forces and airborne units (Figure 6.1).[66] He noted that the adoption of the beret by these units in World War II 'signified new organisations with unique capabilities' and that so too would the adoption of the black beret symbolise 'a changing (transforming) Army that promotes pride, professionalism and *espirit de corps* that soldiers will be proud to wear'. This 'rapid change' would be another indication how 'the Army is transforming into a more decisive, responsive, and versatile force'.[67]

Making a headdress change a priority for his tenure as Army chief of staff was an odd move for Shinseki. Given the widespread anxiety within the Army about the state of the force and its future, swapping patrol caps for berets seemed to be a weak response. Yet, as the furious reaction to the move made clear, Shinseki was certainly getting at

---

[66] Eric Shinseki, 'CSA Sends: The Army Black Beret', The United States Army: Army Black Beret, 11 November 2000, https://web.archive.org/web/20010624053826/http://www.army.mil/features/beret/beret.htm.

[67] 'Beret Implementation Plan', 26 October 2000, Eric K. Shinseki Papers; Box 75, Folder 15, Official Papers AC of S, Briefing and Information Paper on the Black Beret, 26 October 2000, AHEC.

Figure 6.1 Soldiers donning their berets during a beret transition ceremony marking the Army's 226th birthday on 14 June 2001

something fundamental in Army culture, even if the move did not promote the unity he expected. His primary motivation in pushing for a new and distinctive Army-wide headdress was to give the organisation a new symbol that would help to transcend the factionalism that he felt was bogging it down and slowing its adaptation to necessary change. The rationale for choosing the black beret in particular was twofold: the black beret was the traditional headdress of armoured units in many armies and berets had been worn by the Special Forces and the Rangers, the most versatile, deployable and agile units in the Army, for many years. By combining the traditions of these different branches, much as he wanted to combine their capabilities in the medium-weight Stryker Brigades, Shinseki argued that 'the Army Black Beret will represent and honor the best of both our dismounted infantry and our mechanized forces as we transform today's Army into one force'.[68] While it was not apparent in his public remarks, Shinseki's objective was very much tied to the idea of creating 'one force' within the Army, to take the sting out

[68] Eric Shinseki, 'Letter to Senator Bob Dole', 27 February 2001, Eric K. Shinseki Papers; Box 22, Folder 5, Official Correspondence, AC of S, incoming and outgoing, 22–8 February 2001, AHEC.

of some of the cliquish attitudes that were prevalent in the organisation. He had read and reread Mark Bowden's account of the disastrous 1993 raid in Somalia, *Black Hawk Down*, and he talked off the record to reporters about how he had been affected by a passage that described how a Delta Force sergeant first class refused to take an order from a Ranger master sergeant in combat because he saw the Rangers as an inferior unit.[69] That the troops in Somalia had arranged along a well-understood pecking order – Delta, then Rangers, and then all other soldiers – that trumped all other aspects of military professionalism had caused immense damage, and Shinseki wanted one less reason for tribal posturing and bickering.[70]

More than anything though, Shinseki saw the black beret as a way of providing a needed psychological jolt to an Army that was struggling to adapt to a post–Cold War world. Speaking about the move later to a reporter, he characterised his thinking as, 'you sort of come to the point where you need to reach inside the chest cavity of the institution and give it a good squeeze'.[71] Writing in support of Shinseki's decision, Army War College researcher Leonard Wong wrote that the move to the black beret 'is not about fashion. It is about change and the resistance to it.' Wong wrote that 'just as some animals shed their winter coats to acclimatize to the onset of spring, the Army must shed the assumptions and habits of the Cold War in anticipation of peacekeeping, humanitarian assistance, disaster relief and asymmetrical warfare of the future'. For Wong, the beret was 'a small shift in attitude preparing the Army for the larger paradigm shifts of the future'. While admitting that 'there were gasps when the beret policy was announced', he predicted that 'eventually the Army will catch its breath and get on with soldiering'.[72]

Outside the military and the veteran community though, the decision was greeted with bemusement more than gasps. The *New York Times* chose to cover of the decision and the subsequent controversy in its 'Style' section, where their reporter observed that 'the beret brings with it many overtones and subliminal links with many wearers: Che Guevara, Huey P. Newton, and Saddam Hussein, for instance. Monica

---

[69] Chris Lawson, 'Email to Lewis M Boone: For the Chief', 11 December 2000, Eric K. Shinseki Papers; Box 75, Folder 17 reference file on the black berets, December 2000–March 2001, AHEC.

[70] Bowden, *Black Hawk Down*.

[71] Peter J. Boyer, 'A Different War', *New Yorker*, 23 June 2002, www.newyorker.com/magazine/2002/07/01/a-different-war.

[72] Leonard Wong, 'Why the Beret Makes Good Sense for the Army', n.d., Eric K. Shinseki Papers; Box 23, Folder 8, Official Correspondence, AC of S, Incoming and Outgoing, 22–6 March 2001, AHEC.

Lewinsky, and Groucho Marx as an old man.' *The Times* interviewed a fashion consultant who enthused about the versatility of the beret and the facility for the wearer to create his or her own look, noting that '[i]t's the only part of a uniform you can do that with'. Clearly having fun, the journalist claimed that 'a twist here, a little angle there, and the beret wearer can evoke either Field Marshal Montgomery searching the North African horizon for Rommel's tanks, or Jean-Paul Sartre, resistance fighter and existentialist, sipping espresso and smoking Gauloises at Les Deux Magots'.[73] To civilians looking on, the beret controversy seemed to be taking place in another world.

In some ways, the beret was an odd and impractical choice of head-dress. One former British soldier complained that 'it soaks up rain like a sponge, provides no shade for the eyes, hardly gives any protection from cold weather, cannot be cleaned easily, whilst the colours of the beret worn by most regiments today defy camouflage'.[74] The whole point of the beret, though, was its distinctiveness. The British regimental system had always encouraged distinctive uniforms and traditions, with soldiers taking great pride in their 'cap badge' and unit history.[75] Indeed, a previous attempt to introduce the beret into widespread American use had such a regimental system in mind. In the nadir of the post-Vietnam Army of the 1970s, with its widespread morale problems and its issues with race and drugs, units were encouraged to adopt their own head-dress to create some unit pride. Beginning in 1973, different units chose a wide variety of coloured berets, from the maroon of the airborne forces to the black of the 75th Ranger regiment and the armoured forces to the red of garrison troops in Fort Campbell. The American proliferation of berets also brought a tremendously complicated and mushrooming array of insignia to be worn with this headgear. All of this was ended by an order from the Department of the Army in 1979, with most units reverting to the patrol cap.[76] But the airborne troops and the Rangers continued to wear their berets, along with the Special Forces, who had

---

[73] Phil Patton, 'Some Ex-G.I'.s Say Berets Are Not for General Issue', *New York Times*, 11 March 2001, www.nytimes.com/2001/03/11/style/noticed-some-ex-gi-s-say-berets-are-not-for-general-issue.html.

[74] Walter H. Bradford, 'Clothing and Equipment Board: Historical Uniform Study' (U.S. Army Center of Military History, 12 August 1988), 36, Eric K. Shinseki Papers; Box 75, Folder 15, Official Papers AC of S, Briefing and Information Paper on the Black Beret, 26th October 2000, AHEC.

[75] Walter H. Bradford, 'Information Paper: Historical Background of the Green Beret as Distinctive Unit Headgear', 30 July 1993, Eric K. Shinseki Papers; Box 75, Folder 15, Official Papers AC of S, Briefing and Information Paper on the Black Beret, 26th October 2000, AHEC.

[76] Bradford, 'Clothing and Equipment Board: Historical Uniform Study', 33.

been wearing green berets since President Kennedy authorised them to do so, over the objections of the joint chiefs of staff, in 1961.[77]

It was these units – particularly the 75th Ranger Regiment, which had been wearing the black beret since 1975 – that caused the most problems for Shinseki's plan for an Army-wide introduction of the black beret. The reaction among Rangers, and particularly Ranger veterans, was predictably furious. While a gagging order prevented serving Rangers from speaking to the press about the decision, veterans' groups were quick to speak out. Emmett Hiltibrand, president of the 75th Ranger Regiment Association, and Jim Grimshaw, president of the US Army Ranger Association, established Save Our Beret to lobby against the wider adoption of what they regarded as their symbol. The Ranger veterans wrote to General Shinseki in protest, declaring that 'giving soldiers a symbol which has served as a mark of distinction for others to aspire to will merely cheapen the symbol'. As they put it, 'when everyone has it, it won't mean anything'.[78] One former Ranger used a high school analogy, saying 'it's like you're in school, and you aspire to earning a letter jacket. Then they change the rules and give everybody a letter jacket …. These small symbols are the things that drive people to excellence.'[79]

Several congressmen and senators, including Senators Strom Thurmond and Chuck Grassley, along with the former senator and Republican presidential candidate Bob Dole, joined the veterans' groups in their protests. Dole wrote to Shinseki arguing that the beret would dilute the elite status of the Rangers, a status that 'translates into pride, extraordinary performance of duty and willingness to face personal pain, hardship and even death on a foreign battlefield and behind enemy lines'. Invoking his status as a World War II veteran who had served in the 10th Mountain Division in Italy under General Darby, the founder of the modern Rangers, Dole asked Shinseki to open the decision for review.[80] Remarkably, amid all the impassioned responses to the beret plan, no one seemed to make the case that the Army had bigger problems to deal with.

The public affairs team in the Army Staff were caught somewhat off-guard by the vehemence of the reaction to the plan to introduce the black beret. They asked researchers from the Army's Center for Military

[77] John Prados, *The US Special Forces: What Everyone Needs to Know* (Oxford: Oxford University Press, 2015), 30–4.
[78] Patton, 'Some Ex-G.I.'s Say Berets Are Not for General Issue'.
[79] Matthew Barakat, 'Rangers Don't Want to Share Black Berets', *Fox News*, 10 March 2001, Eric K. Shinseki Papers; Box 75, Folder 17 reference file on the black berets, December 2000–March 2001, AHEC.
[80] Bob Dole, 'Letter to General Eric Shinseki', 20 February 2001, Eric K. Shinseki Papers; Box 22, Folder 5, Official Correspondence, AC of S, incoming and outgoing, 22–8 February 2001, AHEC.

History to investigate what uniforms were worn by the original World War II–era Rangers and pointed out that the Rangers had only been wearing the black beret since 1975.[81] This argument had little effect, and larger veterans' organisation, such as the Veterans of Foreign Wars and the American Legion, also moved to oppose the change. Ray G. Smith, the commander of the American Legion, issued a press release stating that 'the American Legion stands for a strong national defense; the welfare, well-being and morale of the troops is a part of that'. Smith argued that 'the Army cannot support morale by undermining cherished traditions, and that is why the Rangers must exclusively wear their historic – and I might add hard-earned – black beret'. The distinction between earned and unearned symbols was what was at stake, and so Smith suggested a compromise: 'If Army brass insists that the total force must wear the black beret, then the Rangers should be authorized a distinctive colour of their own.'[82] The Rangers must be allowed to retain their distinctive headdress, much as the Special Forces had their green beret and airborne troops had their maroon beret.

This notion that one had to earn the right to wear the black beret via sacrifice was perhaps the most potent weapon the veterans' groups had to protest the decision. Given this logic, it was somewhat inevitable that someone would link the beret issue to a specific incident to highlight the ways in which the Rangers had earned the right to wear their headdress. The parents of Private First Class James Markwell, a 19-year-old Ranger medic who had been killed in the invasion of Panama, wrote to both Shinseki and the Chairman of the Joint Chiefs of Staff General Hugh Shelton, to claim that Shinseki's decision belittled their son's sacrifice. Sandra Rouse wrote to Shelton: 'I sent this to you so you could see exactly how the decision being made is affecting all of us who have never worn the black beret but who regard it as an emblem of those elite soldiers who have. Those of us who have given much so that someone we love could wear that beret.' She described the death of her son and his funeral, where she was presented with two mementoes: an American flag and her son's black beret. She emotively closed her letter with a plea that 'with all that's going on in the world today you shouldn't have to deal with this but then neither should the Rangers knowing at any moment

---

[81] Walter H. Bradford, 'Information Paper: Q/A on US Army Ranger Military Beret', 26 October 2000, Eric K. Shinseki Papers; Box 75, Folder 15, Official Papers AC of S, Briefing and Information Paper on the Black Beret, 26 October 2000, AHEC.

[82] 'Legion to Army: Respect Ranger Black Beret Tradition', *Yahoo! Politics*, 1 February 2001, Eric K. Shinseki Papers; Box 75, Folder 17 reference file on the black berets, December 2000–March 2001, AHEC.

you may be asking them to perform as warriors, treat them with the respect they desire I beg you'.[83]

The letter reached Shinseki's desk very quickly, with a note that it demanded an immediate and tactful response. One staffer also noted that the family had ties to President-elect Bush, making a good response all the more vital.[84] In his letter to Rouse, Shinseki tried to console the bereaved mother by claiming that 'in adopting the black beret as a symbol of excellence army-wide, we will not diminish its value or meaning. Rather, we intend to underscore its significance, its history, and the memory of men like PFC [Private First Class] Markwell who have proudly worn it'.[85] In other venues, though, Shinseki and the supporters of the new beret policy had to invoke the same language of sacrifice as the grieving mother, with Shinseki – a twice-wounded Vietnam veteran – telling an *Army Times* journalist off the record that 'all soldiers have the ability to rise to the occasion when called upon regardless of their particular roles within our formations. Twice soldiers personally have carried me off the battlefield. They weren't "special" in any way. They were regular soldiers doing the right thing at the right time.'[86] Senator Daniel K. Inouye invoked *his* status as a World War II veteran to advocate for the introduction of the beret, claiming that 'the black beret demonstrates, first, an excellence which everyone in today's Army can claim. Second, it also demonstrates that all who wear the beret belong to the same team. In the Navy, all wear the same distinctive cap, whether they are a gunner's mate or a cook.'[87]

This line of argument seemed to have some effect, with the *Army Times* in particular starting to give more space to Shinseki's views, after some fraught exchanges between their journalist covering the story and the public affairs staff.[88] The newspaper ran an editorial by Army Vice

---

[83] Sandra Rouse and William Rouse, 'Letter to General Hugh Shelton', n.d., Eric K. Shinseki Papers; Box 75, Folder 17 reference file on the black berets, December 2000–March 2001, AHEC.

[84] 'Note to Colonel House', 14 December 2000, Eric K. Shinseki Papers; Box 17, Folder 10, Official Correspondence, AC of S, Incoming and Outgoing, 27–9 December 2000, AHEC.

[85] Eric Shinseki, 'Letter to Sandra Rouse', 27 December 2000, Eric K. Shinseki Papers; Box 17, Folder 10, Official Correspondence, AC of S, Incoming and Outgoing, 27–9 December 2000, AHEC.

[86] 'Memorandum: Army Times Interview', n.d., Eric K. Shinseki Papers; Box 75, Folder 17 reference file on the black berets, December 2000–March 2001, AHEC.

[87] Daniel K. Inouye, 'Letter to Donald Rumsfeld', 20 March 2001, Eric K. Shinseki Papers; Box 25, Folder 1, Official Correspondence, AC of S, Incoming and Outgoing, 16–17 April 2001, AHEC.

[88] Lewis M. Boone, 'Email to Chris Lawson', 12 December 2000, Eric K. Shinseki Papers; Box 75, Folder 17 reference file on the black berets, December 2000–March 2001, AHEC.

Chief of Staff General Jack Keane that managed to convey Shinseki's argument in a more direct and less diplomatic fashion than his boss had managed. The op-ed opened with: 'say this aloud: "American soldiers don't deserve to wear the black beret": Listen to yourself. How does that sound? Say it again. That sentiment is the fundamental premise of those who oppose the Chief of Staff's decision to make the black beret the Army's standard headgear.' The soldiers in question were not just 'peacekeeping troops, the soldiers who are in Kosovo and Bosnia. Or Kuwait or Saudi Arabia or the Sinai or Korea', they were 'the soldiers who won Desert Storm, the Hundred Hours' War, the most complete battlefield victory of the twentieth century'.[89] The soldiers of the contemporary Army were the 'direct heirs of the warriors of the Cold War, Korea, and Vietnam' and there was no question that they deserved to wear the black beret.

While the *Army Times* editorial had taken some of the pressure off and slowed the rate of negative letters coming to Shinseki's office, this changed drastically with the news that the parents of PFC Markwell had given their dead son's black beret to two former Rangers, who planned to walk the 750 miles from Fort Benning, Georgia, the home of the Rangers, to Washington, DC where they would present the beret to President Bush and ask him to overrule the Army's decision. One staffer immediately recognised the problem this could cause, writing that 'in my estimation, this march has enormous potential to become a "cause célèbre" with the media – there are just too many "hooks." (It's Day 25 of the march and the exhausted Rangers are now just 57 miles from Washington, D.C. ...).'[90]

And indeed, the story did prove irresistible to the media, starting with the *Fayetteville Observer* (the home of Fort Bragg and the Special Forces), which carried an interview with one of the marchers, David Nielsen.[91] Nielsen invoked the Ranger's heritage to explain his march: 'there's something about the sound of the word Ranger, what it means ... The Rangers are older than the country, older than the Constitution. I wanted to wear a black beret.'[92] Nielsen was, in fact, the soldier who had carried

[89] John M. Keane, 'Why Black?', *Army Times*, 25 December 2000, Eric K. Shinseki Papers; Box 75, Folder 17 reference file on the black berets, December 2000–March 2001, AHEC.

[90] Tom Begines, 'Re-surging Media Interest in the Black Beret', 23 January 2001, Eric K. Shinseki Papers; Box 75, Folder 17 reference file on the black berets, December 2000–March 2001, AHEC.

[91] J. S. Newton, 'Ex-Ranger Prepares Beret Protest March', *Fayettesville Observer*, 25 January 2001, Eric K. Shinseki Papers; Box 75, Folder 17 reference file on the black berets, December 2000–March 2001, AHEC.

[92] Barakat, 'Rangers Don't Want to Share Black Berets'.

PFC Markwell's body off the battlefield in Panama, standing vigil over the corpse wrapped in a poncho until it was evacuated, giving added gravity to his protest. There was heavy press coverage of the march, with the *New York Times*, *Washington Post*, *Fox News* and *CNN* all giving the story plenty of attention.[93] Nielsen's pilgrimage – a 750-mile march with a 55 lb pack – was likened to Ranger training, where the aches, pains and blisters of the march were akin to the rite of passage needed to earn the black beret. Just as in Ranger training, Nielsen was joined by 'Ranger buddies' and three of them entered Washington, DC on 10 March 2001, surrounded by a growing crowd.

The protestors led a rally of some 200 people at the foot of the Lincoln Memorial (chosen because Lincoln had been in a Ranger-like unit during the Black Hawk War). There the protestors echoed the same argument about sacrifice and heritage. 'Why would someone harm such a noble heritage?' former Ranger Bob Black asked the crowd. Protestors rejected the idea that issuing the black beret to all soldiers would boost morale and promote unity. 'It's just not the way to do it', said former World War II Ranger John Kormann of Chevy Chase, Maryland. 'I've seen young soldiers almost transformed during Ranger training. To some nice person sitting behind a desk, what will it mean to them?' 'My reaction would be it's in keeping with the politically correct stupidity that the Army has been going along with', said Bob Pace of Chapel Hill. 'After all, it's difficult to buck a commander in chief or a chief of staff.'[94]

The rally was accompanied by days of lobbying Congressmen on Capitol Hill, where Nielsen met with over thirty representatives and senators. However, much of the sting of the protests was taken away by the Army's announcements that while they would still issue the black beret Army-wide, the Rangers would change the colour of their berets to tan, maintaining their elite status as a unit apart.[95] This at least partially

[93] Steve Vogel, 'Foot Soldier in Fight for Black Beret; Ex-Ranger Treks 750 Miles to Protest Plan to Make Elite Symbol Standard Issue', *Washington Post*, 10 March 2001, www.proquest.com/docview/409126279/abstract/632F698857184358PQ/1; 'Army Rangers Gather to Fight Beret Order', *New York Times*, 10 March 2001, www.nytimes.com/2001/03/10/us/army-rangers-gather-to-fight-beret-order.html; 'Former U.S. Amy Ranger Road Marches to Protect Black Beret', *Yahoo! Finance*, 9 March 2001, Eric K. Shinseki Papers; Box 75, Folder 17 reference file on the black berets, December 2000–March 2001, AHEC; Barakat, 'Rangers Don't Want to Share Black Berets'.

[94] 'Beret March Ends', *Fayettesville Observer*, 11 March 2001, Eric K. Shinseki Papers; Box 75, Folder 17 reference file on the black berets, December 2000–March 2001, AHEC.

[95] 'Hat of a Different Color: Army Rangers Allowed to Adopt Tan Berets', *Newsday*, Combined Editions, 16 March 2001, www.proquest.com/docview/279457152/abstract/588CF4FD8E09437FPQ/1.

assuaged some of the concerns of protestors, but the overriding sense among conservatives that the black beret decision represented political correctness gone mad still resonated.

The news that some of the berets the Army had ordered would be manufactured in China did nothing to help this situation, with Shinseki and Secretary of Defense Donald Rumsfeld called to testify on the contracts (and the broader decision) before two House Committees: the Committee on Small Business and the Committee on Government Reform.[96] Both committee chairmen used the fact that some of the berets would be Chinese-made as a way to reopen the debate over the entire decision. Many in Congress questioned the cost of the uniform change – at some \$29.6 million.[97] Rep Roscoe Bartlett (R-MD) introduced a bill that would prevent the Army from purchasing any black berets or authorising their use until the Secretary of the Army certified that any shortfall in Army ammunition stockpiles had been eliminated.[98] Shinseki was further damaged by the fact that his testimony had to be postponed at the request of President Bush by the ongoing delicate negotiations with the People's Republic of China over the release of several US Navy personnel who had been detained on Hainan Island in the first major foreign crisis of the Bush administration. Only by cancelling the Chinese portion of the beret order, and thus delaying the planned introduction of the black beret on the Army's 14 June birthday, was the Department of Defense able to escape a lengthy congressional investigation of their procurement decisions.[99]

All of this was used as a stick to beat Shinseki by the conservative press. The *Washington Times*, an outlet that had frequently aired grievances against the Army in recent years, was particularly vehement in its coverage, printing a cartoon of Shinseki that caused the Acting Secretary

[96] Dan Burton, 'Letter to Eric Shinseki', 15 December 2000, Eric K. Shinseki Papers; Box 17, Folder 8, Official Correspondence, AC of S, Incoming and Outgoing, 19–22 December 2000, AHEC; Donald A. Manzullo, 'Letter to Eric Shinseki', 5 April 2001, Eric K. Shinseki Papers; Box 24, Folder 3, Official Correspondence, AC of S, Incoming and Outgoing, 1–5 April 2001, AHEC.

[97] Edward Walsh, 'Army and Rangers Compromise on Beret', *Washington Post*, 17 March 2001, www.washingtonpost.com/archive/politics/2001/03/17/army-and-rangers-compromise-on-beret/cb54b561-a03a-44ba-8451-1e3a9dab1a18/.

[98] Roscoe G. Bartlett, 'Actions – H.R.1770 – 107th Congress (2001–2002): To Prohibit the Purchasing, Issuing, or Wearing of Berets as Standard Army Headgear (Other than for Certain Specialized Units) until the Secretary of the Army Certifies to Congress that the Army Ammunition Shortfall Has Been Eliminated', legislation, 14 May 2001, 2001/2002, www.congress.gov/bill/107th-congress/house-bill/1770/all-actions.

[99] 'Army Recalling China-Made Black Berets', *New York Times*, 2 May 2001, www.nytimes.com/2001/05/02/world/army-recalling-china-made-black-berets.html.

of the Army to write a letter of protest.[100] The cartoon not only mocked Shinseki's choice of headdress but the Army's new 'Army of One' advertising campaign, which had replaced the popular 'Be All You Can Be' recruiting slogan.[101] Like the black beret, the 'Army of One' was seen as pandering to a selfish, spoiled generation.[102] Columnist (and disgraced former Marine) Oliver North thought that the black beret symbolised an Army that was being irrevocably weakened in service of what he called 'Kofi Annan's "Meals on Wheels" contingent'. North saw himself as giving voice to 'service men and women returning for repeat assignments to Kosovo and Bosnia [who] wonder why we continue to send troops into this Balkan aberration where all we do is protect ourselves against the Albanians we came to save'. According to North, 'all Soldiers ask: "What the hell is an Army of One?" Rangers, proud of their hard-won, distinguishing head gear wonder why every cook and "Remington Raider" in the Pentagon will now be wearing a black beret made in – of all places – communist China.'[103]

His fellow *Washington Times* columnist Suzanne Fields argued that the black beret controversy symbolised the decline of the warrior culture within America and worried that not enough Americans were now made of 'the right stuff'. She decried the fact that *Shakespeare in Love* had won more Oscars than *Saving Private Ryan* and that the latter movie didn't offer a heroic depiction of war in any case, with Tom Hanks playing a regular guy rather than a hero. She worried that 'the contemporary Army must depend on costume for definition, to sort the men from the girls, you might say'. The fact that the 'Army of One' campaign ran not just during Sunday football games but also during midweek sitcoms, such as *Friends*, *The Simpsons* and, worst of all, *Buffy the Vampire Slayer*, was a cause for concern. According to Fields, this focus on television popular with both men and women and the 'Army of One's alleged playing up to potential recruits' desire for instant gratification was a deeply worrying trend. Quoting from the new ad, where a corporal, a solitary runner with a backpack, declares that 'even though there are 1,045,690 soldiers just

---

[100] Joseph Westphal, 'Letter to Helle Bering', 22 March 2001, Eric K. Shinseki Papers; Box 75, Folder 17 reference file on the black berets, December 2000–March 2001, AHEC.
[101] 'General Shinseki: "An Army of One"', *Washington Times*, cartoon, March 2001, Eric K. Shinseki Papers; Box 75, Folder 17 reference file on the black berets, December 2000–March 2001, AHEC.
[102] For a fuller treatment of the 'Army of One' campaign, see Bailey, *America's Army*, 236–44.
[103] Oliver North, 'Listening to the Troops', *Washington Times*, 11 March 2001, Eric K. Shinseki Papers; Box 75, Folder 17 reference file on the black berets, December 2000–March 2001, AHEC.

like me, I am my own force', Fields closed one of her columns with 'Are you listening, Gen. Shinseki? That means berets in 1,045,690 shades of khaki, black – and pink.'[104]

The implication of this conservative critique was that *contra* the *Army Times* editorial, most American soldiers did not in fact deserve to wear the black beret. To these critics, the adoption of the black beret was not a symbol of an Army transforming itself or adopting the warrior spirit of the units that had previously worn this headdress, but of an institution that had lost its way and was lowering standards in order to accommodate political trends. Somehow, the change in headdress further demonstrated that the feminisation of the military was continuing apace. Not only that, but it signalled a diminution rather than an improvement in the elite status of America's soldiers. If Shinseki's purpose in adopting the beret was to signal both to the Army itself and American society more broadly that a serious cultural change was underway, then the response that his initiative received was a sure sign that the Army had more work to do in defining itself for the twenty-first century.

6.3   The Warrior Ethos Programme

Even if Shinseki had provoked a severe backlash by choosing the black beret as his preferred symbol of a transforming Army, it was no surprise that he looked to elements of the Army's Special Operations Forces for inspiration. As well as their obvious cultural cachet, these soldiers had a reputation for being flexible and adaptable: exactly the sort of qualities that would be needed amid uncertainty over the Army's future missions. The Army Special Forces, whose iconic green beret remained unthreatened throughout the entire controversy, had already formally adopted a 'warrior ethos' as part of their enumerated core values. As an article in *Special Warfare*, their in-house professional journal, put it, the warrior ethos meant that 'military service is more than a job. Winning the nation's wars calls for total commitment, and the core of the warrior ethos is the refusal to accept failure.'[105] The Army Special Forces defined themselves as a 'brotherhood of warriors who are bound by their dedication to mission accomplishment, by their loyalty to one another, and by their moral and physical courage' where the 'warrior ethos is embedded in everything we do'. This warrior ethos was made up of intangible

[104] Suzanne Fields, 'The Army's New Clothes', *Washington Times*, 19 March 2001, Eric K. Shinseki Papers; Box 75, Folder 17 reference file on the black berets, December 2000–March 2001, AHEC.
[105] Salvatore F. Cambria, Edward M. Reeder and James E. Kraft, 'Warrior Ethos: The Key to Winning', *Special Warfare* 13, no. 2 (Spring 2000): 2.

factors, such as 'unit cohesion, integrity, physical and moral courage, dedication, commitment, and leadership'.[106]

This language reflected the fact that the 'warrior ethos' had made its ways into parts of Army doctrine. The Aberdeen Proving Ground scandal had led to a renewed focus on Army values, with recruit training being extended by a week to dedicate more time to classes on moral standards. Doctrine writers followed suit and worked to refresh leadership and values doctrine. While the previous edition of *FM 22-100 Military Leadership* (published in 1990) only made a single reference to a 'warrior spirit', the 1999 edition mentioned the warrior ethos twenty-four times and defined it as 'at its core' grounded 'on the refusal to accept failure'.[107] This is what made the military and its values different from other organisations. The manual declared that 'military service is much more than just another job: the purpose of winning the nation's wars calls for total commitment' and that this 'desire to accomplish that mission despite all adversity is called the warrior ethos and makes the profession of arms different from all other professions'.[108] A later study noted that the Army values that were inculcated throughout basic training essentially reflected 'societal beliefs to which most American citizens would subscribe' and therefore were not combat- or even Army-specific. By contrast, a warrior ethos would provide a 'unique set of values' that would be 'peculiar to the needs of an Army which is required by the Nation to fight'.[109]

This was not just about physical courage in close combat: the warrior ethos applied 'to all soldiers and [Department of the Army] civilians, not just those who close with and destroy the enemy'.[110] Not only that, but the doctrinal version of the warrior ethos differed from that described by many critics of Army culture in that it was grounded much more explicitly in ethics. The manual talked about the difficulties of 'such complex arenas as peace operations and nation assistance', and noted that 'in such ambiguous situations, decisions to use lethal or nonlethal force severely test judgement and discipline'. Therefore, the warrior ethos was to act as a moral guide so that 'in whatever conditions Army leaders find themselves, they [could] turn the personal warrior ethos into a collective

---

[106] Cambria, Reeder and Kraft.
[107] United States Army, *FM 22-100 Army Leadership* (Washington, DC: Department of the Army, 1999), secs. 2–21; United States Army, *FM 22-100 Military Leadership* (Washington, DC: Department of the Army, 1990), 54.
[108] United States Army, *FM 22-100 Army Leadership*, 2-21, 1-1.
[109] Gary Riccio et al., 'Warrior Ethos: Analysis of the Concept and Initial Development of Applications' (Fort Benning, GA: U.S. Army Research Institute for the Behavioral and Social Sciences Infantry Forces Research Unit, 1 September 2004), 1.
[110] United States Army, *FM 22-100 Army Leadership*, 4-1.

commitment to win with honour'.[111] Crucially, this meant that the warrior ethos in doctrine was not just a reflection of traditionalist complaints about a supposedly softer Army, even if it affirmed that the military was an institution apart. A warrior ethos that emphasised good judgement as much as it did physical valour and sacrifice was one that could apply in almost all situations. While the doctrinal version of the warrior ethos did not specifically reject the complaints of those who felt that the Army had become too soft, it offered a broader vision of Army values than those who wanted to focus exclusively on combat.

That FM 22-100 spent so much on time on the warrior ethos spoke to the fact that wider institutional interest in the concept was growing. The 2002 Army Training and Leader Development Panel final report on NCO training argued that 'all soldiers need to clearly accept and internalize the warrior ethos' and reported that while the Army's NCOs clearly understood Army values, they were 'not as clear about the concept of the warrior ethos'.[112] The panel noted that 'doctrine on warrior ethos is limited in the Army's training, leadership, and operational field manuals. Warrior ethos does not have a shared meaning, nor is it a well-understood term'. Further, 'many soldiers believe that it applies only to combat units' and the NCO education system did not 'reinforce the warrior ethos throughout its curricula'.[113] As one of his last acts as chief of staff, Shinseki formally initiated the Warrior Ethos Study to define what being a soldier now meant. In a June 2003 memorandum for the Army, he declared that 'a true Warrior Ethos must underpin the Army's enduring traditions and values' and that soldiers needed to be imbued with an 'ethically grounded Warrior Ethos [that] clearly symbolize[s] the Army's unwavering commitment to the nation we serve'.[114] After years of agitation about the lack of such a spirit in the Army, the warrior ethos was now at the core of the Army's officially defined identity.

The process of defining and embedding this warrior ethos was immediately taken up by Shinseki's successor as Army chief of staff, General Peter Schoomaker. Brought out of retirement to replace Shinseki after the presumptive replacement, Vice Chief of Staff General Jack Keane, declined the role, Schoomaker had spent much of his career in Special Operations Forces units, and he made the Warrior Ethos programme his

[111] United States Army, 2-21.
[112] 'The Army Training and Leader Development Panel Report (NCO)' (Fort Leavenworth, KS: US Army Combined Arms Center, 2 April 2002), 3, https://apps.dtic.mil/sti/citations/ADA401192.
[113] 'The Army Training and Leader Development Panel Report (NCO)', 16.
[114] Eric Shinseki, 'Warrior Ethos: Memorandum for the Army' (Department of the Army, 3 June 2003).

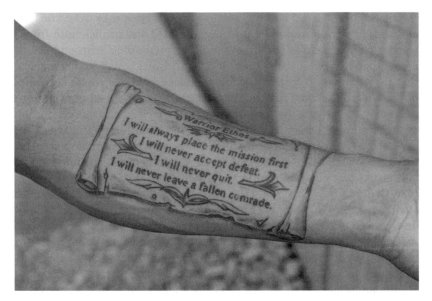

Figure 6.2 The Army's Warrior Ethos tattooed onto the forearm of First Sergeant Aki Paylor

own. In his arrival message to the Army in July 2003, he emphasised that 'our values will not change, and they are non-negotiable. Our Soldiers are Warriors of character.'[115] Schoomaker established Task Force Soldier to examine the needs of the contemporary soldier and folded Shinseki's Warrior Ethos Study into a Team Warrior subgroup to produce clarity on the Warrior Ethos and ideas for how to disseminate it throughout the force.[116] By November 2003, this group had come up with the Soldier's Creed, an affirmation of Army values, which began with 'I am an American soldier. I am a warrior and a member of the team' and went on to define a new officially endorsed warrior ethos (Figure 6.2):

> I will always place the mission first.
> I will never accept defeat.
> I will never quit.
> I will never leave a fallen comrade.[117]

[115] Peter Schoomaker, 'Arrival Message', Task Force Soldier – CSA Quote & Warrior Ethos, 15 October 2004, https://web.archive.org/web/20041015172237/http://www.infantry.army.mil/taskforcesoldier/content/warrior_ethos.htm.

[116] Brown, *Kevlar Legions*, 279.

[117] 'Warrior Ethos – Army Values', n.d., www.army.mil/values/warrior.html.

The Soldier's Creed also had soldiers promise that they would be 'disciplined, physically and mentally tough, trained and proficient in [their] warrior tasks and drills', that they would maintain their arms and equipment, that they were 'an expert and ... a professional' and, crucially, that they that stood 'ready to deploy, engage, and destroy the enemies of the United States of America in close combat'.[118] All enlisted personnel would be taught this creed, and would recite it at the conclusion of their training, while candidates at NCO promotion boards would be expected to know it, and, from 2004 onwards, wear Army dog tags featured the Warrior Ethos.[119] Speaking to reporters, basic-training recruits and instructors alike fully endorsed it, with one staff sergeant declaring that '[w]hen I read that Soldier's Creed, the hair on the back of my neck stood up ... It's making everybody think as one.'[120] Lieutenant Colonel John Carothers, warrior ethos team leader for Task Force Soldier, believed that this new ethos could be transformative, claiming that 'this is the wedge in the door, and that door is open. And when people start living this and absorbing it, it's going to change the Army.'[121]

Fundamentally, as the Soldier's Creed made clear, what this meant in practice was imbuing all soldiers with a psychological orientation towards combat. The very recent experience of the wars in Afghanistan and Iraq made it clear that the distinction between rear and front echelons was now blurring. Nowhere was this clearer than in the ordeal of the 507th Maintenance Company, who got lost during the advance to Baghdad in March 2003 and were ambushed by Iraqi forces outside of Nasiriyah, leading to most of the unit being killed or captured.[122] This experience plainly demonstrated that basic combat skills were now a necessity, no matter what a soldier's primary specialisation. Ironically, this meant that the warrior ethos that critics of the Army wanted to promote – one that celebrated martial masculinity and sought to fortify the female combat exclusion policy – was untenable, given that Army leaders had shown no sign that they wanted to go back to the pre-Gulf War status quo and start the messy, disruptive and controversial work of removing women from every conceivable situation in which they might come under enemy fire.

---

[118] 'Soldier's Creed – Army Values', n.d., www.army.mil/values/soldiers.html.
[119] Reginald P. Rogers, 'New Values Cards, Warrior Ethos "Dogtags" Available to Army Units', TRADOC News Service, 24 September 2004, https://web.archive.org/web/20060920203933/http://www.tradoc.army.mil/pao/TNSarchives/September 04/092304.htm.
[120] Matthew Cox, 'Defining a Soldier-Warrior in 121 Words', *Army Times*, 22 March 2004.
[121] Cox.
[122] Eric Schmitt, 'After the War: Inquiry; Report Says Errors and Fatigue Led to Ambush of Convoy', *New York Times*, 10 July 2003, www.nytimes.com/2003/07/10/world/after-the-war-inquiry-report-says-errors-and-fatigue-led-to-ambush-of-convoy.html.

As the Army's official history put it, 'the Warrior Ethos was not about women in combat. It was about preconceptions that some soldiers would fight, and others would not. It was also about instilling a personal commitment "to win" in the heart of every soldier and rejecting notions that military service was just "a job."'[123]

Even before the Army had experienced first-hand in Iraq how the front lines were now blurred, there had been an impetus to change this mindset. In 2001, in language that echoed the rhetoric of unity in Shinseki's beret policy, the ATLDP argued that 'all Army leaders must be warfighters' with officers competent in conducting small-unit operations and bonded to the Army 'before, and as a higher priority than, their branch'.[124] To achieve this, the Infantry School had begun to develop a Basic Officer Leader Course to make sure that fundamental combat skills and basic small-unit tactics were inculcated in all junior officers. Commander of TRADOC, General Kevin P. Byrnes, cited Special Operations Forces as the model for this training in a conversation with reporters: 'they are very agile, very adaptive ... They're intelligence collectors, they're war fighters.' The question was 'how can we take some of that goodness and bring it into our regular force?'[125] The panel called for the Army to create a training and leadership development model that would achieve these broad objectives by emphasising 'values, service ethic, warrior ethos and commitment to lifelong learning'. As part of this model, they proposed an Army-wide online 'Warrior Development Center' that would support lifelong learning that focused on developing leaders would embody these attributes.[126]

The place where the Warrior Ethos was made most visible, though, was in recruit training. The Team Warrior study recommended making training more stressful and lengthening basic combat training from nine weeks to twelve. Schoomaker refused to agree to the longer training, as it would have disrupted the flow of new soldiers into their units, but he approved the tougher field-training exercises.[127] Speaking of these changes, Byrnes told reporters that 'we took a look at a lot of areas, and warrior ethos was one we wanted to strengthen. They'll tell you "I'm a mechanic," not "I'm a soldier," and we've got to change that.' Byrnes looked outside the Army for inspiration, claiming that 'the Marines do

---

[123] Brown, *Kevlar Legions*, 279.
[124] Steele and Walters, 'Training and Developing Leaders in a Transforming Army', 6.
[125] Vernon Loeb, 'Army Plans Steps to Heighten "Warrior Ethos"', *Washington Post*, 8 September 2003, www.washingtonpost.com/archive/politics/2003/09/08/army-plans-steps-to-heighten-warrior-ethos/aafb2625-a33d-48ca-8fcf-3ef2747f1243/.
[126] Steele and Walters, 'Training and Developing Leaders in a Transforming Army', 10.
[127] William Donnelly, *Department of the Army Historical Summary, Fiscal Year 2004* (Washington, DC: U.S. Army Center of Military History, 2015), 34, https://history.army.mil/html/books/101/101-35-1/index.html.

a good job on their basic combat training, and we're trying to pull the better aspects out and embed them in our training'.[128] The Army added five hours of formal training on the warrior ethos to the basic combat training course and embedded the warrior ethos principles throughout the course, with soldiers expected to recite the Soldier's Creed and Warrior Ethos throughout their training. Army training doctrine emphasised the need for all soldiers to understand the nine Warrior Drills and forty Warrior Tasks, which were effectively basic infantry skills such as moving under fire, reacting to contact and evacuating wounded personnel.[129]

The Army Behavioral Research Institute commissioned a study in 2004 to examine how well these drills and tasks worked to inculcate a warrior ethos, and its authors found that results were mixed. The authors of this report noted that while Schoomaker had made such a move a major goal of his tenure, 'what that means, and how it is to be accomplished is not particularly clear'.[130] They remarked that the concept of a warrior ethos was not particularly difficult to understand, but 'far more difficult are decisions on how to ensure the effective dissemination of the overall ethic of a Warrior'.[131] They found that average soldiers were not continually exposed to 'conditions that foster Warrior Ethos', even in combat, which meant that the onus was internalising this ethos 'to the greatest extent possible during the limited timeframe' of basic training and that, even then, the Warrior Drills and Warrior Tasks were not sufficiently specific to fully impart what being a warrior meant. To further embed this ethos, the 'Warrior Ethos must continue with the Soldier to his or her advanced individual training programme location, then to the unit', and the Army would need develop more 'training curricula which foster the development and sustainment of Warrior Ethos'.[132]

Certainly, the institution as a whole moved quickly to make sure that talk of this ethos was widespread. Army advertising changed to reflect this message, with recruiting ads that (temporarily) focused less on the monetary and educational benefits of service and depicted soldiers serving in Iraq and Afghanistan.[133] Team Warrior also recommended that soldiers with combat experience be assigned to all training centres, and that training become more realistic with enhanced with combat marksmanship and

---

[128] Loeb, 'Army Plans Steps to Heighten "Warrior Ethos"'.
[129] Janet Kirkton, 'Warrior Ethos, Tasks and Drills Spiral into Initial Entry Training', *Engineer* 35 (March 2005): 18–21.
[130] Riccio et al., 'Warrior Ethos', v.
[131] Riccio et al., 2.
[132] Riccio et al., 3.
[133] Bailey, *America's Army*, ix, 244–5.

combat life-saver training a requirement for all soldiers.[134] In an effort to improve soldiers' aggression and close fighting abilities, the Modern Army Combatives Program, a hand-to-hand combat training programme developed at the 75th Ranger Regiment, was rolled out across the entire Army.[135] The Army's Infantry Center at Fort Benning also opened up their arduous Ranger School to non-combat arms soldiers, although they continued to exclude women.[136] The Army also revamped its entry-level NCO training course to spend more time on 'warfighting skills' and renamed it the Warrior Leader Course in 2005. The language of warriors was now everywhere. The centres where wounded soldiers recovered from their injuries became Warrior Transition Units, while the Army's soldier of the year programme was named the 'Best Warrior' competition.

The Warrior Ethos became fully enshrined in Army doctrine too. Whereas the 2001 edition of *FM 1 The Army*, the Army's capstone doctrinal manual intended to explain 'who we are, what we do, and how we do it', mentioned the term 'warrior' only once, it appeared thirty-two times in the 2005 edition, including a section that recapitulated the definition that been circulating since 1999, describing the Warrior Ethos as 'the frame of mind of the professional soldier', something that was 'at its core … [about] the refusal to accept failure and instead overcome obstacles with honor'.[137] The manual also explicitly committed the Army to cultural change and declared that dedicating the force to 'the ideals of the Warrior Ethos' would be part of that change.[138] In contrast to the 2001 edition, which mentioned 'the American people' fifteen times, the 2005 edition used this phrase only four times, despite being 50 per cent longer than the earlier edition. Its opening pages began with the Soldier's Creed and the Warrior Ethos, whereas the 2001 version began with an anecdote about George Washington that emphasised the importance of civilian control and the role of a military in a democracy.[139] The latter anecdote, along with references to civil society, was still present in the newer edition, but it was relegated to page ten.[140] This shift in emphasis

134 Matthew Cox, 'Army Goes on the Warrior Path', *Army Times*, 22 March 2004.
135 James F. Blanton, 'Hand to Hand Combatives in the US Army' (Fort Leavenworth, KS: Army Command and General Staff College, 12 December 2008), https://apps .dtic.mil/sti/citations/ADA511484.
136 Matthew Cox, 'Ranger School, Anyone? Army Leaders Would Like Support Soldiers to Earn Tabs', *Army Times*, 12 April 2004; Victoria A. Hudson, 'Women Unfairly Denied Shot at Ranger School', *Army Times*, 31 May 2004.
137 *FM 1 The Army* (Washington, DC: Department of the Army, 2001); *FM 1 The Army* (Washington, DC: Department of the Army, 2005), 1–18.
138 *FM 1 The Army*, 2005, 4–11.
139 *FM 1 The Army*, iv; *FM 1 The Army*, 2001, 2.
140 *FM 1 The Army*, 2005, 1–4.

was subtle, but denoted an institution that was beginning to talk more and more about the values that set it apart from broader American society rather than those that connected it to its fellow citizens. With its emphasis on legitimate violence, self-sacrifice to the point of death and the centrality of combat to the soldier's identity, the warrior ethos deliberately marked soldiers as a group apart from their fellow Americans.

6.4   Conclusion

The groundswell of discussion about a 'warrior ethos' (or lack thereof) in the Army brought together many of the fault lines that had riven Army culture in the wake of the Cold War's end. Concerns over gender, future missions and the nature of military service combined to produce anxieties about a missing 'warrior ethos' and calls for its reaffirmation. Critics differed in the particulars of their complaints, but they all wanted some sort of commitment from the Army to ensure that it was producing 'warriors' that were universally capable of engaging in close combat. Here, they found some sympathy from Army leadership, as their critiques paralleled internal studies commissioned by the Army chief of staff that were calling for the same thing. The debacle over the black beret policy did not necessarily speak well of the Army's abilities to navigate institutional change amid the broader culture wars and ongoing angst about the Army's role, but it did at least show that, under Shinseki, the Army was trying to find a way to articulate a major shift in its culture and ethos. The almost universally enthusiastic embrace of the Warrior Ethos programme after its official promulgation in the summer of 2003 suggested that Shinseki and his successor had hit upon a more effective vehicle for that cultural shift. It is also worth noting, though, that the gap between the universal ethos of Army doctrine and the one that critics described as being exclusive to the 'band of brothers' who inhabited combat units meant that many of the tensions that had brought the Army to this moment of turmoil were left unresolved. What was clear, though, was that the warrior ethos was about promoting a specific organisational subculture and a particular vision of the profession. Even if the choice wasn't immediately obvious to all concerned, the debate over the warrior ethos did fundamentally pose the question of whether or not the Army should widen or shrink the gap between itself and broader society. In promoting an officially sanctioned warrior ethos, Army leaders effectively chose the former course of action, a decision whose consequences would reverberate for years to come.

Epilogue

On 30 June 2012, Lieutenant Clint Lorance arrived at Strong Point Payenzai in Zharey District, south of Kandahar. He was there to take command of First Platoon, C Troop, of the 4th Squadron, 73rd Cavalry Regiment of the 82nd Airborne Division, whose previous platoon commander had just been wounded in a roadside bombing. In the three short days that he commanded that platoon, Lorance committed one war crime per day.[1] On the day he arrived, he threatened to shoot a four-year-old Afghan boy in front of his father. On 1 July, he directed his troops to fire harassing shots within ten to twelve inches of civilians in a neighbouring village. Most consequentially, on 2 July, while on patrol, he ordered his soldiers to shoot and kill two unarmed Afghan men. That evening, his men turned him in, and he was relieved of command. Fourteen of them testified under oath against him, and it took a military jury three hours of deliberations to find him guilty of a host of offences, including second-degree murder. Lorance received a twenty-year sentence to be served at Fort Leavenworth.[2]

Although the Army later issued a letter of reprimand to Lorance's platoon sergeant for not reporting him after the incidents on 30 June and 1 July, the system had moved with reasonably alacrity once his crimes had been disclosed. Lorance's appeals went nowhere, and reviews of the case by both the commanding general of the 82nd Airborne Division and the Army Court of Criminal Appeals affirmed his guilt. However, his story had been resonating outside of the Army. Lorance became a *cause célèbre* for conservative groups who argued that he was a victim of 'Obama's rules of engagement', restrictions on the use of force which, in their telling, valued the lives of the enemy more than it did American

---

[1] Greg Jaffe, 'He Was Convicted of Murder, Then Pardoned by Trump: His Troops Suffered a Different Fate', *Washington Post*, 2 July 2020, www.washingtonpost.com/graphics/2020/national/clint-lorance-platoon-afghanistan/.

[2] Jaffe; Nathaniel Penn, 'The Last Patrol: The Pardon of a Convicted War Criminal', *California Sunday Magazine*, 27 September 2020, https://story.californiasunday.com/clint-lorance-court-martial-pardon-the-last-patrol.

soldiers.[3] This story was amplified by commentators such as *Fox News'* Sean Hannity and promoted by conservative members of Congress who later founded the 'Congressional Justice for Warriors' caucus. Around 124,000 people signed a petition to the White House demanding a pardon for Lorance. In an *amicus curiae* brief to the Court of Appeal for the Armed Forces, a group of retired officers argued that 'not only is the Appellant's conviction morally and legally wrong, but that it also has a chilling, dangerous impact on our Nation's warriors' ability to defend themselves in combat'.[4]

This campaign culminated on 5 November 2019, when President Donald Trump, who had been vocal about what he saw as an overly cautious attitude towards civilian casualties by the Obama administration, granted Lorance and two other convicted war criminals a full pardon over the objections of the Secretary of Defense and Secretary of the Army.[5] Trump's decision provoked outrage. Former Chairman of the Joint Chiefs of Staff General Martin Dempsey tweeted that 'absent evidence of innocence or injustice, the wholesale pardon of US service members accused of war crimes signals [to] our troops and allies that we don't take the Law of Armed Conflict seriously' and called the decision an 'abdication of moral responsibility'.[6] Senior officers weren't the only ones angered by the decision: those who served with Lorance were disgusted by the pardon. Staff Sergeant Mike McGuinness, who had been a squad leader in First Platoon, complained that 'I've buried people that struggled with what happened, and whether through their own hands or their actions, they're gone ... I'm not going to sit quietly while he gets paraded around and they're not recognized'.[7] His former company commander in Zharey, Captain Patrick

[3] Dave Philipps, 'Cause Célèbre, Scorned by Troops', *New York Times*, 24 February 2015, www.nytimes.com/2015/02/25/us/jailed-ex-army-officer-has-support-but-not-from-his-platoon.html.
[4] Clint Lorance, 'Petition for a Writ of Habeas Corpus under 28 U.S.C. § 2241' (United States District Court for the District of Kansas, 18 December 2018), https://ab9a3241-2e45-441f-953b-59d0ec440449.filesusr.com/ugd/d89b70_91186bd7f7374bb28447626a1d28fce9.pdf.
[5] Dave Philipps, 'Trump Clears Three Service Members in War Crimes Cases', *New York Times*, 15 November 2019, www.nytimes.com/2019/11/15/us/trump-pardons.html.
[6] GEN(R) Martin E. Dempsey [@Martin_Dempsey], 'Absent Evidence of Innocence or Injustice the Wholesale Pardon of US Servicemembers Accused of War Crimes Signals Our Troops and Allies That We Don't Take the Law of Armed Conflict Seriously. Bad Message. Bad Precedent. Abdication of Moral Responsibility. Risk to Us. #Leadership', Tweet, *Twitter*, 21 May 2019, https://twitter.com/Martin_Dempsey/status/1130809276191035392.
[7] Jaffe, 'He Was Convicted of Murder, Then Pardoned by Trump: His Troops Suffered a Different Fate'; Mike McGuinness, 'Clint Lorance Ordered Me to Kill Afghan Civilians: I Still Live with that Guilt Today', *Task & Purpose* (blog), 19 November 2020, https://taskandpurpose.com/news/clint-lorance-war-crimes-essay/.

Swanson, told a reporter that 'he sees Lorance on TV and on Twitter, and it's crushing to watch someone soil what he – all of the guys – tried so hard to deliver on: a certain promise of duty'.[8] Meanwhile, Lorance joined Trump on stage at a campaign rally and was invited onto the morning show *Fox and Friends* to tell his story. Trump, Hannity and the legions of people who had signed petitions on behalf of Lorance were willing to ignore the voices of the soldiers who had actually served with him in order to validate their own vision of what war and warriors should be.

The Lorance case is illustrative not only of the gaping divide in American society between those who went to war and those who cheered them on from a distance, but of the equivocal meaning of the warrior ethos. For most in the Army, Lorance was an ill-disciplined leader not ready for the pressures of combat, despised by his troops and prone to panic and overreaction. For his chain of command, his actions were not only criminal but abhorrent to Army values. However, for his supporters, including President Trump, Lorance was the epitome of what a warrior was supposed to be: he had gone where others would not go to fight America's enemies, and his decisions, made in the heat of the moment in a warzone, should not be questioned. Lorance's defence attorney argued that he had been put in an impossible situation and maintained that 'it's hard to be an ethical warrior when you're pitted against an enemy with no ethic'.[9] In discussing the pardon of Lorance and two other war criminals, Trump claimed that 'these are not weak people. These are tough people ... Somebody has their back, and it's called the president of the United States.'[10]

Lorance himself understood his experience in similar terms. He later told a reporter that 'one of the things that the average American does not understand is you can't use the same filter that we use in the Western world in Afghanistan. At the risk of sounding like some sort of racist, those people are barbarians.' He rejected the population-centric counterinsurgency approach of his brigade commander, arguing that 'we lost the Vietnam War because of people like Colonel Mennes .... I came in strong .... I know I am not the only one that fought the war that way.'[11] Even those who supported Lorance admitted that some of his actions could be understood as an attempt to perform toughness. Don Snyder, a Maine-based novelist who started the petition drive asking Obama to pardon him, said that Lorance was 'trying to appear tough for his men and got caught up in his own act'.[12] As a gay soldier who had joined

[8] Penn, 'The Last Patrol: The Pardon of a Convicted War Criminal'.
[9] Penn.
[10] Penn.
[11] Penn.
[12] Philipps, 'Cause Célèbre, Scorned by Troops'.

the Army before Obama repealed 'Don't Ask Don't Tell', Lorance said
that he was driven by a desire to be accepted 'into perhaps the most
hypermasculine society in America'. He told a reporter that 'to compartmentalize such a big part of yourself is incredibly difficult and requires
an incredible amount of energy' but that the need to live in secrecy and
fear pushed him on: 'that would be the thesis statement of my life: If I
can't be perfect in that way, I'll be perfect in every other way'.[13] Perhaps
more pertinently for his troops, he was also one of the rare infantry officers not to have a Ranger tab, so he may have had something to prove
when he finally took command of a combat unit. In any case, this desire
for acceptance and to live up to the perceived ideals of what it meant to
be a tough soldier combined with contempt for Afghans and for 'hearts
and minds' – style counterinsurgency produced a commander who not
only committed murder, but who celebrated his actions before his troops
turned him in.

The Lorance case may have been an outlier, but the pathologies it
revealed – a subset of the civilian population ready to revere and applaud
literally any action taken by soldiers in war, and an officer who similarly believed his situation to be so exceptional that it justified any deed
he committed – were anything but. The tensions between notions of
citizen-soldiers who were only roused to fight by a need to defend their
way of life and of tough professional warriors who would go anywhere
in pursuit of whatever mission had been given to them had been evident
though the entire post–Cold War period, but these tensions were clearly
exacerbated by the long years of the War on Terror, where rhetoric about
soldiers as 'warriors' and 'warfighters' blossomed. In both popular culture and within the military itself, imagery such as Spartan helmets and
skull logos derived from the Marvel comics character 'The Punisher'
became ubiquitous.[14] Indeed, Steven Pressfield's fictional account of the
battle of Thermopylae, *Gates of Fire*, made it onto the chief of staff of the
Army's professional reading list in both 2011 and 2017.[15]

Not only that, but the Special Forces, whose subculture was most
responsible for promulgating the warrior ethos, enjoyed widespread
acclaim. As a group that was vital to the conduct of the War on Terror,

---

[13] Penn, 'The Last Patrol: The Pardon of a Convicted War Criminal'.
[14] Jim Gourley, 'Welcome to Spartanburg! The Dangers of This Growing American Military
Obsession', *Foreign Policy* (blog), 22 April 2014, https://foreignpolicy.com/2014/04/22/
welcome-to-spartanburg-the-dangers-of-this-growing-american-military-obsession/.
[15] Steven Pressfield, *Gates of Fire: An Epic Novel of the Battle of Thermopylae* (New York:
Bantam, 1999); Martin Dempsey, 'The U.S. Army Chief of Staff's Professional Reading
List' (Washington, DC: U.S. Army Center for Military History, 2011); Mark Milley,
'The U.S. Army Chief of Staff's Professional Reading List' (Washington, DC: U.S.
Army Center for Military History, 2017).

not just in Iraq and Afghanistan but all over the globe, its image was being monetised seemingly everywhere, from movies to best-selling memoirs to coffee companies to craft beer breweries.[16] Virtually all of these cultural products depicted the soldier or special operator as a tough, violent and hypermasculine character. Surveying the War on Terror–focused output of Hollywood and TV networks, the journalist James Fallows noted that while 'cumulatively these dramas highlight the damage that open-ended warfare has done – on the battlefield and elsewhere, to warriors and civilians alike … they lack the comfortable closeness with the military that would allow them to question its competence as they would any other institution's'.[17] To the extent that the warrior ethos had ever been a project of the Army's leadership, the culture of the War on Terror saw it escape their control and become an organic phenomenon that resonated with elements of the public and the ranks of the military itself in ways they had not predicted.

The long years of the War on Terror also brought with them fears that a 'warrior caste', a prospect that had worried everyone from the founding fathers to contemporary scholars of civil–military relations, had finally come into being. Research indicated that a growing percentage of soldiers were themselves the children of veterans. In 2015, fully 36 per cent of Army recruits had a father who had served, while 6 per cent had a mother who served.[18] This phenomenon has been even more pronounced in the upper ranks: an Army study from 2007 noted that of the 304 general officers then serving in the Army, 180 had children serving as well.[19] When surveys asked about family members who had served rather than just parents, 83 per cent of recruits reported a family connection to the military.[20] Since less than 1 per cent of the population was currently serving in the military in 2017 and only 7 per cent of the US

---

[16] Chris Kyle, Scott McEwen and Jim DeFelice, *American Sniper: The Autobiography of the Most Lethal Sniper in U.S. Military History* (New York: Harper, 2012); *Lone Survivor* (Film 44, Emmett/Furla/Oasis Films (EFO Films), Spikings Entertainment, 2014); Jason Zengerle, 'Can the Black Rifle Coffee Company Become the Starbucks of the Right?', *New York Times*, 14 July 2021, www.nytimes.com/2021/07/14/magazine/black-rifle-coffee-company.html; James Clark, 'Navy SEAL Who Shot Bin Laden in the Face Wants You to Invest in This Beer Company', *Task & Purpose* (blog), 9 July 2021, https://taskandpurpose.com/news/navy-seal-team-6-robert-oneill-beer-company/.

[17] James Fallows, 'The Tragedy of the American Military', *The Atlantic*, February 2015, www.theatlantic.com/magazine/archive/2015/01/the-tragedy-of-the-american-military/383516/.

[18] Amy Schafer, 'Generations of War: The Rise of the Warrior Caste and the All-Volunteer Force' (Washington, DC: Center for a New American Security, 8 May 2017), 7, www.cnas.org/publications/reports/generations-of-war.

[19] Schafer, 7.

[20] Schafer, 7.

adult population consisted of military veterans (a percentage that will
likely drop precipitously as the draft-era veterans of World War II, the
Korean War and the Vietnam War die off), the growing insularity of the
Army, as well the military more broadly, is remarkable.[21] Not only that
but, as of 2015, half of all military recruits came from the South, meaning that the military was becoming isolated in a geographical as well as
a familial sense.[22] In this gap between those with a direct connection to
the military and those without one, all sorts of ideas about the nature of
military service could flourish.

This sense of isolation was compounded by the relentless tempo of
deployments. While veterans of peacekeeping missions in the 1990s had
complained about an unsustainable operational tempo, the various wars
of the post-9/11 era were unprecedented in terms of the sheer time commitment they demanded. A 2019 Pew survey revealed that while 58 per
cent of veterans who had served only before 9/11 had deployed overseas,
fully 77 per cent of post-9/11 veterans had deployed,[23] while 29 per cent
of veterans reported that they deployed three or more times.[24] Some had
deployed even more than that. The *New York Times* reported in 2016
that 90,000 soldiers and Marines had deployed overseas more than four
times.[25] Many of these were likely members of the Special Operations
community, a group that put up with a relentless cycle of deployments,
which could typically involve six months overseas followed by six months
at home before the next deployment. By 2011, a spokesperson for Army
Special Forces Command confirmed that many Special Operations
troops had completed deployments in the 'double digits' and one Delta
Force veteran told a reporter that he was home for a total of only eighty-
nine days between 2002 and 2011.[26] While Army leaders had planned
for an expeditionary Army in the late 1990s, this tempo was far beyond
anything they had imagined.

[21] Schafer, 11.
[22] Schafer, 5.
[23] Kim Parker et al., 'The American Veteran Experience and the Post-9/11 Generation',
Pew Research Center's Social & Demographic Trends Project (blog), 10 September 2019,
www.pewresearch.org/social-trends/2019/09/10/the-american-veteran-experience-and-
the-post-9-11-generation/.
[24] Parker et al.
[25] Benedict Carey, 'Those with Multiple Tours of War Overseas Struggle at Home',
New York Times, 29 May 2016, www.nytimes.com/2016/05/30/health/veterans-iraq-
afghanistan-psychology-therapy.html.
[26] Yochi J. Dreazen, 'For Elite U.S. Troops, War's End Will Only Mean More Fighting',
The Atlantic, 25 October 2011, www.theatlantic.com/international/archive/2011/10/for-
elite-us-troops-wars-end-will-only-mean-more-fighting/247309/; W. J. Hennigan, 'Inside
the New American Way of War', *Time*, 30 November 2017, https://time.com/5042700/
inside-new-american-way-of-war/.

Unsurprisingly, the combination of widespread public adulation and the unsustainable pace of their deployments led to serious morale and discipline problems within the Special Operations Forces. Ironically for a group that epitomised the warrior ethos in both popular culture and Army doctrine, Special Operators began to garner a reputation for ill-discipline and misconduct. Their misdeeds included multiple cases of murder, both of detainees and civilians overseas and of other American service members at home and abroad.[27] Indeed, the other two service members who were pardoned along with Clint Lorance were Special Operations troops: an Army Special Forces major accused of murdering an Afghan man, and a Navy SEAL chief petty officer who had been accused of murdering a detainee and killing civilians and was convicted of posing with a dead captive's severed head.[28] These units also suffered from widespread drug and alcohol abuse, with one Navy SEAL team ordered to leave Iraq in 2019 due to the extent of its misconduct.[29] Indeed, at several junctures in the war in Afghanistan, conventional unit commanders found their counterinsurgency campaigns disrupted by Special Forces raids that would attack 'high-value targets' without any coordination with local units.[30] In both Iraq and Afghanistan, commanders also had to grapple with the conduct of private military security companies, which recruited heavily from the ranks of Special Forces units and were prone to firing at civilians.[31]

---

[27] Nicholas Kulish, Christopher Drew and Matthew Rosenberg, 'Navy SEALs, a Beating Death and Claims of a Cover-Up', *New York Times*, 17 December 2015, www.nytimes .com/2015/12/17/world/asia/navy-seal-team-2-afghanistan-beating-death.html; Dan Lamothe, 'Navy SEAL Pleads Guilty in Hazing Death of Special Forces Soldier in Mali', *Washington Post*, 16 May 2019, www.washingtonpost.com/world/national-security/navy-seal-pleads-guilty-in-hazing-death-of-special-forces-soldier-in-mali/2019/05/16/9482a d52-77f9-11e9-b3f5-5673edf2d127_story.html; Helene Cooper, Michael Tackett and Taimoor Shah, 'Twist in Green Beret's Extraordinary Story: Trump's Intervention after Murder Charges', *New York Times*, 16 December 2018, www.nytimes.com/2018/12/16/ us/politics/major-matt-golsteyn-trump.html.

[28] Philipps, 'Trump Clears Three Service Members in War Crimes Cases'.

[29] Dave Philipps, 'A Navy SEAL Platoon Is Pulled from Iraq over Misconduct Reports', *New York Times*, 25 July 2019, www.nytimes.com/2019/07/25/us/navy-seal-platoon-withdrawn-iraq.html; Catherine Herridge, Andrew Bast and Jessica Kegu, 'Navy SEALs Tell CBS News "Lawless" Members Plague Teams with Criminality, Drug Abuse and Profiteering', *CBS News*, 30 April 2021, www.cbsnews.com/news/navy-seals-tell-cbs-news-alleged-criminality-drug-use-exploitation/; Betsy Woodruff Swan and Lara Seligman, 'Internal Study Highlights Struggle over Control of America's Special Ops Forces', *Politico*, 7 May 2021, www.politico.com/news/2021/05/07/internal-study-defense-special-operations-forces-485825.

[30] Pratap Chatterjee, 'Killing the Wrong People in Afghanistan: How Task Force 373 Became a Metaphor for an Aimless Afghan Policy', *CBS News*, 20 August 2010, www .cbsnews.com/news/killing-the-wrong-people-in-afghanistan/.

[31] Matt Apuzzo, 'Blackwater Guards Found Guilty in 2007 Iraq Killings', *New York Times*, 22 October 2014, www.nytimes.com/2014/10/23/us/blackwater-verdict.html;

A congressionally mandated ethics review blamed the state of Special Operations units partly on an operational tempo that eroded unit integrity and leader development, but also on a widespread sense of entitlement among Special Operations troops who not only believed themselves to be part of a separate warrior caste but looked down on the conventional military as well.[32] Even by the generous standards of post-9/11 defence budgets, these units had lavish facilities, including their own special gyms and dining facilities and access to dieticians and fitness trainers, and unlimited quantities of expensive equipment.[33] These perquisites, combined with the pressure of constant deployments and the drumbeat of casualties that did not let up even when major combat operations drew down, helped to produce a culture that encouraged these troops to literally think of themselves as special: as superior troops who were entitled to behave however they wanted while still receiving the respect and admiration of outsiders.

This sense of entitlement may have been more acute among Special Operations troops, but the phenomenon certainly existed elsewhere. As early as 2003, a *Military Times* poll commissioned on the eve of the invasion of Iraq showed that two-thirds of the newspaper's active duty subscribers felt that military members had higher moral standards than the nation they served.[34] Over the years, the everyday gestures of American capitalism, from airlines allowing active duty military to board first and waiving excess baggage fees to countless businesses offering discounts for veterans and even for military family members, helped to reinforce this idea of the military as a class apart.[35]

David Zucchino, 'Deadly Contractor Incident Sours Afghans', *Los Angeles Times*, 16 September 2014, www.latimes.com/la-fg-afghan-contractors13-2009aug13-story.html.

[32] Woodruff, Swan and Seligman, 'Internal Study Highlights Struggle over Control of America's Special Ops Forces'.

[33] David Barno and Nora Bensahel, 'How to Fix U.S. Special Operations Forces', *War on the Rocks*, 25 February 2020, https://warontherocks.com/2020/02/how-to-fix-u-s-special-operations-forces/.

[34] Cited in Susan Bryant, Brett Swaney and Heidi Urben, 'From Citizen Soldier to Secular Saint: The Societal Implications of Military Exceptionalism', *Texas National Security Review* 4, no. 2 (23 February 2021): 9–24.

[35] Anne Schrader, 'Airlines Cut Military Bag Fees after Colorado Soldier Posts Video', *Denver Post*, 8 June 2011, www.denverpost.com/2011/06/08/airlines-cut-military-bag-fees-after-colorado-soldier-posts-video/; Dave Duffy, 'No Room for Sense of Entitlement among Veterans and Military Families', *Washington Post*, 16 March 2015, www.washingtonpost.com/news/checkpoint/wp/2015/03/16/opinion-no-room-for-sense-of-entitlement-among-veterans-and-military-families/; Carl Forsling, 'Military Families Need to Get Over Their Sense of Entitlement', *Task & Purpose* (blog), 25 March 2015, https://taskandpurpose.com/news/military-families-need-to-get-over-their-sense-of-entitlement/; Carl Forsling, 'Unpacking the Veteran Entitlement Spectrum', *Task & Purpose* (blog), 6 October 2014, https://taskandpurpose.com/military-life/unpacking-veteran-entitlement-spectrum/.

Even if Special Operations Forces became culturally ubiquitous in the post-9/11 years, their experiences were far from typical. Many of those who benefitted from free meals at Applebee's and complimentary admission to theme parks may have indeed spent years of their lives overseas, but they had experienced war in relative comfort. The historian Meredith Lair has written about how the US military arrived in Vietnam 'armed with abundance' and the same was doubly true of the wars in Iraq and Afghanistan, where the military went to great efforts to ensure that the troops had ample creature comforts.[36] The author David Abrams lampooned this culture in his novel *Fobbit* (a term used in Iraq to describe soldiers who deployed but never left the safety of the Forward Operating Base) in which he detailed the lives of those 'in the war, but not of the war' and honed in on material abundance as one of the key characteristics of the Fobbit's existence.[37] The dining hall, the PX, the gym and the swimming pool were all central locations in his rendition of the war. Offering readers a tour of a lightly fictionalised Camp Victory in Baghdad, Abrams described an area 'lined with a series of small trailers that house a Burger King, a What-the-Cluck Chicken Shack, and a Starbucks, where you can purchase a venti caramel macchiato and, with the first sip of the froth and sugar, be transported to within an inch of java heaven' and a PX stocked with virtually the same variety of consumer goods that could be found at home, but with bargain prices on consumer electronics.[38] These soldiers lived in air-conditioned trailers and commuted to work along neatly maintained gravel footpaths. If the war intruded on their existence, it came via the occasional rocket attack, or the more frequent sound of vehicle-borne improvised explosive devices exploding in the distance.[39]

The stability of daily life on these large bases was made possible by the long-term nature of these wars. While the planners of the late 1990s had envisioned creating a rapidly deployable, expeditionary-focused Army for the twenty-first century, these expeditionary capabilities were only needed on an episodic basis as the wars in Iraq and Afghanistan settled into their routines and troops rotated on predictable, if sometimes arduous, schedules. Similarly, while the promulgation of a warrior ethos was based on a belief that soldiers of all specialities might be called upon to

---

[36] Meredith H. Lair, *Armed with Abundance: Consumerism and Soldiering in the Vietnam War* (Chapel Hill: The University of North Carolina Press, 2014).

[37] David Abrams, *Fobbit* (New York: Grove Press, Black Cat, 2012), 366.

[38] Abrams, 52.

[39] The journalist Rajiv Chandrasekaran has written an excellent nonfiction account of life in Baghdad's 'green zone'. Rajiv Chandrasekaran, *Imperial Life in the Emerald City: Inside Iraq's Green Zone* (New York: Alfred A. Knopf, 2006).

fight – an assumption reinforced by the ambush of the 507th Maintenance Company during the invasion of Iraq – the experience of combat
was still generally confined to combat arms units. It was true that artillery troops unexpectedly found themselves conducting foot patrols as the
Army scrambled to make up for the shortfall of forces needed to conduct
counterinsurgency campaigns, but the day-to-day lives of the support
troops that made up the overwhelming majority of the deployed army
were more comfortable and predictable, and less fraught with danger,
than the promoters of the warrior ethos had assumed they would be.[40]
Even many of the logistical convoys that supplied both large bases and
small outposts were staffed by 'third country national' contractors, who
lived in less secure quarters and took on more risks than their American
counterparts.[41]

If these contractors are included in the figures, then the actual proportion of the Army in Iraq that was made up of combat and combat support troops was at a historical low of 25 per cent.[42] The sheer logistical
footprint required by contemporary operations necessitated a vast infrastructure to support those doing the fighting. We can trace this growing complexity of the Army's organisational structures by looking at the
growth in the size of headquarters' elements. The sociologist Anthony
King noted that by 2015, a typical American divisional headquarters
'was at least four times the size of its Cold War predecessor and some
ten times the size of a 1940s headquarters', consisting of 400 staff officers rather than forty.[43] The notion of a warrior culture implies that all
soldiers are heroic, or 'secular saints' as one political scientist put it,
but the people required to sustain the post-9/11 wars often carried out
work that was virtually indistinguishable from what their civilian counterparts did.[44] Indeed, many of these people *were* in fact civilians. The
self-deprecating term 'fobbit' undercut notions of soldiers as supermen,
while the phrase 'we went to war and garrison broke out' was frequently
seen graffitied in porta-potties or displayed on T-shirts on sale in the

---

[40] Kandi Huggins, 'From Artillery to Infantry: Soldier Finds Purpose in Mission Change',
www.army.mil, 23 August 2011, www.army.mil/article/63103/from_artillery_to_infantry_
soldier_finds_purpose_in_mission_change.

[41] Sarah Stillman, 'The Invisible Army', *New Yorker*, 30 May 2011, www.newyorker.com/
magazine/2011/06/06/the-invisible-army.

[42] John J. McGrath, *The Other End of the Spear: The Tooth-to-Tail Ratio (T3R) in Modern
Military Operations*, electronic resource, Long War Series Occasional Paper 23 (Fort
Leavenworth, KS: Combat Studies Institute Press, 2007), 66–7, http://purl.access.gpo
.gov/GPO/LPS91108.

[43] Anthony King, *Command: The Twenty-First Century General* (Cambridge: Cambridge
University Press, 2019), 302.

[44] Bryant, Swaney and Urben, 'From Citizen Soldier to Secular Saint'.

PX, hints at their frustrations at how the petty proclivities of the Army persisted even in a war zone. Satirical websites such as *Duffel Blog* lampooned absurdities such as the presence of senior NCOs in the dining hall to ensure that uniform standards were being maintained, and the universally mocked requirement to wear reflective safety belts while out for a run.[45] The world of weekend safety briefs and mandatory reflective belts was one far removed from popular images of bearded Special Operators killing high-value targets during night raids.[46]

Nonetheless, the Army persisted with the warrior ethos. In 2018, it replaced its 'Army Strong' recruiting slogan, which had been in use since 2006, with 'Warriors Wanted', before updating this to 'What's Your Warrior?' in 2019.[47] Strikingly, the 'What's Your Warrior?' campaign focused on twelve different soldiers from a variety of roles.[48] The ever-present Special Forces were represented, but so were microbiologists, surgeons, chefs, intelligence analysts, drone operators, cyber operations officers, technical engineers and signal specialists. Even as Army recruiting efforts made use of the exceptionalist rhetoric of 'warriors', they embraced a very capacious definition of what the term might actually mean. Army Recruiting Command founded an 'Army Warrior Fitness Team' to compete in functional fitness competitions (Figure E.1), and the Army's dining facilities, the site of so much abundance on large bases overseas, were renamed 'warrior restaurants' in 2019 as part of a healthy-eating drive.[49]

Recruiting Command's move to establish a 'warrior fitness team' was a telling one. The very popularity of the sports that this team would compete in, from CrossFit to Hyrox to Spartan races, was due to the fact that they emphasised 'tactical fitness' and often mimicked the combination

[45] 'You Know What? Screw It, Everyone's Gonna Wear Three Reflective Belts At All Times', *Duffel Blog*, 2 May 2013, www.duffelblog.com/p/sergeant-major-chandler-you-know-what-fuck-it-everyones-gonna-wear-three-reflective-belts-during-pt; 'The Reflective Belt: An Icon of the Global War on Terror', *Task & Purpose* (blog), 26 October 2015, https://taskandpurpose.com/culture/the-reflective-belt-an-icon-of-the-global-war-on-terror/; 'Sergeant Major Diverts Surveillance Drone to Check for Uniform Violations', *Duffel Blog*, 9 July 2014, www.duffelblog.com/p/sergeant-major-uav.

[46] 'DUFFEL BLOG PRESENTS: Ernest Hemingway Gives Your Weekend Safety Brief', *Duffel Blog*, 12 May 2017, www.duffelblog.com/p/ernest-hemingway.

[47] Matthew Cox, 'Army Launches New "Warriors Wanted" Campaign Aimed at Generation Z', Military.com, 19 October 2018, www.military.com/dodbuzz/2018/10/19/army-launches-new-warriors-wanted-campaign-aimed-generation-z.html.

[48] U.S. Army, 'Next Chapter Of "What's Your Warrior?" Offers Deeper Look at Army Careers', *PR Newswire*, 12 January 2021, www.prnewswire.com/news-releases/next-chapter-of-whats-your-warrior-offers-deeper-look-at-army-careers-301205755.html.

[49] 'U.S. Army Warrior Fitness Team', U.S. Army Recruiting Command, n.d., https://recruiting.army.mil/functional_fitness/; Paul Szoldra, 'The Army Is Trying to Make "Warrior Restaurant" Happen, and It's Not Gonna Happen', *Task & Purpose* (blog), 19 March 2021, https://taskandpurpose.com/news/us-army-dfac-warrior-restaurant/.

Figure E.1 A soldier taking part in Recruiting Command's Warrior Fitness Team try-out

of strength and endurance common in Special Forces physical training. CrossFit, by far the most popular of this genre of sports, was founded in 2000 and grew exponentially along with the cultural popularity of Special Forces in the post-9/11 era.[50] It promoted itself as offering training designed for the armed forces and those preparing for 'unknowable' military challenges and attracted large numbers of military and law enforcement personnel to its classes. As CrossFit methodologies made their way into military gyms, the company became the largest fitness franchise in the world. Its ubiquity put it into the category of the largest corporate chains in the world, with its 15,500 global locations only narrowly outstripped by Pizza Hut's 16,796 locations and Burger King's 16,859 outlets.[51] Central to CrossFit's methodology is a high-intensity 'workout of the day' (WOD), which is completed by members on the same day. Among these are several highly popular 'Hero WODs', named after military service members killed in the United States' post-9/11 wars. Several

[50]   Thomas E. Ricks, 'The Relationship between the U.S. Military and the CrossFit Program', *Foreign Policy* (blog), 16 December 2014, https://foreignpolicy.com/2014/12/16/the-relationship-between-the-u-s-military-and-the-crossfit-program/.
[51]   Scott Henderson, 'CrossFit's Explosive Affiliate Growth by the Numbers', *Morning Chalk Up*, 23 October 2018, https://morningchalkup.com/2018/10/23/crossfits-explosive-affilaite-growth-by-the-numbers/.

of these, such as 'the Murph', 'the Hidalgo' or 'the Taylor', are supposed to be completed while wearing weighted vests or body armour, to simulate the loads carried by troops in combat.[52] While American sports have long made a point of honouring the military at their events, what is remarkable about CrossFit and its equivalents is that they are designed not only to honour the military but to mimic them as well.

The popularity of 'functional fitness' sports did no more to bridge the gap between the military and broader society than did veteran discount programmes. For many veterans, these conspicuous acts of gratitude were ostentatious or even grating. Articles with titles such as 'Don't Thank Me for My Service' were almost as ubiquitous as the phrase they protested against, and books such as Ben Fountain's novel *Billy Lynn's Long Half-Time Walk* and David Finkel's non-fiction *Thank You for Your Service* (both later made into films) highlighted the extent to which the experience of war had created a chasm between the small number of those who had served and the vast majority who had not.[53] In a series of speeches in 2011, Chairman of the Joint Chiefs of Staff Admiral Mike Mullen declared himself to be gravely worried about this trend. Speaking at a conference on civil–military relations at the National Defense University in January of that year, he noted that 'the American people are extraordinarily supportive of our men and women' but that 'we cannot afford to be out of touch with them. To the degree that we're out of touch, I think it's a very dangerous course.'[54] Speaking in May of that year to West Point's graduating class, he said, 'I fear they do not know us. I fear they do not comprehend the full weight of the burden we carry or the price we pay when we return from battle.' Mullen believed the fault here lay not on the civilian side but with the military, whose members were 'fairly insular, speaking our own language of sorts, living within our own unique culture, isolating ourselves either out of fear or

---

[52] 'Hero and Tribute Workouts', CrossFit, accessed 26 August 2022, www.crossfit.com/heroes.

[53] Jake Wood, 'Don't Just Thank Me for My Service: Ask Me About It', Military.com, 18 August 2022, www.military.com/veterans-day/dont-just-thank-me-for-my-service.html; 'Don't Say "Thank You for Your Service" This Monday', NPR.org, accessed 19 August 2017, www.npr.org/2017/05/28/530504781/words-youll-hear-memorial-day-dos-and-donts; Buttrick, 'My Turn: Please Don't Thank Me for My Service', *Concord Monitor*, 15 May 2020, www.concordmonitor.com/Do-not-thank-me-for-my-service-34293506; Ben Fountain, *Billy Lynn's Long Halftime Walk* (New York: Ecco, 2012); David Finkel, *Thank You for Your Service* (New York: Sarah Crichton Books, 2013); *Thank You for Your Service* (Dreamworks Pictures, Reliance Entertainment, Dune Films, 2017); *Billy Lynn's Long Halftime Walk*, 2016.

[54] Charley Keyes, 'Joint Chiefs Chair Warns of Disconnect between Military and Civilians', *CNN*, 10 January 2011, www.cnn.com/2011/US/01/10/us.military.disconnect/index.html.

from, perhaps, even our own pride .... We haven't exactly made it easy for them.'[55]

Others put the blame more squarely on warrior culture. The historian and Army veteran Rob Williams wrote for *Stars and Stripes* that 'warrior classes rarely integrate well into the societies they protect. They are, by definition, separate.'[56] He argued that 'the use of the term "warrior" has had detrimental effects on the post 9/11 military, as the burden of the wars has fallen on an ever-smaller segment of the population' and that 'dropping the warrior narrative ... is essential to long-term societal health'. For Williams, this state of affairs was not just bad for civil–military relations and the strength of American democracy but, paradoxically, for the veterans who were being treated as secular saints. The transition from military to civilian status was a difficult one, and the tendency to uncritically revere veterans led to 'feelings of isolation, unequal burden-sharing, and a sense of superiority among veterans'.[57] The solution to this state of affairs was clear: 'rather than isolating the service member and the veteran from society through emulating Spartan warriors, the Army should instil in its members the idea that they, too, are part of a longstanding citizen-soldier tradition'. Williams argued that 'the Army, after all, is full of soldiers charged with upholding and defending the Constitution of the United States – a microcosm of American society. It is not full of individual warriors fighting for personal gain.'[58]

This notion that the Army should be a microcosm of broader American society remained contested. Survey data from 2021 indicated that service members who were underrepresented in the military thought that the organisation should look more like the rest of society while those who were in the majority were less invested in the idea.[59] This was an area where the general public reverence for the military did not preclude pressure to diversify its ranks. Public opinion polling was strongly supportive of such efforts and sympathetic to the longstanding efforts of those within the military who had sought to make it more inclusive.[60] When significant change eventually

[55] Thom Shanker, 'Admiral Mullen Urges West Point Graduates to Bridge Gap with Public', *New York Times*, 21 May 2011, www.nytimes.com/2011/05/22/us/22mullen.html.

[56] Robert F. M. Williams, 'The Warrior Problem and the American Veteran', *Stars and Stripes*, 2 July 2021, www.stripes.com/opinion/2021-07-02/opinion-warrior-problem-american-veteran-2029803.html.

[57] Williams.

[58] Williams.

[59] Bryant, Swaney and Urben, 'From Citizen Soldier to Secular Saint'.

[60] Alyssa Davis, 'Americans Favor Allowing Women in Combat', Gallup.com, 25 January 2013, https://news.gallup.com/poll/160124/americans-favor-allowing-women-combat.aspx; Lymari Morales, 'In U.S., 67% Support Repealing "Don't Ask, Don't Tell"', Gallup.com, 9 December 2010, https://news.gallup.com/poll/145130/Support-Repealing-Dont-Ask-Dont-Tell.aspx; 'Broad Support for Combat Roles for Women',

began to come, it happened rapidly. The Obama administration repealed Don't Ask Don't Tell in 2010, to little protest in the ranks. In 2013, the administration ended the combat exclusion policy that prevented women from serving in combat units, and in 2015 Lieutenant Shaye Haver and Captain Kristen Griest became the first women to pass Ranger School. Both went on to command infantry units shortly afterwards.[61] The extent to which the views of senior military leaders had changed since the 1990s was made starkly clear by the controversy over transgender military service in recent years. The Obama administration had ended the ban on transgender personnel serving in 2016 only for President Trump to announce its reinstatement via a tweet a year later. Where military leaders had been staunchly opposed to the Clinton administration's attempts to end the gay ban, here the joint chiefs proclaimed themselves blindsided by Trump's announcement and all four service chiefs made a point of telling the Senate Armed Services Committee that they were unaware of any negative effects of transgender personnel serving the military.[62] Senior leaders now seemed to be acutely conscious of the pressing need for diversity in the armed forces, notwithstanding the seemingly endless problems with sexual assault and ongoing efforts to eliminate racial bias in the organisation.

The experience of war in Iraq and Afghanistan may have demonstrated that soldiers of all genders and sexualities were perfectly capable of carrying out whatever roles were assigned to them and produced a consensus among the senior leadership in favour of building a diverse force, but this did not exempt the Army, or the military more broadly, from the culture wars. Senator Ted Cruz (R-TX) fanned the flames of these controversies when he shared a video on Twitter which ostensibly revealed

Pew Research Center – U.S. Politics & Policy (blog), 29 January 2013, www.pewresearch .org/politics/2013/01/29/broad-support-for-combat-roles-for-women/; Jeff Krehely and Ruy Teixeira, 'Americans Support Repeal of "Don't Ask Don't Tell"', Center for American Progress (blog), 17 February 2010, www.americanprogress.org/article/ americans-support-repeal-of-dont-ask-dont-tell/.

[61] Scott Neuman, 'First Female Soldiers Graduate from Army Ranger School', NPR, 21 August 2015, www.npr.org/sections/thetwo-way/2015/08/21/433482186/first-female-soldiers-graduate-from-army-ranger-school.

[62] Tara Copp, 'All 4 Service Chiefs on Record: No Harm to Units from Transgender Service', Military Times, 25 April 2018, www.militarytimes.com/news/your-military/2018/04/24/ all-4-service-chiefs-on-record-no-harm-to-unit-from-transgender-service/; Barbara Starr, Zacahary Cohen and Jim Sciutto, 'Trump Transgender Ban Blindsides Joint Chiefs', CNN, 27 July 2017, www.cnn.com/2017/07/27/politics/trump-military-transgender-ban-joint-chiefs/index.html; '56 Retired Generals and Admirals Are Warning Trump over His Transgender Ban', The Independent, 1 August 2017, www.independent.co.uk/news/world/ americas/us-politics/donald-trump-transgender-ban-us-military-56-generals-admirals-criticise-palm-center-a7871641.html; Sam Levin, 'Top Military Officials Call on Trump to Reverse Transgender Ban', The Guardian, 1 August 2017, www.theguardian.com/us-news/2017/aug/01/donald-trump-transgender-ban-us-military.

ongoing concerns with feminisation in the armed forces, aired especially by those on the right. The video offered a comparison between a US Army recruiting commercial that told the story of Corporal Emma Malonelord, a soldier who enlisted after being raised by two mothers, and an advertisement for the VDV, the Russian Airborne Forces, which featured shaven-headed and shirtless men doing push-ups, jumping out of planes and aiming a sniper rifle. Cruz remarked: 'perhaps a woke, emasculated military is not the best idea'.[63] Facing criticism for unfavourably comparing the US military with the Russian armed forces, he claimed that he appreciated the military, 'but Dem politicians and woke media are trying to turn them into pansies'.[64] Cruz's comments did not age well, as the VDV, famous for its hypermasculine image and public martial arts displays, fared atrociously in the Russian invasion of Ukraine, which began in February 2022, failing to take key objectives and suffering heavy losses at the hands of Ukraine's gender-integrated armed forces.[65]

This did not stop the drumbeat of conservative criticism of the military, though. Reacting to news that the Army was projecting a major recruiting shortfall in 2022 and 2023 due to the tight labour market conditions in the aftermath of the COVID-19 pandemic and a broader decline in the physical fitness of the recruiting pool, the *Wall Street Journal* ran an opinion piece titled: 'What if They Gave a War and Everybody Was Woke?'[66] The author, a former Army armour officer, claimed that 'one of the reasons the military has been among the most trusted institutions in America in recent decades is that it stands apart from the rest of society' and that it was endangering its reputation by embracing 'woke politics'. In language reminiscent of conservative arguments about how Clinton's attempts to

---

[63] Ted Cruz [@tedcruz], 'Holy Crap. Perhaps a Woke, Emasculated Military Is Not the Best Idea …', Twitter, 20 May 2021, https://twitter.com/tedcruz/status/1395394254969753601.

[64] Katie Shepherd, 'Sen. Ted Cruz Insulted a "Woke, Emasculated" U.S. Army Ad. Angry Veterans Fired Back', *Washington Post*, 21 May 2021, www.washingtonpost.com/nation/2021/05/21/ted-cruz-russia-army-emasculated/; Ted Cruz [@tedcruz], 'I'm Enjoying Lefty Blue Checkmarks Losing Their Minds over This Tweet, Dishonestly Claiming That I'm "Attacking the Military". Uh, No. We Have the Greatest Military on Earth, but Dem Politicians & Woke Media Are Trying to Turn Them into Pansies. The New Dem Videos Are Terrible', Twitter, 21 May 2021, https://twitter.com/tedcruz/status/1395586598943825924.

[65] Brendan Cole, 'Putin's Elite Soldiers Getting Wiped out as Russia Makes Mistakes – U.K.', *Newsweek*, 26 May 2022, www.newsweek.com/putin-russia-air-forces-ukraine-unbalanced-vdv-ministry-defense-british-1710275.

[66] Barbara Starr and Ellie Kaufman, 'US Army to Likely Miss Recruiting Goal of New Troops by Nearly 40,000 over the next 2 Years', *CNN*, 20 July 2022, www.cnn.com/2022/07/19/politics/us-army-recruiting-numbers-fall/index.html; Jimmy Byrn, 'What If They Gave a War and Everybody Was Woke?', *Wall Street Journal*, 29 July 2022, www.wsj.com/articles/what-if-they-gave-a-war-and-everybody-was-woke-military-recruitment-crt-training-obesity-reading-labor-market-11659108526.

end the gay ban would drive away the conservative southerners on whom the All-Volunteer Force had come to rely to fill its recruit platoons, the piece claimed that 'a military that appears to abandon its apolitical role will have a harder time attracting large numbers of warriors and patriots to its ranks. Welcoming woke policies under a warped idea of inclusion may serve to exclude those who are traditionally more likely to serve.'[67]

While his tone was less strident and less directed at the question of who should serve in the military, retired Lieutenant General H. R. McMaster sounded a similar warning in an essay on 'preserving the warrior ethos', published in 2021 by the conservative outlet *National Review*.[68] McMaster – whose career spanned tank combat in the Gulf War to counterinsurgency in northern Iraq to leading an anti-corruption task force in Afghanistan, and whose days in uniform ended in the Trump White House where he served as national security advisor – had been a longstanding critic of the putative RMA and of an overreliance on technology in warfare, but his concerns were now more focused on morale and cohesion. He warned that 'the warrior ethos is at risk' and that 'if lost, it might only be regained at an exorbitant price'.[69] McMaster bemoaned the fact that fewer Americans were serving in the military, leading to an 'unfamiliarity with the warrior ethos'. The crux of his critique, however, was the notion that recent years had seen 'the promotion of philosophies inimical to the sacred trust foundational to it'. Referencing Christopher Coker's work on the warrior ethos, McMaster objected that the most 'damaging misconception of warriors and the warrior ethos may be the tendency to portray warriors as victims who enjoy no authorship over their future'.[70] More worrying for McMaster was 'the erosion of trust and America's shrinking confidence are diminishing the trust that binds warriors to one another and to society at a time when dangers to our security are increasing'. Here, he largely lay the blame on 'critical race theory', the *New York Times*' 1619 project and scholars such as Ibram X. Kendi.[71] He complained that 'postcolonial and New Left history is often warped by the desire to support social and political agendas in the present such as advocacy of social-justice activism and demands to "decolonize" everything from academic curricula to scientific

---

[67] Byrn, 'What If They Gave a War and Everybody Was Woke?'

[68] H. R. McMaster, 'Preserving the Warrior Ethos', *National Review*, 28 October 2021, www.nationalreview.com/magazine/2021/11/15/preserving-the-warrior-ethos/.

[69] McMaster.

[70] McMaster; Christopher Coker, *The Warrior Ethos: Military Culture and the War on Terror*, new edition (London: Routledge, 2007).

[71] Nikole Hannah-Jones, *The 1619 Project: A New Origin Story*, ed. Caitlin Roper, Ilena Silverman and Jake Silverstein (New York: One World, 2021); Ibram X. Kendi, *How to Be an Antiracist* (New York: One World, 2019); Ibram X. Kendi, *Stamped from the Beginning: The Definitive History of Racist Ideas in America* (New York: Nation Books, 2016).

research to hairstyles'. Talk of structural inequalities was inimical to the warrior ethos because it denied individuals agency and because it taught 'children in our free society that their nation is not worth defending'. Ultimately, McMaster wanted American society to pull itself together for the sake of its warriors. He argued that 'all Americans have a role in preserving the warrior ethos', which would 'require efforts to better understand war and warriors, a rejection of the destructive elements of critical theories, and a concerted effort to improve not only our nation's strategic competence but also our confidence in our democratic principles and institutions'.[72]

For someone as well versed in historical scholarship as McMaster to deliver such a scathing critique of American society after decades where that society had deified its soldiers and supported enormous funding for its military was a remarkable development. McMaster's essay put the warrior ethos forth as a totemic concept that had to be protected and demanded that broader social phenomena such as the racial reckonings provoked by the uprisings of the summer of 2020 be subordinated to its needs. Whatever the specifics of the historiographical debate on the 1619 project and the merits of an often vaguely defined 'critical race theory', McMaster's essay demonstrated a strange solipsism in its claims that America's warriors had been let down by their society and that the road to national redemption in part lay in combined civil–military effort to tend to the warrior ethos.[73]

What was also remarkable about McMaster's essay was that it described this warrior ethos both as though it was a constant that had existed largely unchanged through time and that it was the naturally occurring fundamental covenant that bound soldiers to each other and to the citizenry in general. In calling for a move away from 'postmodernist' history, McMaster elided the fact that the warrior ethos was itself quite a recent innovation, and one that does not have a straightforward history. Certainly, the basic components of that ethos could be found in military organisations across time, but concepts such as heroism, sacrifice, honour and integrity could just as easily encompass these components as well and are not as freighted with notions of exceptionalism and entitlement as the warrior ethos too often is. While the comparison would no doubt be odious to McMaster, Clint Lorance and his supporters claimed the warrior ethos too. And on the other side of the spectrum, many of the essential support troops that are vital to the functioning of the army find the moniker of 'warrior' to be faintly ridiculous.

---

[72] McMaster, 'Preserving the Warrior Ethos'.
[73] For overviews of the debate over the 1619 project, see Adam Serwer, 'The Fight Over the 1619 Project Is Not About the Facts', *The Atlantic*, 23 December 2019, www.theatlantic.com/ideas/archive/2019/12/historians-clash-1619-project/604093/; Matthew Karp, 'History As End: 1619, 1776, and the Politics of the Past', *Harper's Magazine*, 8 June 2021, https://harpers.org/archive/2021/07/history-as-end-politics-of-the-past-matthew-karp/.

What this book has sought to show is that the warrior ethos was not a timeless phenomenon, but one that emerged at a particular place and in a particular era in response to specific challenges. In the aftermath of the Cold War, the United States Army was confronted with a severe identity crisis as it struggled for relevance. It found itself to be a revered institution, yet it often struggled to fill its recruiting quotas. It planned for a future where sophisticated sensors and weapons systems would make the battlefield visible with startling clarity, and yet it found itself immersed in murky and difficult operations in the grey areas between war and peace. Its leaders thought that the all-recruited Army that won the Gulf War was a winning formula, yet marginalised groups demanded that the force be made more equitable, and conservative culture warriors lambasted the 'kinder, gentler military' that had given in to political correctness. Part of the response to these challenges was to put forth a warrior ethos that could perhaps unify the force, move past the debates about who should serve and orientate soldiers towards the unknown challenges of the twenty-first century. In the aftermath of the 9/11 attacks, an era that saw the Army constantly deployed, this warrior ethos became something bigger, and became enmeshed with a broader culture of entitlement and exceptionalism that it helped to fuel.

If Army leaders felt that a warrior ethos was of value in that moment, the question is now whether or not it is still useful. Much as the Army sought to redefine itself after the end of the Cold War, it is doing so again today, as the Wars on Terror have come to a protracted and uneasy close. Although the terms of the debate are now different as the unipolar moment has decisively ended and 'history' has restarted again, the Army still struggles in many ways to define its role in the world as it reckons with the legacies of the wars it lost, the myriad geopolitical challenges it faces and the ever more acute question of its relationship with American society. If the warrior ethos helped to drive a wedge between the Army and American society, even if it was more symptom than cause, and if talk of a 'warrior caste' contributed to the disproportionate number of veterans being charged for participation in the 6 January insurrection at the US Capitol, then the answer to any questions about its utility must be negative.[74] Soldiers will always define themselves by what they do on the battlefield, but the unhappy career of the warrior ethos has surely demonstrated that they do better when they think of themselves simply as soldiers rather than warriors.

---

[74] 'Veterans and Extremism: What We Know' (New York: Anti-Defamation League, 16 June 2021), www.adl.org/resources/reports/veterans-and-extremism-what-we-know; Eleanor Watson and Robert Legare, 'Over 80 of Those Charged in the January 6 Investigation Have Ties to the Military', *CBS News*, 15 December 2021, www.cbsnews .com/news/capitol-riot-january-6-military-ties/.

Index